Reality Squared

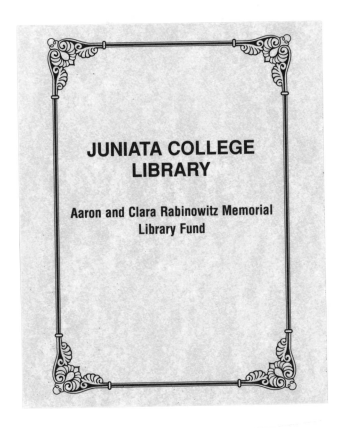

**JUNIATA COLLEGE
LIBRARY**

Aaron and Clara Rabinowitz Memorial
Library Fund

D1113847

Reality Squared

Televisual Discourse on the Real

EDITED BY JAMES FRIEDMAN

RUTGERS UNIVERSITY PRESS
New Brunswick, New Jersey, and London

Library of Congress Cataloging-in-Publication Data
Reality squared : televisual discourse on the real / edited by James Friedman
p. cm.
Includes bibliographical references and index.
ISBN 0-8135-2988-3 (cloth : alk. paper)—ISBN 0-8135-2989-1 (pbk. : alk.
paper)
1. Realism on television.   2. Reality television programs—United States—
History and criticism.   I. Friedman, James, 1958–
PN1992.8.R4 R43   2002
791.45'6—dc21

2001031787

British Cataloging-in-Publication information is available from the British Library.

This collection copyright © 2002 by Rutgers, The State University
Individual chapters copyright © 2002 in the names of their authors
Arild Fetveit, "Reality TV in the Digital Era," *Media, Culture, and Society* 21(6)
(1999), reprinted by permission of Sage Publications, Ltd.
All rights reserved.
No part of this book may be reproduced or utilized in any form or by any means,
electronic or mechanical, or by any information storage or retrieval system, with-
out written permission from the publisher. Please contact Rutgers University
Press, 100 Joyce Kilmer Avenue, Piscataway, NJ 08854-8099. The only exception
to this prohibition is "fair use" as defined by U.S. copyright law.

Manufactured in the United States of America

PN
1992.8
. R4
R43
2002

For Ava and Aaron,
who ground me in reality, inspire me to explore,
and are part of everything I do

Contents

THREE Real Discourse

FOUR Real Fiction

Acknowledgments

This project would not have been possible without the support and advice of many of my friends and colleagues. The concept for the book itself evolved from discussions with Daniel Bernardi, whose enthusiasm and advice was instrumental throughout the project. In addition to being a great friend, Daniel's effort and commitment epitomize the finest qualities of academia and remind me why I chose this field. I am fortunate to have had the opportunity to work with the committed and distinguished group of scholars at UCLA. Vivian Sobchack and John Caldwell's support were instrumental in getting the project off the ground. Both have influenced my thinking on live television and have consistently encouraged my research in this area. Vivian and John have been available whenever I needed them, and I am grateful for the time, guidance, and feedback they have provided. Nick Browne and Peter Wollen have spent countless hours discussing and debating my writings on live television, and their contributions have informed as well as inspired my research. I am also grateful to Laura Mulvey for her support and enthusiasm during the project's earliest stages. While the time frame for the publication prevented her from contributing, our conversations and correspondences helped move the book forward. Mimi White also supported this project form the earliest stages, and I was fortunate to have her participation as well as her patience in breaking in a first-time editor.

During this process I have been fortunate to work with Leslie Mitchner at Rutgers University Press, who has been thorough and professional throughout this project. Her support has helped keep the project on track, and her input has been extremely valuable. In fact the entire staff at Rutgers has been great to work with. Theresa Liu and Marilyn Campbell provided guidance through the production process and helped me to avoid unnecessary pitfalls, and Ann Youmans did an outstanding job copyediting the essays for this volume.

It would have been difficult to complete this project without the support of several of my coworkers within the UCLA Film and TV Archive. Jim Williamson provided valuable feedback and advice on proposals and potential contributors during the early stages of this project. Zoé Burman's editorial input and advice was extremely helpful. And Luana Almares helped review documents and manage the logistics required in putting together an anthology of new essays. I am fortunate to be able to work with such a talented and professional group of individuals. My pursuit of academic activities would not be possible without the support of management within the Archive. Timothy Kittleson, director of the Archive, has made it possible for me to continue teaching and researching within my areas of interest, and from my first day at the Archive, Steven Ricci has always supported and encouraged my academic work. This project would not have been possible without his support. I am also grateful to Robert Rosen, dean of UCLA's School of Theater, Film, and Television, whose support of the 1999 Visible Evidence Conference helped me solicit scholarship for this book.

The cover art and design for this volume was created by two talented and energetic artists/designers: Josh Rose and Scott Grossman. I am extremely fortunate to have them as contributors to the project as well as friends. I will always be thankful that we were able to work together on this project and proud to have my name next to theirs in this book. Finally, and most importantly, I need to acknowledge my wife, Ava Rose, who literally helped with every stage of this book. I simply could not have done this without her support, input, advice, patience, and editorial feedback.

Thank you!

Reality Squared

Introduction

JAMES FRIEDMAN

Debates concerning the relationship between representational media and reality are neither new nor limited to television. In the past century, discussions of mediated reality have ranged from the modernist position that reality existed yet could not be represented, to the claims of some postmodernists that simulation has replaced the real. Over the years, culture and media theorists from André Bazin to Roland Barthes to Jean Baudrillard have routinely contemplated the complicated set of relations encountered when a medium (re)creates images to reflect, suggest, or construct reality. These theoretical discussions have occupied scholars as well as some artists and have occasionally penetrated popular public discourse where, since the 1980s, the television industry and its critics have identified, labeled, and begun promoting a reemergence of "reality-based" television. Indeed, during the past two decades, reality-based programming has come to play a major role in production decisions, promotion, and even network strategy. As we enter the new millennium, the networks' emphasis on and viewers' apparent desire for "reality TV" show no signs of diminishing.

Although the issue of representing reality is frequently addressed by scholars writing on television, a surprisingly small number of books and anthologies have focused directly on this subject. In fact, a subject search on the terms "television" and "reality" produces only one result from UCLA's library database.[1] However, the limited number of scholarly writings specifically addressing television and reality should not be attributed to a lack of interest in the subject but rather to an inherent difficulty in describing and containing the ideological, economic, cultural, technological, and political influences that impact televisual representations of real events. No single methodology or theory can adequately contain the varied forms and fluctuating nature of television's relationship with reality. Therefore, the construction of this volume includes contributions approaching television and reality from a number of disciplinary perspectives. Although many of the contributions that follow are from film and television scholars, an analysis of television and reality is necessarily interdisciplinary.

The tone, style, and orientation may vary slightly between essays, but the commitment to an interdisciplinary approach has allowed for a more expansive exploration of the medium, which ranges from textual analysis within an historic context to the impact of new technologies upon representations of reality and investigations of the semiotics of the television image. By examining texts ranging from early westerns to the weather, from news to New Year's Eve montages, this collection of essays addresses the representation of reality on television; the ways in which socio-political reality impacts television programming; and the impact of televisual reality on the socio-political world. In this way, the collection builds on the insights of postmodernism in order to examine the construction of reality on television while simultaneously seeking to incorporate something of the modernist conviction that there is still a reality "out there" — outside of, or at least not entirely subsumed by, representation.

Taken as a whole, *Reality Squared* is situated squarely along a dialectical continuum of contemporary discourses about representation and reality. As the volume's title suggests, the essays that follow will examine the representation and containment of issues or events within the squared frame of televisual viewing space, as well as the exponential growth of these representational programs on broadcast and cable TV. In this sense, the volume will examine the ways in which reality is reflected by and refracted through television programming as well as the ways in which television serves to frame and fuel discussions about events in the world. Like the exponential "squared" of the title, *Reality Squared* is more than the sum of its parts: taken as a whole, the book will synthesize diverse discourses about reality and representation, history and fiction, text and context, and the "inside" and "outside" of that box we call television.

Real from the Start

Television's link to reality emanates from its ability to render realistic audio and visual representations and to do so in real time, as events occur. It is this capacity for liveness that separates television from other representational media such as the cinema or even the computer, and it is often cited when discussing television and the real. As Robert Stam has suggested, "Although live transmissions form but a tiny proportion of programming, that tiny portion sets the tone for all of television."[2] However, while it is true that television has been and remains the only medium capable of broadcasting both sound and images as they occur, it is important to remember that this capability emerged from a nexus of interests (economic, technological, political, industrial) that determined the form, function, and practice of television. Jane Feuer rightly tells us, "to equate live television with 'real life' is to ignore all those determinations standing between the 'event' and our perception of it — technology and institutions to mention two."[3]

In fact, early prototypes of television, such as those produced in Germany and Great Britain during the 1930s, were not based upon today's electronic model but instead depended upon recorded images. Before television broadcasting had been approved in the United States, John Logie Baird of Great Britain had already used his disk model of television to provide entertainment and information for airline passengers. Although some scholars have suggested that Germany provided live broadcasts of the 1936 Berlin Olympics in salons throughout the city, and images from these broadcasts have been referred to in films like *Contact* (1997), the German model of television did not in fact allow for live broadcasting. Rather, the Olympics were shot on film, processed in a remote laboratory, and broadcast as soon as the film was developed.[4] If television had continued to develop along these early technological paths, the reliance on prerecorded images would undoubtedly have had a major effect on the early types of programming produced and broadcast.

Instead, television's ability to electronically transmit live images was preferred in the United States, and that ability had a substantial impact on the formation of the networks and dominance of the television industry. Drawing upon their technical and structural experiences in radio, network broadcasters conceived electronic television as a means of transmitting images from point to point. This conception by no means limited the medium to live transmission, but it offered the networks a means to build upon existing radio formats and programs as well as to differentiate television's product from that of the cinema. As Robert Vianello has demonstrated, broadcasters during the U.S. television industry's infancy strategically used the live program as a tool to coerce affiliates into alignment with the networks. According to Vianello, live programming was less expensive to produce and was "instrumental in establishing a TV aesthetic which avoided unfavorable comparison with the high production value movies."[5] More importantly, however, Vianello describes how the use of live shows positioned the networks as the programming source and helped to make local stations dependent upon their product.[6] This was the same strategy that the networks had successfully employed years before while establishing dominance in the radio industry. Ironically, when, in the mid-to-late 1950s, the television networks were securely established, live prime-time programming began to slowly disappear. Not only did the production costs associated with live programming increase, but live programs became less profitable since they had limited value for rebroadcast (reruns).

Significantly, networks found another use for regularly scheduled live programming during the late fifties, when it was strategically used to help change the industry's sponsorship practices. While live television had originally been inexpensive to produce, increased viewer expectations and technological improvements made regularly scheduled live programs more expensive than their filmed counterparts. By the late fifties, programmers such as Pat Weaver (NBC) began to produce extravagant live spectacles, which rendered the existing model of single program sponsorship cost prohibitive, and thus helped the networks to wrestle control from the sponsors.[7] Once the network structure was securely established, and the networks had regained program control, regularly scheduled live primetime programs quickly faded away. It is clear that once live programming had exhausted its strategic potential, industry economics dictated that more profitable filmed (or taped) material dominate the airways. Live broadcasting was therefore not television's technological destiny but rather an identifying characteristic that could be used when strategically necessary, convenient, or profitable.

In addition to serving the strategic needs of the television networks, live programming during the fifties also helped established the medium's link to reality. Live dramas, morning shows, and sporting events all offered viewers the opportunity to experience the events being broadcast as they took place. In each case, these live programs were connected to a real event, and the viewer's participation in its unfolding made possible what Robert Stam has identified as "real, as opposed to fabricated suspense."[8] Following the disappearance of regularly scheduled live programming in the late fifties, televisual representations of real events were limited to broadcasting such special occasions as the Academy Awards or presidential debates, sports coverage, the emerging news broadcasts, and occasional documentary productions. Of these broadcasts, news would continue to be the only regularly scheduled program to air near the industry's most popular prime-time viewing hours (currently 8:00 P.M. to 11:00 P.M.). During the early sixties, the network's overall strategy moved away from direct representations of real events as they offered more conventional dramas, westerns, and sit-coms instead.

Contemporary Televisual Reality

As the essays in this volume demonstrate, television as an institution is ideologically, technologically, and programmatically linked to the presentation of reality. This is not to suggest that the presentation of reality reflects the medium's "true nature" but to acknowledge the concerted effort—by critics and producers—to differentiate television from other media and create its unique identity. Although "reality-based" TV has attracted a great deal of attention in the new millennium, it by no means represents a sudden shift in the programmatic landscape. *Los Angeles Times* critic Brian Lowry, for example, reminded readers how reality-based programs became instant hits in 1980 (*Real People* and *That's Incredible*) and again in 1990 (*America's Funniest Home Videos*).⁹ While there may be more reality-based programs in the year 2000 than in the past, promotional references to "reality" and viewer attraction to so-called reality shows have a long and well-documented history.¹⁰ William Boddy has noted that writers such as Gilbert Seldes were arguing as early as 1952 "that television's technological immediacy gave the medium an 'overwhelming feel of reality.'"¹¹ In his valuable study of early television, Boddy cites a multitude of voices, including *New York Times* critic Jack Gould, script editor Edward Barry Roberts, writer Donald Curtis, and others who echoed Seldes's technological essentialism between 1950 and 1952. These early writers were attempting to define the nature of the emerging medium, but the dangers and limitations of this sort of technological determinism have been persuasively articulated by Boddy, Jane Feuer, and others. The essays that follow will not, therefore, seek linkages between the representation of reality and an essential technological basis. At the same time, it is clear that technology plays a significant role in the formal development of televisual styles, and the proliferation of stories and events, linked to a temporality of the present.¹²

Technological innovation does not simply emerge, nor can it be studied apart from the social context in which it is used. Given that the idea almost always precedes the invention, we must view technology as a tool that is marshaled, developed, and deployed within a specific social/cultural context. A discussion of technological change or influence without full exploration of the intersections between economic, social, and technological forces would be misguided and perhaps even misleading. However, while it may be valuable to examine the development of representational reality on television from a technological perspective, such an inquiry is not within the scope of this volume. Rather, the essays that follow will serve to outline, or map, the manner in which style, formal conventions, and program content serve to articulate a representational real, which obfuscates the boundaries between reality and fiction. Television cannot bring "reality" to viewers; it can only provide a representation of an event. But if we wish to distinguish between the representation of real events and the representation of fictional drama, we must wade into the murky space between reality and representation, between event and history, between objectivity and experience.

Beginning in the eighties, television has been in a period of transition and transformation. The growth of cable, video technology (including camcorders), industry mergers, the birth of new networks, the proliferation of satellite broadcasting, and even the personal computer have challenged the industry's monopoly on home entertainment. Both the networks and their new competitors have gained valuable insight from the industry's formative years, and, not surprisingly, reality-based programming has grown exponentially during this period. For fledgling networks such as Fox reality-based programs provided inexpensive shows capable of attracting a sizable audience in terms of ratings and key demographics.[13] Indeed, aside from a few notable exceptions, Fox has seemed to sustain itself through reality-based shows such as *America's Most Wanted* and *Cops,* and the now-familiar "shockumentaries" such as *World's Wildest Police Videos* and *When Animals Attack.*

The resurgence of reality-based programming on television has not, however, been limited to exploitative "shockumentaries," questionable exposés, staged spectaculars and sports but has also become more prominent in prime-time dramatic programming. By the 1980s, references to lived reality were no longer limited to live performances, news, or special events, and reality had become a prominent source of subject material for a number of fiction programs. Certainly shows could always be read in the context of their contemporary social reality, but now the real world had become the explicit source for TV. In addition to made-for-TV movies, which can take topical subjects and bring them to the air faster than other media, regular prime-time series such as *Law and Order, NYPD Blue, The X-Files,* and *Homicide* have routinely based their stories upon topical events. Of these contemporary dramas, *Law and Order* draws most obviously from daily news events, with the tag line for their advertisements, "ripped from the headlines," promoting the show's re-presentation of "real" stories. Indeed, when the show's producer, Dick Wolf, was asked, "What's the bible for this show?" he responded "The front page of the *New York Post.*"[14] Programs drawing upon topical issues are certainly not new to television, but this regular and explicit reference to news stories became commonplace by the 1990s. Furthermore, in the late 1990s, established networks began experimenting with live productions: the 1997 season premier of *ER* and the live drama *Fail Safe* (2000) were both a novelty for the audience that harkened back to the "Golden Age" of the fifties, allowing critics to remind viewers of the industry's unique potential for, and rich history of, "quality" live programming.[15]

As we embark upon a new century of broadcasting, it is clear that no genre, form, or type of programming has been as actively marketed by producers, or more enthusiastically embraced by viewers, than reality-based TV. During the first nine months of the year 2000, programs presented as reality-based have dominated the airways, and inspired more than five hundred articles in major U.S. newspapers.[16] Much of this discussion has focused on the summertime hit *Survivor,* but the success of the game show *Who Wants to Be a Millionaire* has been equally impressive. These programs along with other newcomers such as *Johns Hopkins 24/7* (NBC), *Arrest and Trial* (syndicated), *Confessions* (Court TV), and *Big Brother*

(CBS) have left programmers and viewers wondering if reality-based television will displace dramas and sit-coms as the staples of prime-time U.S. television.

The contemporary popularity of so-called reality-based programming is by no means limited to U.S. broadcasting, and in fact, the most popular of these programs have been imported, and even franchised, from Europe. *Survivor* was created in England and originally aired in Sweden. By July 2000, five countries had purchased the *Survivor* concept for television. Even more impressive is the *Who Wants to Be a Millionaire* franchise, which also originated in England, and is currently on the air in twenty-nine countries and has been sold to fifty others.[17] While *Survivor* may be more interesting to cultural scholars and critics, *Millionaire* was nothing short of an economic and cultural phenomena, as it occupied nearly 20 percent of ABC's 2000–2001 prime-time fall lineup and has regularly maintained top-ten ratings for all four of the nights on which it is broadcast. Even though the ratings for *Millionaire* had begun to slide by October 2000, suggesting that viewers may have begun to satiate their appetite for this program, it continues to be a top draw in the United States and has commanded even larger audiences in other countries such as India.[18]

The proliferation of reality-based programming in the year 2000 does not represent a fundamental shift in television programming, but the industry's reliance on "reality" as a promotional marketing tool is unprecedented. What separates the spate of contemporary reality-based television from its predecessors is not the form or content of these programs (although there are certainly some interesting experiments taking place) but the open and explicit sale of television programming as a representation of reality. Media scholars have often argued that the primary objective of U.S. television is to deliver viewers to advertisers, and in order to realize this objective, it is necessary for broadcasters to attract viewers to their programs or product.[19] Whereas in the past, critics and producers enticed viewers with the shared experience (between actor and viewer) of a live broadcast, or the temporal simultaneity between representation and event, viewers are now sold reality-based television as a form of televisual neorealism. The term "reality-based" is bandied about as a description for everything from video compilations to made-for-TV spectacles, newsmagazines, and game shows. Although these programs share a few characteristics such as participants who are not actors, minimal scripting, and drama or narrative created through structure and editing, none of these shows represent real events as they occur. Game shows like *Millionaire, Survivor,* and *Big Brother,* and newsmagazines like *John Hopkins 24/7* have been on television for years. But in the year 2000, new shows in these formats are being promoted as "reality" programming. What is new and fresh about these programs is not their allegiance to reality but the marriage of reality conventions with dramatic structure. Amitabh Bachchan, the host of India's *Kaun Banega Crorepathi?* (India's franchise of *Millionaire*) describes his program's phenomenal success as a result of the show's "sense of drama," which he opposes to "the flashing lights, fast action and buzzers that are part of most game shows."[20]

Few people confuse "reality-based" programming with a representation of reality. As Stu Bloomberg, cochairman of ABC Entertainment Television, stated in reference to the contemporary game show *Survivor,* "I don't think people eating rats and termites with a camera on them is experiencing 'reality.'"[21] Caryn James of the *New York Times* adds that "*Survivor* is as remote from reality as its setting."[22] By August 2000, Brian Lowry of the *Los Angeles Times* seemed exasperated when he quipped, "Someone needs to come up with a better name for the stuff than 'reality' programming. Reality? Please. No one in my reality has ever suggested I eat larvae or be locked in a house for 90 days without contacting the outside world."[23] Rather than "reality," these programs are using seemingly "normal" (real) people rather than professional actors for the production of televisual drama.[24] The construction of *Survivor* demonstrates this point most clearly. *Survivor* was taped on the remote island of Pulau Tiga, where production was completed more than a month before the program premiered. According to Bill Carter of the *New York Times,* "Within the first few weeks, Mr. Hatch [the eventual winner] set himself up as the center of the drama on the deserted island where *Survivor* takes place. He created an alliance—and boasted about it on camera—with three others who have consistently voted together to eliminate opponents as designated by Mr. Hatch."[25] When Carter describes the program, he speaks of these events as if he is watching them unfold, as if he is witness to the game being played on the island. But Caryn James astutely points out that "each episode was edited into a swift hour. *Survivor* never spent more than a few seconds watching someone eat rice. . . . Take away the ruthless editing, and you end up watching people feed the chickens."[26] James recognizes that it was not Hatch "who set himself up," but the *editors* who foregrounded specific actions while building their narrative to a known conclusion. James adds that "of course the editors knew the winner in advance: they clearly edited to focus on Rich and make him the audience-drawing villain."[27]

As is well documented, the producers of *Survivor* chose contestants who would maximize drama and conflict on the program. Not entirely confident that their selections would be successful on their own, however, they taped the entirety of the show so that it could be edited it into tightly constructed episodes that built suspense, provided viewers with necessary clues and insights, and dramatically presented the winning and losing contestants. This is "reality" programming in the year 2000.

While this brief discussion of *Survivor* demonstrates the recent promotional use of reality, it is not applicable to all contemporary reality programming. Another recent reality-based show, *Johns Hopkins 24/7,* is a documentary-format newsmagazine that is restricted to a single institution. Like a Frederick Wiseman documentary, *Hopkins* focused upon "real-life" dramas (patients) and "real-life" heroes (doctors) within the hospital, turning the camera on the institution, and letting it run. Later, the editors assembled this footage to carefully construct individual stories (usually three that are interwoven for each episode) from the events that have been documented. Notwithstanding the deliberate storytelling, the people and their illnesses are real. This is to say that the individual awaiting an organ donation would have needed a transplant, and would have been waiting, whether or not this show was on the air. Similarly, another contemporary reality-based show, *Confessions* (Court TV) broadcasts edited, taped confessions from actual criminal cases in New York City. This program airs without an editorializing voice-over and allows viewers to hear confessions made by convicted criminals as they were delivered (although some of the tapes are edited for length and content, these are allegedly "faithful" representations of public records). As was the case with *Hopkins,* the events depicted occurred irrespective of the television program.

In addition to these documentary-format programs and the game shows masked as reality, another form of so-called reality programming are the dramas based on "real-life" events. Programs such as *Cops, L.A. Detectives,* and *LAPD: Life on the Beat* require producers to work closely with the institutions who provide access to stories or events these shows are dependent upon. As Howard Rosenberg notes, ". . . how truthful and realistic can these 'reality' series be, given the strong likelihood that they will air nothing that would anger and sever access to their subjects? No access, no show."[28] Rosenberg goes on to describe how the Los Angeles County Sheriff's Department has a binding editorial review of *L.A. Detectives* that "allows them to order the deletion of material 'likely to result in legal action against' the department or anything showing an employee 'committing a violation of a significant departmental policy while on duty.'"[29] It stands to reason that New York City's District Attorney's office would similarly select which confessions are, and which confessions are not, aired on television, and that Johns Hopkins Medical Center must have some influence over which stories, physicians, employees, and patients are depicted on a show that bears their name.

What, then, is the "reality" depicted on television, and how can we possibly begin to discuss it? Through the examples above, it is clear that television does not offer direct access to "the real," but works to present *a* reality. The difference lies in a distinction between an idealized objective reality and subjective experience. As Bill Nichols states in his discussion of documentary film, "This is indeed *the* world we see but it is also *a* world, or more exactly, *a* view of *the* world. It is not just any world but neither is it the only view possible of this one historical world."[30] Similarly, "reality-based" television may refer viewers to *the* world, our one world, but their presentation of events is always, necessarily, *a* view of that world. For example, if two networks were to televise a presidential debate from different broadcast feeds, they would undoubtedly present different versions of a single event. Where one network might cut to a reaction shot, the other might stay focused on a speaker. The reaction could certainly influence the viewers' evaluation of the performers and therefore alter their experience of the debate. Because a representation can never be completely faithful to the actual event, it must always be *a* version of the debate rather than *the* presidential debate. This is not to say, however, that we must dismiss the reality depicted in the representation of the debate. Accepting that television can at best present *a* version of reality is the first step in the exploration of the medium's presentation of real events. Just as the medium does not present a singular reality, individual programs neither invoke nor represent "reality" in a unified fashion.

Taken as a whole, television's increasing, and increasingly sophisticated references to lived reality, can be seen as part of what John Caldwell has identified as "televisuality."[31] In his analysis of American television, *Televisuality: Style, Crisis, and Authority in American Television,* Caldwell finds that the industry experienced significant programmatic and aesthetic shifts during the 1980s and 1990s. Caldwell links these changes to the emergence of "televisuality," an historical development that began in the 1980s as a response to increased competition from alternate media sources. According to Caldwell,

> Starting in the 1980s American mass-market television underwent an uneven shift in the conceptual and ideological paradigms that governed its look and presentational demeanor. In several important programming and institutional areas, television moved from a framework that approached broadcasting primarily as a form of word-based rhetoric and transmission, with all the issues that such terms suggest, to a visually based mythology, framework, and aesthetic based on an extreme self-consciousness of style.[32]

Although televisual representations of lived reality defy simple categorization along formal or stylistic lines, news, sports, and reality-based pro-

PHOTOS 1 AND 2. *Homicide: Life on the Street*
(top); *The Practice* (below).

grams all celebrate a heightened sense of what Caldwell describes as televisuality: graphic overlays, replay/reenactment, and manipulations of the
screen are all commonplace on these programs. For example, *ER*'s live 1997
season premiere using handheld cameras self-consciously drew attention to
the show as a production and the camera's role in that process. *Law and
Order, The X-Files, NYPD Blue,* and others not only deal openly with current issues from the news but also include references to other reality-based
programming, for example, by including mock news coverage of events
within the drama, or using characters as participants on reality programs.[33]
   In some instances, these reflexive moments are presented tongue-in-
cheek, in some they are presented as serious elements meant to reinforce the

verisimilitude of the drama, and in others they may be preceded by a warning so as to insure that viewers do not confuse the dramatization with the "real" thing.

Structuring Reality

Examining reality-based programming within a specific historical context helps explain this form's growth and popularity during the Golden Age as well as post-eighties broadcasting, but it does not address the attendant issues raised when media represents real events. To better understand media representations of reality and how these representations impact both events and viewers, the essays that follow examine the medium's role in the presentation/creation of history, discuss the articulation of televisual reality, and provide analysis of reality programming in both fiction and nonfiction genres. The structure of this volume, therefore, begins with a consideration of television's relation to history. The first part, "Constructing/Reconstructing History" examines how televisual representations of reality influence the production and reception of history, considers the development of realist aesthetics, and analyzes programs and events to illuminate the intersections of television, reality, and history. Having examined televisual reality in relation to history, the focus then shifts to a more general discussion of the presentation and structuration of reality. The second part, "Framing the Real" addresses how television identifies programs as "reality-based," investigates formal variations between different types of reality programming, and extends these considerations to new media.

While the first two sections of the volume address theoretical and historical issues associated with the presentation of mediated reality, the remainder of the volume's essays engage in analysis of specific programs or genres. The third part, "Real Discourse" investigates reality-based programming in the United States and Britain and examines the social/political roles these programs play. The fourth and final part, "Real Fiction," considers the use of real stories and reality aesthetics in fiction programming. In approaching the topic in this way, the collection seeks to explore representations of reality from a variety of perspectives and to incorporate a range of programs dispersed over time and across genres.

"Constructing/Reconstructing History" opens the volume by examining relationships between televisual reality and history. Television's unique ability to present real events of social/political importance as they occur is often promoted (in advance of the event) as "history in the making." Although historically "significant" events occur relatively infrequently, the industry regularly capitalizes upon this possibility and promotes everything from hour-long dramas to sporting events to talk shows as "historic." Televisual history has become ubiquitous as several cable networks have been dedicated to its presentation. At the same time, according to some scholars, the medium can be seen as "exemplifying, even propagating, the loss of history."[34] Whether or not television is seen as a recorder or manufacturer of history, broadcasts labeled as "historic" have become some of the most common and recognizable instances of television's representation of the real. While it would be beyond the scope of this volume to thoroughly examine the complex interactions between television, history, and cultural memory, the four essays in this section begin to investigate examples of televisual reality and how programs function to represent, create, and rewrite history.

The section begins with Rhona Berenstein's "Acting Live: TV Performance, Intimacy, and Immediacy (1945–1955)," which examines the creation of a "realistic" acting style that emerged on television during the forties and fifties. Her analysis connects acting styles on the emerging medium to existing production conventions, technology, and the industry's self-promoted ontology of liveness as well as sponsorship. Berenstein examines technical considerations that may have exerted some influence upon the development of television acting styles. More importantly, however, she argues that since many early programs were broadcast live, a natural style of performance suggested an intimacy that reinforced the immediacy generated through a temporality shared between performance and reception. As Berenstein carefully demonstrates, the dominant style of naturalized acting on television can be attributed to a number of factors, but it most importantly emerged from the industry's imperative to effectively sell the sponsors' products and image. In this way, Berenstein is able to describe how a naturalistic acting style helped to solidify a consumer model for the emerging television industry.

The naturalistic acting styles Berenstein describes suggest not only intimacy with the viewer but also a more real (less historic) portrayal of character and events. This style becomes particularly interesting when actors in dramatic programs represent historical agents in real historical events. Alan Nadel examines such occurrences in "'Johnny Yuma Was a Rebel; He Roamed Through the West'—Television, Race, and the 'Real' West," which investigates TV westerns produced during the 1950s and early 1960s Cold War era. Nadel looks at revisionist histories, such as that of Davy Crockett in the TV series *Disneyland,* and also examines episodic programming in the western series *The Rebel.* His analysis provides an exceptional model for examining television in relation to the actual events portrayed, contemporaneous social influences, and industrial/economic imperatives, all of which inform television's entertainment models for revisionist history. In this way, Nadel is able to place the programmer's retelling of history within a context of industrial economic imperatives that demand that programs attract the largest possible audience and that networks present programs conducive to promoting the sponsor's products. Nadel thus analyzes the "real" influences that shape productions and explores how historical events are transformed to better serve popular media within the framework of a specific social/cultural moment.

Having examined acting style and the representation of historic events, the section moves on to consider representations of real events and the construction of history on television. Kristen Hatch's analysis focuses upon two examples of televised Senate hearings that were broadcast to a predominantly female audience during the early fifties. In "Daytime Politics: Kefauver, McCarthy, and the American Housewife," Hatch documents the overwhelming popularity of both the 1951 Kefauver hearings (which investigated politics and organized crime) and the 1954 Army-McCarthy hearings. Daytime broadcasting had never attracted the mass audiences found during prime time, and Hatch demonstrates how, on the one hand, the industry searched for viable daytime formulas, and on the other, it failed to follow up on the overwhelming success of these political hearings. She goes on to argue that the lack of subsequent political programming aired during the day can be attributed to a social desire for maintaining separate gendered spheres within the home and the political/work place. Hatch shows how these daytime broadcasts of political hearings to an audience primarily comprised of housewives were perceived as a threat to the existing status quo, positioning women as participants in the American political process. Her provocative documentation of public response through the popular press suggests how social concerns can impact programming. Like Nadel, Hatch is interested in how social considerations influence programmatic decisions and conversely how television influences/impacts social transformation.

The first section ends with "'Happy New Year and Auld Lang Syne': On Televisual Montage and Historical Consciousness," Vivian Sobchack's analysis of the way in which U.S. local and network news programs' New Year's Eve "montage sequences" create, through a series of iconic and indexical images, a peculiar and interrogative narrative/history for the past year. Sobchack's rhetorical approach to this annual rite of passage is both illuminating and provocative. While her object of study is limited to New Year's Eve montages, her analysis raises more general questions regarding one of news programming's most common storytelling conventions: montage. Sobchack's examination of this atypically structured television montage not only helps explain the power and attraction of these sequences but additionally serves as a smooth transition between the first section's focus on the articulation of reality and the upcoming exploration into televisual construction of history. The New Year's Eve montage purports to present familiar images but creates and defines an ambiguously emplotted historical narrative. Understanding how the combination of images and sounds becomes comprehensible and how it speaks to a geographically, ideologically, and socially dispersed group of viewers is in itself significant. Yet equally important is the way in which these particular images construct and omit what comes to be seen as the history of a given year.

While the first section of this volume looks at the relationships between televisual reality and history, the second part, "Framing the Real," considers the presentation, operation, and multiple functions of reality-based programming. From surveillance to sports to war coverage, television presents a variety of its broadcasts as representations of something real rather than fictive. In some instances, a program's link to reality may be obvious and commonly accepted (such as the coverage of a crisis or catastrophe). In other instances, the reference to reality may be more oblique (as in some fictional programming that addresses/incorporates real issues or events). But in each case, when the media presents programmatic content as real, the link to lived reality is verbally, formally, and/or visually articulated. Thus the second section begins with an exploration of the articulation or the discourse of reality. It then moves to an analysis of how different forms of live broadcasting might influence reception and concludes by extending the discussion to include new media and the Internet.

"Framing the Real" opens with Arild Fetveit's "Reality TV in the Digital Era: A Paradox in Visual Culture," an examination of existing scholarship on photography and realism in relation to reality-based television. Fetveit's analysis emerges from what he identifies as a paradoxical moment: the increased demand for media realism coupled with a heightened awareness and skepticism related to digital manipulations of media. To investigate these seemingly oppositional currents, Fetveit explores the discourse of realism in relation to reality TV. He acknowledges the medium's ability to manipulate and alter images while at the same time recognizing that viewers understand and accept this manipulation in certain circumstances while in others they will not. For Fetveit, the question is not only whether a photographic media can represent real objects or events but how viewers discriminate between attempts to represent reality and programs that allude to real events while including aesthetic or editorial embellishments.

Fetveit's consideration of how viewers come to expect, desire, or trust reality TV is followed by my own analysis of formal variations within live broadcasting. By examining a variety of live programs, "Attraction to Distraction: Live Television and the Public Sphere" demonstrates how varied and often contradictory formal conventions impact viewer's reception and relation to the events depicted. Of specific interest are the ways in which time and space are layered within a broadcast and the way in which these layers suggests proximity or distance between viewer, broadcast, and event. The impact of form upon reception is particularly significant since live broadcasting is most often used to communicate information regarding *real* social, cultural, and political events. If the form influences reception, then programmatic choices not only determine how real events are represented but also influence how viewers understand, respond, and relate to events as well as to each other.

Having traced the debate surrounding representations of reality back to photography and having considered contemporary formal conventions for live broadcasting, the second section concludes with Daniel Bernardi's "Cyborgs in Cyberspace: White Pride, Pedophilic Pornography, and Donna Haraway's Manifesto." Bernardi's analysis of Internet Web sites and chat rooms, extends the discussion of representational reality to include new media. At first glance, an essay exploring the computer and the Internet in an anthology on television might appear misplaced. Although there are considerable differences between television and the Internet, it seems clear that these two industries continue to move towards a converging viewing experience. Indeed, with the dawn of WebTV, Tivo, digital satellite transmission, and cable/DSL Internet access not to mention corporate mergers between film, television, and new media giants, the lines between television and the Internet are increasingly blurred. Bernardi analyzes the representation of race on Internet Web sites and argues that the social reality of cyberspace includes "aesthetically pleasing hate speech and racist pedophilia." To address the proliferation of pornographic Web sites featuring ethnic women, Bernardi extends Donna Haraway's cyborg manifesto into cyberspace, or Internet culture, and notes how utopian visions of this parallel universe ignore the socio-cultural history of racism and misogyny.

Television does not simply portray a window onto a real world "out there," but frames the world, contextualizes the narrative, and argues for the integrity of the reality it depicts. Therefore, the essays in the third part, "Real Discourse," examine several types of programming explicitly linked to lived social reality. Each essay interrogates the role of technology in the representation of this reality and considers how these representations function in relation to ideology and identity and support or help create social communities. The section begins with Marita Sturken's "Television Vectors and the Making of a Media Event: The Helicopter, the Freeway Chase, and National Memory," which analyzes the role live broadcasting plays in the construction of both local and national identities. Sturken juxtaposes the general globalization of media with the specificity of localized events that are broadcast live to a community of viewers who are addressed as members of a national culture. Specifically, she is interested in live programs that marshal multiple technologies in order to broadcast events that, by virtue of their live presentation, are categorized as "historic." To demonstrate the media's role in creating identity, Sturken analyzes the 1994 O. J. Simpson car chase in order to define the virtual spaces into which viewers are inserted. This internationally broadcast story occupied much of the country but particularly mesmerized Los Angelenos who watched, talked, made signs, and themselves became participants in televisual history.[35] Sturken uses the O. J. Simpson car chase to demonstrate the media vectors, or spaces, created by the live coverage of an event. From radio coverage, cell phone calls, preempted national broadcasts, satellite transmissions, the actual freeway, and helicopters recording overhead, Sturken describes how the virtual geography of these media vectors impacts history and memory and helps to create a national space incorporating all viewers as participants.

Live presentations of extraordinary events such as the O. J. Simpson car chase are only one of the ways in which the media constructs and defines space (local or national) for a community of viewers. Toby Miller's essay "Tomorrow Will Be . . . Risky and Disciplined," follows Sturken's analysis by examining one of the most common news segments: the weather. Miller examines the history of weather reporting and its connection to an economy of work and control. Far from a simple factual reporting, Miller argues that the technological knowledge employed in broadcasting the weather relates to our desire to know and control. He further analyses the placement of the weather within news broadcasts and demonstrates how it can serve as a replacement for or diversion from significant events occurring elsewhere. Ultimately, the presentation of the weather functions to define communities and to bind individuals together. Miller's essay demonstrates how the most normal everyday depiction of reality becomes highly politicized as it aids in the construction of community, serves to reinforce dominant cultural ideals, and sometimes deflects attention from man-made social crises.

One of the most complex, yet common, forms for depicting real-life stories has come to be known as reality TV. The final two essays in this section examine two different kinds of reality TV programs: *Neighbours from Hell,* a popular British program, and *America's Most Wanted,* a staple of U.S. broadcasting over the past decade. Gareth Palmer begins the examination of reality TV when he explores the phenomenon of the program *Neighbours from Hell,* a successful ITV network offering that premiered in 1997. Palmer's analysis addresses the context in which the show emerged, the formal elements used to structure reality, and the show's content, which focuses on problems within communities. Palmer contextualizes the program within contemporary British politics and examines the use of reenactment, close-circuit security surveillance footage, video camcorders, and other forms connoting "reality." Like Sturken and Miller, Palmer is also intrigued by the manner in which the show generates communities both within the program and amongst viewers. He demonstrates how, through the use and depiction of selected British communities, the program serves to reinforce dominant cultural ideology regarding proper citizenship. While *Neighbours from Hell* is a British ITV program, Palmer's analysis makes clear the commonalties between culturally specific "reality" programming in the United States and abroad.

Margaret DeRosia is also interested in the construction of community and identity, and in the final essay of this section, "The Court of Last Resort: Making Race, Crime, and Nation on *America's Most Wanted,*" she focuses on the representation of race within these constructs. Much has been written about the racialized representation of criminality prevalent in American television news, dramatic programming, and reality-based crime shows, and DeRosia's contribution brings these commentaries to bear in a well-documented analysis of *America's Most Wanted,* one of the most popular and long-standing examples of reality TV. What makes DeRosia's analysis particularly provocative is her demonstration of the slippage between reenactments, mediated reality, social policy, and real (in this case police) practice. In addition, her documentation of official endorsements of the program, ranging from local law enforcement to President Clinton, demonstrates how its depiction of reality becomes tied to dominant ideology and impacts contemporary social concerns. Whether televisual "reality" focuses upon an ongoing police investigation, a community problem, or the daily weather, the essays in this third section together demonstrate how the media's representation structures and presents information so as to contrast community and national identities, define proper citizenship, present caricatures of otherness, and reinforce dominant ideologies.

The fourth and final section, "Real Fiction," moves away from nonfiction television to investigate representations of reality in dramatic programming. From TV movies based upon real events to programs creating fictionalized accounts of current news stories, reality has become a primary source for and influence upon network television production. The section begins with John Caldwell's insightful investigation of how reality conventions are periodically mapped onto prime-time network serial fiction. In "Prime-Time Fiction Theorizes the Docu-Real," Caldwell notes the appearance of what he refers to as "docu-real" episodes, which the networks often roll out as special events intended to garner critical acclaim and spike viewership for pivotal periods such as sweeps week. His analysis explores self-reflexivity within these programs, the institutional use of reality as a promotional vehicle, and addresses the question of "what is real?" In this way, Caldwell's discussion of the "docu-real" serves as a fluid transition between earlier essays considering more traditional nonfiction programming and the remaining contributions focused on representations of reality in fiction. While Caldwell uses distinctions such as fiction/nonfiction, and examines their hybrids as a distinct genre of television, he also performs an institutional analysis focused on the ways in which the television industry self-consciously produces, promotes, and increasingly combines elements of both fiction and nonfiction within programming.

While Caldwell's analysis incorporates a variety of programs from the fifties through the nineties, Jodi Dean focuses her essay, "Uncertainty, Conspiracy, Abduction," on a single series, *The X-Files*. Dean's analysis connects the form and content of *The X-Files* to contemporary political events as well as to the logic or structure of the Internet. Dean's analysis of *The X-Files* is both engaging and provocative as it focuses on specific paradigmatic episodes of the series. On one level, she connects individual episodes to contemporary news events, while on another level she finds recurrent narrative motifs within the series that present contradictory open-ended conclusions that mirror or are linked to a representation of subjectivity in the Information Age. Although one might not expect a program dealing with aliens to be a prime subject for considering representations of reality, *The X-Files* regularly reinterprets contemporary events. Undoubtedly the program uses known events to lend credibility to the strange and bizarre explanations it offers. In doing so, the show defies the simple truths and reductive explanations of reality offered in the popular press and replaces them with inconclusive readings based on contradictory interpretations of information. As Dean demonstrates, the program suggests that "the truth is out there" while refusing to promote the singularity of truth. Dean's analysis of *The X-Files* describes a programmatic architecture that emerges parallel to, and mirrors, the proliferation of information (and ambiguous truths) found on the Internet.

The final essay in this collection furthers this interest in psychological issues and considers television's presentation of therapy and its impact on social subjectivity. Mimi White has written a great deal on television and therapy, and in her essay, "Television, Therapy, and the Social Subject; or, The TV Therapy Machine," she looks specifically at the representation of therapeutic discourse in daytime programming. White builds upon Foucault's writing on confession and applies it to a variety of programs including talks shows, game shows, and advice programs. Examining the ways in which television employs therapeutic discourse, White finds a conflation of entertainment and medical expertise that stands as an alternate model of the therapeutic process. Emerging in the era of managed care and short-term treatment, television therapy eschews traditional long-term therapeutic models and privileges self-help, quick fixes, and humor instead. White's analysis delves into the contemporary construction of social subjectivity and addresses the changes made possible through new technologies. Building upon Foucault, she suggests ways in which technological advances have altered subject positions within his model of confession. White argues that the confessional model is dominant among therapy programs and describes how shifts in the confessional transaction impact viewers.

The variety of essays included in this collection point to the complexity involved in television's representations of reality. Indeed, future areas of inquiry might include discussions of preproduction—how reality impacts programming prior to its being filmed (or taped)—technology, and industry economics. The avenues for interrogating representations of reality are as limitless as television itself. This collection has been designed to outline many of the concerns related to televisual representations of reality but not to define or exhaust it. The essays that follow only begin an examination of the representation and containment of issues or events within the squared televisual viewing space, as well as the exponential growth of these representational programs on broadcast and cable TV. In this sense, *Reality Squared* elucidates the ways in which reality is reflected by and refracted through television programming; and the ways in which television serves to frame and fuel discussions about events in the world.

NOTES

1. Clearly more than one book addresses this issue, but scholars have generally discussed the issue of reality in relation to other research interests rather than as their subject.

2. Robert Stam, "Television News and Its Spectator," in *Regarding Television*, ed. E. Ann Kaplan (Los Angeles: American Film Institute, 1983), 24–25.

3. Jane Feuer, "The Concept of Live Television: Ontology as Ideology," in *Regarding Television*, 13.

4. According to Professor Dieter Poetsch, who teaches at the Fachhochschule Wiesbaden University of Applied Science in the Department of Television and Multimedia Engineering. Dr. Poetsch helped develop early film-to-video transfer equipment in Germany.

5. Robert Vianello, "The Rise of the Telefilm and the Networks' Hegemony Over the Motion Picture Industry," *Quarterly Review of Film Studies* 5 (summer 1994): 210.

6. It was possible for networks to simply sell live programs to affiliates and become contact providers, but this practice was explicitly prohibited. In fact, prior to the establishment of the transcontinental link in 1951, affiliates on the West Coast had to receive filmed versions (kinescopes) of live programs. Aesthetics were certainly an issue for the networks, since the filmed versions came off rather flat, but this concern was clearly secondary to lining up affiliates and strengthening the network.

7. For a full discussion, see J. Fred MacDonald, *One Nation Under Television: The Rise and Decline of Network TV* (Chicago: Nelson-Hall, 1994).

8. Stam, "Television News," 24.

9. *Real People* had a short run in 1979 and earned a regular spot in the 1980 lineup. The program finished as the fifteenth highest rated show for the 1979–80 season. For 1980–81 it moved up to number twelve. *That's Incredible* was a response to *Real People* and finished the 1979–80 season as the ninth highest rated show on television. In 1990, *America's Funniest Home Videos* premiered and finished the year as the fifth highest rated show.

10. See, for example, William Boddy, *Fifties Television: The Industry and Its Critics* (Urbana: University of Illinois Press, 1993), and Lynn Spigel and Michael Curtin, ed., *The Revolution Wasn't Televised: Sixties Television and Social Conflict* (New York: Routledge, 1997).

11. Boddy, *Fifties Television*, 84.

12. This temporality of the present is ideological rather than actual. News programming, newsmagazines, talk shows, game shows, and others programs are often taped to give a feeling of presence. In this way, broadcasters play upon the medium's potential for liveness and capitalize on the ability to bring stories to air more quickly than print media. The "temporality of the present" should not be, therefore, equated with the representation of reality but seen as a stylistic or formal production choice.

13. Respectable in terms of audience share as well as key demographics. For an example of these statistics, see "Reality Shocks Sweeps. (shock-value reality specials are a major factor in Feb. 1999 TV Sweeps ratings)," *Variety*, March 1, 1999, 70.

14. Richard Firstman, "Justice Rules: Inside Law and Order," *TV Guide*, March 28–April 3, 1998, 14.

15. While there are not many examples of this type of live programming, the shows are highly publicized and clearly linked to television's Golden Age by broadcasters and critics alike.

16. The number of articles is drawn from the Lexus-Nexus Academic Universe database.

17. Bill Carter, "Britons Revamp American TV; Exporting 'Millionaire' and 'Survivor' Was a Hard Sell with Crosscultural Allies and a Detour to Sweden," *New York Times*, July 18, 2000, E1.

18. See, for example, Brian Lowry, "In Early Going, 'Millionaire' Loses a Step," *Los Angeles Times*, October 11, 2000. Lowry discusses recent ratings and *Millionaire*'s 30 percent decrease from the preceding year. Kavita Daaswani, "'Millionaire' Is the Taj Mahal of Indian TV," *Los Angeles Times*, September 30, 2000, F1.

19. See, for example, Thomas Elsaesser, "Through the Looking Glass," in *American Television*, ed. Nick Browne (Langhorne, Pa.: Harwood, 1993), 97–120.

20. Daaswani, "'Millionaire' Is the Taj Mahal."

21. Brian Lowry, "'Reality' Craze Is Nothing New to Some TV Veterans," *Los Angeles Times*, July 1, 2000, F20.

22. Caryn James, "Machiavelli, on a Desert Isle, Meets TV's Reality. Unreal," *New York Times*, August 24, 2000, A1.

23. Brian Lowry, "On TV: Reality, in the Blinded Eyes of the Beholders," *Los Angeles Times*, August 29, 2000, F1.

24. Brian Lowry of the *Los Angeles Times* pointed out that the emergence of programming without actors coincided with a potential strike by the Screen Actors Guild. If actors were to go on strike, production of dramatic programming and sitcoms would be shut down. Reality-based programming, with its use of nonprofessional actors, would be able to continue production if a lengthy strike unfolded. This may be a secondary consideration to producers, but to Lowry it seems more than simple coincidence. For more on this, see Lowry, "Fall Preview/Television, Tossed About in TV's Rough Waters: The conflicting needs of networks, creators, viewers, and critics has resulted in a season of disconnections," *Los Angeles Times*, September 17, 2000, 13.

25. Bill Carter, "TV NOTES: 'Survivor' Star: One Man Is an Island Villain," *New York Times*, August 16, 2000, E1.

26. James, "Machiavelli, on a Desert Isle, Meets TV's Reality," A1.

27. Ibid.

28. Howard Rosenberg, "Reality TV in a World of Strange Bedfellows," *Los Angeles Times*, December 7, 1998, F1.

29. Ibid.

30. Bill Nichols, *Representing Reality* (Bloomington: Indiana University Press, 1991), 115.

31. John Caldwell, *Televisuality: Style, Crisis, and Authority in American Television* (New Brunswick, N.J.: Rutgers University Press, 1995).

32. Ibid., 4.

33. For example, the story line for *The X-Files* episode "X-Cops" presented the program's characters as participants in an episode of another Fox series, *Cops*. While this episode was presented in a self-conscious and reflexive manner, the characters within a "reality-program" gimmick served to heighten the sense of realism within the episode while at the same time promoting another Fox series.

34. Mimi White, "Television Liveness: History, Banality, Attractions" (unpublished essay, 1997). White discusses this position while summarizing postmodernist perceptions of television and history.

35. For more on this topic, see Vivian Sobchack, "Introduction: History Happens," in *The Persistence of History: Cinema, Television, and the Modern Event*, ed. Vivian Sobchack (New York: Routledge, 1996).

ONE

Constructing / Reconstructing History

Acting Live

TV Performance, Intimacy, and Immediacy (1945–1955)

RHONA J. BERENSTEIN

Television will satisfy the deep human desire to look, at times, on the force of reality.
—*Gilbert Seldes, 1949*

To me the great difference between radio and television performance is that television demands honesty. Radio is an escape from reality, whereas good television is reality.
—*George Burns, 1955*

Introducing Television

When television was introduced full force to the American public in the 1940s and early 1950s, the specificities of the medium were debated and delineated by industry professionals, journalists, and academics. Intent upon describing a fledgling technology with an important overarching ontological mandate—namely, to allow people to "see at a distance"—writers addressed TV as a medium firmly linked to attributes of liveness, immediacy, intimacy, and actuality. That is, television was assumed to offer to the viewer a particular temporal and spatial experience, an experience marked by a sense of nowness and hereness and inflected by presumed access to the real.

The dimensions of that experience—as it impacted viewers and as it characterized the medium as a whole—were articulated in both general and specific terms. The most thorough debates about the contours and qualities of television's ontological identity emerged in discussions of TV acting. Determining or analyzing how the TV actor must perform for the little screen—in relation and contrast to how s/he must perform on stage, for radio, or on the cinema screen—became a focal point for industry advocates.

These early discourses offer a rich resource for understanding the assumptions and biases that helped mold television's entry into American culture in the post–World War II era. Often explicitly linked to notions of the real, or "actuality" as it was referred to by a number of writers, television liveness and immediacy served as markers of the medium's assumed calling and as signposts of proper performance skills.

In this article I will explore the nuances of these early TV discussions and, furthermore, argue that liveness and immediacy, especially when combined with descriptions of televisual intimacy, functioned to reinforce American TV's commercial underpinnings by offering viewers performances that were assumed or promoted to be true to life. The study of early TV discourses in general and those centered on television acting in particular is, then, also the study of the establishment of patterns of TV-viewer interaction enmeshed in and with discourses of the real.

Perishable Art

In the opening chapter of *Acting in the Cinema,* James Naremore remarks, "The most interesting figures on the screen often look 'natural,' as if they were merely lending themselves to the manipulation of script, camera, and editing: the work they do is variable and vague, and critics usually discuss them as personalities, rather than as craftspeople."[1] If Naremore's estimation of cinematic performance—specifically, its naturalness and its reception by critics—is correct, then the study of early American television acting is potentially *more* variable and vague, more difficult to fix in place, than the performances captured on celluloid. Upon its widespread commercial inception in the late forties, television had the reputation of being a medium of immediacy: an apparatus that, more than film, offers its viewers live access to the world around them and hence, it was assumed, to reality.

But what do I mean, exactly, by the terms *immediacy* and *liveness*? In part, I am referring to the temporal dimensions of a performance whose specificity depends, at least in early TV terms, on the simultaneity of its production and reception. (*Immediate* is defined as "of or near the present time," in the *American Heritage Dictionary,* while *live* is described as "broadcast while actually being performed; not taped, filmed, or recorded."[2]) Additionally, both *immediate* and *live* resonate in spatial terms, suggesting a physical proximity between the viewer and the performance rendered. (*Immediate* is defined in the dictionary as "close at hand" and "near," while *live* is described as "involving performers or spectators who are physically present.") In fact, some dictionary definitions of immediacy use television as a central example: "Lack of intervening or mediating agency; directness: *the immediacy of live television coverage.*"[3] As these definitions suggest, the qualities of immediacy and liveness—which were attributed to early television by critics and broadcast experts—connote temporal and spatial rela-

tions between the viewer and performance at hand and suggest an unmediated or direct access to those performances. The assumed absence of an
intervening or mediating agency, to borrow the dictionary's phrasing, has
significant implications for the understanding of early television discourses
and presumed relationships among TV, television acting, and the real.

In a *New York Times* article published in 1952, Jack Gould described
the televisual specificity that was popular among journalists and industry
workers: "There is simply no substitute for the intangible excitement and
sense of anticipation that is inherent in the performance that takes place at
the moment one is watching. . . . To regard the [television] medium as
merely a variation on the neighborhood picture house is to misunderstand
the medium."[4] Whether or not Gould's claims about television are accurate
in an ontological sense—that is, whether or not television is *inherently*
live—is, in a way, not nearly as important as the belief in, and commitment
to, liveness and immediacy evoked by comments such as these.

I would like to begin with a brief consideration of some of the debates
about liveness and immediacy that have characterized the field of television
studies in the last fifteen or so years. These debates are noteworthy less for
their determining effect on any theorization of television's relationship to
liveness and more for their impassioned engagement with or against liveness
as a televisual element or construct. Television's status within the family
home, its relationship to the consumer public, and its central positioning in
American society have bestowed upon the medium a level of cultural significance that connotes truth-value, and truth-value and liveness have been
linked in both the cultural and professional television imaginations since the
forties. As Gilbert Seldes, TV writer, critic, and former CBS television executive,[5] remarked in 1952, "the TV camera is an x-ray, penetrating to the
reality behind appearance, showing up whatever is exaggerated and falsi-
fied."[6] While we may read Seldes's words today as a naïve attribution of
realist power to television, I think it would be wiser to understand his comments as continuing guideposts to our enduring social romance in the
United States with television as a realist medium.

In "The Concept of Live Television: Ontology as Ideology," her article
on 1980s morning news programming, Jane Feuer makes a compelling
argument for the construction of liveness on TV. For Feuer, whether or not
TV is inherently live is not as crucial as the impression of liveness manufactured by the various techniques codified into programs and production values. As she remarks: "Indeed, as television in fact becomes less and less a
'live' transmission, the medium in its own practices seems to insist more and
more upon an ideology of the live, the immediate, the direct, the spontaneous, the real."[7] Like Feuer, John Ellis has argued for television's investment in liveness. As he notes, "Television presents itself as an immediate

presence, except when it is borrowing [sic] the cinema with transmissions that are labeled 'films.' Television pretends to actuality, to immediacy; the television image . . . behaves as though it were live."[8] In addition to anthropomorphizing television, Ellis contends that the medium, except under circumstances that link it directly to cinema, is deeply invested in offering viewers impressions of actuality, immediacy, and liveness. The ideology of liveness may take a different form in the eighties and nineties than it did in the forties and fifties, yet it resonates across historical eras in terms of enduring assumptions about the relationships among television, its viewers, and those who perform (and sell wares) on the medium.

Most recently, the valorization of liveness, whether as a critical construct or an ontological imperative, has been scrutinized and critiqued with a view to expanding the consideration of televisual aesthetics. John Caldwell remarks, "As long as high theory continues to overestimate the centrality of liveness in television—even as it critiques liveness—it will also underestimate or ignore other modes of practice and production: the performance of the visual and stylistic exhibitionism."[9] In his call for a shift in evaluative perspectives on American television, Caldwell rejects the primacy of what he calls the "liveness myth"[10] and the "myth of nowness."[11] Yet, in his attempts to shift critical analysis away from liveness and toward televisual style in the eighties, Caldwell underestimates the ways in which the myth of liveness is not only a function of production values but also of reception context. Television images are received, for the most part, in viewers' homes; they become part of their everyday environs, they exist in viewers' present lives, in their experiences of the here and now.

Caldwell's critique also needs to be reconsidered with a view to understanding how writers addressed TV during the fifties. For example, while Gould bemoaned the rise of telefilm and valorized live TV, he also recognized the contributions to liveness that videotape could make: "The day is not far off when a TV picture will be shot in the morning and put on the screen that night. Or even better, a live program can be offered with the knowledge that it can be tape recorded and shown a second time with virtually the same quality."[12] According to Gould, then, the impending development of videotape in the fifties offered the means, unlike film, of maintaining the centrality of liveness even while a TV broadcast was *not* live.

While Gould's perspective predated the use of video, Richard Austin Smith offered a remarkably similar opinion in *Fortune* in 1958: videotape "preserves the subtle but no less important sense of immediacy heretofore found only on live programs."[13] Thus, while a scholar like Feuer may take more recent note of television's continuing investment in the (apparent) oxymoron *live on tape,* critics in the fifties valorized this technological development as a means of maintaining what they assumed were television's most important and unique qualities: liveness and immediacy. In fact, by the late seventies, academics presumed the endurance of liveness in non-live programming. "'Liveness' is a quality that people have come to expect from the TV medium," wrote theater professors James Hindman, Larry Kirkman, and Elizabeth Monk. They continued, "It provides the viewing context of nearly all broadcast programs, since the qualities of a live show can also be imitated in pre-taped or filmed shows that are later edited."[14] Thus, while Caldwell is justified in arguing for a more expansive consideration of televisual aesthetics, his attempts to demote the centrality of liveness and immediacy to our understanding of American television's ideological power and draw are premature.

In focusing on the ways in which TV was discussed in the forties and fifties, I am most interested in addressing both a favored production mode of the early TV era—live programming—and a philosophy of production that has endured since that era—an impression of liveness. No matter what we know about the myriad ways in which TV's texts are constructed, much American television programming remains marked by and invested in an intimate rapport between viewer and actor that depends upon the impression of liveness or, at the very least, immediacy for its effective spectatorial address. As I will argue in the following section, analyzing how that impression was imagined and invested in by writers in the early days of television deepens our understanding of TV's position in postwar American culture as a site of fantasy and commercial potential.

Living-Room Liveness

Prior to the widespread commercialization of television in the United States, Judy Dupuy—a "writer, engineer, news broadcaster, and producer of beauty and fashion trade shows"[15]—described television in 1945 as follows: "Motion pictures, the theater and radio have all contributed to the arts but visual broadcasting is developing a creative form all its own."[16] That form, according to Dupuy, is part of an ancient ontological imperative:

> Man has always wanted to be in two places at the same time and now he can be by means of television. Tele is Greek for "at a distance." Vision, of course, means the "ability to see." Therefore, television is the ability to see at a distance. Man at home pushes a button on his television receiver and he then can see what is being televised in a studio many miles away or he can be a spectator at a Yale Bowl football game or a parade down Fifth Avenue.[17]

Dupuy's description of television posits an overarching ontological fantasy: TV is the result of man's desire to "see at a distance," a venture that does not require him to move physically—or at least not in conventional physical terms—to that distant sight. Furthermore, television allows for ease of operation, as well as instant gratification. The viewer merely presses a button at home and is offered immediately a selection of visual delights. Unlike radio's aural limitations, or the cinema's temporal limits (the schism between the moment of filming and the time of projection), TV offers instant and simultaneous visual transport to faraway places. As Gilbert Seldes asserted in 1952, "The essence of television techniques is their contribution to the sense of immediacy."[18] In 1949, but three years prior to Seldes's pronouncement, Henry Cassirer contextualized television's brand of immediacy by describing the benefits offered to film by the new broadcast medium: "The motion picture cannot be transmitted instantaneously except by television."[19] Like Cassirer, whose focus was TV news, Richard Hubbell, who worked with Seldes in early television production at CBS from 1937 to 1942, was interested in the impact of television on filmed materials. In his 1945 publication, *Television: Programming and Production,* Hubbell drew a significant distinction between TV and motion pictures and outlined his assumptions regarding television's innate attributes: "In short, film can be transmitted over the television, just as easily as a 'live' program. But, *although motion pictures can provide a permanent record for television, they cannot transmit television in its true sense—cannot retain its speed of communication, its immediacy.*"[20]

Hubbell's description of TV is considerably more elaborate than Dupuy's, Seldes's or Cassirer's, and offers a good overview of the main tenets ascribed to TV (some of which were, in fact, also ascribed to radio and cinema). As Hubbell argues:

> Because the process of visual-aural extension is instantaneous, television can achieve the effect of making you feel that you are in two places at one time: watching your receiver at home . . . and at the scene of the telecast. This feeling is most pronounced when you know that you are viewing a "live" program, not a previously exposed motion-picture film. A viewer's reaction to a successful program often takes one of three forms:
>   (1) The effect of "looking in" on the program from the sidelines, without actually taking part in it. . . .
>   (2) The effect of not only "looking in" on the program, wherever it may be, but of actually taking part in it. . . .
>   (3) The person or persons in the program seem to step into your living room and converse with you.[21]

According to Hubbell, the TV viewer is engaged in processes of temporal simultaneity and spatial mobility unlike the cinema spectator. In fact, both Dupuy's and Hubbell's evocation of an ontological dimension to television—the urge to be two places at once and to see at a distance—suggest that the medium's uniqueness, as perceived by industry advocates, resided in its ability to spatialize time and temporalize space.[22] Television renders presence present by ostensibly overcoming spatial distance and time lags by providing the viewer with the experience of immediate and proximate access to the world (that is, to television's world).

According to Hubbell, the quintessential televisual experience is, therefore, marked by immediacy (instantaneous transmission), liveness (versus a pre-filmed motion picture), and physical proximity (being two places at one time). Proximity is, in Hubbell's description, also evocative of a feeling of intimacy: the viewer looks in on, takes part in, or is directly addressed by the program. This aspect of television evokes performance in that viewers are made to feel as if those persons who appear in a program (whether announcers or dramatic actors) actually step into their homes and communicate directly with them (I will return to this point shortly).

Hubbell summarizes these elements of the televisual experience succinctly when he remarks, "The audience can be made to feel a *sense of participation*, of being in two places at one time. . . . In 'live' programs, particularly of news and sporting events, there is that *sense of immediacy, of actuality*. One knows that what he is seeing and hearing is actually taking place at that moment."[23] That knowledge, according to Hubbell, has a realist aspect to it insofar as the viewer's participation in and access to the events that are transmitted via television is also access to actuality. Noteworthy is that while Hubbell highlights news and sporting events, the viewer's experience of actuality is linked more directly to liveness in general (which also took the form of dramatic programming) than to any single TV genre.

This privileging of actuality also appeared in Rudy Bretz's work. For Bretz, who wrote for the *Hollywood Quarterly* and eventually published a coauthored book on the medium, television possesses three primary qualities: immediacy, spontaneity, and actuality. He argues:

> "Actuality" refers to the feeling that what is being seen is real. This enhances the feelings of immediacy and spontaneity. . . . In a live theater where the audience occupies the same room with the actors, there is no particular advantage in the feeling that things are real. The audience knows the actors are real people. . . . An audience before a television screen, however, is fascinated by the actual and the real. The more that they can be kept conscious of the fact that the show they are watching is going on at that very moment in a very real place, the better they like it.[24]

According to Bretz, and in contrast to the perspectives offered by a number of his contemporaries, television's unique performance circumstances—live transmission combined with the viewer *not* being in the actor's presence—fosters an impression of actuality.

Despite the specificity that Hubbell and Bretz attributed to the televisual experience, their descriptions of TV are not entirely unlike some descriptions of radio and cinema. Cassirer, for example, offers a view of television as a mélange of elements: "Combining the instantaneous immediacy of radio with the realism of the motion picture with the personal intimacy of the lecture platform, presentation on television can bring events to life."[25] While Cassirer links TV's impression of intimacy to the lecture platform, earlier critics attributed it to radio. Writing in 1939, John S. Carlile remarked, "Radio dramatists and directors discovered how intimate this new theatre [radio] can be. Despite the unlimited audience, the audience can be brought close to hear the lowest-voiced confidence, the hushed words breathed at a hospital bedside, whispered protestations of love. . . . Such close contacts are not possible in the playhouse."[26] (Or as Arch Oboler noted in 1942, "Radio is a thing of intimacy."[27]) In Carlile's description, as in Hubbell's, intimacy is related to performance.

The term *intimacy* as applied to television (and radio before it) must be understood in multiple ways. At the most basic level, intimacy refers to that which is familiar, private, sexual, or "indicative of one's deepest nature," to quote the *American Heritage Dictionary*.[28] As mobilized in the forties and fifties vis-à-vis television, the term also refers to an emotional and physical proximity between the viewer and TV. Furthermore, televisual intimacy, unlike the intimacy ascribed to radio, was employed as a descriptive tool in contrast to spectacle and artifice. In his analysis of an anthology drama in 1953, theater critic Douglas Mackenzie described the show as follows: "This is just the sort of story that television is gaited to handle well; that is to say, it has intimacy, a small focus, and intensity of interest in one character. No spectacles intrude, nothing that the camera cannot translate into the living-room with simplicity."[29]

As I will explore further below, a number of writers linked television's intimacy to (1) its physical presence in the family home, (2) its technological limitations (for example, small screen size), (3) its specific production requirements (for example, small sets), and (4) the assumed bond created between the medium and viewers. All of these elements also worked in concert with American television's consumerist mandate. Actuality, liveness, and intimacy—although attributes linked to television from an ontological perspective—formed an important triad of qualities that reinforced the medium's focus on selling products. That is, it can be argued that products were sold effectively to viewers because they were linked to the real, to instant gratification, and to a sense of familiarity.

Radio and television's primary positions within the family home, their status as fixtures of a private environment, reinforced their stature as intimate media. As Judy Dupuy wrote, "Like radio, television is an intimate medium which goes into the home and must be welcomed as a fireside guest."[30] Here, Dupuy highlights television's role in the lives of its viewers

and, furthermore, anthropomorphizes the technology so that TV *itself*, and
not only those who appear on it, provides an intimate, domestic performance. In his critique of television for *Harper's*, Bernard Smith similarly took
note of TV's spatial positioning in 1948: "People will look at and listen to
television programs for the same reason that they now listen to the radio:
the television set is placed where it will form a part of the living habits of the
American people."[31] Thus, while cinema could be described as a realist
medium (although a number of critics believed it was less so than radio or
TV),[32] it was not assumed to be intimate—its spectators ventured out into
public for showings and remained at a physical distance from the screen.[33]

Writing in 1956, sociologist Leo Bogart made reference to the relationship between realism and intimacy in television. In a section of his book
entitled "The Illusion of Intimacy," he argued:

> Because the audience projects itself and its wishes into what it hears and sees,
> the broadcast media can create the illusion that their performers or announcers
> communicate directly to the people on the receiving end. This illusion is
> achieved because radio and television have a quality of immediacy. The listener
> or viewer feels that the person he hears is a real individual talking to him
> "right here and now." . . . Moreover, because the receiver is located in the
> home, the act of communication takes place in familiar surroundings. This
> helps create an intimate situation which contrasts with the more formal atmos-
> phere of the theater or with the impersonal symbolism of the printed word.[34]

Bogart captures the nuances of television's address to viewers and ties
together important aspects of the broadcast media's allure. The combination of the site of reception (the home) and the mode of transmission (immediacy) creates a powerful means of engaging and, according to Bogart,
manipulating audiences into believing that what they see (or hear) is real. In
a sense, television might be said to promote the illusion of *intimate realism*,
a form of realism more enhanced than that produced by radio due to the
visual components of television broadcasting.

According to industry advocates, an impression of intimacy was also
fostered in radio and television because of limitations related to amplification and screen size, that is, because they required listeners and viewers to
sit relatively close in order to hear or see performances. As Samuel L.
Becker, director of television, radio, film at the State University of Iowa, and
H. Clay Harshbarger, chair of the department of speech and dramatic art at
the same institution, argued in 1958, "[The broadcaster] will be able to
make [the image] no larger than 21 inches for most audiences."[35] The limited size of the screen required even the best-sighted viewers to position
themselves close to their sets. This physical positioning was presumed to
forge a close bond between the broadcast media and those who listened to

or watched them. For example, Arch Oboler described the situation with radio thus: "In the medium of radio every listener is standing right before an actor and there must be an underemphasis in both the coloring and the projection of the speech." For Oboler, who goes on to refer to radio as "an intimate medium," performers must modulate their voices because their audiences are physically proximate.[36] Ignoring the possibility of variations in amplification (either via the manipulation of sound levels or of the actor's distance from the microphone), Oboler removes all physical space and, indeed, all barriers between the radio actor and listener.

Television critics, too, imagined this sort of physical proximity between the medium and viewers, as evidenced by Jack Gould's claims: "Both the player in the studio and the audience at home have an intuitive awareness of being in each other's presence. . . . The foundation of this rapport [between TV performer and audience] is a shared experience of the immediacy of the present."[37] Here, television's ability to render presence present—that is, to temporalize space and spatialize time—is what accounts for its presumed intimacy and, in fact, offers an added dimension impossible with radio: visual intimacy. Writing of live television performances, Walter Kingson, Rome Cowgill, and Ralph Levy similarly privileged proximity: "In a live television program, you don't let the viewer sense that you're surrounded by well-ordered chaos, and in some filmed programs you can't let the viewer sense that you're playing to a cast and crew instead of to a live audience. You must seem to have audience *contact*."[38]

According to a number of writers, that contact was reinforced by the intimacy between the actor and the camera. In his television production manual, Melvin White mentioned the "close-up intimacy of the camera" and indicated that the actor, due to this technical aspect, must avoid overacting and mugging.[39] Orrin Dunlap Jr., too, remarked upon the camera's role in TV performance: "Television is different from stage acting because the nearness of the camera makes it more intimate."[40] Offering a generalized estimation of television, Giraud Chester and Garnet R. Garrison mentioned that the "intimacy of the medium calls for naturalness in bodily action."[41] To a remarkable degree, television was assumed to engage viewers by addressing them as people who existed in physical proximity to their television sets and, therefore, to the programming and performers that appeared on their consoles.

As this discussion of the intimate rapport between TV performances and viewers suggests, the positioning of television in the home is a practical arrangement but one with significant ideological consequences. TV not only collapses the private and public spheres but, as Lynn Spigel has shown of early televisual discourses, it provided the viewer, especially the housewife, with the illusion of escape into the world at large. As Spigel remarks:

"Women's home magazines displayed television sets in decorative settings that created the illusion of spatial conquests. The television set was often placed in rooms with panoramic window views, or else installed next to globes and colorful maps. . . . The depiction of domestic space [on situation-comedies] appears to have been based in part upon those utopian predictions that promised that television would provide for its audiences a view of outside spaces."[42] Television's spatial positioning—as a domestic fixture coincident with 1950s' architectural trends toward picture windows, for example—and its promise of spatial mobility—as a means of visually transporting the viewer to faraway places—fostered an environment in which domestic entrapment was figured as televisual wanderlust and an illusive form of spatial empowerment. Like the consumerist mandates developed in the twenties, one of which promised women liberation when they exercised their choice among consumer products,[43] television provided viewers with a veritable window on the world, an initially cost-free immobile shopping spree.

At the same time that television offered this grand and grandiose access to a world "out there," it also suggested—by its intimate presentation of images—that the world existed not as a space for physical exploration (except via consumerism) but as a space that has already been conquered. Television achieved this impression by its ability to temporalize space and spatialize time and its mobilization of the impression of being two places at once. This was reinforced by the fact that this impression depended, to a degree, on the assumption that what the viewer sees is really taking place in the here and now. As I will argue in the remaining sections of this article, these qualities of early television—its immediacy, intimate placement in the home, and evocation of actuality—are criteria for both early televisual acting techniques and, in TV's links to consumerism, ideologically charged descriptions of the medium in the forties and fifties.

Understanding Acting

While there exist a number of books that address cinematic performance, such as James Naremore's *Acting in the Cinema* and Carole Zucker's anthology, *Making Visible the Invisible*,[44] moving image performances remain an understudied area of inquiry in large part because acting poses significant challenges to the critic. Dramatic performances regardless of the medium are, if not immune to evaluation, then so intangible as to be difficult to describe. In fact, a qualitative vocabulary designed to evaluate the nuances of performance remains lacking. "She gave a good performance" or "He was believable in the part"—standard modes of describing acting accomplishments—offer little in the way of qualitative detail.

The absence of a critical vocabulary has been unimportant in some discussions of acting. This is especially true when the dominant perspective has been that there is no object to analyze. As Fanny Kemble, a stage actress, wrote in *The Cornhill Magazine* in 1863, acting is an "art that requires no study worthy of the name: it creates nothing; it perpetuates nothing."[45] Kemble's comments were taken up over sixty years later by Montrose J. Moses, a critic for *Theatre Arts Monthly*, who used them in 1926 to inspire a suggestive question: "Is it true that acting creates nothing definite, that it is all perishable?"[46]

For Montrose, who is invested in raising acting to a lofty plateau (the title of his article is "The Royal Roads to Acting"), the perishability of acting is deeply distressing; so distressing, in fact, that he offers a passionate argument for the enduring power of noteworthy performances. Montrose's response to Kemble's dismissal of acting as unproductive and ephemeral is a testimony to the power of performances to inspire both an impassioned reaction on the part of the audience as well as a desire to capture those performances in critical and descriptive terms.

In spite of this urge to fix, to name, to describe performances, the lessons of early American television acting might be said to celebrate precisely the opposite quality: namely, the perishable and ephemeral. That ephemerality helped shape the medium's acting principles and, as noted earlier, was assumed to reinforce a privileged relationship with and to the real. I do not mean to suggest that early TV critics were not invested in naming and describing the performances rendered. However, a presumed and crucial element of many of those performances, an attribute valorized as a sign of skilled acting, and as an ontological signifier of the medium as a whole, was an immediate and fleeting quality. In addition, as I will argue shortly, the qualitative discussion of early television performances, most notably the creation of a critical vocabulary for teaching TV acting techniques in manuals, *depended,* to a degree, upon the perishable nature of the medium's best-loved productions.

TV or Not TV

"*Acting is acting,* wherever you find it, whether on stage or screen," wrote drama coach Lillian Albertson in 1947, but "there are differences in stage and screen acting . . . and they are important ones."[47] Albertson's comments, which appeared in her book *Motion Picture Acting,* are a means of attributing both universality and specificity to dramatic performances. The paradox that she presents appears with some frequency in writings about acting, whether their focus is the theater, cinema, radio, or television. One of the few exceptions to this paradox was offered by stage, screen, and, later, TV actor Hume Cronyn. Unlike Albertson, he privileged the universalizing approach in 1949: "The difference between acting for the screen and acting for the stage is negligible and the latter is, despite the exceptions, the best possible training for the former."[48]

Albertson's paradoxical approach to acting, though, was far more popular, especially in early writing about radio and TV. As radio critic Raymond Tyson noted in 1939, "Although the basic tenets of acting are the same regardless of the medium, each one—stage, screen, and radio—puts entirely different demands upon the player. . . . The actor in radio in many ways faces problems more formidable than those encountered in the theatre. . . . In radio the actor has only his voice to realize the fullest expression of character and situation."[49] While Tyson's comments can be read as a defensive effort to attribute skill to the radio actor, an enterprise in which other critics joined him,[50] his remarks also delineate the particular demands made by a solely aural medium on performers. In his 1950 manual, *Radio and Television Acting*, drama coach Edwin Duerr provides an equally paradoxical vision of performance: "Radio and television acting, though new to the theatre, are not so unique that they can be separated from the general field of acting."[51] He continues, "The basic differentiation between radio acting and all other kinds of acting is, of course, that it is only auditory, that it forfeits all visual appeals for an audience." While the difference between acting for radio and acting for the stage or cinema may be apparent, Duerr also highlights the skills demanded by television:

> The television actor, in order to know his specific business, needs to discover wherein video acting differs, although not in essentials, both from acting in general and from acting in radio. . . . Unlike radio acting:
> (1) Television acting depends on the memorization of the words of the script.
> (2) Television acting is directed simultaneously at both the ear and the eye of the audience, is seen as well as heard. Like radio acting, it differs from acting in general in [the following ways]: bondage to a clock, quick and arbitrary transitions, huge audiences not assembled in a theatre, and a lack of traditional theatre projection.[52]

Duerr's discussion of television marks out a performance space that has much in common with other media. Like the stage and movies, TV acting requires memorization and engages aural and visual stimuli. Like radio, however, televisual performances are "bound to a clock" and require "quick transitions"—that is, Duerr assumes they are live.[53] Duerr's characterization of the similarities and contrasts between TV and the acting techniques that are reserved for other media recalls the remarks made by drama coach Josephine Dillon Gable a decade earlier. As Gable noted in 1940,

"The technique of acting in television is a combination of radio dialogue and motion picture photography."[54]

If Gable was correct in describing television acting as a means of conjoining radio with film techniques, how, specifically, does TV put that combination into effect and what unique performance elements are, then, constructed? Here I want to return to Duerr's assumption that television acting is, necessarily, live, and re-invoke a claim I made earlier—namely, that at least one of the criteria employed to teach acting in the era of early television *depended* on the real or assumed-to-be ephemeral quality of productions. By being in "bondage to a clock," the television actor, like the radio performer, had to develop a technique that would allow for live broadcast, that would suit the demands of the medium and still engage viewers. According to William C. Eddy, that technique must remain believable: "The actor must always remember that the main factor of all successful television productions is the element of naturalness, and he must work toward this end. The closer that the actor, by reason of his experience and knowledge of the system, can approach this goal, the higher will rise his star in the new firmament of the video arts."[55] Richard Hubbell, too, was convinced that television demanded a more naturalistic performance style, one that "rejects many purely theatrical conventions," such as projecting one's voice and making sudden or expansive gestures.[56] Hubbell's TV actor must also be expertly trained to deal with the quick temporal transitions demanded by the switcher in live productions: "We must look for more expert acting than is called for in either theatre or motion pictures. The actor must be able to sustain his technique for the moving camera, now in close-up, now in long shot."[57] This combination of naturalistic acting styles with assumptions regarding live performance points to the medium's privileged relationship to techniques of realism and naturalism. It also indicates the degree to which preconceptions about television acting were part of a larger ideological project—a project linked to mandates of consumerism— that demanded that television foster a unique and intimate relationship between TV (and TV actors) and viewers/consumers.[58]

The attempts by early television advocates to espouse a televisual performance technique are nowhere more focused than in Judy Dupuy's work. In a detailed description of the relationship between production mandates and performance, Dupuy notes:

In developing an acting technique for television it is first necessary to understand the basic principles of the medium which affect picture composition. These basic factors are:

(1) Television is an *intimate medium.* The home audience sees performers on a *small screen in close-up* from a distance of three to five feet or at most from

across the room. Performers, under these circumstances, must appear *natural* to viewers.

(2) The camera lens has a narrow field. This means that performers must learn to act with restricted gestures in close grouping. . . .

(3) The perspective of the television picture appears to the eye to have depth and space. . . . Performers, required by the narrow field of the lens to be crowded against each other, appear on the screen to be comfortably chatting in an *intimate* group.

(4) Television shows go on the air in *one continuous performance*, hence, the television actor must memorize his part to the letter perfect in all lines, gestures and area playing positions.[59]

Dupuy's comments, like Hubbell's, serve multiple purposes. First, they appeared just prior to the mass marketing of television and, therefore, helped establish the medium as a viable, and impressive, platform for talented dramatic performers. Second, they detailed the specific skills required for acting success on TV, skills that promoted a new televisual performance style. Finally, Dupuy's comments confirmed the primacy of television as a *live* and *intimate* medium; a medium that required performance techniques to match those qualities and reinforce an impression of naturalism. The assumption was that TV actors were required to be natural *and* accessible for the benefit of viewers.

As I remarked earlier, this sense of intimacy is repeated with great regularity in early television manuals. It was touted, in fact, as a warning to film actors who, naïvely it seems, believed they could make the transition from the large to small screen without retraining. As Jan Bussell, an early television producer and performer, wrote in 1952 of the different speech skills demanded of film and TV: "Film actors may consider they have already acquired this technique, but the home screen goes a great deal further than the cinema in intimacy and quietness."[60] Actors themselves became aware of precisely this mandate, as articulated by TV performer Patricia Murray in 1944: "The intimacy of television cannot be over-emphasized. . . . So far as the performer is concerned, he is working for a small group of people assembled in a cozy living room."[61]

Close-Up and Personal

The natural and accessible qualities attributed to performers link television acting not only to production values in general, but to American TV as a specific ideological form. The development and function of the television close-up, for example, can be understood as both a technical necessity (camera work was developed, in part, to accommodate the screen's small size) and an ideological effect (camerawork was coincident with selling products to viewers via intimate and realistic means). Here, I want to address the close-up as a visual technique that, while an element of cinematic style, was especially well suited to, and exploited by, the consumerist impulses of TV. The use of the close-up as a filmmaking device, one that demanded specific responses on the part of the motion picture actor, was noted by Lillian Albertson in 1947: "The camera . . . comes up close to the actor, and registers every fleeting expression."[62] Hume Cronyn, too, emphasized this technique in "Notes on Film Acting": "In 'closeup' very little becomes very much; a whole new range of expression is opened to the actor."[63]

Discussions of television performance established not only the importance of the close-up to the medium but also emphasized its popularity with viewers. As Josephine Gable remarked, "Most of the scenes are close-up and three-quarter shots as in the motion pictures, and will be more and more . . . as television develops, for more and more the audience wishes to see the expression of the faces, and cares less for the settings of the room or location."[64] Like film acting coaches before him, Edwin Duerr emphasized the performance techniques demanded of the close-up: "Most faces, it is true, can register the most obvious emotions, such as anger, horror, great joy, pain, and the like; but for television they must be trained to show all the more subtle shades of meaning and feelings. The actor's face must be so sensitive that it can reflect a character's every thought and emotion until the viewers can literally *see* the personality." Gable and Duerr suggest that television's use of the close-up is both more frequent and necessary than the cinema's appeal to the same technique. For Duerr, this was a function of screen size, which meant that the medium was "compelled to use more close-ups than are ordinarily used on the motion-picture screen."[65]

Duerr was joined by other industry experts in his equation of screen size with shot size. For example, Rudy Bretz, who worked with Richard Hubbell as part of Gilbert Seldes's CBS Television Program Department in the late thirties and early forties, made the following pronouncement in 1950–51: "A large deterrent to the full enjoyment of any program is, of course, the small size of the average television screen. . . . This restriction has led to a great concentration on close-ups and a hesitancy in the use of long shots, simply to make sure that the audience is able to see the subject properly."[66] While screen size cannot be overlooked entirely as a motivation for favoring the close-up, television's fondness for it during the heyday of live TV must be understood as more than the result of technical necessity: it was an ideological tool as well.[67]

Thus, part of early television's intimacy in dramatic and variety shows was created by its conditions of performance, and the close-up facilitated an intimate rapport between viewer and performer. Early television programs were, in most cases, sponsored shows in which an announcer, the sponsor's representative, spoke directly to the viewer in a bid for her consumerist response. While the announcer did not always serve as an emissary for the sponsor, broadcasting's economic paradigms in the United States ensured that radio listeners and TV viewers encountered many product advocates. Thus, Richard Tyson's 1939 description of the radio narrator resonates when read with radio and then television's consumerist impulses in mind: "The use of a narrator in the role of a 'storyteller' helps to develop that sense of intimacy to the drama broadcast. This quality of intimacy permits characters in the radio play to get closer to the individual members of their audience."[68]

In television terms, the close-up helped facilitate the spatial proximity described by Tyson. William Eddy details this process of spatial closeness:

> In television, the audience is brought into a new close-up intimacy with the actors in the play. . . . Under these circumstances, the actor would do well to play his part to the cameraman behind the lens, as representative of the unseen audience seated before the television receivers in the home. Television has brought about this new intimacy between player and audience, not only because of the predominating technique of close-up photography used, but even more because of the environment in which the average set owner will see the program.[69]

Television's commitment to the close-up and its reception in the home were, as Eddy remarks, crucial for actors. But they were also crucial for audiences. For they created a comfortable rapport between viewers and performers, a relationship that could be exploited for the sale of products. Thus, when Gilbert Seldes noted that "no matter how big the [TV] screen [becomes], the medium shot cannot supplant the *close-up* in its . . . [function] *to concentrate attention*,"[70] he spoke directly to the technique's importance as a means of drawing viewers into the performances rendered—performances that helped showcase consumer wares. In this way, the acting techniques aligned with television and the ontological descriptions of the medium, both of which presumed as well as fostered a reliance on what I referred to earlier as *intimate realism,* reinforced a rapport between the viewer and TV/actor that implicitly reinforced consumerism.

Tube Stars

Television's unique, intimate mode of cultivating star personalities magnified the viewer's impression that performers were accessible, real people. In her discussion of the transition by a number of film stars from motion pictures to television, Denise Mann remarks upon the different personae

demanded by each medium. Movies create "auratic stars,"[71] constructed in
a complex and often contradictory manner, that remain at a distance from
their fans. Because of the consumerist impulses of American commercial television, however, early TV stars were constructed as "ordinary individuals—frustrated butchers and homely aunts—[which can be seen as] . . . a
compensatory gesture designed to counteract the celebrity's status as either
upper class, *or* as corporate property."[72] She continues, "By contrasting the
TV stars to their Hollywood counterparts, the believability and trustworthi-
ness of the former were reinforced. . . . [This] encouraged women to
empathize with TV stars as sincere product salespersons."[73] Mann adds that
TV stars were also promoted according to their "naturalness,"[74] which was
meant to contrast with the glamorous image perpetuated by, and for, film
stars.

In his analysis of the discursive construction of cinematic stardom, John
Ellis reinforces Mann's perspective when he notes that the film "star is at
once ordinary and extraordinary, available for desire and unattainable."
This process is not uniform across media, however: "A similar creation of
stars is impossible for broadcast TV."[75] The movie star's persona is impaired
by television because of the specifics of the viewer-TV relationship. Ellis
argues: "The television performer exists very much . . . in the same space as
the television audience, as a known and familiar person rather than as a
paradoxical figure."[76] As TV actor Bill Lawrence remarked in 1949, "You
become recognized as a person on TV. . . . People know who you are and
what you look like."[77] Jack Gould phrased the contrast between TV and
film spectatorship succinctly in 1956: "It is the difference between being
with somebody and looking at somebody."[78] Like Gould, early TV producer
Fred Coe recognized the uniqueness of this viewer-TV relationship when he
commented, "The faces and figures and voices that travel our coaxial cables
have achieved a rapport with American audiences that no other medium of
communication has ever equaled."[79]

While Mann focuses on the ways in which character types and TV's
generic contexts, such as the comedy-variety show, contributed to this
process of bringing the film star "down to earth," or down to TV, there is
every indication that the general skills demanded of actors also impacted
this process. In the making of the television star, for example, Judy Dupuy
offered a scenario in 1945 remarkably compatible with Mann's: "Television
will develop its own coterie of stars—stars that may rival the Hollywood
colony in fan popularity. The television actor and actress, however, meet
their public on a small screen in the intimate circle of the family, during a
performance of a show that demands continuous action."[80] Thus even in the
case of TV personalities destined to reach star status, including those who
had not succeeded in motion pictures, early television's call for natural, live,

and intimate acting styles, combined with production values that reinforced immediacy, succeeded in constructing the medium's performers as accessible, ordinary folk. They were people who had much in common with viewers. Perhaps no other early TV critic articulated this phenomenon better than Orrin Dunlap Jr., who remarked, "On both sides of the Atlantic it is generally agreed upon that a star of the silver screen will not necessarily be a star of the radio screen. . . . On the more intimate home screen [of television] the artist becomes a member of the family circle; he or she enters the home more as a friend or neighbor than as a performer."[81] The very accessibility of television stars, their construction as ordinary, as friends and neighbors, as opposed to performers (that is, as opposed to those who feign emotions and actions), reinforced their presentation to the American public as real people. In contrast to the artifice and distance that characterized movie stars, TV personalities were credible product salespeople precisely because they appeared on a medium and employed acting principles that rendered them believable, accessible, and hence real to viewers.

By drawing out the ideological significance of early television acting, though, I do not want to suggest that the qualities attributed to early TV and, hence, to performances on this new medium were not enjoyable to and entertaining for viewers. On the contrary, an acting style (and a medium) devoted to fostering a sense of immediacy and intimacy was, in all likelihood, quite satisfying to those who watched TV. But it is also an acting style that meshed perfectly with television's commitment to selling products, a commitment that depended on targeted viewers (especially white, married women) identifying with, and relating to, the impulses, personalities, and lifestyles of those who were depicted on the small screen.

In this way, acting techniques not only fit the visual limits of the TV set but also fit the mandates of a consumerist philosophy dependent on intimacy and realism as selling ploys. Accomplished TV actors, then, learned to portray their characters naturalistically, to deal with the spontaneous changes required of live productions, and they learned the facial and emotional nuances demanded of the TV close-up. As Molly Berg, star and writer of *The Goldbergs*, noted of her cast in 1949, "Our actors seem to live their roles, and I am fortunate indeed in television to have life breathed into my creations."[82]

It was not only actors who learned to develop their craft in the context of a medium motivated by advertising principles. Writers, too, were trained to approach their work as both drama and business. In fact, the language of business was a prominent part of discourses of the time. As Gilbert Seldes remarked in his 1952 book, *Writing for Television,* "All the elements in television production are directed to the ultimate consumer and the writer must keep that consumer constantly in mind; so it might be a good exercise to approach writing for television first by way of the living room instead of the studio where programs originate."[83]

If TV performers learned the techniques demanded of the new, intimate and immediate medium of television properly, they succeeded in providing viewers with performances destined to reach them in the privacy of their own homes and to speak to them as intimate and living emissaries of TV. In the case of *The Goldbergs*, this meant that Berg's cast brought Sanka coffee, in addition to the dramatic twists and turns of the family portrayed, into the homes of its viewers. In the case of other early television shows, this meant that intimate and immediate performances also fostered intimate and immediate contact with the products touted or used by the actors on television's small screen. In early TV terms, then, effective acting must be viewed as more than technical prowess. It was also a signpost of the medium's economic basis, a signifier of consumerism that was disguised, or served simultaneously, as a dramatic yet realistic art designed to speak to the hearts, minds, and pocketbooks of its viewers.

NOTES

I would like to thank Vivian Sobchack for our engaging conversations about many of the ideas explored in this article. Thanks, too, to James Friedman for his excellent editorial suggestions, which greatly improved this piece. Finally, thank you to Lia Hotchkiss, Azin Samari, and Allison Spencer for their greatly appreciated research assistance.

1. James Naremore, *Acting in the Cinema* (Berkeley: University of California Press, 1988), 1.

2. *American Heritage Dictionary of the English Language,* 3d ed., s.v. "live."

3. *American Heritage Dictionary,* s.v. "immediacy."

4. Jack Gould, "A Plea for Live Video," *New York Times,* December 7, 1952, 17. Another strong advocate of live television was Rod Serling. As he remarked in 1957, "Whatever memorable television moments exist were contributed by live shows. Whatever techniques were developed that were television's own are live techniques" ("TV in the Can vs. TV in the Flesh," *New York Times Magazine,* November 24, 1957, 49). While a number of journalists favored live over filmed TV, others remarked upon the audience's inability to differentiate between the two approaches: "Five years ago, New York was treating Hollywood's infant telefilm industry with disdain. TV had to be live, it claimed, because only then would it have impact, reality, and empathy. . . . The public apparently couldn't tell the difference between film and live and did not seem to notice the lack of realistic impact" ("Film for '52," *Newsweek,* August 11, 1952, 54). Here, film on TV is addressed in terms of its ability to maintain the medium's realistic impact on viewers.

5. Throughout this article, I will be quoting from a range of authors who wrote about radio and television in the thirties, forties, and fifties. Whenever pos-

sible, I will include information regarding their professional credentials, as in the case of Seldes. Unfortunately, not all articles and books from this era include biographical information. As a result, the credentials of some industry advocates or critics, i.e., their claimed expertise (or lack thereof) vis-à-vis radio, television, or acting, will remain a mystery.

6. Gilbert Seldes, *Writing for Television* (Garden City, N.Y.: Doubleday and Co., 1952), 81.

7. Jane Feuer, "The Concept of Live Television: Ontology as Ideology," in *Regarding Television*, ed. E. Ann Kaplan. American Film Institute Monograph Series vol. 2 (Frederick, Md.: University Publications of America, 1983), 14.

8. John Ellis, "Stars as a Cinematic Phenomenon," *Star Texts: Image and Performance in Film and Television*, ed. Jeremy Butler (Detroit: Wayne State University Press, 1991), 313.

9. John Thornton Caldwell, *Televisuality: Style, Crisis, and Authority in American Television* (New Brunswick, N.J.: Rutgers University Press, 1995), 30.

10. Ibid., 27.

11. Ibid., 29.

12. Jack Gould, "'Live' TV vs. 'Canned,'" *New York Times Magazine* (February 2, 1956): 37.

13. Richard Austin Smith, "TV: The Light That Failed," *Fortune* 63, 6 (December 1958): 171.

14. James Hindman, Larry Kirkman, and Elizabeth Monk, *TV Acting: A Manual for Camera Performance* (New York: Hastings House Publishers, 1979), 23.

15. Judy Dupuy, *Television Show Business* (General Electric, 1945), n.p.

16. Ibid., 3.

17. Ibid., 140.

18. Seldes, *Writing for Television*, 85. Appropriately enough, Seldes's comment appeared in a section of his book entitled: "TV is 'Now.'"

19. Henry R. Cassirer, "Television News: A Challenge to Imaginative Journalism," *Journalism Quarterly* 26 (September 1949): 280.

20. Richard Hubbell, *Television: Programming and Production* (New York: Murray Hill Books, 1945), 40.

21. Ibid., 12–13.

22. In 1939 Philip Kerby, too, applied an ontological mythology to television: "To marry sight with sound and transport both across invisible waves of ether with the speed of light has been man's greatest dream. . . . Television is the practical fulfillment of that dream—and television today is an accomplished fact." *The Victory of Television* (New York: Harper and Brothers, 1939), 1.

23. Hubbell, *Television*, 24.

24. Rudy Bretz, "TV as an Art Form," *Hollywood Quarterly* 5 (1950–51): 154.

25. Cassirer, "Television News," 278.

26. John S. Carlile, *Production and Direction of Radio Programs* (Englewood Cliffs, N.J.: Prentice-Hall, 1939), 639.

27. Arch Oboler, *This Freedom* (New York: Random House, 1942), xiv.

28. *American Heritage Dictionary,* s.v. "intimacy."

29. Douglas Mackenzie, "Drama from a Vacuum Tube," *Theatre Arts* 37, 2 (May 1953): 31.

30. Dupuy, *Television Show Business,* 5.

31. Bernard Smith, "Television: There Ought to Be a Law," *Harper's* 197 (September 1948): 37. Or as Hoyland Bettinger remarked, television is a "powerful sociological source. Like radio, it reaches into the home and thus into the heart of the nation." *Television Techniques* (New York: Harper and Brothers, 1947), 11.

32. Radio realism was passionately argued by Merrill Denison. He noted that the broadcast play is "able to convey a greater sense of reality than any other form of dramatic expression" ("The Broadcast Play," *Theatre Arts Monthly* 15, 12 [December 1931]: 1008). Gilbert Seldes made similar claims about TV. He argued for television's privileged relationship to the real: "The other great side of television—its function as a reporter of actuality—is distinct from all other forms because it is complete *and* instantaneous whereas movies and radio are either one or the other." *Writing for Television,* 152.

33. Bernard Smith notes the public/private divide between cinema and TV: "What the [film] exhibitors overlooked was the fact that television has a cardinal advantage over motion pictures, the fact that the television receiver is in the living room of the American home and not in the public auditorium some distance away." "Television," 37.

34. Leo Bogart, *The Age of Television: A Study of Viewing Habits and the Impact of Television on American Life* (New York: Ungar, 1956), 29.

35. Samuel L. Becker and H. Clay Harshbarger, *Television: Techniques for Planning and Performance* (New York: Holt, 1958), 3.

36. Oboler, *This Freedom,* xiv–xv.

37. Jack Gould, "'Live' TV," 37.

38. Walter K. Kingson, Rome Cowgill, and Ralph Levy, *Broadcasting Television and Radio* (New York: Prentice-Hall, 1955), 32. Emphasis added.

39. Melvin R. White, *Beginning Television Production* (Minneapolis: Burgess Publishing Co., 1953), 79.

40. Orrin E. Dunlap Jr., *The Future of Television* (New York: Harper and Brothers, 1942), 65.

41. Giraud Chester and Garnet R. Garrison, *Television and Radio* (New York: Appleton-Century-Crofts, 1956), 534.

42. Lynn Spigel, *Make Room for TV: Television and the Family Ideal in Postwar America* (Chicago: University of Chicago Press, 1992), 104–105.

43. Stuart Ewen remarks of the trend in the 1920s that linked consumerism to empowerment, "If consumption of mass-produced goods could be equated with free choice, then the direction of consumption could appear to be a new and liberated role." *Captains of Consciousness: Advertising and the Social Roots of Consumer Culture* (New York: McGraw-Hill, 1976), 171.

44. Carole Zucker, ed., *Making Visible the Invisible: An Anthology of Original Essays on Film Acting* (Metuchen, N.J.: Scarecrow Press, 1990).

45. Fanny Kemble quoted in Montrose J. Moses, "Royal Roads to Acting," *Theatre Arts Monthly* 10, 12 (December 1926): 832.

46. Moses, "Royal Roads to Acting," 833.

47. Lillian Albertson, *Motion Picture Acting* (New York: Funk and Wagnalls, 1947), 8.

48. Hume Cronyn, "Notes on Film Acting," *Theatre Arts* 33, 5 (June 1949): 46.

49. Raymond Tyson, "Acting for Radio," *Quarterly Journal of Speech* 25, 4 (1939): 636–37.

50. Critical arguments for the merits of radio acting were numerous in the 1930s. Merrill Denison, for example, noted in 1933 that "the actor alone . . . can lift the radio from a mechanical sound-transmitting device to a dramatic vehicle capable of creating for the listener a world of reality and of emotional intensity" ("The Actor and Radio," *Theatre Arts Monthly* 17, 11 [November 1933]: 852). Val Gielgud remarked in 1934 that American critiques of radio performances make "depressing reading," and he encouraged an assessment of radio acting based on the British context ("What Hope Radio Drama?" *Theatre Arts* 18, 4 [April 1934]: 307). At the end of the decade, Raymond Tyson reiterated Denison's high estimation of radio acting: "In many respects, radio drama offers to the actor a medium for the fullest expression of his art" ("Acting for Radio," 636). The urge to reinforce radio's stature as a performance medium was reiterated as late as 1955: "Radio acting is an art in itself, and pays well" (Merrill E. Joels, *Acting Is a Business: How to Get into Television and Radio* [New York: Hastings House, 1955], 25).

51. Edwin Duerr, *Radio and Television Acting: Criticism, Theory, and Practice* (New York: Rinehart and Co., 1950), 1.

52. Duerr, *Radio and Television Acting*, 6.

53. Writing five years before Duerr published his book, William C. Eddy began his discussion of television by universalizing performance: "Our limited experience in commercial television programming has so far given no indication that the art of acting or producing this medium will require radical change in the accepted stage habits or techniques of either the actor or director" (*Television: The Eyes of Tomorrow* [New York: Prentice-Hall Inc., 1945], 270). However, as I will indicate later in this section, Eddy, too, points to the impact of specific televisual attributes on acting.

54. Josephine Dillon Gable, *Modern Acting: A Guide for Stage, Screen, and Radio* (New York: Prentice-Hall, 1940), 17. Comparative descriptions of TV acting endured in the 1950s. As Merrill E. Joels remarked, television "combines movements of the stage, camera work of the screen and the intimate technique of delivery used in radio." *Acting Is a Business*, 26.

55. Eddy, *Television*, 283.

56. Hubbell, *Television*, 29.

57. Ibid., 43. The valorization of the TV actor, like the radio actor before him/her, appeared in a range of early television discourses. Taylor Vaughn, for example, made the following pronouncement in 1950: "As far as the actor is con-

cerned, television is the most difficult of all mediums" ("The Television Actor," in *The Best Television Plays of the Year 1950–1951*, ed. William I. Kaufman [New York: Merlin, 1950], 313). And Melvin R. White was similarly impressed two years later: "Television acting may well be the most difficult of the acting arts." *Beginning Television Production*, 77.

58. While I realize there is definitional danger in conflating realism and naturalism, especially in discussions of acting techniques, their common commitment to developing means of representing "the real" is what I am most concerned with in the context of this article. That is, the early assumptions about television as providing viewers with (immediate and intimate) access to reality, combined with discussions promoting a naturalistic acting style, converge in their shared assumptions that TV is a realist medium.

59. Dupuy, *Television Show Business*, 175. Emphasis added.

60. Jan Bussell, *The Art of Television* (London: Faber and Faber, 1952), 39.

61. Patricia Murray, "A Performer Speaks," *Televiser* 1, 1 (fall 1944): 19.

62. Albertson, *Motion Picture Acting*, 8.

63. Cronyn, "Notes on Film Acting," 46.

64. Gable, *Modern Acting*, 17.

65. Duerr, *Radio and Television Acting*, 356.

66. Rudy Bretz, "The Limitations of Television," *Hollywood Quarterly* 5 (1950–51): 251. Bretz reiterated his equation of technique with technology in a coauthored book. "Close-ups are particularly important in television," wrote Bretz and Edward Stasheff, "not only because of the small size of the average receiver screen, but because of the poor resolution which is displayed" (*Television Scripts for Staging and Study* [New York: A. A. Wyn, 1953], 28). Performers also emphasized the relationship between televisual technique and screen size as evidenced by this comment from actress Patricia Murray: "Due to the small screens in television receivers, close-up shots are much easier on the televiewers, [and] it is desirable to use as many of these as possible." "A Performer Speaks," 18.

67. Actually, the assumed relationship between screen size and shot size was articulated a number of years earlier. As John Western remarked in 1939, "Long shots and crowd scenes [on television] provide insufficient detail on the present small screens. There is a consequent bias toward foreground action, a profusion of close-ups and medium shots." "Television Girds for Battle," *Public Quarterly* 3 (October 1939): 557.

68. Tyson, "Acting for Radio," 639.

69. Eddy, *Television*, 270–71.

70. Seldes, *Writing for Television*, 55.

71. Denise Mann, "The Spectacularization of Everyday Life: Recycling Hollywood Stars and Fans in Early Television Variety Shows," in *Private Screenings: Television and the Female Consumer*, ed. Denise Mann and Lynn Spigel (Minneapolis: University of Minneapolis Press, 1992), 46.

72. Ibid., 51.

73. Ibid., 52.

74. Ibid., 55.

75. Ellis, "Stars as a Cinematic Phenomenon," 303.

76. Ibid., 313.

77. Quoted in Edmund Leamy, "TV Speeds Up Climb to Fame," *New York World-Telegram* (November 18, 1949), n.p. Clippings brochure on a career in television 1940–49. New York Public Library for the Performing Arts, Theater Division.

78. Gould, "'Live' TV," 34.

79. Fred Coe, "TV Drama's Declaration of Independence," *Theatre Arts* 38, 6 (June 1954): 29.

80. Dupuy, *Television Show Business*, 177.

81. Dunlap, *The Future of Television*, 80.

82. Gertrude Berg, "TV and Molly," *Variety* 175, 7 (July 27, 1949): 46.

83. Seldes, *Writing for Television*, 17.

"Johnny Yuma Was a Rebel; He Roamed through the West"—

Television, Race, and the "Real" West

ALAN NADEL

The television industry has from its beginnings distinguished its medium from film by claiming a unique and intimate connection to "reality" arising from its ability to broadcast "live," a crucial difference that, despite numerous negotiations and accommodations, it has maintained.[1] This distinction has been maintained even though the shift of network programming from a chiefly live to chiefly filmed medium occurred in the mid-1950s. Important to maintaining television's privileged relationship to "reality" during that shift, I believe, was the advent of the adult western, a genre that helped popularize filmed television shows while still claiming to represent the "real west" in a historical sense, the "real" American spirit in a mythic sense, and, more subtly, the Western Bloc in a (Cold War) geopolitical sense.

If during this period significant debate arose over what characterized the adult western, more fundamentally the Cold War evoked general questions about what comprised Western values and how to represent the West. Although the twentieth-century geopolitical West may seem easily distinguished from the nineteenth-century geographical West, in many ways—especially during the peak years of the Cold War—the narratives attached to these discrete spaces unavoidably commingled such that the conquest of the American West and all its attendant mythology functioned as a cogent scaffold for Cold War America's national narratives. At the end of the decade, John F. Kennedy made explicit this connection between the West of America's mythic history and the West of Cold War alliances in an inaugural speech that united America's future and past, its domestic and global agendas, its history and its destiny under the rubric "The New Frontier." Kennedy, who is generally thought to be the first television president, gave his address at the end of the 1959–60 television season and could be seen as articulating the implicit premise of a season that had thirty-two adult western series in prime time and had eight westerns among the year's top ten shows.[2] At the moment of Kennedy's speech—roughly the moment when virtually all households had acquired television sets—the greatest common denominator was the West.

The full cultural implications of the adult westerns, of course, are far too vast to be discussed here. Rather I am going to look at the development of the adult western specifically in relation to the shifting racial realities of American life that occurred simultaneous to the rise of that genre and to the conversion of prime-time television into a predominantly filmed medium. First I will look at that conversion as it relates to some of the unique commercial conditions that circumscribed television. Within those parameters, Walt Disney was particularly important in providing a range of mediations that not only eroded distinctions between fantasy and reality but also demonstrated, through the Davy Crockett trilogy, that the myth of the West could breach the gap between competing commercial and social realities that informed television programming and production. In this context, the proliferation of adult westerns that followed closely on the success of Disney's Crockett episodes helped television retain its claim on reality by promoting national narratives that did what the founding fathers were incapable of doing: excluding blacks. The problem thus posed by the Civil War, according to television, was not confronting slavery or racism but uniting southern and northern Americans in the interests of the West.

Live Television and Telefilm

Several factors, both aesthetic and economic, at first resisted and then contributed to the development of telefilm programming. Since television as film's competitor could not deliver an image of comparable quality—the size and resolution of the early television screen being vastly inferior to even the most slipshod black-and-white B movie—competing solely on the basis of visual quality gave television little chance of winning a broad audience. Nor could television produce on a weekly basis an adequate number programming hours if it attempted to replicate the quality of cinematic mise-en-scène, as the cost in time and material would have been prohibitive. Since film products, furthermore, could be stored and shown at will, reliance on film would make individual television affiliates less dependent on a network than would a regular feed of live programs.

The film industry, for its part, was equally antipathetic to television. That attitude, as Robert Vianello has pointed out, was not, as has been commonly argued, the result of "blind indifference or foolish ignorance."[3] For several reasons, nevertheless, television and film were promoted through the early 1950s as alternative rather than complementary media, with television providing "live" entertainment in small parcels for families with a presumed low attention span, and movies providing large-scale, elaborate productions that demanded and earned full attention. Television fore-grounded its immediacy—consider such titles as *See It Now, You Are There, Today,* or *Tonight*—while films often emphasized the length of production time ("two years in the making"); television worked to improve its delivery mechanisms (for example, the coaxial cable connection coast to coast), while film stressed the way in which it contrived to amplify its projected image (for example, 3-D, Cinerama, or CinemaScope).

If rapprochement between the two entertainment industries, as Vianello makes clear, was inevitable, and if, as Douglas Gomery reminds us, the "Hollywood movie makers did not have to be dragged, kicking and scream-ing (or with their heads buried in the sand) into the television age,"[4] it is still important to understand that one of the obstacles to that merger was the perception of difference in the minds of the public produced by the early rivalry.[5] So strong was television's myth of immediacy that well into the late 1950s, long after the bulk of prime time was broadcast in telefilm format, *TV Guide* still notified viewers that a show was not "live" with a paren-thetical "film" in its listing, thus indicating that the show would not contain the "sense of immediacy" that Gilbert Seldes described as the essential con-tribution of television techniques.[6]

Nor were those techniques without recognizable commercial value, since television provided advertising an immediate conduit into American households. Television's "immediacy" functioned, at least in theory, not only to create a sense of shared experience between a small household unit and a set of narratives, but also a closeness between sponsor and consumer, between entertainer and consumable. "Even in its earliest years," Fred Mac-Donald cogently reminds us, "TV was more than a device for home enlight-enment; it was also a persuasive conduit for the propaganda of mass marketing."[7] To put it another way, what Seldes saw as television's essential contribution could equally be seen as the essence of consumerism, that is, as an ongoing reminder of the viewer's capacity for immediate consumption, be it of products or narratives, sports or politics.

This capacity was the governing reality of broadcast television. Instead of delivering entertainment to audiences, it constructed "reality"[8] as a form of entertainment, allowed free consumption of that entertainment, and then delivered the consumers to the organizations who sponsored the delivery of that reality. This set of conditions mandated many programming decisions. For instance, because the efficacy of delivering consumers to sponsors seemed, at least ostensibly, connected to head counting, the network or pro-gram that could deliver the largest audience was the most valuable. Unlike industries that rely chiefly on niche audiences—including, to some extent, the film industry—television, especially in the first decades, delivered vast numbers and sought a degree of universality. The consequent pressure to maintain huge audiences resulted in an effort to offend the fewest number of people. In an exemplary case, Rod Serling's attempt to dramatize the story of Emmett Till (a northern black teenager lynched while visiting family in the South) underwent so many changes that, in the final version, the victim was no longer black and the locale was not southern.[9]

In addition to being inoffensive, shows had to encourage consumption, and since people were more likely to consume when happy, happy endings were favored. Viewers also had to consume the appropriate products. Nina Leibman cites, in this regard, a 1959 memo from the J. Walter Thompson advertising agency to the Screen Gems advertising liaison, regarding an episode of *Father Knows Best,* sponsored by the agency's client, Scott Paper:

> Unfortunately, I notice there is a very grievous error on Page 2, namely the business where Margaret wipes the paint off the refrigerator. The author has boldly written, "She gets a *cloth* and wipes off the paint." Were Mr. Elliotte a new and untried author I would not have been so shocked. Surely this young man has been most derelict in failing to watch the Scott commercials. Else, he would not possibly have failed to realize that no material performs the disagreeable task of absorbing paint so well as a Scott Paper Towel.
>
> From past experience I am sure that when this scene is shot Margaret will instinctively use a Scott Paper Towel. Correct? If so, you may consider this letter to constitute client approval. (111)

Notably, by indicating that the writer was being unrealistic, this memo situates the sponsor as the protector of reality rather than the promoter of contrivance. In reality "no material performs the disagreeable task of absorbing paint so well as a Scott Paper Towel," a fact established by Scott commercials. Ignoring the commercials, the writer was not being true to life, thus differentiating himself from the character, Margaret, who in reality would never succumb to the writer's unnatural instructions. Margaret, the ad man was sure, remaining true to her instinct, would use a Scott paper towel. The script, from this viewpoint, does not provide an artificial display for consumer products but rather reflects accurately the truth contained in the Scott commercials.

Television, as the memo illustrates, uniquely merged the economic realities that circumscribed its production with the reality it professed to deliver, establishing itself in the postwar American scene as a two-way circuit. It professed to bring the real world to the viewers and to bring the viewers to the realities that informed their consumption. Since television's capacity for live presentations or immediate broadcasts served only to bolster this circuit of consumption, it was probably inevitable that television's claim on reality would transcend changes in its principal mode of presentation and thus that the specifics of its transition to telefilm would work to gloss over any perceived movement away from "reality."

Disney to the Rescue

Even in the earliest days of television, of course, television programming
included televised films and filmed programs, the most successful being *I
Love Lucy,* one of television's highest rated shows from its premiere in
1951. Despite the success of *I Love Lucy,* however, in 1953 less than a fifth
of NBC's and less than a seventh of CBS's programming was film. ABC,
with almost half of its shows filmed, posed little competition for the two
major networks.[10] In 1954, however, in conjunction with Disney Studios,
ABC spearheaded the large-scale transition to telefilm. At that time, as the
result of a merger with United Paramount Theaters, ABC was heavy in capital and lean in competitive programs. In order to compete with NBC and
CBS, ABC sought connections with motion picture studios, using as bait its
ability to help bankroll the studio's television projects. In a 1953 deal with
Hal Roach Jr., for example, ABC help fund production in exchange for
"syndication rights and a profit share in the series."[11]

The arrangement for Disney's weekly show, *Disneyland,* ABC's first
bona fide hit, was somewhat different. Disney Studios had negotiated with
all three networks, but only ABC would help finance the huge amusement
park, Disneyland, for the construction of which Disney had acquired 160
acres in Anaheim (two thirds of the acreage intended as parking space).
Given the high production cost of the film series, Disney had not expected
to turn a profit on the actual show, even though only about 60 percent of
the material would be new and more than half of the broadcasts would be
reruns.[12] Rather, Disney expected the value of the show to come from ancil-
lary benefits. As *TV Guide* explained:

> By an odd coincidence, both the amusement park and the TV show will be
> called "Disneyland." By another coincidence, both the amusement park and
> the TV show will be divided into four parts: Fantasy Land, Adventure Land,
> Frontier Land, and the World of Tomorrow. The amusement park will be
> opened to the public July 1955, just nine months after the television show goes
> on the air.
>
> "By that time," a Disney aide muses, "there will be hardly a living soul in
> the United States who won't have heard about the Disneyland amusement park
> and who won't be dying to come to see it. Yessir, television is a wonderful
> thing."[13]

The wonderful thing about television, in other words, was its ability to
turn a dream into a reality, and thus at every turn television and Disneyland
were interconnected. ABC's financial backing enabled the construction of
the amusement park that provided the basis for the ABC television show,
and the show served as an elaborate commercial for the amusement park
(from which ABC received profits from food concessions). The success of

the show, moreover, established the network that had backed it, making that network a platform for promoting the products of Disney Studios. The success of that symbiotic relationship, moreover, initiated the rush of movie studios into telefilm production that, in about half a decade, reformulated television programming. As *TV Guide* reported in 1955:

> It all started, of course, with Walt Disney, whose incredible success with *Disneyland* forced the hand of the other studios. All by itself, *Disneyland* made a senior partner out of what had been a junior TV network, provided an unparalleled publicity platform for the Disney theatrical pictures [and] won two Emmy awards.[14]

It might seem ironic that Disney, the film studio most heavily dependent upon the overt production of fantasy, would initially be the studio most incisive in the history of a medium fundamentally invested in its superior ability to communicate "reality." Disney, however, could also be viewed as being uniquely in sync with television's understanding of reality, that is, with the understanding of reality expressed in the memo regarding Scott paper towels. The reality of palpable commercial products entering into a flow of economic exchange through the immediacy of television arose only secondarily out of its "live" broadcasts and primarily out of its insertion into the living situation of consumers, such that they were constantly reminded of the material world to which the broadcasts—whether "live" or film, fiction or nonfiction—connected them.

In this regard, *Disneyland* used several strategies to link the show to "reality." First of all, Disneyland was a real place, with a geographical design and mapped coordinates, even though, when *Disneyland* (the show) first aired, Disneyland (the park) was only an image, designated by that design and those coordinates. The image, however, was the real dream of a real man, Walt Disney, who was the live host (recorded on film) of *Disneyland* (the show) and the real mind behind the show's (and the planned park's) animated characters. That real man had the same name as the trademark that connected those characters to all the material uses of their images. Looking directly at the camera, the real Walt Disney spoke to the real boys and girls of America (and many of their parents) about his real plans to build a Fantasy Land (as well as an Adventure Land, a Frontier Land, and a World of Tomorrow). These imaginary lands were also, the show constantly reminded its audience, segments of the television show they were really watching.

That show, moreover, strategically blurred the boundaries of the real. Under the trademark "Walt Disney," the man of the same name was constructing a real park that did not exist but that was represented by a television show that did. The show did not have the actual rides and restaurants that its namesake would have, but in their stead it had the real narratives upon which those amusements would be based, real narratives about fantasies, adventures, dreams for the future, or legends from the past. Those narratives were being brought to life through the reality of film production and brought home through the reality of television technology.

The financial and communicational realities derived from that technology may have bankrolled the construction of Walt Disney's dream, securing the dream's realization as well as helping to guarantee its financial success, but the blending of dream and reality, narrative as commercial promotion and as commercial product, exceeded Disney's greatest expectations, when, on December 13, 1954, the Disney studio premiered the first of three "Frontier Land" episodes based on the life of Davy Crockett. Nothing to date had suggested the immense commercial potential of television, not only to deliver audiences to sponsors but also to create commercial products. In addition to helping ABC become a viable network and *Disneyland* become, according to a *TV Guide* poll of 45,000 readers, the most popular show of the 1954–55 season (it was rated second by Neilsen), the Davy Crockett episodes set off a craze that gave television, in the words of *TV Guide,* its "first genuine overnight star"[15] and "provided the nation with a new hero and a new song hit, both named Davy Crockett."[16] The hero and the song, reciprocally, became endorsements not only for *Disneyland* (the show) and Disneyland (the park), but also for countless products such as T-shirts, lunch boxes, toy rifles, and the ubiquitous coonskin caps.

If the "flow" that Raymond Williams identified as characterizing television could be imagined as a Mobius strip in which the "inside" and the "outside" of American experience—the reality of consumerism and the reality that circumscribed the consumer's material life with informing narratives—became a seamless continuum, the case could be made that *Disneyland* in general and the Davy Crockett episodes in particular marked the moment when the ends of the strip were cemented together. One reason was that the show occurred when television was starting to occupy the attention of a majority of Americans, making it perhaps the single most common experience of Cold War America. It created, in other words, a kind of public space heretofore inaccessible, given the United States' spatial and temporal vastness and diversity. Within the parameters of that public space, moreover, it targeted that huge demographic bubble, the baby boomers, who throughout the second half of the twentieth century would critically inflect America's cultural norms. *Disneyland* provided this generation with a common past and with informing myths based on rereadings of a privileged set of fairy tales.[17]

It also, as *TV Guide* pointed out, provided a national hero grounded in the allegedly "true" adventures of a real person who lived on the American frontier. This frontiersman was particularly well suited at that moment to represent the quintessence of America. Like the parents of his chief audience, he was a recent war veteran (the Indian Wars), and like their president he had moved into a political career. The last episode, which recounted Crockett's journey to and death at the Alamo, moreover, constructed Crockett's memory in the image of the cold warrior, drawn to foreign soil by the cause of "freedom."

Another factor that contributed to the Crockett craze was that even prior to the *Disneyland* episodes, American culture in general and television in particular had drawn its heroes from the frontier. The western had been, without doubt or serious competition, the most prolific genre in American film history, especially when one includes B pictures. "Because new movies couldn't be found," *TV Guide* explained,

> stations were forced to use old ones, just to have something to show [before the coaxial cable allowed national network shows]. They soon found that cowboy movies, no matter how ancient, invariably built a regular audience.
>
> A psychiatrist once accounted for the popularity of westerns by saying that the hero represents a "father image," the incorruptible leader with whom all viewers want to identify themselves.[18]

The availability and popularity of westerns made Hopalong Cassidy (William Boyd), Roy Rogers, and Gene Autry superstars among the children in the early television audience.[19] "Children Made Roy King of the Cowboys," a *TV Guide* article announced explicitly in the summer of 1954,[20] but a few months later Davy Crockett moved the western hero from the world of children's fantasy to that of adult nation making. In replacing Roy Rogers, "King of the Cowboys," with Davy Crockett, "King of the Wild Frontier," *Disneyland* was providing the American public space of TV land with a "father image" who combined fantasy with history, adventure with Manifest Destiny. Although the product of Frontier Land, Davy Crockett's mythic status, his heroic adventures, his concern with western expansion, and his final devotion to the cause of Texas and thus the future of American borders and influence, made him equally well a representative from Fantasy Land, Adventure Land, and the Land of Tomorrow. To the extent, therefore, that Crockett represented Disneyland, he helped Disneyland represent America. And from the perspective of the 1950s, representing the West was not only America's role in popular culture and its destiny in nineteenth-century history, but also its charge in the Cold War. In Cold War terminology, to represent the West was to be the "leader of the Free World."

Unremembering the Alamo

In this context the final episode of the Crockett trilogy, "Davy Crockett at the Alamo," is particularly interesting. Host Disney introduced the episode, which aired on February 23, 1955, by drastically inflating Crockett's role in the siege of the Alamo:

> If he had done nothing else in his brief, adventurous life, Davy Crockett's courage and daring during the immortal battle of the Alamo would have earned him an honored place in American history. In tribute to this frontier hero, we present another story based on Davy's own journal.

For several reasons, Disney was describing neither the episode that would follow nor the facts upon which the episode was based. In the episode, Crockett's behavior was not significantly different from any of those at the Alamo, a situation that did not significantly allow for individual heroics. The Alamo, after all, was not a fort but an abandoned mission, ill-equipped to withstand the onslaught of thousands of Mexican troops. The 182 people there simply manned the walls until they were overrun. Since all those who fought at the Alamo were killed, moreover, no one could record Crockett's "courage and daring," and hence we cannot possibly know if it would have "won him an honored place in American history." Nor, of course, could that aspect of the story have come from "Davy's own journal." No doubt Disney was referring to "*Col. Crockett's Exploits and Adventures in Texas,* Written by Himself," published the summer after the Alamo fell. That book—one in a long array of increasingly outlandish (and racist) publications about Crockett that proliferated throughout the nineteenth century—was completely bogus, a "long-lived hoax," as James Shackford has shown.[21]

Disney's introduction also implies that the battle of the Alamo was, in and of itself, a significant part of American history, a questionable point. Jim Bowie had been sent to Alamo with orders to destroy it, but for reasons that remain unclear, he could not get himself to do so. Nor could the Alamo have provided a practical site from which to forestall the advance of Santa Anna's troops. The revolutionary troops under Sam Houston's command at the time of the siege, moreover, were neither sufficient nor sufficiently well organized to engage Santa Anna's army.[22] If anything, the Alamo had symbolic significance, providing a rallying cry for the emerging Texas army and for the press in the United States.

One needs to ask, as well, in what sense was the event part of *American* history? In 1836, when the Alamo fell, it was located on Mexican soil, the site of a conflict initiated between the Mexican Army and *Mexican* citizens (of American origin). The Mexican government had, from the 1820s on, encouraged the settlement of Texas by making generous land offers—one tenth the price of public land in the United States, in parcels nearly sixty times larger[23]—conditioned on the settlers becoming Mexican citizens and Catholics. American land agents (or *empresarios*) commissioned by the Mexican government—the most successful being Stephen Austin—encouraged settlement by advertising widely through the Untied States. As a result, by the 1830s 75 percent of the Texas region's population was Anglo American.

This Texas population, however, by no means represented the United States but rather a specific segment of its population, as T. R. Fehrenbach reminds us, inordinately prone toward aggression and violence: "No matter how many historians prefer to gloss over the fact, the first Trans-Appalachian-born or –bred generation was an extremely tough and violent race. Texas was where the action was."[24] They included an array of opportunistic scoundrels, many of whom, such as Jim Bowie, Sam Houston, and William Travis, figured prominently in the Texas Revolution. Bowie, a financially bankrupt slave runner, smuggler, and land scammer was, by 1834, severely alcoholic.[25] So too was Houston, the former governor of Tennessee, who in the 1830s lived among the Arkansas Cherokee, with a drinking problem so severe that the Cherokee dubbed him Oo-tse-tee Ar-de-tah-skee (meaning "Big Drunk"). Travis, who had abandoned his son and pregnant wife to seek his fortune in Texas, there "conducted a thriving legal practice, gambled heavily, and bedded as many women as he could, making notes in Spanish in his diary of each conquest."[26] Travis became a leader among the Anglo settlers known as the War Dogs—almost all of them young southern lawyers—who favored for financial reasons open rebellion from Mexico. Hardly a cross section of America, either demographically or philosophically, Austin's immigrants, moreover, were inordinately dominated by Southerners.[27] "The great difference between Texas and the other regions of the West was that Texas had a planter class," Fehrenbach explains, "[that] stamped the lasting standards of conduct upon the Lone Star State. . . . [B]oth because of early settlement and social financial prominence, the planter formed the apex of society in Texas."[28] Texas did not attract those governed by democratic principles and certainly—given that they changed religion and nationality—not governed by faith or patriotism. They wanted land and power.

So did Crockett. Like Houston, Crockett was a failed Tennessee politician; like Houston and Bowie, he had had a serious drinking problem; and like Austin, Travis, Bowie, and Houston, he had come to Texas for material gain. As Jeff Long succinctly put it:

He was sick and tired of being broke. Texas seemed like a good solution. . . .
    Crockett didn't go to Texas to fight a revolution. He didn't go to sharp-
shoot tyrants or defend liberty. He went for himself.
    He wanted land.
    He wanted money.[29]

In the Disney episode, however, Crockett is drawn by a newspaper headline:

Texas Independence Threatened
General Santa Anna Vows to Expel Settlers

Since at the time Texas independence did not exist, it certainly could not
have been threatened. Nor was "expulsion" exactly the issue. Mexican officials, concerned, as Mark Deer explains, "at what they saw as an American
takeover, . . . outlawed immigration from the United States *and banned
slavery in the province.* They also sought to break the settlers' monopoly on
shipping and levied taxes, in an attempt to pressure people into leaving. The
colonists ignored the new laws, and the Mexicans strengthened their gar-
risons to enforce them" (emphasis added).[30] By the mid-1830s, as Long puts
it, "Texas was being radicalized by men who stood to gain fortunes if they
could cut it loose of the Mexican republic."[31] Hence, Mexico's attempt to
regain authority over the region and over the Mexican citizens (of American
origin) who lived there led to the Texas Revolution.
    When, in the Disney episode, Crockett's sidekick, George Russell (Buddy
Ebsen), accurately responds to the newspaper headline, "There's nothing
there but a mess a trouble," Crockett reflects the tone of 1830s propaganda
when he tersely replies "Americans in trouble." No doubt this was the way
these expatriates were regarded by many Americans in that their nationality
had little to do with citizenship and everything to do with race and national
origin. "Americanness" was something the Texas colonizers in effect carried
with them, the inalienable right to be Americans, regardless of their citizenship or their location. Texans thus extended the borders of the nation
simply by being American, by claiming the rights of Americans, even when
technically they were Mexicans. If they believed that the quintessential right
of the American was "freedom," in this case that entailed freedom from
obeying Mexican law. In other words, they regarded the Mexican laws as
local and American privilege as universal.
    Even after the Texas Revolution, moreover, the Texas territory (includ-
ing the Alamo) did not become part of the United States, instead functioning as an independent country, the Lone Star Republic, for nearly a decade.
Only after the Mexican War of 1846 did Texas join the Union. The Alamo
thus was a part of *American* history only in terms of the way in which it
manifest the continental destiny of the United States.

"Manifest Destiny," however, as Reginald Horsman has shown, was lodged from its beginnings in a notion of a superior "Anglo-Saxon race." This notion justified the subordination of non-Anglo-Saxons in the name of freedom, so that the American history of which the Alamo comprised a part was a history based not on nation but on race. "The Texas Revolution," Horsman makes clear, "was from its beginnings interpreted in the United States and among Americans in Texas as a racial clash, not simply a revolt against unjust government or tyranny."[32] The actual term "Manifest Destiny" first came into use in the 1840s in regard to the annexation of Mexico. Drawing as it did on early-nineteenth-century concepts of racial supremacy, the phrase quickly gained currency, evoking the sundry concerns felt to be implicit in the dangers of a racially mixed nation and focussing on what Horsman identified as the "general low regard in which the people of Mexico were held by the government and people of the United States. . . . Since the time of the Texas Revolution, the Mexicans had been repeatedly attacked in the United States as a degenerate, largely Indian race unable to control or improve the territories it owned."[33]

Because Manifest Destiny entailed that inferior peoples would "naturally" be replaced by or subordinated to superior Anglo-Saxons, the term "American," in the sense that the Disney episode employs it, describes a political mandate arising out of genetic inevitability. That inevitability, moreover, is proved through a temporal inversion that retrospectively extends America to the sites it was (historically? biologically? theologically?) "destined" to acquire. The successful annexation of Texas that followed ten years after the Anglos' successful subordination of the Mexicans, according to this logic, proved that the Alamo was American.

This fulfillment of racial "destiny" effectively freed the repatriated Americans from the restrictions of Mexican law, including the law abolishing slavery. If destiny declared that the Texans were fighting for freedom, that freedom was defined racially, and the issue of Texas annexation was linked from the outset to the struggle between pro-slavery and abolitionist forces over the potential expansion of slavery into western regions of the United States. Thus the Alamo was important to American history because history was the product of a destiny that was the function of race, and freedom represented the ability to distribute rights and define property along racial lines. To this concept of freedom, the idea of the Alamo as a site in a civil war among Mexican citizens was an anathema, for it precluded the narrative in which the Alamo signified the triumph, even in defeat, of America's racial destiny. Russell reflects this universalizing narrative of America's destiny in his reply to Crockett:

Yeah, a bunch of crazy fools that'r trying to take on a whole army. They're so far away from the rest of the country that they know they ain't gonna get no help—a bunch of rock-headed idiots that won't quit because they think they're right. . . . How soon you reckon we'll be headed out that way?

We can clearly see the Cold War narrative implicit in this interchange between Crockett and Russell, enacted through the bonding in danger and death of white men who are investing a small frontier community with the quintessence of America. Because America is not a place but a set of values, a dedication to the cause of freedom, Americans feel obliged to fight for freedom wherever its cry is heard. As this show aired, we should remember, American soldiers had just returned from a "police action" in Korea, and Vietnam was being divided, with American support and blessing, into North and South zones in concurrence with the 1954 Geneva accord. The episode's final image—Davy Crockett swinging his rifle against an onslaught of Mexican soldiers dissolving into a Lone Star Republic flag—blends the defeat at the Alamo into the long-term triumph of Manifest Destiny at the same time that it obscures the aporia between the sign of freedom and the expansion of slavery that the history surrounding the Alamo entailed. This image indeed captures the spirit in which Lyndon Johnson is believed to have equated the Alamo with Vietnam[34] and also suggests how the Alamo signified television itself, that emerging public space of the 1950s that replaced regional interests with national narratives.[35]

The frontier, the "real" West, Davy Crockett, *Disneyland,* the effectiveness of telefilm, the power of television, consolidate vividly at the Alamo. With the advent of *Disneyland* (the show) and, as its most consumable image, Davy Crockett, Disney had found his metier. The show identified the frontier—imagined through the relentless and relentlessly anachronistic middle classism of Walt Disney—as connecting the hero of the baby boomers with the hero of their parents, America as fantasy land with America as tomorrow land, television as source of real life with television as producer of filmed fantasy.

Desegregation and the Cold War

Another dramatic event, simultaneous to the development of *Disneyland* and the production of the Crockett episodes, had profound national and international impact. Four months before the premiere of *Disneyland* (and fourteen months before the opening of Disneyland), the Supreme Court delivered its decision in the case of *Brown v. the Board of Education of Topeka* overturning the principle of "separate but equal" racial treatment established in the 1896 *Plessy v. Ferguson* decision. The unanimous 1954 decision not only mandated drastic alterations in educational policy for large segments of the country but also opened the door to changes in myriad aspects of racial discrimination.

The decision also had important international implications, as *Newsweek* was quick to note: "[O]ver the years, segregation in the public schools has become a symbol of inequality, not only to Negroes in the United States but to colored peoples elsewhere in the world. It has also been a weapon of world communism. Now that symbol lies shattered." So important was the Cold War symbology of *Brown v. the Board of Education of Topeka* that, "within an hour after the Supreme Court decision," the *New York Times* indicated in a separate article, "the Voice of America sent a news broadcast by short-wave radio" in thirty-four languages. Lost neither on *Newsweek* nor on the Voice of America was the decision's role in representing the West because America, strategically and paradigmatically, was synonymous with the West in the geopolitical organization of the Cold War. This role may shed light on the arguments made in the court's decision, arguments lodged not in legal precedent but in perceived social realities. As James Reston pointed out, "relying more on the social scientists than on legal practices—a procedure often in controversy in the past—the court insisted on equality of the mind and heart rather than on equal school facilities."[36] The decision is striking, in other words, in its subordination of statutory precedent to social necessity and its substituting psychological concerns for material consequences. To put it another way, the decision represents the West as privileging what is ultimately a spiritual and individualistic interest in its citizens over a general concern with their material conditions, locating class in the state of mind of the individual. Noting that "the policy of separating the races is usually interpreted as denoting the inferiority of the Negro group," the decision states, "A sense of inferiority affects the motivation of the child to learn. Segregation with the sanction of law, therefore, has a tendency to retard the educational and mental development of Negro children."[37] The "real" problem with segregation, the decision indicates, can be found in mental rather than material realities. The decision, in fact, made fundamental connections between a pupil's state of mind (and its concomitant educational consequences) and being a citizen: Education "is the very foundation of good citizenship."[38] The good citizen of the West, the decision assumes, cannot be marked by a sense of inferiority. An inequality inherent to segregation, then, is that it fosters a state of mind incompatible with being a leader of the Free World. This type of leadership finds its ideal in the American western, that is, in the story of individual leadership, "manliness," "toughness," and violence underwritten by superior technology.[39]

The western as a genre thus serves as the apotheosis of Cold War narratives such that one could say much of American Cold War rhetoric and cul-

ture attempted to affirm the reality of the western. Since television, as I have
noted, touted its capacity for presenting unmediated reality, in many ways
by the mid-1950s it started to comprise the common space of America's
quotidian reality in the same way that the western constituted the space of
the country's mythic reality. It is not surprising, then, that the privileged
genre of late-1950s television was the adult western, for which the success
of the Crockett series paved the way. In 1956, at the beginning of the adult
western craze, *TV Guide* indicated the connections to Disney's Crockett:

> [T]he adult western has more in common with "Crockett" than man-sized
> budgets. As producer Walt Disney points out:
>   "The 'Crockett' show was based on historical frontier stories. It's not a story
> about bad men. Rather, Davy Crockett sets himself toward constructive
> causes."[40]

The "constructive" cause for which Crockett gave his life, however, was
tainted heavily by pro-slavery interests and the notions of racial superiority
underpinning the idea of Manifest Destiny. In reinventing the Alamo as a
Cold War icon, Disney de-racialized its history, suggesting that real Americans were defined by their willingness to fight for the freedom of others. In
this Cold War narrative, the cause of slavery dissolves into a national cause,
something that, regardless of one's regional affiliation, evokes transcendent
American idealism.

Adult Westerns in Black and White

Starting in 1955, with the shows *Gunsmoke* and *The Life and Legend of
Wyatt Earp,* adult westerns came by the end of the decade to dominate
prime time and the Nielsen ratings. These series differentiated themselves
from children's westerns (such as Roy Rogers, Hopalong Cassidy, Gene
Autry, and Annie Oakley), by claiming to be grounded in realistic, even
true, stories about heroes like Davy Crockett.

The character of Davy Crockett might have been seen as having
"inspired" the trend, a Disney spokesman contended in 1956. Like the
Crockett series, *TV Guide* pointed out, the adult westerns had a "relative
absence of 'bad men' and [an] emphasis on historic atmosphere."[41] They
also emphasized psychology over action and shunned the use of chases and
shootouts for their own sake. Particularly, they were united by at least an
ostensive commitment to "realism," that is, to the idea that the West was a
real place, populated by more or less ordinary people (who nevertheless
often did extraordinary things). An article accounting for *Gunsmoke*'s success, for example, explained that the concept for the show was that "everyone would behave more or less as human beings behave in real life, where

characters would resemble the real articles . . . the show would operate on the revolutionary but entirely valid principle that in the early West the most hated man in town was usually the marshal."[42]

According to a review of *Wyatt Earp*, "Earp's exploits as a frontier marshal were so crammed with gun-slinging action, suspense and excitement that a producer could hardly go wrong basing a show on his life . . . The scripts . . . adhere to reality with only an occasional foray into fiction."[43] In January 1956, Hugh O'Brien, the star of *Wyatt Earp,* wrote on article on the real Earp, indicating that the series used Stuart Lake's biography of Earp as its guide.[44] That article was paired with "My Cousin Wyatt," an article by a distant relative of Earp's who happened to be on *TV Guide*'s staff.[45]

Articles continued to emphasize the adult westerns' foothold in reality. A *TV Guide* description for the premiere episode of *Bat Masterson* indicated, "Reports differ on how this actual incident ended. Tonight's show offers dramatizations of two different versions of the windup."[46] And in February 1959, in an article entitled "The Facts Are Enough," the producer of *Bat Masterson* indicated that the show wanted to be as accurate as possible.[47]

Throughout the late 1950s, the number of adult westerns continued to proliferate so that in 1957 there were twenty adult westerns per week on prime-time network television, in 1958, twenty-six (with thirty or forty in syndication), and 1959 a peak of thirty-two. The migration to the West of prime-time television between 1954 and 1960, however, was not marked by commensurate racial integration of the space delimited by that westward expansion. While courts, legislatures, attorneys general, and even some U.S. marshals throughout the nation were engaged in ending the principle of "separate but equal," the television networks continued to remember the Alamo and the unfinished work Disney started there. "The Disney Company," as Henry Giroux has perceptively noted, "has become synonymous with a notion of innocence that aggressively rewrites the historical and collective identity of the American past. . . . The strategies of entertainment, escapism, historical forgetting and repressive pedagogy . . . produce a series of identifications that relentlessly define America as white and middle class."[48]

By the end of the decade, in other words, on television the history of the American West had merged thematically with the desired future of the West. To the extent, then, that the televisual West continued to represent both the history and the ethos of America, it solved America's twentieth-century race problems in the same way that Manifest Destiny solved its the nineteenth-century land problems: by accepting as fact the inevitability of Anglo-Saxon domination. Although historically blacks, Hispanics, and native Americans comprised a significant percentage—over a third—of actual cowboys,[49] one

rarely if ever found a black face in a prominent television cattle town such
as Dodge City. It is important to remember that the historical reality of the
adult western narratives shared its authority with the commercial reality
responsible for producing and delivering those narratives. That commercial
reality, as we have seen, was inextricable from the reality that the narratives
reflected. Thus, according to a 1957 *Ad Age* article, "in the matter of segregation, it would be difficult to present a dramatization dealing with some
aspects of this problem on a sponsored program, particularly at a time when
the subject is considered highly inflammatory. . . . It would be impossible to
maintain any balance of dramatization highlighting one side of such a currently explosive issue as segregation in a sponsored *entertainment* program."[50]

But what is being weighed in this desire for "balance" if not the heft of
the segregationist position? Although the courts had ruled that separate but
equal was *not* equal, television and its sponsors continued to give equal
weight to the arguments for segregation or, more accurately, to the people
who made those arguments. In terms of the realities that governed television
programming, they comprised a much more lucrative audience than did
black America. In the first decade of the black-and-white era, as MacDonald points out, "whites were the main consumers of TV programming and
of the corporate advertisers' products, and by the early 1950s ratings illustrated that white Americans preferred shows with blacks in traditional
roles."[51] In 1949, few television stations and less than five percent of the TV
receivers were located in the South. However, "once the FCC freeze [on station licenses, from September 1948 to April 1952] was lifted and TV spread
beyond the West Coast, Midwest, and Northeast, networks and advertisers
became increasingly sensitive to regional racial attitudes. . . . [T]he white
South was especially influential as a force for segregation, asserting its own
world view and demanding the acquiescence of national video."[52]

If television "entertainment" programming thus rendered race invisible
in the West, the medium's eclectic mode of presentation[53] necessarily juxtaposed adult westerns with reportage of civil rights conflicts. Those conflicts
operated in the same rhythm as the television season, with more of the
major events occurring in September, things winding down as summer
approached, and late summer providing previews of the coming season. For
two very well publicized years, Orval Faubus, the governor of Arkansas,
waged a war with federal authorities over the integration of Little Rock
Central High School. The conflict was marked by outbreaks of violence,
school closings, and state and national troops used both to prevent and to
permit black students from studying at Central High. Particularly striking
was the way in which Faubus constantly cast himself in the position of the
aggrieved victim. In his narrative, blacks were treated well by Arkansas
whites while Southerners were treated unfairly by the federal government.

Under the rubric of "states rights," in other words, Faubus claimed the same privileges as did the Anglo Americans at the Alamo.

This theme was iterated throughout an array of television narratives that delivered the "true" West to the adult viewers of America. Episodes of top western shows set in artificially white societies repeatedly redeemed aggrieved Southerners by uniting them in the common cause of the wagon train, cattle drive, or western settlement. Or these "good" Southerners were distinguished from the aberrant "bad" Southerners (for example, Jesse James, Quantrill, or some local "enforcers"). One adult western hero, Bronco Lane, was a former Confederate officer, now working as a federal undercover agent reporting to his former Confederate commanding officer who occupied a high post in a proto-FBI branch of the government. The adult western thus repeatedly worked to construct an image of the historically and symbolically true West as the place where the Northerner and Southerner united to recognize their common interest in the welfare of the West. An implicit compromise—one that indeed reflects the actual compromise of the post-Reconstruction era—is that the price of this reunification was the acceptance of segregation. In such a context, the rejection of segregation could be viewed as a breach of contract, a reneging on the compromise that settled the 1876 Tilden-Hayes election, an unfair impingement on the rights of the South, a return to the time when the South was controlled by occupying armies. Throughout the South, in the aftermath of *Brown v. Board,* these charges were repeated constantly on the floors of Congress, in legal briefs, at public meetings and mob actions, in school doorways. While, through the second half of 1950s, the conflict between North and South grew in these venues, television's vision of a white West proliferated with concomitant tenacity. It was almost as if television were keeping the promise that unified the nation while the federal government and the Supreme Court were undermining it.

The most astounding example, I think, of this identification between the aggrieved Southerner and the interests of the West was the television show *The Rebel.* The show, which premiered on October 4, 1959, chronicles the adventures of Johnny Yuma, a veteran of the Confederate Army. "Johnny Yuma," the title song tells us, "was a rebel; he roamed through the West." Yuma's identification with the Confederacy, however, was not regional. Rather, it reflected his commitment, like Crockett's at the Alamo, to a generic American sense of justice and fair play. His leaving his western hometown to enlist in the Confederate Army thus signified his integrity. Like all true Americans, he could be drawn to the cause of freedom, wherever it took him, whatever it cost.

In the series' premiere episode, the important link of the rebel to the West rather than the South is established quickly and emphasized repeatedly. Before the opening credits appear, we see this rebel fending off an Indian attack using his dead horse as a shield, shooting one Indian and killing the other in hand-to-hand combat. Clearly, this is not the land of cotton but a more unsettled Indian territory. The locale, moreover, is arid, suggesting the Southwest, a suggestion reinforced by the Rebel's having the same name as an Arizona city. Johnny Yuma's outfit also identifies him with the frontier rather than with Dixie. He wears his Rebel enlisted man's cap— certainly in this climate something with a brim wide enough to shield him from the sun would be more sensible (and look less stupid)—and gray Confederate Army pants, but his shirt is fringed buckskin. Although with forty years perspective this mix-and-match may seem more apt for the Village People than for an adult western hero, in the context of its time, it probably seemed no more ludicrous than Crockett's coonskin cap, and further echoed a fashion motif that scattered remnants of Confederate Army garb over an array of shows and characters to indicate, if nothing else, that the settling of the West represented the unification of (white!) Americans in the interest of the nation. To put it simply, in the West of the adult western, Confederate symbology was far more commonplace than black cowboys. The combination of cap and buckskin thus marked Johnny Yuma as that quintessentially American combination of idealism and pragmatism in the mold of his buckskinned (television) ancestor, Davy Crockett.

After the titles, the episode begins with Yuma carrying his saddle, walking down a dusty road into a small town. As it turns out, this is his hometown and although its location is not specified, it is clearly not in the South. No one in the town has a Southern accent and, more importantly, the town seems to contain no Confederate sympathizers. The thugs now running the town, having killed the former sheriff (Yuma's father), are in fact overtly hostile to Yuma even before they know his name, based simply on his outfit. (This hostility should not, of course, be viewed as a fashion statement but as an act of prima facie prejudice.) When the parched and exhausted Yuma dunks his head in a water trough, Jess (Strother Martin), says to his boss (Dan Blocker), "I think I need to have me some fun with that little Rebel . . . can I have me some fun?" He then approaches the trough and the following interchange takes place:

> Jess: Hey you, Reb, hey you, Reb—This here water's for horses; it ain't for no jackasses. I come here to water my horse.
> Yuma: Then you do that.
> Jess: Well, not with your face in it. I don't want him contaminated.
> Yuma: Don't push.
> Jess: Why Reb you oughta be used to being pushed. Why we pushed you clear from Gettysburg though Georgia. You gotta admit you've been pushed real good.

Yuma: Yeah. The war's done.
Jess: So it is, but I'm not. I'm going to enjoy pushing you pretty good.

This interchange ends when Yuma draws a (huge) gun and threatens to blow Jess's eyes out, a perfectly appropriate threat, since Yuma's transgressions are purely in the eyes of the beholder; he is not being threatened because he drank from the trough but because, based on his appearance, he can be presumed to have contaminated it. The trough, Jess has pointed out, is a segregated drinking place, reserved for horses and restricted from rebels. Clearly the irrational restriction is motivated not by the practical threat Yuma poses to the water supply but by the symbolic threat his appearance poses to the post–Civil War hierarchy. That hierarchy is connected to the violation of southern soil and southern rights as underscored by Jess's direct reference to Union Army as an invading force. When Yuma says that the war is done, he is asserting the restoration of his rights as an American, rights that he enjoyed before the war. Jess acts villainously in refusing to acknowledge those rights, insisting that the war has forever changed the rebel's status.

But that is exactly what the Civil War did. It legally negated some privileges of the Southerner, chiefly in regard to slavery and more generally in regard to race, even if the legal sanctions were not enforced and the practices of the South allowed the reinstitution of laws that normalized racism. Our introduction to the rebel, however, rereads this history, seeing the rebel as the victim rather than the perpetrator of blind prejudice, extended even to the sphere of public facilities.

This western town, it turns out, is, like the South, an occupied place, and the men who torment Yuma simply on the basis of his appearance are also those who have killed his father and are continuing to exploit the town. For example, they are using supplies without paying for them. In the context of the tenant farmer economy that arose in the South after the war, this detail provides another reversal of southern conditions, for here instead of the store's being the source of exploitation, it is the victim of exploitation. This capacity for exploiting the rebel's hometown, moreover, is directly linked to the consequences of the Civil War. When Yuma asks the editor of the newspaper (John Carradine), "Why haven't you sent for government troops?" he is told, "We have. . . . I guess they're too busy attending to the defeated South or the undefeated Indians."

The inversion of the southern rebel and the southern black is further suggested when Jess later torments Yuma with a variant of "Dixie" — "I'm glad I'm not in a land of cotton. / The Rebs lost the war and their bones are rotten" — and then yells, "Hey you cottontail, you better scat while you can." The cottontail rabbit suggests not a Rebel soldier but a character out of slave folklore. The rebel, in this unjust world, has thus become the cottontail, the oppressed minority figure, subject to the ridicule and violence of the majority.

For Yuma, of course, the solution is simply to get new clothing, that is, to show he submits to post–Civil War authorities and values. But as the series represents it, that would be wrong and cowardly. No matter how much the Southerner may suffer from prejudice, harassment, discrimination, or violence, the interests of the West require that he stick to his principles. After he rids the town of the bullies, therefore, he turns down the offer to stay on as sheriff, opting instead to display his rebel hat and the principles they signify in whatever part of the West needs him, as a kind of knight errant, going where there's nothing but a mess of trouble—Americans in trouble. "He packed no star as he wandered far," his theme song tells us. "He searched the land, this restless land. / He was panther quick and leather tough, / And he figured that he had been pushed enough."

This theme song is marked by a confused sense of direction. As a wanderer, Yuma has no direction, only a sense of motion, but as someone who has been pushed enough, his motion is characterized by resistance to mobility. Once again, we see his thematic kinship to the defenders of the Alamo, who have wandered to Texas so that they can refuse to be pushed, thus effecting the intransigent claim of Manifest Destiny. In Texas, as in the Indian Territory, it is the *settlers* who have been pushed enough. In the contemporary South, it is the Southerner who has been pushed beyond reason to abandon rights and privileges. Through his identification with the South as the beleaguered victim of prejudice and violence, Yuma can bring to the West the principle of resistance—a wandering, expansionist resistance—out of which the destiny of the West will be forged.

This inversion is not just about civil rights but rather it is the political reality of American mythology in which the Southerner, as the representative of the Manifest Destiny of the Anglo-Saxon race, becomes the paradigmatic hero of the West and by extension of the Free World. That world, moreover, is committed to the absolute value of whiteness, a point underscored at that moment in the premiere of *The Rebel* when the reality of the adult western enfolds into the other realities that circumscribe the narrative, the reality of performer making direct address to real people in their real homes, conveying the commercial truths that underwrite the medium. In this moment of truth, when the network meets its real obligation to deliver the audience to the sponsor, we make direct eye contact with Nick Adams, the star of *The Rebel*, sitting next to a box of Cheer: "Hi. I'm Nick Adams and this is tonight's sponsor, Cheer, the folks who know how to get a white shirt really white. Just check mine. Cheer gets it so white that even I can see

Cheer gets it whiter." Since *The Rebel* is broadcast in black and white, we can't tell if Nick Adams's shirt is really white. We only have the authority evoked by his direct address, as though he were really speaking to us, augmented by the residual authority he accrues from his role. No doubt his association with the Confederate cause helps us understand why he values whiteness so much, just as, reciprocally, Cheer's sponsoring of *The Rebel* helps prove the detergent's commitment to the cause of whiteness. As a commercial earlier in the show proclaimed, "Cheer washes so white you can tell the difference," and "Try Cheer and see the difference in whiteness for yourself!" In comparison to Cheer's pure white, the commercials imply, items washed by other products are just passing for white. But users of Cheer will be able to segregate the true white from the ersatz and make their sheets (and hoods?) as white as the true white of Nick Adams's shirt.

Nor should we forget in stressing the important difference of Nick Adams's shirt that the whole series depends on the crucial difference effected by sartorial decisions. Adams's shirt is no less important in the commercial than Yuma's hat is in the series, for without the sign of the rebel, Yuma cannot evoke the acts of prejudice around which the dramatic action revolves. The messages of Yuma's hat and Adams's shirt are more than parallel; they are synonymous, both attesting to the wearer's commitment to the supremacy of whiteness. It is fitting, moreover, that Adams and Yuma should share a common distinction because, as the opening credits inform us, Adams was the cocreator of the series.

If *The Rebel,* like all the adult westerns, owed a debt to *Disneyland,* that debt, by 1959, had in part been repaid by turning a significant chunk of prime time into "Frontier Land" while it advertised the West as the place where one could tell the difference in whiteness. At the same time, because the status of American civil rights was important to both East and West Cold War propaganda, television became a cogent interpreter of America's historical and racial realities, representing those realities in one way on news shows and in another on the western. In many ways, this juxtaposition allowed the image of the West reflected by the adult westerns to contextualize the image of a racially torn nation reflected by the evening news. The adult westerns conflated America's history and destiny into a mythic "truth" against which the conflicts over racial discrimination could be read as inaccurate or as partial, both in the sense of being incomplete, like the story of the Alamo, and of being biased, like the treatment of Johnny Yuma, as he implicitly remembered the Alamo in the process of representing the values of the South in the name of the West. The adult western thus effected the same segregation that the courts had outlawed in schools and the congress was in the process of outlawing in public facilities. In the face of legal decisions and social protest, television remained throughout the black-and-white era of the 1950s the United States's real separate but equal public space.

NOTES

1. For further discussion of the ontology of television's real, see Jane Feuer, "The Concept of Live Television: Ontology as Ideology," and Robert Stam, "Television News and Its Spectator," in *Regarding Television: Critical Approaches—An Anthology,* ed. E. Ann Kaplan (Los Angeles: American Film Institute, 1983).

2. John Cawelti, *The Six-Gun Mystique* (Bowling Green, Ohio: Bowling Green University Press, 1975), 30.

3. Nick Browne, ed., *American Television: New Directions in History and Theory* (Chur, Switzerland: Harwood Academic Press, 1994), 13.

4. Ibid., 33.

5. William Boddy, *Fifties Television: The Industry and Its Critics* (Urbana: University of Illinois Press, 1990), 80–90.

6. Gilbert Seldes, *Writing for Television* (New York: Doubleday, 1952), 32.

7. J. Fred MacDonald, *One Nation Under Television: The Rise and Decline of Network TV* (Chicago: Nelson-Hall, 1994), 93.

8. Ibid., 63–95.

9. Boddy, *Fifties Television,* 201.

10. MacDonald, *One Nation Under Television,* 114.

11. Boddy, *Fifties Television,* 146.

12. "Disney in TVland," *TV Guide,* January 23, 1954, 5.

13. Ibid., 5.

14. "Love That Television," *TV Guide,* August 13, 1955, 4–5.

15. "Fess Parker: King of the Wild Frontier," *TV Guide,* April 30, 1955, 6.

16. "Love That Television," 4–5.

17. See Jack Zipes, "Breaking the Disney Spell," in *From Mouse to Mermaid: The Politics of Film Gender and Culture,* ed. Elizabeth Bell, Lynda Haas, and Laura Sells (Bloomington: Indiana University Press, 1995), 21–42.

18. "Old Horse Operas Never Die: They Just Go On Making Hay," *TV Guide,* January 15, 1954, 20–21.

19. Rogers and Autry built on their exceptional movie popularity of the preceding decade while Boyd was turned into a major children's star by virtue of his seizing the moment of early television.

20. Dan Jenkins, "Children Made Roy King of the Cowboys," *TV Guide,* January 17, 1954, 5.

21. James Atkins Shackford calls *Col. Crockett's Exploits and Adventures in Texas,* written by Crockett, "the source of so many errors, fabrications, and misrepresentations that . . . it deserves . . . its final refutation." James Atkins Shackford, *David Crockett: The Man and the Legend* (Chapel Hill: University of North Carolina Press, 1956), 273–81.

22. Houston's primary strategy in the early part of the revolt was continuous retreat.

23. Mark Deer, *The Frontiersman: The Real Life and the Many Legends of Davy Crockett* (New York: William Morrow, 1993), 230.

24. T. R. Fehrenbach, *Lone Star: A History of Texas* (New York: Macmillan, 1968), 196.

25. Deer, *The Frontiersman*, 231.

26. Ibid., 234.

27. See Lawrence D. Rice, *The Negro in Texas, 1874–1900* (Baton Rouge: Louisiana State University Press, 1971), 3–4.

28. Fehrenbach, *Lone Star,* 305.

29. Jeff Long, *Duel of Eagles: The Mexican and U.S. Fight for the Alamo* (New York: William Morrow, 1990), 100.

30. Deer, *The Frontiersman,* 232.

31. Long, *Duel of Eagles,* 51.

32. Reginald Horsman, *Race and Manifest Destiny: The Origins of American Racial Anglo-Saxonism* (Cambridge, Mass.: Harvard University Press, 1981), 213.

33. Ibid., 231.

34. Paul Andrew Hutton, "David Crockett: An Exposition on Hero Worship," in *Crockett at Two Hundred: New Perspectives on the Man and the Myth,* ed. Michael A. Lofaro and Joe Cummings (Knoxville: University of Tennessee Press, 1989), 23.

35. As MacDonald notes, "The victory of national entertainment was striking not only in its destruction of local initiative but also in its influence on the way viewers lived and thought." *One Nation Under Television,* 93.

36. "A Sociological Decision," *New York Times,* May 18, 1954, 1.

37. "Text of the Supreme Court Decision Outlawing Segregation in the Public Schools," *New York Times,* May 18, 1954, 15.

38. Ibid.

39. See Richard Slotkin, *Gunfighter Nation: The Myth of the Frontier in Twentieth-Century America* (New York: Athenaeum, 1992).

40. "Hold Her Cowboy," *TV Guide,* March 31, 1956, 4.

41. Ibid., 5.

42. *TV Guide,* December 6, 1958, 10.

43. *TV Guide,* October 8, 1955, 18.

44. Hugh O'Brien, "Marshal Earp," *TV Guide,* January 21, 1956, 8.

45. Welcome Ann Earp, "My Cousin Wyatt," *TV Guide,* January 21, 1956, 9.

46. *TV Guide,* October 4, 1958, A-39.

47. Robert Stahl, "The Facts Are Enough," *TV Guide,* February 21, 1959, 12–14.

48. Henry Giroux, "Memory and Pedagogy in the 'Wonderful World of Disney': Beyond the Politics of Innocence," in *From Mouse to Mermaid,* 45, 47.

49. See Philip Durham and Everett L. Jones, *The Negro Cowboys* (New York: Dodd, Mead, 1965); Kenneth Wiggins Porter, *The Negro on the American Frontier* (New York: Arno and the New York Times, 1971); William Loren Katz, *Black People Who Made the Old West* (Philadelphia: Africa World Press, 1992); William H. Leckie, *The Buffalo Soldiers: A Narrative of the Negro Cavalry in the West*

(Norman: University of Oklahoma Press, 1967); Rice, *The Negro in Texas*; Gina DeAngelis, *The Black Cowboys* (Philadelphia: Chelsea House, 1988).

50. Boddy, *Fifties Television*, 202.

51. MacDonald, *One Nation Under Television*, 93.

52. Ibid., 94.

53. See Raymond Williams, *Television: Technology and Cultural Form* (Hanover, N.H.: University Press of New England, 1974); John Thornton Caldwell, *Televisuality: Style, Crisis, and Authority in American Television* (New Brunswick: Rutgers University Press, 1995); John Fiske, *Television Culture* (London: Metheun, 1987); John Ellis, *Visible Fictions: Cinema, Television, Video* (London: Routledge, 1982).

Daytime Politics

Kefauver, McCarthy, and the American Housewife

KRISTEN HATCH

During the 1950s, television networks struggled with a nagging question: what do women want? Daytime television was searching for a means of capturing the attention of housewives who were accustomed to turning on the radio as they worked during the day. As the *Hollywood Reporter* described it, "The networks are having a devil of a time with their daytime programming. No one can quite pinpoint what the daytime viewers are looking for."[1] However, daytime viewers had already demonstrated overwhelmingly what it was they wanted. It was the networks that failed to perceive the full range of women's desires and translate them into commercial programming.

In March of 1951, daytime television became a national obsession. As many as thirty million people in twenty-one cities on the East Coast of the United States turned on their televisions daily to see Senator Estes Kefauver lead a Senate investigation into the relationship between politics and organized crime. In New York alone, the Hooper rating was 26.2 as compared to an average morning rating of 1.5.[2] One woman in New Jersey described the experience of millions of women when she explained, "I never look at television in the daytime ordinarily, but for the past week I have done little else."[3]

And yet, despite women's obvious interest in politics, regular network television remained void of extended political news and discussion during the day.[4] Why is it that the networks ignored all indications that daytime audiences were interested in political programming? The answer lies, in part, in the fact that the broadcasts significantly disrupted the imagined social order; the very categories that defined American society were challenged by the daily intrusion of live political proceedings into the middle-class home. In response to this challenge, the popular press resituated the housewife as an aberrant viewer, who consumed political events in a distinctly feminine manner.[5] The sponsors, who continued to dominate daytime programming long after the networks had gained control over prime time, relied heavily on an ideology of separate spheres, wherein the housewife's duty to society lay in cleaning the single-family home and seeing to the health and well-being of her husband and children. Given the needs of social critics to reassert the established social order and of sponsors to maintain an ideology of separate spheres, there is little wonder that, until the advent of cable, political news during the day took the form of an interruption of regular daytime schedules.

Following a pattern established in radio, sponsors and networks based their programming strategies on a very narrow vision of the television audience. As it has developed in the United States, network television works to preserve a specific fantasy of the American family. Nick Browne explains, "the position of the programs in the television schedule reflects and is determined by the work-structured order of the real social world. The patterns of position and flow imply the question of who is home, and through the complicated social relays and temporal mediations, link television to the modes, processes, and scheduling of production characteristic of the population."[6] During the 1950s, the television networks developed programming to conform to the imagined routines of an audience that was narrowly constructed as white, Christian, and middle class, living in single-family homes that were paid for by men employed in white-collar jobs that kept them away from home from 9:00 to 5:00 and were cleaned by their wives (as opposed to paid domestic laborers) who stayed home during the day. Everyone could be defined by his or her relationship to the nuclear family, which consisted of the breadwinning father, homemaking mother, and their school-aged children,[7] and network television programming corresponded to the rhythms of this imagined family. Weekday programming was devoted to the entertainment of housewives. Periodically throughout the day, shows for preschoolers gave Mom a break from childcare. At 4:00, when school was out, the children's shows began in earnest while Mom prepared dinner. At 7:00, the news entertained husbands while their wives washed the dishes. At 8:00, the family could gather together around the television set to watch family-oriented programs. On Sunday mornings, Christian religious services were televised. And on weekend afternoons, Dad could relax in front of a sporting event or news analysis, resting up for another week at the office.

The preemption of regular weekday programming by the Senate hearings upset this tidy pattern, and the disruption of the American home that resulted from the housewife's consuming interest in the telecasts became the subject of widespread commentary. During the Kefauver hearings, the *New York Times* ran a front-page headline proclaiming "Home Chores Wait, Shopping Sage." The article explained that during the telecasts, "Housewives skimped on their household chores and offered no guarantee that dinner would be ready on time."[8] In another front-page story, the *Washington Post* warned, "The dust got swept under the rug yesterday, if it got swept at all. . . . Glued to their TV sets by the Senate Crime Committee hearing . . . housewives gave scant attention to their chores."[9] The *Chicago Daily Tribune* explained that "women by the thousands deserted their household duties, afternoon bridge, and canasta for the second day to eavesdrop on the big show. . . . There will be more watching today. The women may not even get the dishes done."[10] And the *New York Herald Tribune* described a city caught in the grip of television, "Beds went unmade and pots boiled over as housewives sat absorbed and fascinated [in front of their television sets]. 'My wife hasn't been out of the house for a week,' said a letter carrier . . . 'All the women in the neighborhood are the same. They just don't go out while this is going on.'"[11]

In the years following the Kefauver hearings, an increasing number of American households acquired television sets, television stations began operations throughout the country, and AT&T's coaxial cable made coast-to-coast live broadcasts feasible.[12] As a result, during the spring of 1954, the Army-McCarthy hearings reached an even larger audience than had Kefauver's investigations. Again, major city newspapers complained that televised hearings were disrupting the housewife's chores. "Some suburban merchants found that housewives did no shopping during the broadcasts and then raced to the stores in the late afternoon."[13] The *Chicago Daily Tribune* reported a return to the clutter of the Kefauver investigations, "Housewives, recalling days and days of stacked dishes in the sink during the Kefauver hearings, yesterday were spellbound by this tremendous tug-of-war on TV."[14] And the *Washington Post* ran a front-page headline, "McCarthy-Army Telecasts Disrupt Housework Routines," followed by a story explaining:

One duty-bound housewife even got up early to get the housework cleared away before the telecasts began at 10:30 a.m. Another had the day's schedule planned to sandwich her marketing between the morning and afternoon sessions. Others admitted the housework might have gotten just a lick-and-a-promise as they kept one eye on the doings on Capitol Hill. One said the McCarthy-Army telecasts were the biggest show on morning and afternoon TV since the Kefauver Senate Crime Committee hearings pulled her away from her ironing board and kitchen sink three years ago.[15]

The hyperbolic headlines suggest more than mere peevishness brought on by cold dinners and cluttered homes. They are expressions of concern not only about the value of the housewife's labor in a postindustrial economy but about the manner in which television appeared to be challenging the categories that help to define American society. In the face of these concerns, it was the stereotype of the housewife that permitted social critics to simultaneously acknowledge and disavow the threat that television represented to the perceived order of American society. Within the cultural imagination, the stereotyped figure of the housewife performed the vital function of drawing off these anxieties. The sense that television would indelibly change American life and politics became less threatening when the uncontrollable aspects of those changes were perceived to be the outcome of the housewife's lazy viewing habits and her misinterpretation of public events. The apparent disruption of the social order seemed less overwhelming when women were perceived to behave in a feminine manner even as they consumed televised political events.[16]

Television, even as it represented American ingenuity and business acumen, threatened the very definitions upon which a middle-class sense of superiority was based—the capacity to differentiate between scientific truth and superstitious fiction and to clearly distinguish the masculine public sphere of politics from the feminine private sphere of the home. News reports on the hearings suggest a widespread perception that the broadcasts had wreaked havoc on American society. The dirty world of politics had infiltrated the well-maintained privacy of the single-family home; likewise, the housewife's gaze threatened to trivialize the nation's most serious business.

The broadcasts disrupted the division of public and private spheres. There was a sense that public figures were becoming too intimately familiar to viewers. The *New York Herald Tribune* celebrated the fact that "[m]en who had been entire strangers, or mere names, had become acquaintances."[17] However, others expressed unease about this newfound intimacy. As the *New York Times* put it, neither Joseph McCarthy nor Roy Cohn could "blow his nose or mop his brow but the news of this gesture goes out to the waiting millions."[18] The unease bordered on a now-familiar sense of paranoia when one viewer wrote to the *Washington Post* that the broadcasts of the Army-McCarthy hearings "make every onlooker feel he himself is being investigated."[19]

Further, the broadcasts posed a threat to masculine authority, both in the political realm and within the home. Because the cameras captured and disseminated testimony at the same moment it was being heard by the senators themselves, it became difficult to contain or control the flow of information, creating a sense that "video [had taken] away the walls around the hearing room."[20] It was no longer up to Congress to determine what the public record of the proceedings should consist of. During the Army-McCarthy hearings, the chair, Karl Mundt, ordered that certain testimony be stricken from the record. But one senator objected, asking how "could Mundt strike something that had already been heard across the Nation via radio and television. The Chairman thought this one over for a moment and said: 'Leave it in the record.'"[21]

Just as U.S. senators could not control the information that flowed from the hearing rooms, so the American patriarch could no longer protect his wife and children from the information piped into the home via the television set. During the Kefauver hearings, women's familiarity with the underworld figures who were called in as witnesses became suspect: "Housewives from Minneapolis to Miami let the dishes pile up in their sinks . . . while gangsters, gamblers, and hoodlums 'dropped in' in their living rooms."[22] Worse, children were exposed to these shady figures. The *Chicago Daily Tribune* complained of the language employed by witnesses, expressing concern about the "profanity and obscenity that burst out in the air occasionally"[23] at an hour when children could be watching. Parents were concerned that their children might be influenced by the gangsters who appeared on the witness stand. When the hearings ran late into the afternoon, the *Washington Post* reported that irate mothers had called in to the local television station demanding that *Howdy Doody* be shown on schedule. According to the *Post,* their complaints arose partially from the fact that they "didn't want their little ones watching Howdy Costello."[24]

The broadcasts of Senate hearings further threatened masculine authority by conferring political expertise onto the women who watched them. Television had expanded the definition of the public sphere to include the home, since the broadcasts "enable[d] the US to reach a private verdict right in its own living room."[25] But because men were assumed to be away from home during the day, it was widely understood that their knowledge of the hearings rested on reports published in the print media.[26] With the role of the television audience likened to that of a jury, women understood themselves to be participants in a national drama. Countless women wrote to newspapers and magazines offering their opinions of the hearings. They described themselves as active participants in the proceedings, as witnesses or jurors. And they clearly felt that the experience of watching the telecasts rendered them qualified to evaluate the manner in which the proceedings were reported in newspapers. "I am really glad for the opportunity to view these hearings over the television, for I can see for myself what the true story is in this controversy,"[27] one woman wrote. "Just want you to know how fortunate I think it is that the hearings are televised so that the public can get the true picture and make up their own minds. It is a protection against slanted, biased editorials such as appear in your paper."[28] Their letters convey the seriousness with which they approached their role as observers of the hearings. "I have watched the entire committee proceedings by television and reviewed the texts. Then I have read carefully the comments, editorials, and front-page articles upon them. . . . I was thoroughly misled and have been for

months by [the] consistent slanting and misrepresentations and juggling of
what should be factual reporting. . . . I am only now at last learning the truth
by following the actual texts."[29] And the difference in degree of access to the
information disseminated during the hearings became apparent in the different interpretations of Senator Joseph McCarthy's testimony during the Army-
McCarthy hearings. Public opinion was reported to be divided along gender
lines. According to *Newsweek,* "the anti-McCarthy women lined up solidly
against the pro-McCarthy men" and "[a] factor here, particularly among women
was the impression made by the principals over television."[30]

Just as the broadcasts obfuscated the margin between public and private
spheres and challenged masculine authority within the realm of politics, the
stability of the category of fact was thrown into jeopardy when viewers read
about the hearings in the press and found that the written accounts did not
conform to their own interpretation of the proceedings. One reader voiced
the frustration of many who recognized a disparity between what they saw
and what they read when he complained that, having watched most of the
hearings on television, "the resemblance of what I have seen and heard,
compared with what I have read from newspapers and magazines, is purely
academic."[31] Further, by virtue of their being broadcast through a medium
that was already associated with entertainment, the line separating the factual recording of important events from the frivolity of fictional entertainment seemed to be in danger of disappearing altogether. *Newsweek*
complained, "Many didn't care who was right, who was wrong, but turned
on their TV sets merely for the spectacle. . . . What it would prove in the
long run was moot—except that for every spectacle there is a spectator."[32]
In the case of the Kefauver hearings, the similarity between underworld witnesses and Hollywood portrayals of mob bosses was widely commented
upon. Was Hollywood imitating reality, or had reality taken on the contours of Hollywood? The question plagued viewers who followed the
Kefauver hearings on television. "Humphrey Bogart, the tough man of the
movies, would be hard put to match Dapper Joe Adonis in arrogant defi-
ance."[33] Virginia Hill's "brazen performance as the gangsters' gal . . . made
Claire Trevor's playing of similar roles in movies seem pale by comparison."[34] A viewer wrote to the *New York Herald Tribune* that

> the leading "heavy," Frank Costello, suave, sinister, faultlessly garbed, impec-
> cably groomed. . . . Haven't we seen [him] on the screen? Then of course, the
> "big shot" must have a "mouthpiece" and here he is on the stage sitting at the
> side of his client having numerous whispered conferences. . . . How often have
> you seen him in your favorite gangster thriller? And who can ask for a better
> "gun moll" than Virginia Hill? What Hollywood movie lot could have given
> us a better "type" or what script writer could have given her better lines?[35]

The problem was compounded when the participants in the hearings became television celebrities as a result of the broadcasts. Senator Kefauver was the mystery guest on an episode of *What's My Line?* (which prompted commentators to retitle the hearings "What's My Crime?"). According to the *Chicago Daily Tribune,* the audience laughed uproariously when the contestants asked, "Are you in the entertainment business?" and "Have you ever been on television?"[36] To further blur the distinction between the reality of the hearings and the fictional nature of most television fare, Kefauver and other members of the Senate Crime Investigating Committee also appeared on the CBS series *Crime Syndicated,* which featured fictionalized stories about organized crime. Television left its mark on the Senate testimony, as well. When one witness repeatedly invoked his right not to testify on the grounds that he might incriminate himself, the senators asked him where he had learned about the Fifth Amendment. He replied that he had seen it used on crime shows on television. However, television's ability to manipulate the proceedings was no laughing matter. Objective truth was being mediated by technology that was otherwise devoted to commercialized entertainment. One viewer complained to the *New York Herald Tribune* that "TV—whose crews will be able to edit the 'show' like a film cutter—can make a jackass out of any innocent man."[37]

If the Kefauver hearings' claim to reality seemed jeopardized by the broadcasts' relationship to fictional television programming, the line between reality and fiction was further obscured by television technology itself during the Army-McCarthy hearings, during which a U.S. senator and representatives of the United States Army argued over different versions of the truth. The veracity of the technology used to transmit the hearings to millions of television viewers was thrown into question by virtue of the fact that one of the charges against McCarthy was that he had entered a doctored photograph into evidence. Debates ensued over the question of the manner in which photographic representations could be manipulated. Likewise, commentators noted that, through the choice of angles and images, the television camera was able to shape the proceedings. According to the *Chicago Daily Tribune,* the camera's ability to transmit the hearings truthfully was open to debate, and "the public will judge whether the camera covered the hearings fairly."[38] Indeed, the hearings were staged with the television cameras in mind. Senator McCarthy and representatives from the Army sat next to one another, rather than taking their customary places across the table from one another, for the convenience of the cameras. Their positions at the table were reversed daily so that each side would have equal time being shot full face and in profile. However, viewers remained unconvinced of the impartiality of the broadcasts.

Finally, television threatened to pervert government through the association of the nation's business with the crass commercialism of network broadcasting. There was widespread concern that commercial sponsorship of political broadcasts would pervert government, that it would be harmful to the nation if businesses made a profit off of official government procedures. But it wasn't just any form of sponsorship that was at issue. Critics were not outraged when the televised Kefauver hearings were sponsored by *Time* magazine. In fact, the magazine was praised for underwriting the broadcasts. Likewise, local newspapers' sponsorship of the Army-McCarthy hearings was not considered cause for worry. What was of concern, in article after article, was the possibility that in the future such proceedings might be sponsored by the manufacturers of soap, a fear that stemmed in part from the fact that sponsorship of daytime radio programming was dominated by General Mills and Proctor and Gamble. Airing advertisements for their products during the Senate hearings would suggest the unseemly juxtaposition of national politics with the intimate concerns of the housewife. It would be demeaning to a senator if his testimony were interrupted by an advertisement for soap or antacids.

The commercialism of American broadcasting had already been the subject of widespread debate with the development of network radio. During those debates, the dangers of commercialism had been strongly associated with female listeners. Michele Hilmes argues that the development of daytime programming in the 1930s reflected not only the advertisers' desire to appeal to viewers who were responsible for most household purchases, but grew out of the networks' more complicated needs as well. During a period in which radio's commercial base was being hotly debated, the networks were at pains to define their programming in terms of their social function. As a result, the broadcasting schedule was split. Prestige shows were reserved for prime time, leaving daytime the domain of shows that were widely criticized for their base appeal to housewives. In this way, Hilmes argues, the networks were able to displace criticism of commercialism in broadcasting onto daytime programming:

> Broadcasters during this period of contested credibility had two formidable projects to take on. One was exploiting an economic base that clearly rested on the female purchaser of household products. . . . The other . . . [was to] convince regulators that their mission consisted as much of public service programming as of sheer commercialism . . . in order to rebuff educational broadcasters' claims on the spectrum. . . . [A] way of achieving this end was to create a differentiation between daytime and nighttime programming, by which daytime became the venue for a debased kind of commercialized, feminized mass culture—heavily dominated by advertising agencies—in contrast to the more sophisticated, respectable, and masculine-characterized

arena of prime time, also dominated by agencies but subject to stricter network controls.[39]

Thus, daytime television programming was shaped as much by the widespread denigration of the housewife as it was by her perceived desires.

Once again in the 1950s, when network broadcasting posed a challenge
to American ideals, the image of a feminine mass audience helped to resolve
the contradictions embodied in the new medium. The image of the undisciplined housewife surfaces in countless stories about the televising of the
Kefauver and Army-McCarthy hearings. And through the repeated use of
this stereotype, we can discern a society struggling to restore the sense of
order that was challenged by the new medium. The invocation of the housewife did not just help to reassure the nation that women themselves
remained the same despite the profound social changes that the television
set was producing. Stories about female viewers also helped to reestablish
the categories that the broadcasts had threatened to destroy.

Offsetting the disruption caused by the transformation of government
into spectacle, several newspaper and magazine accounts took pains to
reassert the difference between masculine and feminine modes of looking.
Women were repositioned as the object of the gaze even as they participated
in the political drama. Virginia Hill, a key witness in Kefauver's crime investigation, became a national sensation during the broadcasts largely because
she fit so well the popular image of the gangster's moll. The Army-
McCarthy hearings had no comparable witnesses to call. Instead, the
women on the sidelines became news. The hearings were framed by the television cameras in such a way that a woman—Ruth Watt—appeared at the
center of the screen whenever the cameras turned to the chair of the Senate
inquiry, Karl Mundt. Stylishly dressed, her pose suggested self-conscious-
ness in the face of the television cameras as, according to the *New York
Times,* she attended to the needs of the busy senators (a reprimand, perhaps, to the slothful housewife watching at home). By virtue of her seat
behind the senator, she had become "one of the nation's newest television
personalities, though her official role in the hearings was limited to supply-
ing the participants with pencils, paper, and water."[40]

The female spectators in the hearing room also became the object of the
nation's collective gaze. A *New York Times* article reported that the spectators in the hearing rooms "feel like actors rather than spectators in this
drama. The spotlight may fall upon any one of them at any moment. This is
especially true of the ladies, and especially true of the pretty ladies."[41]
Newsweek turned to the women in the audience for reassuring reminders
that, despite the cameras' preoccupation with the senators, women's primary public function remained the same; women were there to be looked at,

even when they comprised the audience for the hearings. In a half-page pictorial entitled "Every Day Is Ladies' Day," the magazine showed photographs of well-dressed and attractively posed women in the hearing room. The caption reads, "Outnumbering men, the women from far and near who get seats in the Army-McCarthy hearing room usually dress up for their appearances at the most-publicized Congressional hearings in history."[42] Two weeks later, several letters were published praising the beauty of the women who had appeared in the pictorial.

While the continued positioning of women as objects of the collective gaze helped to appease fears about the disruption of masculine and feminine roles, those who observed the proceedings from the privacy of their own home also helped to assure readers that the world was not significantly changed. If the broadcasts posed a threat to the stability of American life, newspaper and magazine articles suggested, it was because the housewife was an undisciplined viewer. She was described as taking an unhealthy interest in the proceedings, treating them as entertainment rather than serious business. "Some housewives held television parties yesterday, and . . . the ladies were inclined to be critical. One woman . . . called the bureau and complained that Ambassador O'Dwyer was talking too much. 'Can't you tell him to shut up and get Frank Costello back on the stand?' she said."[43] The newspapers suggested that the spectacular nature of the broadcasts arose from the fact that women were attuned to their theatrical quality rather than focusing on the political importance of the proceedings. "An informal poll among viewing housewives would seem to indicate that Kefauver is the most telegenic of the [senators] and that Tobey looks most like a movie version of a politician."[44] During the Army-McCarthy hearings, one taxi driver summed up the widespread perception that women focused on feeling to the exclusion of fact when he told a *Newsweek* reporter, "My wife doesn't know anything about politics, but she sure has gotten to hate these guys McCarthy and Roy Cohn."[45] To this day, historical accounts of the effect of the broadcasts on McCarthy's political career point to housewives' disgust at the senator's poor manners—rather than their assessment of the issues—as a decisive factor in his loss of power.

More precisely, the housewife's interest in national politics during this period was interpreted less as an awakening interest in the affairs of state than as an extension of her deeply flawed devotion to soap operas. While both broadcasts were likened to everything from a wrestling match, circus, or minstrel show to Broadway theater and Hollywood film, more than anything else, they were compared to soap opera. The misperception of politics as soap opera seemed to explain why housewives took such an unlikely interest in the proceedings. According to the critics, women consumed the hearings as though they were akin to the serialized dramas to which housewives had already become accustomed through years of radio listening. "Thousands of housewives, turning on their television sets yesterday to catch up with the latest in cookery and soap opera adventures, found something considerably more dramatic—the Senate's crime investigating committee with Sen. Kefauver in charge."[46] Kefauver's investigation was facetiously retitled "Costello Faces Life" or "Just Plain Bill O'Dwyer," a play on the popular radio serials *Portia Faces Life* and *Just Plain Bill*. I. F. Stone described McCarthy as a "Soap Opera Hero." And, in a satirical column entitled "One Man's Subcommittee" (after the serial drama *One Man's Family*), Ace Goodman suggested that the networks adopt the techniques used in soap operas to increase the housewife's interest in the Army-McCarthy hearings. Rather than providing political commentary, the newscasters should "recapitulate what happened earlier so as not to confuse McCarthy with [characters from a soap opera]. This show is no *Meet the Press*. It should be sold like daytime soap opera with all the trimmings. . . . 'And now . . . 'One Man's Subcommittee' . . . ORGAN THEME . . . FADES FOR . . .Well, when last we left Bob on the witness stand. . . .'"[47]

The supposed similarities between the housewife's reception of soap opera and politics went beyond the facetious comparison of the hearings to low forms of entertainment. Women were imagined to have consumed the broadcasts much in the manner that they consumed daytime serials. Throughout the popular press, soap opera fans were described as lazy and stupid, devoted to maudlin fantasies to the point of neglecting their duties within the home. The lazy housewife, weeping before her radio or television set as the dishes piled up in the sink and the vacuum cleaner lay idle, was a recurring image and one not far removed, minus the weeping, from the headlines that described her interest in the Senate hearings. Another widely circulated caricature of the soap opera fan had her incapable of distinguishing between soap opera fantasy and the reality of everyday life. Countless articles about soap operas carried the obligatory story of the housewife who thought the characters on her favorite show were real. According to *TV Guide*, "setting the gals straight [on the fictional nature of soap opera is] like tipping off a youngster to the truth about Santa Claus."[48] Housewives' overinvestment in radio soap opera had already been the subject of extensive criticism. In the 1940s, numerous studies were conducted to measure the degree to which serial dramas might harm susceptible listeners. Dr. Louis Berg, for instance, argued that radio serials aggravated the neuroses that lay dormant in female listeners. CBS took his report seriously enough to conduct its own study, which found no significant variation in the mental health of listeners and nonlisteners.

Likewise, there appeared to be something similarly unhealthy about the housewife's intense interest in the televised political proceedings. According

to the *New York Times,* "watching personalities who were real yet had all
the appeal of characters straight out of a mystery thriller had a narcotic fascination on the viewer at home."[49] During the hearings, housewives were
imagined to have misread the broadcasts, limning the senators' every word
and movement for indications of hidden emotional meaning, much as they
would view a daytime serial. The housewife was supposed to have misinter-
preted the hearings, to have focused on the feminine concerns of character
and emotion, translating the broadcasts into gossip as opposed to news.

In this regard, the headlines describing the disruption of household
order—the dusty and cluttered homes, the dish-filled sinks, and idle vacuum
cleaners—are more than a reflection of the social disruption provoked by
the broadcasting of Senate hearings. They also suggest the means by which
the sense of order could be reestablished. The housewife's distraction was
depicted as having dire consequences for the nation. Columnists and political cartoonists joked about husbands surviving on bouillon cubes for the
duration of the hearings. Men told reporters of wives too preoccupied with
the broadcasts to wash and feed their children.[50] The social order of the
nation was perceived to be in jeopardy while the housewife sat at home in
the thrall of the television set. Not only were husbands and children denied
their dinners, but the very lifeblood of the nation was being withheld as
well. During the Kefauver hearings, headlines scolded, "Blood Gifts for the
Wounded in Korea Fall Off; Public Too Busy Watching Inquiry on TV."[51]
The Red Cross enlisted the help of Senator Kefauver, who took advantage
of a recess in the hearings to urge women viewers to "donate blood instead
of sitting at home watching TV."[52] The senator "urged . . . that Brooklyn
housewives work doubly hard on a Red Cross campaign while the Committee is recessed [because] housewives counted on by the Red Cross to conduct a special money-raising campaign have all been glued to their
television sets."[53] Likewise, the housewife's undisciplined consumption of
television had put the economic health of the nation in jeopardy. Numerous
newspaper and magazine articles complained about a drop in business for
the duration of the broadcasts. During the Kefauver hearings, the *Washington Post* reported, "Department stores were not as busy as usual, nor were
theaters."[54] And during the Army-McCarthy hearings, *Newsweek* reported,
"In many . . . cities, department-store sales slumped badly as housewives
neglected not only shopping but dishes and dusting as well."[55]

While such news reports certainly suggest the degree to which the telecasts had disrupted the national sense of order, they also provide reassur-
ance that order would soon be restored. The problems posed by the new
medium were not perceived to be permanent. Rather, they were the temporary product of aberrant behavior on the part of the housewife. As soon as

she resumed her position within the home, American life would return to normal.

Television had invited women to participate in national politics. An editorial in the *New York Herald Tribune* explained, "Aristotle long ago defined the size of a democratic community as the area within which the citizens could know the *character* of their public servants. A lot about the character of men in public office is being learned these days by the television watchers."[56] Housewives, the target audience for regular daytime programming, were thus offered entry into the democratic citizenry in a way Aristotle never imagined. While it is impossible to gauge the extent to which the broadcasts actually did incorporate women into national politics, it is apparent that women were beginning to perceive themselves as capable of analyzing public events, not in spite of but because of their feminine skills. Women wrote numerous letters to the editor to express their views on the proceedings. They drew upon a familiar feminine role—that of upholding the moral order of the nation—in their critiques of men elected to national office. And, when one editorial complained that the Army-McCarthy hearings amounted to the public airing of dirty laundry, several housewives wrote in reply that, in their experience, laundry requires airing.[57]

Occurring during television's infancy, before the network's daytime programming had become established, there was some speculation that the networks and sponsors might respond to housewives' overwhelming interest in the broadcasts by developing programs that would continue to elicit the "glowing sense of civic purpose" that the televised hearings had aroused. Commentators wondered how "televiewers [would] like returning to the insipidity of the average daytime TV show when the hearings were over."[58] Newspapers editorialized on the possibilities that lay dormant in the new medium: "If television can educate . . . the whole population on crime and politics, why not take in Congress, the Legislature . . . or even our Board of Estimate and City Council? For that matter, a further expansion might include the court trials of broad and legitimate interest."[59] And one man wrote to the *New York Herald Tribune*, "My wife and a friend of hers have kept their eyes glued to the television ever since the hearings here in New York started. They are convinced that the Kefauver committee should be a permanent Congressional committee and are thoroughly aroused about the criminal condition in the United States."[60]

However, after the live broadcasts ended, national politics disappeared almost completely from daytime network television. Clearly, the housewife's active participation in the political process, even as a distant observer, was hardly conducive to the selling of household products. The countless newspaper and magazine articles describing her preoccupation with the hearings—at the expense of her ironing, vacuuming, and scrubbing—offer evidence as to why the sponsors that dominated daytime radio would not be eager to promote political programming on television during the day. If housewives were too enthralled by the program to tend to their chores, and if the program were one that encouraged her to develop political rather than homemaking skills, housewives would hardly be receptive to advertisements for household cleaning products.

Further, daytime sponsors were unlikely to have recognized the over- whelming ratings for the live hearings as evidence that the political arena might be an exploitable source of programming content. In one sense, they must have even interpreted the broadcasts to have affirmed the suitability of daytime serial drama for homemaking listeners, since women's interest in the political proceedings was interpreted to be a perversion of their ongoing devotion to soap operas. More to the point, the national sense of stability and order rested, in part, on the image of the undisciplined housewife. Adapting daytime television schedules in response to the considerable inter- est that women had exhibited during the hearings would require a radical reassessment of the housewife's interests and abilities, a reassessment that would undermine the precarious social balance that had been achieved at the housewife's expense.

After the live broadcasts ended, national politics disappeared almost completely from daytime network television; the void was filled once again with soap operas, game shows, variety shows, household advice, and Holly- wood movies. By 1956, two years after the Army-McCarthy hearings, the networks had established the pattern of daytime programming that would remain in effect until the advent of cable. And when national news did return to daytime, it did so in the form of interruptions, with apologies, of the regular daytime schedule.

NOTES

1. Leon Guild, "On the Air," *Hollywood Reporter* (April 8, 1954): 8.
2. "Crime Hearing Is TV Smash in District, 20 Other Cities," *Washington Post,* March 20, 1951, 1. Different sources report different Hooper ratings for the broadcasts, but the *Washington Post* suggests the range that most sources were reporting.
3. Florence Hay, letter to the editor, *Time,* April 2, 1951, 6.
4. The Crackerbarrel Interviews on the *Kate Smith Hour,* in which cohost Ted Collins discussed controversial topics with political figures, were a rare and popular exception.
5. It is worth noting the commercial interests of the newspapers and maga- zines in which these reports appear. Television's broadcast of the hearings posed a threat to the print media's absolute authority over political news coverage.
6. Nick Browne, "The Political Economy of the Television (Super) Text,"

American Television: New Directions in History and Theory, ed. Nick Browne (Langhorne, Pa.: Harwood Academic Publishers, 1994), 71.

7. Of course, this was little more than a fantasy of American family life. Not only did it eliminate anyone who was not Christian, middle class, or monogamously heterosexual, it also mischaracterized even those who did conform to such standards, since during this period an unprecedented number of middle-class married women worked outside the home.

8. Jack Gould, "Millions Glued to TV for Hearing: Home Chores Wait, Shopping Sags," *New York Times,* March 20, 1951, 1.

9. "Crime Hearing Is TV Smash," 1.

10. Larry Wolters, "Gambling Boss' Hands Betray His Fears to TV," *Chicago Daily Tribune,* March 14, 1951, II, 8.

11. Gordon Allison, "Fascinated City Sees O'Dwyer Testify on TV," *New York Herald Tribune,* March 20, 1951, 8.

12. During the Kefauver hearings, the live broadcasts had been an East Coast phenomenon. In Los Angeles, the independent station KTLA broadcast live testimony during the Army-McCarthy hearings accompanied by still photographs of the participants rather than the moving images seen on television in eastern states.

13. Richard T. Baker, "Public Accepts Inquiry in Stride," *New York Times,* April 23, 1954, 9.

14. Larry Wolters, "Big Show Plays to Standees," *Chicago Daily Tribune,* April 23, 1954, II, 8.

15. "McCarthy-Army Telecasts Disrupt Housework Routines," *Washington Post,* April 23, 1954, 1.

16. I am borrowing from Homi Bhabha's analysis of stereotypes in "The Other Question: Difference, Discrimination, and the Discourse of Colonialism," in which he examines the function of the stereotype in the cultural imagination. Bhabha argues that, in Western culture, stereotypes operate much in the manner of the Freudian fetish, serving as a means by which a society can simultaneously recognize and disavow knowledge that threatens its sense of mastery and control. The stereotyped figure is regarded with ambivalence, an equal mix of affection and disdain, because it is both dangerous and controllable. Ultimately, the characteristics that constitute the stereotype reveal a great deal about the fears and anxieties of the culture that created it. Homi Bhabha, "The Other Question: Difference, Discrimination, and the Discourse of Colonialism," in *Out There: Marginalization and Contemporary Cultures,* ed. Russell Ferguson (New York: Museum of Contemporary Art, 1990).

17. "The Great Show," *New York Herald Tribune,* April 23, 1954, 16.

18. R. L. Duffus, "Millions of Eyes Are Footlights for Inquiry Dramatis Personae," *New York Times,* May 27, 1954, 21.

19. Prudence Ellis Kinsley, letter to the editor, *Washington Post,* May 7, 1954, 15.

20. Jack Gould, "The Crime Hearings," *New York Times,* March 18, 1951, 18.

21. "Cameraman 'Steals' Secrets Before Eyes of Probers," *Washington Post,*

April 24, 1954, 6. The article's title, referring to Cold War fears about the nation's ability to prevent the illicit flow of information across its borders, suggests the degree of paranoia the cameras' presence at the hearings had inspired.

22. Larry Wolters, "Probe Gives TV Its Best Show—And Showoffs," *Chicago Daily Tribune*, March 13, 1951, II, 1.

23. Ibid.

24. "Crime Hearing Is TV Smash," 8.

25. "The U.S. Gets a Close Look at Crime," *Life*, March 26, 1951, 33.

26. A parallel story to that of housewives neglecting their chores in the home was that of their husbands arriving late to work and taking long lunch hours so that they might watch the hearings. Men were photographed crowded around television sets in public bars, train stations, and stores. Nonetheless, they were not described as having the degree of access to the broadcasts that was assumed to be enjoyed by their wives.

27. Queene C. Brookshire, letter to the editor, *Washington Post*, May 10, 1954, 10.

28. Marie Muldoon, letter to the editor, *New York Herald Tribune*, May 5, 1954, 12.

29. Lucia Hull, "Reactions to the Hearings," *New York Herald Tribune*, May 8, 1954, 10.

30. "Army-McCarthy: Clouded Verdict" *Newsweek*, June 28, 1954, 20.

31. Bob D. Wright, "Cast of Characters," *Newsweek*, May 31, 1954, 2.

32. "The Country: Looking and Deciding for Itself," *Newsweek*, May 3, 1954, 28.

33. Larry Wolters, "Housewives See Kefauver and Hoodlums on TV," *Chicago Daily Tribune*, March 13, 1951, II, 8.

34. Wolters, "Probe Gives TV Its Best Show," II, 1.

35. Michael Grubnick, "The Hollywood Reality," *New York Herald Tribune*, March 22, 1951, 12. Likewise, during the Army-McCarthy hearings, the *Chicago Daily Tribune* described special counsel Ray Jenkins's performance as akin to that of a venerable stage actor: "Jenkins made a strong TV appearance. Granite-faced and impassive, he spoke deliberately, forcefully and with precise diction that might have won applause from the late John Barrymore." Wolters, "Big Show Plays to Standees," *Chicago Daily Tribune*, April 23, 1954, II, 8.

36. Larry Wolters, "Here's a Switch: Kefauver Gets Quizzed on TV," *Chicago Daily Tribune*, March 19, 1951, III, 10.

37. Martin Proctor, "The Kefauver Committee and TV," *New York Herald Tribune,* March 20, 1951, 15.

38. Wolters, "Big Show Plays to Standees," 8.

39. Michele Hilmes, *Radio Voices: American Broadcasting, 1922–1952* (Minneapolis: University of Minnesota Press, 1997), 153–54.

40. "Chief Clerk of Inquiry Now a TV Personality," *New York Times,* April 24, 1954, 11.

41. Duffus, "Millions of Eyes," 21.

42. "The Hearings: Every Day Is Ladies' Day," *Newsweek* (June 7, 1954, 26.

43. Allison, "Fascinated City," 8.

44. Wolters, "Gambling Boss' Hands Betray," II, 8.

45. "Army-McCarthy: Clouded Verdict," 20.

46. Wolters, "Housewives See Kefauver and Hoodlums on TV," 8.

47. Goodman Ace, "One Man's Sub-Committee," *Saturday Review* (May 15, 1954): 28.

48. "Why Housewives Holler," *TV Guide,* June 11, 1954, 21.

49. Jack Gould, "The Crime Hearings," 18.

50. Olliee Crawford, "Fine Tuning," *TV Guide,* June 11, 1954, 23; "The Country: Looking and Deciding for Itself," 28.

51 "Blood Gifts for Wounded in Korea Fall Off; Public Too Busy Watching Inquiry on TV," *New York Times,* March 21, 1951, 15.

52. "Biggest Show on Earth," *Time,* March 26, 1951, 80.

53. "TV Wives Reminded to Help Red Cross," *New York Herald Tribune,* March 17, 1951, 9.

54. "Crime Hearing Is TV Smash," 8.

55. "The Country: Looking and Deciding for Itself," 28.

56. "The Great Show" *New York Herald,* April 23, 1954, 16.

57. "Dirty Linen," *Washington Post,* April 28, 1954, 14. In this regard, it is interesting to note that the women's magazines failed to report on the Kefauver or Army-McCarthy hearings. However, they did include numerous stories on the war in Korea. Women's roles in times of war were already well established. But the reconciliation of white, middle-class femininity with participation in the political sphere was less clearly defined.

58. "Biggest Show on Earth," 80.

59. "Kefauver and TV," *New York Herald Tribune,* March 15, 1951, 9.

60. Allison, "Fascinated City," 8.

"Happy New Year and Auld Lang Syne"

On Televisual Montage and Historical Consciousness

VIVIAN SOBCHACK

Can we view seriously, with reverence, the discarded material objects of mass culture as monuments to the utopian hope of past generations, and to its betrayal? Who will teach us *these* truths, and in what form shall they be passed on to those who come after us?
—Susan Buck-Morss

The dialectical optics of the historical gaze arrests the movement of ("natural," archaic, mythical, dreamlike) images in the moment of their "coming into legibility"; it gives them a "shock," that is, it allegorizes them into quotability. But only "at a standstill" can they become genuinely historical images, monads that resist the catastrophic continuity of time. "The first stage in this voyage will be to carry the montage principle over into history."
—Miriam Hansen (quoting Walter Benjamin)

In its incessantly busy "flow" of image and sound "segments" and "bites,"[1] in its distracting insistence on the present moment of its ephemeral presence, in its excessive and noisy disciplinary action upon raw materials that threaten to escape its overdeterminations, television only rarely allows us sites for reflective meditation. And, given television's quotidian situation in our lives and its constant self-promotion and presentation of "the real" and "the historic," this lack of meditational space seems particularly problematic in our increasingly mediated—but nonetheless consequential—relation to the past and future. However, there do exist some such televisual sites. They are usually constructed as (and by) what, in a related context, John Caldwell has called "self-conscious presentational rituals."[2] For some years now, I have been fascinated by one of these self-conscious presentational rituals—particularly insofar as it uses represented fragments of the "real" past to construct a televisual site in which popular consciousness has at least some chance to emerge and reflect upon what it means to live both in historical time and in medias res—that is, in the middle of things and through the things that mediate. This ritual, meditational, and highly paradoxical site is the New Year's Eve montage that, on December 31 in the United States, ends nearly every evening television news broadcast and gathers together the "historic events" of the year for our contemplation.

In the essay that follows, I want to worry over the New Year's Eve montage from a number of perspectives for the form raises significant questions about television's use of real events, about its narrative construction of the historically real, and about the nature and function of visual abstraction and "intellectual montage."[3] Indeed, I will say at the outset that one of the reasons I am so fascinated by the New Year's Eve montage is that it seems at once both overdetermined and underdetermined: a ritual, highly manipulated, and closed construction of the year's History (with a capital "H") and yet also an ambiguous and open coalescence of multiple and complex events that—through its relative discontinuity—begs both historical and historiographic questions regarding just what constitutes an "historical event," the periodization and/or teleology of "the year," and a unitary and/or otherwise "coherent" historical narrative.

Indeed, the paradox presented by these New Year's Eve montages (perhaps a necessary one that accrues to the decontextualized abstractions of every "intellectual montage") is that they can be read in two seemingly irreconcilable ways. On the one hand, by virtue of their televisual style, not only are they major examples of what Caldwell sees as "historical exhibitionism," but they also seem to "rip history from any connection to the real world by endlessly ritualizing its formal permutations."[4] That is, one could argue that the New Year's Eve montage is historicist and nostalgic: providing "the disembodied signs of history rather than history itself," and functioning as both a "mass-produced textual therapy" and a site meant for the construction of "hegemonic consensus."[5] On the other hand, these montages might also be read as the site of potential "historical awakening," their abstracted and discontinuous images and sound bites making visible "the gap between sign and referent,"[6] or as Walter Benjamin has put it, the "jagged line of demarcation between physical nature and meaning."[7] (In this regard, it is important to emphasize that I am privileging the New Year's Eve news montage as qualitatively different from those "year in review" programs produced as discrete and lengthier news presentations; while the latter have much in common with the former in terms of material content, they also differ greatly in their much higher degree of narrative coherence, expository and explanatory commentary, and strategies of closure.) Thus, following Benjamin's lead, we might well argue that the particular abstractions, fragmentation, and discontinuities of the New Year's Eve montage use "dream images" and "decaying fragments" of the "real" events of the past year so that (whether purposefully or not) they become "dialectical images" that quicken—rather than lull—the viewer's historical consciousness. For Benjamin, montage was a privileged form for generating such images, which become historical (rather than historicist) insofar as their "ideational elements remain unreconciled, rather than fusing into one 'harmonizing perspective.'"[8] Through montage, "dialectical images were to draw dream images into an awakened state, and awakening was synonymous with historical knowledge."[9]

Given the object of my discussion here, a passage in Susan Buck-Morss's *The Dialectics of Seeing: Walter Benjamin and the Arcades Project* seems quite uncanny. Interrogating the "dialectical image," she might well be describing and interrogating the image fragments of a New Year's Eve montage when she asks:

> Was "dust" such an image? fashion? the prostitute? expositions? commodities? the arcades themselves? Yes, surely—not, however, as these referents are empirically given, nor even as they are critically interpreted as emblematic of commodity society, but as they are dialectically "constructed," as "historical objects," politically charged monads, "blasted" out of history's continuum and made "actual" in the present.[10]

Yet Buck-Morss is also somewhat uncertain, aware that such abstracted image fragments, such "monads," are not in themselves historical objects but must be made so "through the active intervention of the thinking subject."[11] Thus the paradox of the New Year's Eve montage turns out to be less a paradox than, as Buck-Morss suggests, "a dilemma in interpretation."[12] And thus this preamble has served not only to announce and justify my fascination with one televisual object among many but also to indulge and foreground my own dilemma of interpretation in tackling this particular televisual object. Now, however, as any good historical materialist (or for that matter, any good phenomenologist) would say, "To the things themselves!"[13]

Image Fragments and Sound Bites

Benjamin has written, "History decomposes into images, not into narratives."[14] On December 31, 1996—New Year's Eve—in Los Angeles, the local NBC affiliate offered a very brief litany of unidentified images accompanied only by music in a montage that memorialized the year and made its passing significant (if not, indeed, momentarily sacred). Marking not only the year's end but also the beginning of my interest in the historical nature and function of the New Year's Eve montage, consider the following images (single shots unless otherwise specified):

- Shots of flood waters and partially immersed homes (presumably in the Midwest)
- Airplane wreckage (presumably from TWA Flight 800)
- Shots showing a massive blizzard (presumably in the Midwest)
- Hostages (presumably) leaving a building (presumably the Japanese embassy in Peru)
- Bill Clinton speaking from a podium
- Bob Dole campaigning, shaking hands in a crowd
- O. J. Simpson leaving a building
- Shots of a raging brush fire or fires (presumably in Southern California)
- Michael Jackson smiling with his new wife
- Michael Jackson smiling with his new baby
- Madonna dressed in 1940s clothing (possibly a shot from *Evita*)
- Madonna smiling and holding her new baby
- Princess Diana looking grim (presumably after her divorce from Prince Charles has been granted)
- Boris Yeltsin dancing (presumably after his recovery from heart surgery)
- A mass of people dancing the "macareña"
- A rooftop with people looking upward at a giant spaceship (definitely from *Independence Day*)
- Shots of Yankee ballplayers hugging each other (presumably after winning the World Series)

Perhaps because it was made by the local affiliate's own editorial staff, this particular montage kept to a bare minimum the kind of "televisual excess" that certainly marks most of the New Year's Eve montages I've seen since. It lacks the identifying textual overlays of moving graphics, the polyphonic mixture of voice-overs, diegetic sound bites, selective (and often ironic) use of popular song, the optical layering of images, and the exhibitionist computer-graphic transitions that are characteristic of most New Year's Eve montages. Nonetheless, as a relatively simple example of what we might now call a televisual "genre," it foregrounds certain of the genre's major features: a high degree of abstraction in the image fragments, many with no marked identifying features; a nonlinear and acausal structure; a mixture of official and popular, high and low, historical and cultural events; weak thematic organization; and a vague emplotment that offers up no grand, teleological, or unified historical narrative.

I will elaborate these and several other generic features of the New Year's Eve montage, but first I want to present another montage much more characteristic of the genre as a whole in its length, complexity, and use of sound bites and graphics. Here, I will focus description primarily on the images. Nonetheless, the montage is filled with sound from a variety of sources: diegetic sound bites from the event's participants on site, voice-over fragments of news commentary, voice-overs from the featured figures, and various kinds of music. The montage also features graphic devices, most used to identify locations and people—although there are just as many instances in which the viewer's knowledge of a person or place or event is presumed and no identification is provided. In this regard, although I will indicate some of the montage's aural and graphic features where pertinent, please note that when I use a proper name ("Winnie Mandela"), unless otherwise indicated, this identification has been made by me as a viewer and not within the montage itself. (Thus, in some instances, my own ignorance prevents identification of some people and events, an important issue to which I shall return.) These, then, are the images of the "special presentation" of "The Year that Was" offered at the end of the CBS Evening News broadcast on December 31, 1997:

- President Clinton being sworn in (becomes part of a split-screen interior montage of Washington images)
- Newt Gingrich apologizing to House (diegetic sound bite)
- Clinton with Asian visitors at the White House (voice-over fragment on "influence peddling")
- Flooded streets in Grand Forks, North Dakota (identified by diegetic sign)
- Shots of a tornado and devastation (no identification)
- Computer-graphic image of Earth and oceans (voice-over introduces El Niño)
- Shots of floods and devastation (graphic indicates Mexico)
- Women crouching on parched earth (graphic indicates Turkey)
- Volcano belching smoke (graphic indicates Montserrat)
- Shots of interior of old church and rubble (presumably) from earthquake (graphic indicates Italy)
- Soldiers crowding a truck for food supplies (graphic indicates North Korea)
- Emaciated children looking at camera (graphic indicates Zaire)
- Shots of dead bodies on ground (graphic indicates Albania; voice-over fragment speaks of "near collapse of the government")
- Winnie Mandela speaking angrily (graphic indicates South Africa)
- People (presumably hostages) leaving building (graphic indicates Peru)
- Split screen shots of Benjamin Netanyahu and Yasser Arafat (graphic indicates Israel and Palestine)
- A man at Promise Keepers gathering (diegetic sound bite)

- A woman at a black women's march (diegetic sound bite)
- Madeline Albright being sworn in (diegetic sound bite)
- Saddam Hussein
- An angry crowd (presumably) in Iraq (no identification)
- Shots of Hong Kong's return to China (split-screen images of Prince Charles, pomp and circumstance, fireworks)
- Shots of the stock market (with voice-over sound bites indicating "skyrocketing" and "falling" and "records being broken")
- A racing car in the desert (presumably) breaking land speed record (no identification)
- Gary Kasparov leaving championship chess match (voice-over sound bite says he "resigns")
- A sheep (presumably Dolly) splits into four images
- A baby (presumably a septuplet) serially followed on split-screen by six others
- A computer screen showing America On Line's home page (voice-over indicates "overload")
- Queen Elizabeth opening "royal Web site" (diegetic sound bite)
- Pathfinder, Mars explorer, on Mars's soil
- Shots of space station *Mir* (voice-over indicates "*Mir* is wobbling through space")
- Simulation of a hurtling asteroid (possibly from *Armageddon*)
- Photograph of a comet in the night sky (presumably Hale-Bopp)
- "Heaven's Gate" leader speaking on television about "Planet Earth . . . about to be recycled")
- Shots of covered dead bodies (presumably "Heaven's Gate" suicides) being removed from house
- Gianni Versace at some event (no identification)
- Photo of his killer, Andrew Cunanan (voice-over sound bite that "now the reign of terror is over")
- Shots of Los Angeles bank robbery street shoot-out (diegetic shots and yelling)
- A videotaped beating of a man (no identification)
- "Nannygate" defendant hearing sentence in courtroom
- Patsy Ramsey denying she killed her daughter, JonBenet
- Car on freeway shoulder at night and cops (voice-over sound bite "Ennis Cosby"), followed by
  - Bill Cosby looking grim
  - Photo of Ennis Cosby
- Betty Shabazz speaking (voice-over indicating "death from arson"), followed by
  - Little boy shrinking from camera

- O. J. Simpson (voice-over indicating "found guilty")
- Timothy McVeigh walking in chains (voice-over indicates he received the death penalty)
- Interior of tunnel in Paris (unidentified), followed by very long mini-montage of car wreck, Princess Diana, funeral, et al.
- Mountain and plane wreckage (voice-over comment "search for suicide pilot")
- Uniformed female army officer (voice-over fragment "not just a case of adultery")
- Shots of military hazing (no identification)
- Shots from footage of various military sex scandals
- Black officer denying he committed rape
- Tearful Paula Jones with her attorney
- Clinton announcing a "balanced budget," followed by
  - Clinton with Buddy, the dog
  - Hillary Clinton on the Rosie O'Donnell show
  - Two shots of Chelsea Clinton (her voice-over saying "We can do it for ourselves regardless of what we're given.")
- Tiger Woods after winning the Master's golf tournament
- Mike Tyson on top of Evander Holyfield (and presumably biting his ear)
- Sportscaster Marv Albert
- Clip from *Xena, Warrior Princess* with Xena brandishing lance
- Close-up of Bruce Willis with a big gun (from a movie)
- Clip from *L.A. Confidential* of a group of men with guns
- Extreme close-up of the alien from one of the *Alien* movies
- Extreme close-up of Arnold Schwarzenegger
- Clip of Will Smith from *Men in Black*
- A trio of "cowboys" in a western setting running from a canyon (from a movie? a music video?)
- The rock group Hansen
- The Spice Girls in concert
- A clip from *Ellen*, with Ellen saying "I'm gay."
- A clip of Mike Meyers as *Austin Powers*
- Howard Stern
- A moment from the Broadway production of *The Lion King*
- Frank Geary's Guggenheim museum in Bilbao (not identified)
- Clips from *Titanic* including Kate Winslett and Leonardo DiCaprio
- Musician from *Kiss* "kissing" camera
- Last shot from the last episode of *Seinfeld* (the group sitting in a jail cell)
- A necrology of those who died during 1997 with images and identifying graphics as follows:
  - Chris Farley

- James Stewart
- Red Skelton
- John Denver
- Robert Mitchum
- Pamela Harriman
- Notorious B.I.G.
- Jacques Cousteau
- Alan Ginsburg
- Deng Xiaoping
- Brandon Tartikoff
- Charles Kurault
- William Brennan
- James Michener
- Mother Teresa (A mini-montage of images much shorter in length than that for Princess Diana)
- General Colin Powell with a group of people (his voice-over speaks of "volunteerism" and "helping others")
- Several shots of people helping with rescues, relief, etc. in various catastrophes (voice-over speaks of "lifting somebody up in need")
- Princess Diana on one of her charitable missions to Africa lifting up a native child (ending the montage in freeze frame)

How might we characterize the two montages I've described as well as others like them? First, there seems very little reason—if some rhyme—in their sequencing of images meant both to evoke the year's "history" and to provide the site for its remembrance. "History" here resolves itself into no grand narrative. Indeed, it is not even offered up in the "primitive," acausal, but chronological list of "events" that forms the chronicle. No chronology, no linear temporality, dictates the editorial order of these images that mark the year's "historic" moments. Instead, images of people and events tend to adhere to each other in sporadic and ephemeral attachments that seem based on no consistent principles.

For example, in the second montage, we begin in Washington, D.C., with what seems a "proper" historical moment: not only is a President's inauguration of historic importance, but it also takes place in January at the start of the year thus promising a chronology. However, we next move to catastrophic flooding in Grand Forks for no apparent reason. Later, we shift from the last of a series of internationally inflected images—a split screen shot in both Israel and Palestine—to a men's Christian gathering in the United States (is the connection here based loosely on religion?). And from that to the black women's march (an "easy" move for its gendered and racial opposition to the previous shot and its conceptual connective of "mass gathering"), followed by Madeline Albright being sworn in as secretary of state (here the connection seems only to be gender), and then we see images of Saddam Hussein and Iraq (a shift made comprehensible by virtue of Albright's new position—but only if one already has the basis for identifying Albright and Hussein).

Elsewhere, we move from a split-screen spectacle of Hong Kong's return to China to the floor of the U.S. stock market by virtue of (one supposes) the "rhyming" connection between a fireworks display also heard in the former and the soundbite about the stock market "skyrocketing" in the latter, as well as through the most general conceptual linkage of Hong Kong to business. The stock market shot moves us to the breaking of the land speed record (with no identification of the event) by virtue of the voice-over in the stock market shot mentioning "records being broken"—and then we move from the racing shot to Kasparov conceding a championship chess match (are the connectives here the idea of "competition" and the notion of Kasparov as "being broken"?) and on from there to a split screen and multiplied images of the cloned sheep, Dolly. (This last transition is most difficult to fathom: does it emerge formally from the patterned repetition of the chessboard?) The move from the cloned sheep (all four of them) to the seven babies is simple enough—its numerical (and genetic) reasoning made explicit by the visual and analogical device of split screen. Later we are given a trio of images—golfer Tiger Woods and boxer Mike Tyson explicitly plying their respective trades and unidentified sportscaster, Marv Albert— all connected by "sports." Here, however, the really informed can take particular pleasure in the subtle slide from the image of Tyson biting opponent Evander Holyfield's ear to disgraced sportscaster Marv Albert (who, involved in a sex scandal, apparently had bitten his partner on the back). I could go on, but space does not permit.

Certainly, this is no academic or official way of constructing "History" or historical narrative. The world and history turn on the slimmest of signifiers and rhymes: a word or sound here, an image there, a vague relationship of content or concept elsewhere. Thus, in a mere five shots, we can get from a computer-simulated asteroid to murderer Andrew Cunanan—much as we did playing those children's word games where one five-letter word is changed into a completely different and semantically unrelated word in only five moves by replacing one letter each time, but each time also rearranging the letters into a comprehensible lexeme. There is a similar logic of transition and transformation operating in the New Year's Eve montage although it connects signifiers and co-constitutes meaning with its viewers according to an eclectic variety of strategies (rather than rules). Furthermore, these strategies are ephemeral, contingent, and capricious—and based as much on the materiality of representation as on its historical and cultural "content."

A second major feature of the New Year's Eve montage (and it follows from the first) is that emplotment is vague and sporadic.[15] Story fragments are presented but they are minimally plotted. For example, many montages are organized briefly around the trope of "catastrophe" and occasionally seem to be inscribing a certain narrative trajectory that takes us from natural disasters (floods, earthquakes, fires) to man-made and cultural disasters (war, terrorism, starvation), a narrative potentially emplotted as both ironic and cautionary in its movement and dénouement. Similarly, the rise and fall (or, alternatively, the "comeback") of the famous is also a familiar potential plot that, given the amount of time devoted to celebrity in these montages, would seem central to the New Year's Eve montage. Indeed, in the two montages described above, we do find loose organization around both the tropes of "catastrophe" and "celebrity"—yet this organization is not coherent or its trajectory sustained enough to narratively comprehend the "year" as a whole, or even to serve as a secure containment for what could be seen as a unified and emplotted "segment."

Thus, while almost all the montages organize many of their images in very loose categories—"politics," "popular culture," "international events," "natural catastrophe," "violent events," "deaths"—these "segments" tend to be very brief, or interrupt themselves, or cede some of their "proper" images to other segments. In the first and shorter montage, for example, the shot of a raging fire is *not* included in the loose grouping of catastrophes but *does* interrupt a potential segment on celebrities, coming as it does between shots of O. J. Simpson and Madonna. Furthermore, the loose categories or tropes that hold a cluster of images together are often so broad in conception they continually threaten to disperse: "catastrophe" can begin as "natural" but then is "internationalized" and begins to include "starvation" and "war" and dissolves into yet something else. A "science" segment passes through the tail of Hale-Bopp comet and transforms into a segment on "irrational" acts and "violence."

Overall, then, however marked off and contained it is by style from typical televisual representation, however much it points to its own historicity, the montage's temporal organization and emplotment of worldly events does not resolve itself into a grand narrative: as a whole, it cannot be characterized as tragic, comic, romantic, or epic. Certainly, if (for a variety of reasons) an event and/or person has sufficient "historical" significance, a segment of the montage might occasionally cohere as an emplotted narrative. In the second montage, the relatively lengthy Princess Diana sequence is emplotted as a tragedy. Nonetheless, this kind of coherent narrative trajectory and view on events is relatively rare. For example, however lengthy, the Monica Lewinsky/Bill Clinton/Kenneth Starr sequence in several 1998 montages was *not* emplotted, did not cohere in narrative and narrational stance: indeed, its trajectory shifted from moment to moment from tragic ("the fall of a great man") to romantic ("poor young Monica") to comic ("I'm not going to parse that statement, parse that statement" repetitions) to epic (an image ribbon of all the historical "players" and much ado at the Capitol). Even the "endings" of the New Year's Eve montage function less in relation to either a grand historical narrative emplotment of the particular year or of the montage as a whole than to open-ended temporal questions of beginnings and ends, lasts and firsts, the cyclicity or teleological extension of time. Thus, some of the montages end with death (the nearly omnipresent necrology), some with birth (one showed the scene from Broadway's *The Lion King* with the new baby and king-to-be lifted upward, followed by a closing image of the septuplets) , some with both (the image of Diana holding up a child)—and some with a pensive, ambiguous, and open-ended image (in 1998, Clinton walking alone on the White House veranda).

A third significant characteristic of the New Year's Eve montage is that what constitutes the "stuff" of the year's "history" is various and selected according to no overarching historiographic principle. Some of the events represented in the montage are given to us—insofar as we know what we are looking at—for their particularity and specificity: the crash of TWA 800, the hostages walking out of the Japanese embassy. Some images, however, are selected for their generality: this year "everyone" is dancing the macareña, this year there were "several" devastating floods in various places. Furthermore, while some of the images selected would seem to represent what academic historians would deem a "proper" historical event such as the swearing in of a president or the signing of a peace accord, others mark "only" a cultural event *en passant*: a dance craze, a personal episode in the life of a pop star. Similarly, the New Year's Eve montage makes no distinctions among its forms of "documentation." That is, it mixes "real" news footage and photographs (whatever their acknowledged problematic status, generally regarded as "legitimate" historical records of "real" people and events) with clips and characters from fiction films and television shows and with computer simulations (representations seen less as historical documentation of the "real" than as real historical artifacts). In sum, images in the New Year's Eve montage fluctuate between making specific and general claims about the year, between focusing on official and popular culture, between offering up "historic" events and "trivial" instances, between representing the "real" though documentation and artifact. Here, the "stuff" of history is an eclectic and incoherent collection of materials similar to those Benjamin saw in the variegated debris of his Arcades or in the buildings and shops along his "one-way street."[16]

A fourth characteristic of the New Year's Eve montage is that the abstraction of most of its images from a broader context (of visual and aural information, of narrative) forces the viewer (however "intuitively") to inform them with historical and cultural meaning derived from external knowledge. Stanley Fish has noted: "Abstractions do not declare their own meaning."[17] Most montage images are individually hermetic and vague (however concrete): a man (unidentified Bill Clinton) taking an oath (only presumably, of office); "any" brush fire (most fires look the same); "some" moment of a woman's (unidentified Madonna) life, "some man" (whom I cannot identify) speaking both as himself and for his "function" (as "on the scene," as a solider, as a voter). Thus—and, indeed, because of their abstraction and vagueness—these images provoke us to "name" and "place" them in space and time, to activate them into narratives (of which there might be many). They require our intervention and information. They appeal to and provoke our knowledge and presumption of the very contexts they lack— and thereby become informed with a historical specificity that, given their abstraction, is relatively absent from the images themselves. In sum, I am put to historical work by these images. And what seems, through much of the montage, an "immediate" and "intuitive" apprehension of people and events and their historical narratives and relevance to "the year" is, in fact, belied by all those moments in which I cannot "re-cognize" an abstract image as meaningful. ("Who" or "What" or "Where" or "When" remain hollow forms.)

In this regard, along with its appeal to and provocation of my contextual knowledge to provide historical specificity and narrative potential to its abstract images, the New Year's Eve montage also appeals to the illusion of self-identity.[18] Here, I am referring to a logic that has less to do with the viewer confusing the televisual image with its real-world referent than it has to do with a particular referent being "definitively" equated by the viewer with itself—in the one instance, a shot from *Independence Day* exactly identical to itself as confirmed through my previous experience of the film; in the other, the people I "recognize" exactly identical to themselves by virtue of my familiarity with their particular and habitual denotation: that is, their "singular" image and their "proper" name.[19] (Hence, no matter how abstracted their image from a context, I see "Bob Dole," not "some man" and "Madonna," not "some woman" and thus I can—once I "name" them—effortlessly "place" them in an off-screen narrative.)

Finally, the New Year's Eve montage, as a stylized whole, serves a ceremonial function in relation to the conundrum of the meaning of historical time and human presence. It marks both a temporal ending and beginning but, through its lack of linear chronology and a grand narrative, it blurs the difference between them: are we mourning or celebrating the end of the beginning or the beginning of the end? The montage is temporally open-ended and yet closed. On the one hand, it suggests not merely a progression, but an endless series ("Time marches on"); on the other, it suggests an eternal structure ("Shit happens"; "In the end is the beginning").[20] Like Janus, the New York's Eve montage faces in two temporal directions (toward "Auld Lang Syne" and toward the "New Year") and yet, like the *uroboros*, it encircles itself to eat its own tale. A "self-conscious presentational ritual" framed as it is, yet framing that which frames it, the New Year's Eve montage is formally—and "eventfully"—generic and yet historically singular, mass-produced for the masses and yet nonetheless unique and "auratic." This is to say that the New Year's Eve montage not only *presents,* but also *is* what Samuel Weber says "aura" always has been: *"the singular leave-taking of the singular,* whose singularity is no longer that of an original moment but of its posthumous aftershock."[21]

Icons and Mediaphemes

Given the achronological structure of the New Year's Eve montage as well as its high stylization and ceremonial function, how might we approach it as an historiographic text—or, perhaps, more aptly, as provoking historical consciousness in its viewers? In some ways, the montage as both ceremonial ritual and formal structure seems precisely an evocation and expression of what Claude Lévi-Strauss has identified as "primitive thought," whose peculiarity is that "its object is to grasp the world as both a synchronic and a diachronic totality."[22] And yet, the montage's organizing schema for creating order and making meaning is neither totalizing nor analogic (as Lévi-Strauss characterizes the primary logic of the "savage mind"). Instead of constituting *cosmological* meaning from the "natural" and materially iconic correspondences and indexical continuities visibly found "in the middle of things," we who live in the mass-mediated culture of images constitute *contingent* meaning from iconic and indexical correspondences found not in the "natural" symbolic world, but rather in a world of symbols that have been "naturalized." That is, we are immersed not in the signifying materiality of trees and clouds and animals but in the signifying materiality of their images: a second "order of things" always already analytically abstracted and understood as visual signs, always already repeatedly circulated in medias res.[23]

While the New Year's Eve montage as a whole does seem to "grasp" the past year as "both a synchronic and diachronic totality," most of its iconic and indexical images of "the real" are hermetic—temporally and spatially discontinuous, if formally contiguous, with the others that surround them. Furthermore, these images are temporally encrypted—the historical and cultural events of which they are a part (and for which they stand) are condensed in the small but densely charged space of the fragment. Thus both the parts and the whole of the montage call forth a temporalizing hermeneutic, one bent less on understanding the montage's analogical correspondences and reference to "the real" than on unpacking the very logics and symbolic meanings of its iconic abstraction and density. The New Year's Eve montage, then, engages us not only in a *historical* reading of the world (its abstracted fragments and density provoking us to narrative), but also urges us toward a *historiographic* reading of its reading as historiographic. (Just look at my discussion above.) Thus, despite what might seem the montage's overarching "primitive" historiographic form and logic, we are far removed from Lévi-Strauss's discussion of analogy and correspondence—and much closer to Caldwell's discussion of "televisuality." Caldwell not only argues that the "excessive visuality" that marks the form and logic of much contemporary television "actually enhances the sense of narrativity since its sensory appeals make narrative spectatorship more overt and demanding," but also that "viewer pleasure and engagement depend upon the skilled discrimination and consumption of narrational fragments and stylistic flags."[24]

However, although Caldwell foregrounds how "the televisual flow demands active decipherment and critical facility on the part of the viewer," he himself is highly critical of the way in which the medium's "excess visuality" and "stylistic density" are also used to foreclose and overdetermine what initially might seem "the heterogeneous and dense flow of epic televisuality" and its opportunities for "counter-readings" and a plurality of narratives. In this regard (and apposite to the New Year's Eve montage), he is particularly hard on the medium's representation of "real" and significant worldly events—its "excess visuality" in this instance a form of "historicist hyperactivity," and its "stylistic density" a way of spectacularizing such events and overdetermining their textual meaning.[25] Indeed, Caldwell calls the regular application of such formal strategies "historification," and he warns us:

> Televisuality may deal with the wrong history, but academics are misguided if they ignore the fact that historification is very much a central preoccupation of the televisual apparatus. . . . The possibilities for historification now seem tantalizingly limitless, for most major stations have amassed large amounts of archival material from years of news production. Proprietary access to this raw material provides endless possibilities for historical reworking and hybridization.[26]

Nonetheless, despite his recognition that television's formal strategies of historification tend to overdetermine the multiple narratives and meanings of "real" events, Caldwell ends this passage on a sanguine note: "Constructing a history along binarist or reductive lines is dangerous however, . . . for images can belie the theses that news editors force upon them."[27]

We are yet again brought back to the interpretive dilemma of televisual abstraction and historiographic representation not only in the news broadcast segment, but also in the stylistically hyperbolic and ceremonial New Year's Eve montage. On the one hand, and particularly in relation to its frequently repeated function as an abstract marker of real world events, the individual montage image most often seems overdetermined. Certainly its highly stylized and "histrionic" use as a unit of the montage can be seen as "historicist." Even more significant, however, is that its general repetition and circulation through the mass media as an iconic and indexical image of "the real" *prior to* its inclusion in the New Year's Eve montage enables it to function within the montage also as a visual symbol: in other words, "iconographically."[28] On the other hand, because of its very abstraction and its history of circulation and repetition, the montage image seems underdetermined—escaping containment by any one narrative. As an abstracted fragment, the iconic and indexical image points beyond itself and its use to both a specific absent context and a broad field of other possible historical narratives in which it might play a part. Furthermore, as a historically repeated and circulated image that has been re-cognized as iconographically symbolic, the montage fragment is also implosive: that is, its spatial and symbolic presence "sucks in" and accumulates not only multiple narratives, but also multiple *kinds* of narratives (only some of them "properly" historical). In sum, the abstracted and hermetic quality of the image fragment and its often iconographic status constitute for the viewer an ambiguous and general site (and sight) that tends to undermine its fixation in any given historical narrative.[29]

Is there some other way, then, we might approach the "dilemma of interpretation" that the abstracted montage image presents us—particularly insofar as such images also iconically and indexically represent "fragments" of the historical and cultural "real"? Furthermore, while acknowledging the strategies of textual (and historical) overdetermination characterized by Caldwell as "historification," is there some other way in which we can also think through such overdetermination to something more progressive and provocative? In *American Monroe: The Making of a Body Politic,* a consideration of the use and significance of popular and symbolic visual iconography to American political culture in medias res,[30] S. Paige Baty offers some distinctions that may help us understand how the complex constitution and operations of the New Year's Eve montage not only mobilize different kinds of abstract image fragments of "real" people and events, but also how such image fragments might provoke historical consciousness—particularly in a mass audience in a mass-mediated society.

Baty makes a distinction between two kinds and functions of iconic visual images, both of which have, to varying degrees, become symbolically re-cognized as *iconographic*. One is the "icon"[31]—her paradigmatic example, the mass-circulated iconic image (in varying permutations and abstractions) of Marilyn Monroe, but we might think also here of images of such historical "figures" as Abraham Lincoln or Bill Clinton. The other is the "mediapheme"—a mass-circulated iconic image of some historical specificity that is much more ephemeral in its symbolic and iconographic function than is the "icon." Baty explains:

> For stories, figures, and identities to be transmissible as *icons,* they must first be compressed into units able to quickly circulate through the channels of mass mediation. I call these units *mediaphemes.* The mediapheme is the most common unit of communication in mass-mediated iconographic modes of remembering. I use this term to differentiate them from icons, which I define as circulated figures or characters that become the very surface on which other meanings are communicated. Mediaphemes are quick encapsulations; once a story, person, or event is translated into mediapheme form, it ricochets through the channels of mass mediation with ease. Mediaphemes may become icons, but they rarely do; they tend to last as long as a story, issue, or person is "hot." Icons, in contrast, outlast single, short-lived versions of an event, character, or history: they are the sites for repeated stagings of narratives, the sites on which the past, present, and future may be written. The mass-mediated mode of iconographic remembering relies on both icons and mediaphemes in the construction of the remembered world.[32]

One such "construction of the remembered world" is, of course, the New Year's Eve montage that is historically and iconographically dependent upon both "mediaphemes" and "icons." Mediaphemes are exemplified by such broadly recognized but symbolically short-lived image fragments as people dancing the macareña, Bob Dole shaking hands on the campaign trail, Marv Albert ("Who?" I asked at first—the image on its way out even at its very moment of iconographic significance in the year that was). Icons in the New Year's Eve montage come in two forms—the first exemplified by the kinds of images that concern Baty: Madonna, O. J., and Bill Clinton in further stagings of themselves; and the second exemplified by such unidentified and generalizing images as floods and fires that not only specify but also stand for "natural disaster." Both kinds of icons offer, as Baty suggests, a site and surface open to historical and personal inscription and a broad range of narrative possibilities.

If, as Benjamin believed, "history decomposes into images, not into narratives," we need to consider the historiographic "rationality" of such decomposition—that is, how abstracted images of the "real" (mediaphemes and icons) write histories symbolically through "a visual, not linear logic."[33]

Baty suggests just such a rationality. Arguing that "iconic images, rather than narrativity, . . . communicate explicit messages and histories" by circulating "*as* images" (themselves "objects of memory"), she posits a historiographic logic that, in character and function, "is both *material* and *metaphorical.*"[34] (Given her characterization below, however, in which images become emblematic representations of ideas, we might substitute *allegorical* for metaphorical.) That is, icons and, to a lesser degree, mediaphemes express "a different meaning and mode of organizing culture, of remembering a time or place. They operate as a shorthand for . . . early death, glamour, dissipation, isolation, triumph, youth, fame, domestic violence, racial identity, etc. At the same time, they point back to a particular representative character—a discrete biography."[35] Furthermore, Baty argues that viewers of mediaphemes and icons do not "fix the object of memory outside of the lived world." Rather, they take up that "object of memory"— the image of a discrete but representative identity—as already historicized and historical: not only "part of the common ground on which the present may be articulated, known, and understood,"[36] but also referencing "the economy within which [that object] is produced and circulated."[37] Thus, for Baty, "mass-mediated rememberings [such as the ritual representation of the New Year's Eve montage] both deconstruct and reconstruct dominant frames of knowing and being in our time. They do not escape from the excessive commodification of the real in contemporary life, but neither do they simply reproduce forms . . . that leave the dominant orders unchallenged."[38]

Thus what is evidenced on my television set on New Year's Eve is a faith in the communicative, affective, and reflective power of the *iconographic image as a historiographic form*: on the one hand, its power to condense the diachrony of historical narrative into an abstracted, symbolic, synchronically dense—and thus emotionally moving—fixity of a historical "moment" and, on the other, its power to evoke from this "momentous" density and "monumental" concretion a sense not only of general historical temporality and narrative but also of a certain (yet unfixed) historical specificity. As historiographic (rather than merely poetic) forms, the mediapheme and icon aggregate and constitute as concrete a whole but open historical field. That is, they mobilize both specific historic instants and general historical "eventfulness." They offer up the sight of synecdochic and paradigmatic spatial sites that provoke the syntagmatic unfolding of various possible historiographic trajectories, of multiple temporal narratives. They also evoke the very contexts and forms of historiographic expression that they themselves lack: a specific historical chronology or narrative coherence, an elaboration and interpretation of their historical meaning and usage that demand more thought and more determinate language. Thus, as overdetermined signs of "history," both the mediapheme and the icon are always also insistent (albeit to different degrees) upon their underdetermination. Hence, within their field, it is possible to become truly *trans-fixed*—that is, anchored in the "historified" and symbolically fixed historical present but always also led temporally elsewhere: to historical consideration not only of the past and future and human temporality but also to their historiographic construction by and mediation through yet other images, other words, other narratives.

Montage and Allegory

The iconographic logic of the New Year's montage and its historiographic operations would seem to stand, then, as some new and highly complex mutation of temporal thought immersed and grounded in a pervasive (if generally unselfconscious and "distracted") awareness of visual representation and intertextuality in mass-mediated culture. This mode of thought, I would argue, has become the dominant mode of popular historical consciousness in contemporary America's overtextualized and ever-accelerating mediascape. Indeed, the New Year's Eve montage can be regarded as merely the most blatant and sacrilized articulation of a historical and historicizing logic of images that underlies not only the whole of television but also the whole of contemporary culture. That is, we could say that the fragmented narrative of fragments that is the New Year's Eve montage functions as an *allegory* of both the medium through which it appears and the logic of the culture of which it is a part.

The relationship between montage and allegory is one privileged by Benjamin and critical to our understanding of the progressive historiographic possibilities of the New Year's Eve montage. As Buck-Morss writes: "The allegorical mode allows Benjamin to make visibly palpable the experience of the world in fragments, in which the passing of time means not progress but disintegration."[39] In medias res, it is the deconstructive and abstracting device of montage that allows allegory to emerge from aggregate images. Montage's fragmented and discontinuous structure and practice "denaturalizes" images of people, objects, and events and reveals them as less "natural" than "naturalized." "Intellectual" and cognitive, montage "shocks"—generating meaning and critical consciousness through the juxtaposition and collision of its abstracted images, thus releasing the cultural and historical ideas that they materially embody and enabling their emblematic use. For Benjamin, it was through montage that the "'failed material' of his own historical era could be 'elevated to the position of allegory' . . . [and] allegory was an 'antidote' to myth."[40]

Convinced of the need for a nonlinear, visual logic of history more suited to modern, mass-mediated, commodity culture, Benjamin's "objective was to 'rescue' . . . historical objects by ripping them out of the developmental histories . . . into which fictional and falsifying narratives they had been inserted in the process of their transmission."[41] Thus, Benjamin privileges montage for its deconstructive practice of destroying the "ideological fusion of nature and history,"[42] its cognitive appeal to our critical faculties, and its ability to construct a temporal field that dialectically relates the abstracted and emblematic "decayed fragments" of the past to the naturalized conditions of the lived historical present:

> "In order for a piece of the past to be touched by present actuality, there must exist no continuity between them" . . . Historical objects are first constituted by being "blasted" out of the historical continuum. They have a "monadological structure," into which "all the forces and interests of history enter on a reduced scale." . . . In a tension-filled constellation with the present, this "temporal nucleus" becomes politically charged, polarized dialectically," as "a force field, in which the conflict between its fore- and after-history plays itself out."[43]

As Buck-Morss observes, Benjamin practiced what he preached—not only in his unfinished Arcades project, but in the montage construction and allegorical narrative of his *One-Way Street*. Here, in his confrontation with the lived detritus of commodity culture, "concepts were . . . imagistically constructed, according to the cognitive principles of montage."[44] That is, concrete and material fragments of the historical and cultural "real" become abstracted and collide in Benjamin's juxtapositions: "the images themselves cannot be strung together into a coherent, non-contradictory picture of the whole,"[45] and they become discrete historical emblems of commodity culture that aggregate (rather than cohere) as an allegorical narrative of fragmentation, alienation, and dialectical contradiction. Indeed, Benjamin's *One-Way Street* is a verbal model of "one way" of seeing the disjunctive images, commodity forms, and ideational elements embodied in—and deconstructed by—the New Year's Eve montage. Buck-Morss describes Benjamin's "modernist fragments, images of the city, and of commodities" as they become "emblematic representations of ideas":

> [A] "filling station" . . . depicts the practical role of the intellectual. "Gloves" become the emblem for modern humanity's relation to its own animality. Some titles hang like shop signs over their fragmentary contents ("Optician," "Stamp Shop," "Watches and Jewelry," "Dry Goods"); others are city commands for attention ("Caution, Steps!" "Begging and Loitering Forbidden!" "Post No Bills!" "Closed for Repairs!"), public warnings posted over what might otherwise be mistaken as private practices (writing, dreaming), while "Fire Alarm" is the warning sign over a discussion of revolutionary practice. . . . It is not the desire to rehabilitate an arcane dramatic genre that motivates Benjamin, but the desire to make allegory actual . . . [and] petrified nature and decaying objects provide the imagery adequate to allegory.[46]

The same could be said of the allegorical imagery and actuality of the New Year's Eve montage as images of petrified nature and decaying objects pass us bypassers by to mark the year's passing. As we view it in a "distracted" state (a state of habituated but critical attention "in touch" with "layers of unconscious memory buried in the reified structures of subjectivity"),[47] the montage has the power to "shock" us into historical recognition and reflection through both its fragmented and disjunctive images and its allegorical form. Thus, speaking of "allegorical devices" such as cinematic montage serving a "therapeutic function" more socially positive than that suggested by Caldwell, Miriam Hansen writes:

> The cinema's promise of collectivity resides . . . in the shock-like configuration, or re-figuration, of social documents—images, sounds, textual fragments of an alienated yet common experience. The revolutionary potential of montage thus hinges not only upon the formal rehearsal of the shock-effect but also, and perhaps primarily, upon the mimetic power of its elements, the "complicity of film technique with the milieu."[48]

The mimetic power of its fragmented image "elements" and the "complicity" of its technique with the historical and cultural logic, conditions, and experience of living in medias res constitute the New Year's Eve montage as a "shocking" allegory of contemporary mass-mediated life and history.[49]

And it is the shock and contradictions of montage that allow us the reflective space "out of time" in which to both "read" the aggregate of discrete images and sounds as a coherent allegory, a meta-historical history, and to "re-cognize" the detritus of the past —what Benjamin differentiated as "fossils," "fetishes," "wish images," and "ruins"—represented in the New Year's Eve montage as historical objects. In his "Theses on the Philosophy of History," Benjamin writes of the historical materialist project of historiography: "Where thinking suddenly stops in a configuration pregnant with tensions, it gives that configuration a shock, by which it crystallizes into a monad . . . the sign of a Messianic cessation of happening, or put differently, a revolutionary chance in the fight for the oppressed past."[50] And, in the *Passagen-Werk*, he continues by identifying that crystallized monad as a "dialectical image." The "dialectical image" thus emerges from and as "the caesura in the movement of thought. Its positioning, of course, is in no way arbitrary. In a word, it is to be sought at the point where the tension between the dialectical oppositions is the greatest. The dialectical image . . . is identical to the historical object."[51]

The "dialectical image," then, is, at once, a static and crystallized temporal "moment" transformed and stilled by the shock of discontinuity and contradiction into an historical *object* and the very subjective *act* of re-

cognition that both shocks and is shocked by it.[52] In this way, the "dialectical image" is more than an image. As Buck-Morss writes, "It is a way of
seeing that crystallizes antithetical elements by providing the axes for their
alignment" rather than for their synthesis.[53] That is, antithetical "forces"
and "interests" are circumscribed and concreted in the "dialectical image"
—that historical object or field that contains without resolving the historical and cultural contradictions of the commodified image object. In the
New Year's Eve montage, insofar as we are shocked into historical consciousness and meditative reflection by its discontinuities and contradictions (both in part and as a whole), we come to re-cognize its own status—
and the year's—as a commodity form. In the stilled time and space of a
moment, "where thinking suddenly stops in a configuration pregnant with
tensions," we can see both the parts and the whole of the New Year's Eve
montage as representing not only the "petrified" or fixed objects of our culture's "natural" and "mythic" history—the *fossil* and the *fetish*—but also
the more transient objects of its "mythic" and "historical" nature—the
wish image and the *ruin.*

Indeed, this is the "stuff" of the New Year's Eve montage and its discrete
images. As *fossil,* both parts and whole of the montage are "traces" of a
"natural history," "visible remains of the ur-phenomena," the past year. As
fetish, both parts and whole are also "phantasmagoria," marking a
"mythic" or "arrested form of history" which presents "the new as always
the same." As *wish image,* both parts and whole also function as "symbols"
that constitute a "mythic nature" as a dream form of revolutionary potential and "the 'dialectic' of awakening." And, as *ruin,* both parts and whole
become "allegories" of an "historical nature," appearing not only as the
rubble of the past, but also as "loosened building blocks (both semantic and
material) out of which a new order can be constructed."[54]

However crude, then, the New Year Eve's montage seems to represent
and strive not merely for the historicist nostalgia of "auld lang syne," but
also for a "dialectic" of historical "awakening." As itself an historical
object in mass culture in medias res, we should take it seriously as Buck-
Morss suggests—that is, "not merely as the source of the phantasmagoria of
false consciousness, but as the source of collective energy to overcome it."[55]
For insofar as we—as academics and viewers— pay attention to it, are dis-
tractedly "shocked" by it, the New Year's Eve montage just might be a televisual primer, educating "the image-creating medium within us to see
dimensionally, stereoscopically, into the depths of the historical shade."[56]

NOTES

1. I am obviously referring here to early debates in television studies about
the medium's construction and reception as a continuous "flow" or a discontinu-

ous series of "segments." For an excellent overview, see Richard Dienst, *Still Life in Real Time: Theory after Television* (Durham, N.C.: Duke University Press, 1994), 25–33.

2. John Thornton Caldwell, *Televisuality: Style, Crises, and Authority in American Television* (New Brunswick, N.J.: Rutgers University Press, 1995), 165. In a section titled "Volume Discounts: History-Narrative (Exhibitionist History)," Caldwell focuses on excessive historical narrative (i.e., the epic form of the miniseries).

3. I am purposefully using the term "intellectual montage" here to distinguish image (and sound) editorial relationships of a particular kind whose aesthetic (based on discontinuity) and rhetorical aim (to awaken cognitive processes and ideological awareness) is quite opposite from those of "classical" Hollywood montage (based on continuity editing and psychological motivations). The term, of course, as well as its elaboration, is attributable to Sergei Eisenstein. See *Film Form and the Film Sense,* ed. and trans. Jay Leyda (New York: Meridian Books, 1957).

4. Caldwell, *Televisuality,* 164.

5. Ibid., 165–66.

6. Susan Buck-Morss, *The Dialectics of Seeing: Walter Benjamin and the Arcades Project* (Cambridge, Mass.: MIT Press, 1991), 68.

7. Benjamin, quoted in ibid., 164. (The epigraph that begins this essay can be found on p. 336.)

8. Ibid., 68.

9. Ibid., 261.

10. Ibid., 221.

11. Ibid., 222.

12. Ibid. She continues by asking: "Are dialectical images too subjective in their formulation? Or, are they not subjective enough?"

13. Edmund Husserl, *Cartesian Meditations,* trans. Dorion Cairns (The Hague: Martinus Nijhoff, 1960), 12–13. (Translated from the German *su den Sachen selbst,* these are the watchwords of phenomenological investigation.)

14. Benjamin, from the *Passagen-Werk,* quoted in Buck-Morss, *The Dialectics of Seeing,* 220.

15. On emplotment, particularly as temporal organization of events embodies a world view, see Hayden White, *Meta-History: The Historical Imagination in Nineteenth-Century Europe* (Baltimore, Md.: Johns Hopkins University Press), 5–11.

16. Walter Benjamin, "One-Way Street," trans. Edmund Jephcott, in *Walter Benjamin: Selected Writings,* vol. 1, *1913–1926,* ed. Marcus Bullock and Michael W. Jennings (Cambridge, Mass.: Harvard University Press, 1996), 444–88. Both the "stuff" and "order" that informs Benjamin's montage-like "monograph" (an uncomfortable designation) follows the same contingent principles of collection that seem to inform the New Year's Eve montage.

17. Stanley Fish, "The Logic of Reciprocal Right(s), or What's Sauce for the Goose," a lecture given for the UCLA Center for Modern and Contemporary Studies, January 28, 1998.

18. For a concise discussion of the major varieties of referential meaning, including self-identity, see Hubert G. Alexander, *The Language and Logic of Philosophy* (Albuquerque: University of New Mexico Press, 1967), 85–95.

19. Of great relevance here is Michel de Certeau's discussion of the function of "proper names" for historiographers in *The Writing of History*, trans. Tom Conley (New York: Columbia University Press, 1988). Referring particularly to the historiographer's "multiplication of proper names (personages, localities, coins, etc.)" and their duplication in the "Index of Proper Names," he writes, "[W]hat proliferates in historical discourse are elements 'below which nothing more can be done except display,' and through which *saying* reaches its limit, as near as possible to *showing*" (100).

20. Of particular relevance to the relation between "series" and "structure," see Umberto Eco, *The Open Work*, trans. Anna Cancogni (Cambridge, Mass.: Harvard University Press, 1989), 217–35.

21. Samuel Weber, "Mass Mediauras, or: Art, Aura and Media in the Work of Walter Benjamin," in *Mass Mediauras: Form, Technics, Media*, ed. Alan Cholodenko (Stanford, Calif.: Stanford University Press, 1996), 104–105.

22. Claude Lévi-Strauss, *The Savage Mind* (Chicago: University of Chicago Press, 1966), 263.

23. In this context, I am using the terms "iconic" and "indexical" (also implicating the term "symbolic") as differentiated in the semiology of C. S. Pierce. The "iconic sign" is based on material or structural resemblance to and stands "as" its referent (a monadic relation of identity between sign and referent). The "indexical sign" is based on existential proximity to its referent and points "to" its referent (a dyadic relation of sign to the "other" thing it references). The "symbolic sign" is based on linguistic convention and stands "for" its referent (a triadic relation of sign to referent by virtue of social agreement). Although Pierce differentiates these three major sign forms (as well as their subsets), he indicates that no sign is purely iconic, indexical, or symbolic. This becomes extremely complicated when dealing with visual signs that are primarily iconic and indexical and then secondarily mobilized in highly conventional and symbolic signifying practices and systems.

24. Caldwell, *Televisuality*, 179, 190.

25. Ibid., 189–91.

26. Ibid., 317–18.

27. Ibid., 318.

28. So as to make a connection (rather than create confusion) with the Piercean notion of the "icon" as a sign (based on monadic relations of resemblance and identity), we can think of the "iconographic" image as the iconic and/or indexical sign that has taken on—along with its visual resemblance and existential connection to the "real"—additional, "re-cognized," and conventional symbolic function and meaning.

29. Here I cannot refrain from illustrating this general conundrum with—and I pun—a particularly "illuminating" example of a televisual mistake. In 1997, a year in which there were many dangerous and newsworthy brush fires raging in Southern California, one local newscast reported on two simultaneous fires by

using two simultaneous "live from the scene" insert shots of the brush fires, each singular location identified by graphic text. At one point in the segment, however, the commentator became confused as the locating text disappeared only to reappear transferred onto the other image. The faulty "fixing" and attempted "repair" of something so general in appearance as the abstracted image of a brush fire (which could be "any" fire "any" where) was not only comic but highly "illuminating."

30. S. Paige Baty, *American Monroe: The Making of a Body Politic* (Berkeley: University of California Press, 1995).

31. Baty uses the term "icon" here as a unitary figure of the "iconographic." In this regard, she does not deny the Piercean notion of the iconic sign but is discussing its primary basis in resemblance and identity as already mobilized into a secondary system of signification. Her usage in context also appropriately evokes and mobilizes the religious and art-historical insofar as the term "icon" also refers to (according to the *Oxford English Dictionary*) "an image in traditional Byzantine style of Jesus or a holy person that is used ceremonially and venerated in the Orthodox church."

32. Baty, *American Monroe*, 60.

33. Buck-Morss, *The Dialectics of Seeing*, 218.

34. Baty, *American Monroe*, 10, 37 (emphasis mine).

35. Ibid., 64.

36. Ibid., 31.

37. Ibid., 60.

38. Ibid., 78. This argument (as well as my own) thus goes against the grain of Roland Barthes's reading of the repetition and circulation of mass-mediated images in his *Mythologies,* trans. Annette Lavers (New York: Hill and Wang, 1972). See particularly the essays "The Romans in Film" and "Myth Today." For a further defense of the historical possibilities of the iconographic image against Barthes's characterization of it as "mythic," see my "The Insistent Fringe: Moving Images and Historical Consciousness," *History and Theory: Studies in the Philosophy of History* 36 (1997): 4–20.

39. Buck-Morss, *The Dialectics of Seeing*, 18.

40. Ibid., 164.

41. Ibid., 218.

42. Ibid., 62.

43. Ibid., 218–19.

44. Ibid., 218.

45. Ibid., 55.

46. Ibid., 18.

47. Miriam Hansen, "Benjamin, Cinema, and Experience: 'The Blue Flower in the Land of Technology,'" *New German Critique* 40 (Winter 1987): 211. (The epigraph that begins this essay can be found on p. 199.)

48. Ibid., 211. (Interior quote is from Benjamin.)

49. For more on allegory, particularly as it is developed in Benjamin and applied specifically to television, see Samuel Weber, *Mass Mediauras* (particularly

his essays "Mass Mediauras" and "Television: Set and Screen").

50. Walter Benjamin, "Theses on the Philosophy of History," in *Illuminations: Essays and Reflections,* ed. Hannah Arendt, trans. Harry Zohn (New York: Schocken Books, 1968), 263.

51. Buck-Morss, *The Dialectics of Seeing,* 219.

52. Although I am following Benjamin's thought here, his recognition of the shock of montage as creating a space out of time, a "Messianic cessation of happening," a "caesura in the movement of thought," bears some resemblance (less Messianic) to the very interesting distinction made by Richard Dienst between two modes of televisual temporality: "still time" and "automatic time," the former a function of televisual image replacement as in montage and the latter a function of an image "left running." See Dienst, *Still Life in Real Time,* 159–67.

53. Buck-Morss, *The Dialectics of Seeing,* 210.

54. Ibid., 211–12. (This is Buck-Morss's schematic of Benjamin's thought in relation to the function and character of the dialectical image and its historical and cultural materials.)

55. Ibid., 253.

56. Benjamin, quoted in ibid., 292.

TWO

Framing the Real

Reality TV in the Digital Era

A Paradox in Visual Culture?

ARILD FETVEIT

It's like they say. The picture's worth a thousand words. The video camera's worth a million words really.
—*Police officer in* Real TV

More real than the real, that is how the real is abolished.
—*Jean Baudrillard*

The advent of digital manipulation and image generation techniques has seriously challenged the credibility of photographic discourses.[1] At the same time, however, we are experiencing a growing use of surveillance cameras and a form of factual television that seems to depend more heavily on the evidential force of the photographic image than any previous form: *reality TV.*

The simultaneity of the digital "revolution in photography" and the proliferation of visual evidence seems paradoxical.[2] It seems as if we are experiencing a strengthening and a weakening of the credibility of photographic discourses at the same time. How are we to make sense of this? Are we, in some sense, at a turning point in visual culture? And, if so, does this entail a strengthening or a weakening of the evidential credibility of photographic images? Or is there a third option available? The aim in this article is to historicize and conceptualize this possible change in visual culture and to suggest plausible explanations for the proliferation of reality TV in the digital era.

I will first present a conceptual framework for assessing changes in credibility for photographic discourses before historicizing this credibility briefly. Then I discuss the use of visual evidence in reality TV and the impact of digitalization. I conclude by suggesting some explanations concerning the initial paradox, the most important one emphasizing the increasingly discourse-specific trust in photographic images and consequently, the need to complement a general technical understanding of photographic images with knowledge of different photographic practices.

Histories of Photographic Images

In order to suggest a conceptual framework for understanding changes in the credibility of discourses based upon photographic images, I find it useful to look at an argument advanced by John Tagg and later developed by Martin Lister.[3] These writers warn against placing too much emphasis on the common characteristics of photographic images. Rather than thinking of photography as a singular medium with unifying characteristics, they encourage us to recognize that there are numerous uses of photography and that the medium changes significantly according to the discourse it is used within. Presenting Tagg's view, Lister claims that

> it is more helpful to think of "photographies" which have different "histories" than it is to think of a singular medium with a singular, grand and sweeping history. The conventional history of photography has been written like The History of Literature or Art. It would be better understood as like a history of writing. By which Tagg means that it is better understood as a technique which is employed in many different kinds of work.[4]

I think Tagg and Lister are right in warning against a too monolithic view of photographic images. A view that is too heavily based upon unique technical features will tend to neglect the amount of convention invested in photographic practices. However, the reverse danger also exists. By emphasizing issues of convention too strongly, the unique iconical/indexical relation to the profilmic—which prepares the ground for the use of photographic evidence—is overlooked. Tagg makes himself guilty of this in claims like the following: "That a photograph can come to stand as *evidence* . . . rests not on a natural or existential fact, but on a social, semiotic process."[5] This conventionalism dismantles any idea of a common technological core unifying photographic practices in different areas. It dissolves photography into a set of faintly related conventional practices constituted by the different conventions at work in the various fields of use.

I want to argue that we should neither opt for a wholesale technologically and existentially based view nor a wholesale conventionalist one. Rather, we ought to see photographic practices as fundamentally based upon existential features involving the iconical/indexical relation to the profilmic but also as strongly invested with conventions. Further, we should be aware that to the extent to which we believe in a common core in photography, changes in our trust in one type of photographic discourse might affect our trust in another. Thus digital manipulation of photographic images within one area might not only affect our trust within that particular area, it might also lead to a declining trust in other uses of photographic images and to an undermining of credibility for photographic discourses in general. The picture I am drawing here is one in which we can conceive of trust in discourses based upon photographic images as existing on two levels:

- trust in discourses based upon photographic images in general
- trust in specific discourses based upon photographic images: documentary film, nature photography, reality TV, news photography, photography used in advertising, and so on[6]

This general framework for writing on the history of photographic images suggests that we can write both the *history* and *histories* of photography—and moreover, it suggests that relationships between these levels might be interesting to explore. It should also be noted that in our understanding of photographic discourses, a historical shift of balance between these two levels is conceivable. At one point in time we may think of photographic practices as fairly unified, but the development of more diversified practices may prompt us to ask questions of trust on a more discourse-specific level.

Before coming to the present changes in credibility, I shall present a brief account of some earlier changes in this field. This might give a better background for understanding the present situation.

The Growth of Credibility

A suitable point of departure would be 1839, when the techniques of two of the inventors of photography, William Henry Fox Talbot and Louis Jacques Mandé Daguerre, were first disclosed. Both viewed photography as a tool that was able to produce visual evidence. Talbot characterises photographic images as unique since they "have been obtained by the mere action of Light upon sensitive paper. They have been formed or depicted by optical and chemical means alone, and without the aid of anyone acquainted with the art of drawing."[7] They are unique, he adds, since an effect is produced "having a general resemblance to the cause that produced it."[8] Talbot thereby prefigures present semiotic conceptions of photography as based upon an iconic/indexical relation to the thing photographed. He goes on to suggest that the images might be accepted in court as "evidence of a novel kind."[9] This view parallels that of Daguerre's representative, the physicist M. François Arago, who argued that the French government should purchase Daguerre's patents on the grounds of their artistic and scientific uses. He argued that the camera would join "the thermometer, barometer, and hygrometer," as well as the telescope and microscope as scientific instruments, and that it will provide "faithful pictorial records" of events.[10] Although early photography was first of all used for making portraits, the evidential power of these images was not neglected. This is apparent not least in the early portraits of criminals.[11]

According to Tagg, a considerable change due to technical development occurred toward the end of the century. "In the decades of the 1880s and the 1890s . . . photography underwent a double technical revolution, enabling, on the one hand, the mass production of cheaply printed half-tone block and, on the other hand, the mass production of simple and convenient photographic equipment, such as the hand-held Kodak camera."[12] The half-tone plates that were introduced enabled the mass production of photographs in books, magazines, and newspapers. Light and inexpensive cameras made photography much more accessible. Both prepared the ground for an increased use of the camera for purposes of surveillance.[13] However, it is important to keep in mind that the early introduction of double exposure, composite images, and other photographic tricks prefiguring film effects made for a complicated field where both issues of what photography should be and issues of its evidential quality was contested.[14]

Though the technical means for using photography in books and magazines were available, according to André Bazin, a "feeling for the photographic document developed only gradually."[15] He supports this claim by pointing to the rivalry between photographic reporting and the use of drawing in the illustrated magazines of 1890 to 1910, with drawings often preferred on account of their dramatic character.[16] The notion that a feeling for the photographic document *developed gradually* is interesting. One way to think of this is that there was an increasing emphasis on the documentary or evidential quality of the images, adding to their illustrative qualities. Another way to conceive of this development would be to see it as a result of a gradual *adoption* of the photographic technology within new areas. This cumulative adoption within different areas of use might then effect a strengthening of the general credibility of photographic evidence. Thus we get interplay between a discourse-specific level and a general level as suggested in the framework above.

The invention of cinema in the 1890s adds new dimensions to the array of visual evidence: time and movement. However, it also invites fictional uses where the evidential, in a sense, is relieved. Without going into the complexities of this, let me point to some major turns in the development of visual evidence within film. Though the first films derived much of their appeal from the sheer fascination with authentic footage, the first powerful interest for the evidential seems to evolve in the 1920s with Dziga Vertov's program for a "true cinema": Kino Pravda. Much as a reaction to fiction, the lives of the people were to be caught "unawares." Still, Vertov was criticized for not going far enough, since he edited his films in a way that made it difficult to identify time and place of the events filmed. In 1926, Viktor

Shklovsky said that "newsreel material is in Vertov's treatment deprived of its soul—its documentary quality."[17] He also complained that "there is no precise determination of the [shots]. . . . The man who departs on broad skis into the snow-covered distance is no longer a man but a symbol of the departing past. The object has lost its substance and become transparent, like a work by the Symbolists."[18] This critique eloquently illustrates a possible spectrum open to actuality footage between the illustrative and symbolic on the one side and the evidential on the other. Later changes in the view of credibility can be understood partly in view of such a spectrum.

Though the term documentary film suggests a genre based on the documentary power of photographic images, manipulations, re-creations, and fakeries were prevalent in these films throughout the 1930s.[19] Thus the illustrative and symbolic function of the images was dominant. After World War II, however, actuality material was strongly preferred over dramatizations (perhaps due to the impact of the authentic war footage).[20] Thus the evidential function of the images was considerably strengthened.

Prefiguring today's reality TV, an even stronger emphasis on the evidential came with the advent of lightweight camera equipment featuring synchronic sound recording in the late 1950s.[21] Increased camera access allied with an epistemological optimism to establish a new documentary aesthetic, strongly based upon observation and interviews, often documenting events as they unfolded through an "objective," "fly on the wall" technique.[22] On the face of it, much of today's reality TV seems to embody aspirations both from Vertov's Kino Pravda to catch life "unawares" and from the verité movements of the 1960s to give an objective view of life as it unfolds. Thus the evidential aspirations of photographic discourse is powerfully carried on—if not stretched to its limits—in reality TV.

I have suggested that a belief in the evidential powers of photographic images might grow through (1) the adoption of photographic techniques in novel areas, and through (2) the shift of emphasis from the illustrative to the evidential power of the images used. The history of photography is filled with examples of the first, with the adoption of photography in illustrated magazines (as pointed to by Bazin) being just one of them. The latter movement is exemplified in the critique of Vertov and, later, in the growing demands for authenticity within documentary film first after World War II, then with the coming of lightweight equipment. Though photomontage, retouching, and other non-evidential manifestations of photography have been around since the first days of photography, in general I think it is fair to say that the evidential view of photography has gained a strong position through the years. However, inherent in the fabric of photographic images seems to lie an unresolvable tension between the illustrative and the evidential, the iconic and the indexical—and it is within this very fabric that digitalization and reality TV now seem to confront each other. The former exerts a pull in the direction of the illustrative and the iconic, the latter in the direction of the evidential and the indexical.

Visual Evidence in Reality TV

Concepts like "reality TV," "reality show," "reality programming," and "neo-verité" have been used to designate this recent trend in television, showing us dramatic moments from police work, rescue operations, accidents, and so forth.[23] *Cops* and *LAPD: Life on the Beat* show us police at work; programs like *Crimewatch UK* re-create unsolved crimes in order to enlist the audience as assistants to the police;[24] *I Witness Video* and *Real TV* show dramatic (and sometimes funny) moments caught on tape. Though some of the reality TV programs employ re-creations—notably *Rescue 911* and *Crimewatch UK*—most rely on visual evidence of the following kinds:

- authentic footage from camera crews observing arrests or rescue operations
- footage from surveillance videos
- recordings (often by amateurs) of dramatic accidents and dangerous situations

Both *Cops* and *LAPD* are based on the recordings of a one-camera unit "riding along" with the police in the patrol car. The chaotic and rough sound track, saturated with white noise from police radios and accidental environmental sounds, testifies to the authenticity of the recordings, as does the ragged movements of the handheld camera. The footage in *Cops* is further authenticated by a voice-over in the opening of the program claiming that "*Cops* is filmed on location with the men and women of law enforcement." In long takes, displaying the action as it unfolds, we are presented with chases, arrests, and police inquiries. Though the camera has good access to events, we might still have a hard time figuring out what is happening through sheer observation. This is solved by having one police officer brief another in front of the camera. In *LAPD*, voice-over narration is also used.

Formats that rely on amateur and surveillance videos are often structured around a single and unique moment caught by camera: a dramatic car crash, a robbery caught by a surveillance camera, or even airplanes colliding in midair. This moment, when "real TV happens," as the announcer in *Real TV* phrases it, is the evidential jewel around which the segment is built.[25] The dramatic footage is often supported by testimonies from people involved. In most cases, we get an account from a surviving victim looking back at the incident. We can also find interviews with friends and family, with accidental eyewitnesses, and in some cases with police or rescue workers. These elements surround and explain the dramatic footage. Repetition and slow motion are often used to help us inspect the visual evidence.

In an episode from the Norwegian version of *Real TV*, we see amateur videos from an air display featuring two MIG 29s doing impressive loops.[26] When the airplanes demonstrate a twin loop, they get too close, and the wing of the leader slices the other plane. As the planes collide, we hear the narrator of *Real TV* say: "During a fatal moment, the overwhelming view of the two gracious airplanes is transformed into an inferno in the air. The cameras capture every single moment." Then we meet two eyewitnesses. First, the announcer for the air display comments on the accident as we see it once more: "In a fraction of a second, these two graceful jets were flaming pieces of rubbish, falling out of the sky." Then a clip from an interview with a fireman is inserted, in order to remind us of the danger and to prolong the suspense: "Looking at the stage of the wreckage—if you would have been in there, there wouldn't have been a lot left of you," he says. We see the crash again, this time in slow motion and from a slightly different angle, as the narrator comments, "but in this video you can see the pilots eject themselves the second after the collision." Two circles are drawn above the planes in order to guide our vision. We can see two faint dots shooting out from the planes before we see the parachutes opening, bringing the pilots safely to the ground.[27]

Here the evidential power of the cameras that capture "every single moment" has become the main issue. The focus is not so much on presenting a story of an air crash as on presenting the audio/visual evidence that shows us what really happened in that decisive moment when the planes crash. The function of the camera is close to that of the scientific instrument, measuring out the concrete details of a particular instant. The format heavily propagates a belief in visual evidence. However, the strong presence of the verbal explanation pointing out what is going on in the footage should not be neglected. The "visual evidence" is not merely visual. Walter Benjamin makes an interesting prediction when commenting on increased camera access in the 1930s: "The camera will become smaller and smaller, more and more prepared to grasp fleeting, secret images whose shock will bring the mechanism of association in the viewer to a halt. At this point captions must begin to function. . . . Will not captions become the essential component of pictures?"[28] Benjamin's observation on the relationship between the visual and the verbal is surprisingly well fitted to reality TV featuring authentic recordings of dramatic events. Much of the blurred and chaotic images at the height of drama seem to need powerful support from linguistic sources for us to make sense of them. The description of what we see helps us to choose the suitable level of perception; it helps to focus not simply our gaze but also our understanding.[29]

The focus on presenting audio/visual evidence as much as "the story" is one of the features that distinguishes reality TV from earlier attempts to "catch the real." This focus also leads to an emphasis on the visible surface of the world rather than on deeper symbolic aspects. Whereas Vertov set out "to fix and organize the individual characteristic phenomena of life into a whole, an extract," reality TV opts for an exploration of the visible surface of the here and now, avoiding abstract, symbolic montage and often pointing to its own status as visual evidence.[30] The goal is "to capture that real TV moment," and audience members are advised to keep a camcorder in the trunk of their cars because you "never know when real TV might happen."[31] Similarly, the producers of *Cops* are looking for "amazing, unusual, exciting or weird videotapes. Crazy arrest, angry suspects, hot pursuits and bloopers from in car cameras" [*sic*].[32] What we get is evidential photography paired with an aesthetics of "liveness," a dramaturgy geared toward keeping alive the question "what happens next?" and often "Will the good guys make it?"—"Will the bad guys fry?" Then the putatively objective eye of the camera provides the answer for us to see. And the TV station will not let us have serious doubts: "Yes, they will."[33] Our two pilots survived against all odds and thereby inscribed themselves into the mythic core of reality TV. The deepest fascination with the evidential—when slow motion and repetition serve a close scrutiny of the footage—seems to occur when death is only inches away.

Nonetheless, how can this almost frantic obsession with the evidential powers of the camera survive in a digital era? Does not digitalization do away with visual evidence?

Digitalization and Visual Evidence

Photographic images cannot account for their own production process very eloquently; they cannot tell us where, when, and how they are taken. Though we are often successful in our guesses on issues like these, our only way of knowing is by way of a truthful account from the producer or some other person who knows. Any serious use of visual evidence has to rely on such knowledge. This means that, in order to be held credible, visual evidence is reliant upon more or less explicit verbal descriptions and personal/institutional warrant that the description is true. Provided that this is taken care of, that the technology works and the people using it are doing what they are supposed to, cameras will still serve their purposes in monitoring us on the street, in the bank, and in prison as they also will surveille physical experiments in the sciences and the inside of our bodies under surgery.

Whereas descriptions of images used for scientific purposes tend to be explicit, standardized, and detailed, the opposite is normally the case for images used in the media. Here we are informed about the status of the recordings either through genre convention or through network and program style. Our belief that television news mainly features authentic recordings, and that some networks tend to stick more firmly to such a policy than others, is established this way. Claims might also be more explicitly stated, like the claim that *Cops* is "filmed on location," or that we see "the pilots eject themselves the second after the collision" in a *Real TV* episode. In the last case we get an interpretation of the footage and no explicit statement about its authenticity, since this is regarded as self-evident. However, later developments of digital techniques have made such assumptions less evident.

The development of computer programs for manipulation and generation of images has made it, at times, very hard to see whether we are looking at ordinary photographic images or images that have been altered. In the latter case, iconicity is sustained whereas indexicality—the causal relation between the profilmic (what was in front of the camera) and the image—partly disappears. In most cases the relationship is still there, but we might have a hard time deciding which parts of an image originate from the profilmic event and which parts are digitally generated or manipulated. Thus the evidential power of composite and digitally manipulated images is lost. It is also important to note that digitalization has substantially expanded the spectrum of photographic techniques available—especially within the increasingly blurred boundaries between painting and photography—though the different practices employed may not be detectable in the images themselves. This makes us more heavily reliant upon the truthfulness of the claims made about photographic images.[34]

We should also note that the impact of "the digital revolution in photography" is contingent upon the use of these techniques within different areas. In some genres, digital manipulation techniques are used extensively; in others such techniques are more or less banned. People engaged in the production of factual discourses like news and documentary tend to shy away from digital imagery whereas those who create commercials and fiction films employ such techniques more freely. Negotiating institutional standards is an important part of adapting to the new situation. Such negotiations have taken place in the press, in television news, and in nature photography, just to mention a few areas.[35] Some argue pragmatically that what is important is that the truth be told not whether the images are authentic, have been subjected to color adjustments, have had disturbing objects removed, or other manipulations done to them. Others seem to think that any conduct transgressing what goes on in a traditional darkroom setting will ruin the credibility not only of the images but also of what is being told.

There have been efforts to communicate the status of the images explicitly by marking manipulated images with "M," but it seems that a more implicit communication has gained the upper hand. There might be limits to the audiences' interest in metacommunication, and besides, arguments have also been advanced against the "M."[36] Following other factual discourses, producers of the reality TV formats discussed here are also careful not to give the impression that their programs have been subjected to image manipulation or that they contain footage that is not authentic.[37]

More research on these institutional negotiations would be welcome. What are the arguments used? Where are the limits drawn? How do agents position themselves in order to protect the credibility of their discourse and distance themselves from less credible discourses? It would also be interesting to know more about how changes in one discourse may bleed over and affect another or affect the credibility of photographic discourses on a more general level.[38]

But let us leave these questions now and turn to some less palpable dimensions of this change within visual culture.

A Psychological Loss

The dissemination of indexicality does not only represent an undermining of evidential power. On a deeper psychological level, it can be argued that it also comes to represent a loss of contact with the world. This is because photographic images come with a promise to provide a certain sense of connectedness. By way of the light rays emanating from the person photographed, the image becomes inscribed with traces from that person: it becomes a relic. As Bazin puts it, a "transference of reality from the thing to its reproduction" takes place.[39] And more than sheer information, what we seem to be attracted to in these images is a form of presence.

> A very faithful drawing may actually tell us more about the model but despite the promptings of our critical intelligence it will never have the irrational power of the photograph to bear away our faith. . . . No matter how fuzzy, distorted, or discoloured, no matter how lacking in documentary value the image may be, it shares, by virtue of the very process of its becoming, the being of the model of which it is the reproduction; it *is* the model.[40]

This deep psychological fascination with the sense of connectedness, of closeness to something infinitely remote, is also what Barthes takes as his point of departure in *Camera Lucida*. Looking at a photograph of

Napoleon's youngest brother, Jerome, taken in 1852, Barthes realizes with amazement, "I am looking at eyes that looked at the Emperor."[41] This sense of connectedness (which in Barthes's phrasing makes the representation disappear and replaces it with the object itself) is an important source of fascination with photographic images. When indexicality is disseminated, this sense of connectedness is also partly lost.

Pursued to a more global level, this is a loss concerning our sense of contact with reality through audio/visual representations. From a McLuhanesque point of view, the media are "extensions of man," prosthetic devices that extend our perceptive apparatus. From this perspective, the loss of indexicality could be interpreted as a powerful refiguration of these extensions, implicating our perceptive apparatus. In this refiguration, representations based upon the iconic/indexical are being replaced by representations sustaining the iconic, but losing the causal connection to reality. Thus, to the extent that indexicality is lost, we might not only lose evidential power, but we might come to feel a sense of losing touch with reality, of being stranded in the world of the simulacrum.

From Technological to Institutional Trust

In view of all this, how can we make sense of our initial paradox, the simultaneous loss of faith in photographic images and the proliferation of reality TV and visual evidence? Rather than a general strengthening or weakening of the evidential credibility of photographic images, I think we are witnessing an *increased compartmentalization of credibility*; a shift of emphasis from general assessments of credibility to more discourse-specific judgments. I am not claiming that a compartmentalized understanding of photographic images is something entirely new, but I believe it is being strengthened currently. A move in our understanding of photography from a general and technically defined level to a more discourse-specific level reliant upon discourse-specific practices and institutional warrant permits the coexistence of reality TV and digital manipulation, since different discursive practices are guided by different rules.

This brings us back to Tagg and Lister. If we regard our initial paradox as solved, I think it is at the price of accepting that the common technological core unifying photographic images across different formats and practices has become less important to us. Thus our understanding of these images has moved some steps in the direction Tagg and Lister are suggesting. With increasing numbers of practices, now expanded by the advent of digital techniques, our understanding of and trust in photographic images must more than ever take varying practices and conventions into account. Thus the credibility of photographic discourses becomes less reliant on an overarching trust in the technology of photography and more dependent upon institutional warrant.

This compartmentalization may go a long way in explaining why the coexistence of digital manipulation and reality TV is no contradiction, but it does not provide an explanation for the obsession with visual evidence and reality expressed in reality TV. Obviously, institutional changes and economical drives should not be forgotten, but I also think the interest for reality TV is feeding upon less tangible aspects of the current changes.

The Ambiguous Longing for the Real

In a deeper psychological sense, the proliferation of reality TV could be understood as a euphoric effort to reclaim what seems to be lost after digitalization.[42] And what seems lost is not only a belief in the evidential powers of photography but as much a sense of being in contact with the world by way of indexicality. The powerful urge for a sense of contact with the real is inscribed in much of the reality TV footage. The rough quality of the hand-held footage draws attention to the issue of contact itself, to what Jakobson calls the phatic function of discourse.[43]

The reality depicted in these formats is most of the time one where other lives are at stake; either people survive accidents that could have been fatal or the danger is provided by police hunting assumed criminals. What most powerfully conveys a sense of reality is, perhaps, the presence of death. It is also where the real ends. In a sense, death cannot be represented, but we still cannot stop representing it.[44] On reality TV, however, death is only depicted when the surviving numbers are astonishing. After all, a major theme in these programs seems to be the good citizen escaping death and the bad citizen being confined.

Reality TV comes with a unique promise of contact with reality, but at the same time it promises a secure distance. Too much reality is easily dispensed with by a touch on the remote control. It is not reality, it is reality *TV*, reality *show*. Kevin Robins points to a "tendency to replace the world around us with an alternative space of simulation."[45] He sees reality TV as "anticipating, ahead of any technological transformation, the experience of . . . virtual-reality systems."[46] He develops this comparison by maintaining that virtual reality "is inspired by the dream of an alternative and compensatory reality . . . so attractive because it combines entertainment and thrills with comfort and security."[47]

This view suggests a complex scenario in which developments in visual culture interact with both technical and socio-political issues. From this perspective, digital manipulation hardly represents any threat against reality TV since both bring us closer to simulation anyway, though admittedly in different ways. I think Robins's analysis is suggestive, particularly the socio-logical and political perspectives that it yields. It points to an increasing compartmentalization of society in which we build up "safe environments" where we no longer need to share physical space with the underprivileged, where the more problematic aspects of reality are locked out. With its focus on rescuing us from nature and technology gone awry and protecting us from criminals, reality TV could easily be interpreted as conveying an ideol-ogy tailored to such a development.

However, I think we should hesitate somewhat toward plainly talking about "simulation," both in regard to digitized photography and reality TV. A partial loss of indexicality does not bring about a state of simulation, at least not in the sense of a generalized suspension of referentiality. After all, the referential image was not invented by Talbot and Daguerre, though, admittedly, their effort of bringing together the iconical and the indexical has powerfully come to shape what we understand by "representing real-ity." Furthermore, rather than simply claiming that reality TV represents simulation, I suggest that we should see it as a representation of reality that is not very useful for developing our understanding of what goes on in the world.[48]

What is at stake here could be reconceptualized as a tension between modes of representation, modes that reflect different views on what reality is, or, perhaps more precisely, different views on which aspects of reality should be represented. Shklovsky, in his critique of Vertov, wanted less sym-bolism and general statements and more concrete accounts. Reality TV seems to have taken us further in such a direction than we have ever been before. Now Robins, however, in the tradition of Plato, Brecht, Benjamin, and others, wants to take us back. This seems like an ongoing struggle within the very fabric of photography—reflecting a similar tension within our understanding of reality—where no level between the symbolic and the concrete is "the right one" except according to the purposes and interests we might have. However, in a culture where critical and independent docu-mentaries have a hard time competing with more flashy reality-oriented programming, it is in our interest not to allow reality TV too much influ-ence on what "reality" should be on our television screens.[49]

Conclusion

I have argued that the coexistence of digital manipulation and visual evi-dence testifies to a transmutation in our visual culture. This is a change in which the credibility of photographic images has become less dependent upon technology and more based upon institutional warrant. Thus we have recently seen efforts to negotiate and communicate standards for photo-

graphic discourses. These changes require us to place greater emphasis on
the differences between photographic practices and less upon the technical
features that unite them. Such a move, from the idea of trust as linked to the
technology itself and toward placing it in a larger techno-institutional complex, largely resolves our initial paradox originating from the simultaneous
proliferation of digital imagery and visual evidence.

Reality TV itself might be read partly as a symptom of unsettled issues in
this transmutation. More precisely, it might express a longing for a lost touch
with reality, prompted by the undermining and problematizing of indexicality. Not only does reality TV powerfully reclaim the evidential quality of
photography said to be lost after digitalization, it also is obsessed with conveying a sense of connectedness, of contact with the world—a trait that also,
albeit on a less tangible psychological level, might seem to be lost in an era
where silicon has replaced the silver of Daguerre and Talbot.

NOTES

Thanks to *Rådet for anvendt medieforskning, Handlingsplanen mot vold i
bildemediene,* and *Institusjonen Fritt Ord* for supporting my research on reality
TV financially. I also want to thank Arnt Maasø, Andrew Morrison, John Corner,
James Friedman, Carol J. Clover, and Kiersten Leigh Johnson for helpful comments and suggestions. This article has been slightly revised since its original publication in Media, Culture and Society 21, 6 (November 1999): 787–804.

1. I prefer talking about the credibility of "photographic discourses" rather
than "photographic images" because it makes no sense to say that an image as
such is credible or not. Only when the image is used within a discursive context
does it make sense to talk about credibility.

2. Fred Ritchin, *In Our Own Image: The Coming Revolution in Photography* (New York: Aperture, 1990).

3. John Tagg, *The Burden of Representation: Essays on Photographies and
Histories* (London: Macmillan, 1988), and Martin Lister, ed., introduction to *The
Photographic Image in Digital Culture* (London: Routledge, 1995), 1–26.

4. Lister, *The Photographic Image,* 11.

5. Tagg, *The Burden of Representation,* 4.

6. This picture could be rendered in several different ways. For example, we
could easily add a third level: either technologically based—photography, film, television, computer—or based on cultural function—entertainment, information.

7. William Henry Fox Talbot, *The Pencil of Nature* (London: Longman,
Brown, Green and Longmans, 1844), n.p.

8. Ibid.

9. Ibid.

10. François Dominique Arago, "Report," in *Classic Essays on Photography,*
ed. Alan Trachtenberg (New Haven, Conn.: Leete's Island Books, 1980), 17, 23.

11. It is hardly surprising that the possibilities of the new instrument were
soon discovered by the legal apparatus. According to Alan Sekula, "The Body and

the Archive," in *The Contest of Meaning: Critical Histories of Photography*, ed. Richard Bolton (Cambridge, Mass.: MIT Press, 1989), 342–89, photographic documentation of prisoners became institutionalized in the 1860s. Susan Sontag notes in *On Photography* (New York: Penguin Books, 1979) that the Paris police were using cameras eagerly in the roundup of Communards in June 1871 (5). A substantial growth in the uses of photographic evidence by the police followed the development of Sir Edward Henry's system of identification by means of fingerprints in 1901. It soon became apparent that the only way to record fingerprints discovered at the scene of a crime was by way of photography (Tagg, *The Burden of Representation*, 75–76).

12. Ibid., 66.

13. Tagg argues that the "democratisation" and proliferation of photography following this "double technical revolution" set the stage for a far-reaching pictorial revolution: "the political axis of representation had been entirely reversed. It was no longer a privilege to be pictured but the burden of a new class of the surveilled" (ibid., 59).

14. James Lastra, in "From the Captured Moment to the Cinematic Image: A Transformation in Pictorial Order," in *The Image in Dispute: Art and Cinema in the Age of Photography*, ed. Dudley Andrew (Austin: University of Texas Press, 1997), points to debates about whether "combined negatives of two or more exposures might still be considered 'photographs,' in light of the proliferation of single-exposure snapshots" (264), citing titles like W. K. Burton, "Combination Printing: Is It Legitimate in Photography?" *Pacific Coast Photographer* 2, 5 (June 1893): 318–20; H. P. Bowditch, "Are Composite Photographs Typical Pictures?" *McClure's* 3 (September 1894): 331–34; and W. deW. Abney, "Are Instantaneous Photographs True?" *International Annual of Anthony's Photographic Bulletin* 2 (1889): 256–57.

15. André Bazin, *What Is Cinema?* 2 vols. (Berkeley: University of California Press, 1967), 1:11.

16. Ibid.

17. Viktor Shklovsky, "Where Is Dziga Vertov Striding?" in *The Film Factory: Russian and Soviet Cinema in Documents 1896–1939*, ed. Richard Taylor and Ian Christie (Cambridge, Mass.: Harvard University Press, 1988), 152.

18. Ibid., 153.

19. Eric Barnouw, *Documentary: A History of the Nonfiction Film* (Oxford: Oxford University Press, 1984).

20. See Bazin, *What Is Cinema?* 1:155–56.

21. This is not the first time sound plays an important role in bringing film closer to tangible reality. With the advent of sound, newsreels like Fox's *Movietone News* were praised for bringing the world closer and feature films like Warner's *Jazz Singer* (1927) for bringing new life to the screen. However, the coming of sound was also heavily deplored by people like Pudovkin, Eisenstein, and Arnheim, who felt that the highly developed abstract and symbolic montage of the silent film was threatened by the blunt closeness to reality brought about by sound.

22. Brian Winston, in *Claiming the Real: The Documentary Film Revisited* (London: British Film Institute, 1995), sees this as a very unfortunate development: "A hundred and thirty years or so after François Arago claimed the camera for science, the documentary purists, essentially American direct cinema proponents, implicitly reasserted that claim on behalf of the lightweight Auricon and the Eclair. In such hands the camera was nothing more than as instrument of scientific inscription producing evidence objective enough to be 'judged' by a spectator" (151). The problem with this, as Winston further argues, is that research, analysis, and social meaning are abandoned in favor of "emotionalism and aesthetic pleasure" (ibid., 154).

23. Intimate talk shows are also often referred to as "reality TV." Though they obviously form part of a general turn toward "reality" within television entertainment, I prefer to reserve the term for programs depicting physical drama on location rather than emotional drama produced in the studio. Formats like *Big Brother* are also occasionally referred to as "reality TV," though a more suitable name would be "experiment TV." *Big Brother* is a social (Darwinist) experiment where ten participants agree to be locked up in a specially designed house for one hundred days and be voted out one by one. In order to secure the sterility of the experiment, the participants have never before met, and they have no contact with the world outside, no telephone, newspaper, radio, or television. Cameras and microphones observe them day and night in every room.

Whereas the intimate talk shows of Jerry Springer and Ricki Lake mostly trigger negative feelings through emotionally violent confrontations, *Big Brother* is also designed to produce romance and sex. With the right casting and the proper impulses and restrictions, this social laboratory will produce "real life soap characters" that quarrel, insult, and seduce each other in front of large television and Internet audiences. The attraction is largely premised on a promise of pornography, and the format is constantly tuned in order to secure delivery (casting a stripper [Norwegian version] or a go-go dancer [French version], or having no single bedrooms and perhaps no single beds [German version] are among the means used to incite close encounters).

It can be argued that *Big Brother* further interrogates issues at stake in the reality TV of violent drama. On one level it is dramatizing and normalizing our lives as fully surveilled and incarcerated. On another level it pushes the interrogation of authenticity on from the level of the image and onto the subjects photographed whose "authenticity" is strongly thematized by participants themselves as well as marketed by producers.

On a more general level Big Brother is like a herald announcing a new creative imagery in television production (with television, Internet, and telephone fully integrated). The matrix of this new creativity is the surveillance of a human experiment. Put ten young people in a house for a hundred days *(Big Brother)*. Put four young couples on a tropical island and have beauties (among them a former Playboy model and Miss Georgia 2000) try to tempt them into committing adultery *(Temptation Island)*. Watch obese people try to earn their weight loss in gold *(The Big Diet)*. Perhaps the deeper experiment here is one in which some people are tested for their willingness to subject themselves to possible humiliation in order to be on television—others are tested for how well they adapt to a Peeping Tom and cannabalist gaze. Television itself is tested for its ability to transform what we would otherwise think of as perverse into something "ordinary" and "normal."

24. The format used in *Crimewatch UK* is employed in local productions throughout the Nordic countries. The various programs are called *Øyenvitne* (Norwegian TV2), *Station 2* (Danish TV2), *Efterlyst* (Swedish TV3), and *Polisii TV* (Finnish YLE TV2).

25. *Real TV*, which in Norway is broadcast as *Fra Virkeligheten* (TV2), also contains more evolving events with longer takes, as did its predecessor *I Witness Video*, in Norway called *Videovitne* (TVNorge). However, these more slowly evolving segments, containing the rescue of animals or showing people doing "weird" things, do not raise issues of evidence in the same way as the dramatic footage of possible death (which most of the time turn out to be footage of survival).

26. Broadcast by Norwegian TV2 on March 5, 1998. In the Norwegian version, the host, John Daly, is replaced by Richard Kongsteien (who used to host *Øyenvitne*).

27. Although our attention is first and foremost directed toward the visual elements, excerpts of authentic sound occasionally also become the focus of special attention. In the example above, as the planes collide, we hear a vague sound, a bit like voices. The speaker says: "That's the sound of 150,000 people drawing their breath in, and gasping at what they've seen, myself included."

28. Walter Benjamin, "A Short History of Photography," in *Classic Essays on Photography*, 215. Working from similar assumptions as Benjamin's, Roland Barthes develops the concepts "anchorage" and "relay" when trying to describe the function of the linguistic message with regard to the iconic. When the linguistic message dominates, Barthes talks of "anchorage." When the iconic and the linguistic are equally important, the linguistic message functions as a "relay." He further claims that "in every society various techniques are developed intended to fix the floating chain of signifieds in such a way as to counter the terror of uncertain signs; the linguistic message is one of these techniques" (1977: 39).

29. The use of replay and slow motion is perhaps greater in sports than any other programming. Decisive moments of failure or achievement can be experienced again and again, extracted from the normal flow of time and projected into the sphere of slow motion for detailed scrutiny and aesthetic admiration. Another place where the aesthetics of slow motion is prevalent is in ultraviolent film scenes. Reality TV seems able to provide a common ground, bringing sports, violent events, and visual evidence together. The present example, the MIGs crashing in an air display, comes close to a merger of these elements.

30. Dziga Vertov, "Fiction Film Drama and the Cine-Eye: A Speech," in *The Film Factory*, 115.

31. http://www.realtv1.com/ (February 15, 1997).

32. http://www.tvcops.com/page_cops.html (February 15, 1997).

33. In the formats where the material has been edited, keeping in line with network policy represents no problem. Another matter is live reports. In early May

1998, in front of a live television audience, a man killed his dog and set his truck on fire before blowing his head off with a shotgun. This incident might induce a change in policy when it comes to transmitting such events live.

34. Again, there is some hesitation (see note 14) toward using the word "photography" in relation to digitally manipulated images, but though terms like "hyper-photography," "post-photography," and "digital photography" have been introduced, I believe the established designations are likely to prevail. More specified designations, as well as metacommunication about how the images were produced, will be required when the audience is frustrated or when those making the images want to distinguish their practices from others.

35. Whereas the issues seem to be resolved within news departments (with a slightly more conservative result in print media than in television), debates within nature photography might not be that settled. The March–April 1997 issue of *American Photography* ran a discussion about the norms of photography related to Barbara Sleeper and Art Wolfe's book *Migrations: Wildlife in Motion* (Hillsboro, Ore.: Beyond Words Publishing, 1994) in which Wolfe has digitally enhanced about one third of the pictures. He claims it to be art while his critics call it fake documentation.

36. Søren Kjørup argues in "Billedmanipulation: Og den indexikalske teori om fotografiet," in *Mediegleder: Et festskrift til Peter Larsen* ("Image Manipulation: And the Indexical Theory of Photography," in *Media Pleasures: A Fiftieth-Birthday Collection for Peter Larsen*), ed. Jostein Gripsrud (Oslo: Ad Notam Gyldendal, 1993), 161–74, against the marking of manipulated images since this might support unrealistic beliefs in the evidential power of other images.

37. The importance of authenticity was strongly emphasized in a personal interview with John Langley, the executive producer of *Cops* (March 4, 1997). The same attitude was expressed by Andrew Jebb, the producer of *LAPD*, in a personal interview (March 3, 1997). It is interesting to note that Jebb gave a substantially lower estimate of the amount of "B-roll" (footage that is not authentic) used than his coworkers did in a less formal meeting (same date). This illustrates the importance for these producers to underline the "realness" of their products.

38. The proliferation of digitized imagery in advertising does not seem to affect our trust in documentary photography too much. But when more of the discourses involving photographic images start using digital techniques, I believe our general trust might be affected—and eventually our trust in documentary photography.

39. Bazin, *What Is Cinema?* 14.

40. Ibid.

41. Roland Barthes, *Camera Lucida: Reflections on Photography* (New York: Hill and Wang, 1981), 3.

42. Jean Baudrillard talks in *Simulacra and Simulations* (Ann Arbor: University of Michigan Press, 1994) about a "[p]anic-stricken production of the real and of the referential" when the simulacrum replaces referential discourses (7).

43. Roman Jakobson, "Lingustics and Poetics," in *Modern Criticism and Theory: A Reader,* ed. David Lodge (London: Longman, 1988), 32–61.

44. As Vivian Sobchack says in "Inscribing Ethical Space: Ten Propositions on Death, Representation, and Documentary," *Quarterly Review of Film Studies* 9, 4 (1984), "nonbeing is not visible. It lies over the threshold of visibility and representation. Thus, it can only be pointed to. . . . The classic 'proof' of the excess of death over its indexical representation was the fascination exerted by the Zapruder film of John Kennedy's assassination; played again and again, slowed down, stopped frame by frame, the momentum of death escaped each moment of its representation" (287). Nonetheless, as Bill Nichols indicates in *Blurred Boundaries: Questions of Meaning in Contemporary Culture* (Bloomington: Indiana University Press, 1994), we don't give up: "at death's door, we find documentary endlessly, and anxiously, waiting. It hovers, fascinated by a border zone it cannot ever fully represent" (48).

45. Kevin Robins, "The Virtual Unconscious in Postphotography," in *Electronic Culture: Technology and Visual Representation,* ed. Timothy Druckrey (New York: Aperture, 1996), 159.

46. Kevin Robins, *Into the Image: Culture and Politics in the Field of Vision* (London: Routledge, 1996), 121–22.

47. Ibid.

48. Documentaries address issues of crime in quite another way than does reality TV. It can be useful to compare the representation of crime in *Cops* and *LAPD* to that offered in PBS *Frontline* documentaries like *Snitch* (Ofra Bikel, 1999), *Drug Wars* (Martin Smith and Lowell Bergman, 2000), *Real Justice* (Ben Gale and Ben Loeterman, 2000), and *LAPD Blues* (Michael Kirk and Rick Young, 2001). A comparison could, for example, focus on differences in the information projected, on the level of generality of the claims made, on the role of stereotypes, and on attitudes towards the police and those who are arrested (see http://www.pbs.org/wgbh/pages/frontline/programs/categories/c.html for more details on the documentaries mentioned).

49. See John Corner, *Television Form and Public Address* (London: Edward Arnold, 1995) and *The Art of Record: A Critical Introduction to Documentary* (Manchester: Manchester University Press, 1996); and Richard Kilborn, "Shaping the Real: Democratization and Commodification in UK Factual Broadcasting," *European Journal of Communication* 13, 2 (June 1998): 201–18, for discussions on how commercial pressures and "reality" orientation affect current documentary production. It is also worth posing the question whether the ideology of reality TV has contributed to a stricter view of what should be admitted in documentary filmmaking resulting in fines to U.K. filmmakers for "breach of public trust." See Brian Winston, *Lies, Damn Lies, and Documentaries* (London: BFI Publishing, 2000). We need an even fuller assessment of this, and also of how the logic of reality TV bleeds into news and nature programming.

Attraction to Distraction

Live Television and the Public Sphere

JAMES FRIEDMAN

Growing up in Portland, Oregon, I became aware of the relationship between television and temporality while watching *Monday Night Football*. Every major television market in the United States watched the NFL's entry into prime-time television live except Portland. For reasons that are still somewhat unclear to me, Portland's ABC affiliate, KATU, decided to present the broadcast on tape one hour after the game actually began. I guess they were trying to maximize the viewing audience by starting at 7:00 P.M. instead of 6:00, but, in practical terms, that meant that the game was really over early in the second half of the broadcast. If television had provided our only access to the coverage of football games (or other events in the world for that matter), it might not have mattered (or more accurately, we might not have known) that the broadcasts of the events were delayed. But years before the Internet made news and information available on demand, there was radio, which in the case of football meant that the game we were watching on television beginning at 7:00 P.M. was already broadcast on the radio an hour earlier.

The radio broadcast of the football game did not in any way change the television broadcast, but it did change the viewer's reception of that broadcast, since it provided us with access to extratextual knowledge about what was going to happen, who was going to win, how they would win, and by how many points.[1] I remember one night, for example, I was working in a restaurant and serving a customer from out of town. We were watching the Oakland Raiders on Monday night, and they were being beaten badly by the Denver Broncos. I had access to a radio, however, and therefore I knew that the Raiders were going to come back in the fourth quarter and win the game. Armed with this knowledge, I jokingly bet with the customer that Oakland would win. After the TV eventually broadcast what I had already heard on the radio, I let the customer in on fact that the game was tape delayed. What I will always remember is that, more that anything, he was dismayed that our community was only offered a taped broadcast of what should have been a *live* event.

Monday Night Football, then, made me aware of the complexity of live broadcasting and stands as a constant reminder that, even though a broadcast has all the markings or conventions of liveness, those trappings do not mean in and of themselves that what we are watching is live. The problem of *Monday Night Football* stems from broadcasters' and team owners' desire to present sporting events—which are usually broadcast live—to a national prime-time audience. When special events such as the World Series are broadcast, it is assumed that people will alter their schedules to accommodate the all-important event. When dealing with ongoing programming, however, such as the fourteen to seventeen weeks of *Monday Night Football,* broadcasters in Oregon seemed to have been less certain that viewers would conform their schedules to accommodate the actual time of the game.[2]

It would seem that the problem, or at least part of the problem, stems from the separation of the viewing audience into four time zones: Eastern, Central, Mountain, and Pacific (Hawaii and Alaska represent additional time zones for U.S. viewers). This was also a problem when broadcasters of the prime-time series *ER* boasted that they would present their 1997–98 season premiere live. Presenting this show—which has an assigned programming slot—live would require either multiple performances or altering the time slot for what was then the nation's most popular program. The presentation of this live extravaganza turned out to be a marketing bonanza, but the idea of airing at 7:00 P.M. on the West Coast (which would be necessary for a live national program at 10:00 EST) seemed less than appealing to advertisers. To reach a compromise, the producers decided to perform the live show twice, once for the East Coast and again three hours later for West Coast viewers. This meant that most of the country (East and West Coasts) could watch the program live in its normal time slot while viewers elsewhere were offered one of the two versions live at a "special" time.

Journalists and viewers around the world anticipated the program and treated it as a special event. Following the episode, news programs on the West Coast presented lead stories comparing the two live broadcasts, and journalists related the event to the Golden Age of television. Lost in the hyperbole and debate was the recognition, by both NBC and television viewers, that "live" meant broadcast at the time it was taped. While creating the impression of liveness has been elevated to an art form by the networks on talk shows, nightly news, and other programs that are either taped live or contain live segments, at this moment the NBC acknowledged the simplicity of the term. The idea of presenting the episode "live on tape" was not an option since the networks had promised a "live" broadcast, and they recognize that taped is not "live." The issue of live broadcasting would be much simpler if networks had a solution for the varied time zones in which viewers watch their programs. While NBC's solution was to perform the program twice, ABC (perhaps benefiting from its years of experience with *Monday Night Football*) later solved the problem another way on New Year's Eve 1997.

I first became aware of the challenge that New Year's presented to broadcasters when Vivian Sobchack posed the question "Where does New Year's occur?" Since the passage from one year to the next is a strictly temporal event—by definition a marking of the passage of time—the question of locating its occurrence in spatial terms was both interesting and provocative. In the case of New Year's Eve, we have become accustomed—especially those of us who have lived in New York—to recognizing the dropping of the ball (now an apple) in Times Square as the icon of time's passage into a new year. Indeed, much of the country watches as Dick Clark annually broadcasts this celebration from New York. But most of the country is in a different time zone from New York, which raises the question: If New Year's is iconically linked to the dropping of the ball/apple in Times Square, does the New Year occur at 9:00 P.M. in Los Angeles (when the apple is actually dropping in New York), or at midnight (when the year actually ends in Los Angeles)? How can a temporally fragmented nation collectively celebrate the accomplishments of the past year and the promise of a new year when the moment that marks this passage occurs three hours earlier on one coast than it does on the other? Perhaps more importantly, how can a network cash in on the commercial potential of this moment and present a program that appeals to viewers on each coast as well as everyone in between?

The answer to these questions eluded me for some time, but was apparently overcome by ABC on New Year's Eve 1997 when the network seized the moment, solved the problem, and presented a grand New Year's celebration thanks to the brilliant creation of a new unifying time zone: "ABC time"! While all the networks—in their various, supposedly live programs—have found a multitude of techniques for feigning liveness, this creation of a virtual time zone was by far the simplest and most direct technique I have witnessed. On New Year's Eve 1997, while Dick Clark and hundreds of thousands of New Yorkers awaited the dropping of the apple, their celebration was linked through the *Dick Clark's Rockin' New Year's Eve* program to New Year's celebrations in Las Vegas and Anaheim (Disneyland). These geographically separated locations, representing three distinct time zones, were not only connected spatially through editing within the program, they were also temporally united as each location appeared with a single temporal marker ("Live 11:59 ABC Time"). Thanks to the miracle of "ABC time," viewers in Los Angeles, New York, and Las Vegas

—and by extension the entire nation—were finally able to share our passage to a New Year "live" on ABC.

In the case of both *Monday Night Football* and *Dick Clark's Rockin' New Year's Eve,* viewers were offered programs that were presented as—and appeared to be—live events. In both cases, however, these "live" programs were broadcast by my local affiliate from tape. Furthermore, despite the delays in their broadcast, many scholars would still consider these programs as examples of "live" television. While it is true that the exact same *Monday Night Football* game is presented to most of the country live, and New Yorkers undoubtedly watched the ball/apple drop in Times Square as the clock struck midnight on the East Coast, it is unlikely that these can be considered live programs when they are viewed via tape in other locations! What these examples demonstrate is the complexity and the variety of programs subsumed under the general heading of "live TV."

Defining Liveness

From its origins as a broadcast medium, television has always played upon its potential for live broadcasting. In fact, many of the significant events of the past decades are remembered primarily through their live representation on TV.[3] From technical achievements like walking on the moon to the civil upheaval in Los Angeles, and from spectacular sporting events such as the Super Bowl to cultural institutions such as the nightly news, live broadcasting has been, and continues to be, the mode of television used by many of the most talked about, written about, and watched programs. It is possible that no other mode of broadcasting has greater impact on viewers, on society, or on history, than live TV.

What I hope to demonstrate in the pages to follow is that the quantity and the variety of live television in broadcast programming today requires a more thorough investigation. "Live television" must first of all be viewed as a mode of broadcasting rather than as a genre of television. When we consider live TV primarily as a mode, we recognize that its defining characteristic is that it is broadcast at the time it occurs. In fact, the *Oxford English Dictionary* defines "live" as "a performance, heard or watched at the time of its occurrence, as distinguished from one recorded on film, tape, etc."[4] Thus the temporal axis is pivotal in identifying and distinguishing between the different forms of live broadcasting. My intention here will be to describe the various modes of live television, to examine viewer attraction to each specific form, and to explore the manner in which each category of liveness functions to promote or restrict public opinion and public action. In this sense I am interested in distinguishing how forms of live broadcasting relate to what Jürgen Habermas has defined as "the public sphere." To that end, I will distinguish between four dominant modes of "live" texts—"(re)presentations," "ceremonies," "unstructured events," and "unscripted events"—and analyze the manner in which their distinct formal properties enhance varied modes of narrative engagement.[5] Of primary concern here is the role of live television; its range of relations to viewers; and the possibilities for participation, dialogue, or interaction. Through this I will demonstrate that, while these categories share—to varying degrees—the element of "liveness," there is a dramatic range of viewer-text relations invited by these connected, yet ideologically contradictory, discourses.

In order to assess television's impact, the theoretical foundation of the formal variations within relevant modes of live broadcasting must first be discussed. Only with a more complete formal analysis can we begin to theorize viewer attraction to the varied forms of live broadcasting as well as the impact each form exerts upon the spectator. The key to my formal analysis is the categorical differentiation between live broadcasts, which is based primarily upon temporality, but also includes considerations of the organization of space between the event and its representation and the form of narrative used in its representation. Categories of live television will therefore be analyzed focusing on the layering of spatial/temporal or visual/verbal components. These components can be seen as constituting the spectrum of possible forms of live broadcasting. They include, for example, the type and prominence of live versus taped segments within the broadcast; the use of language to signal liveness or generate a sense of immediacy; and the spatial organization, or layering, of locations—including the positioning of the interlocutors (announcers) within those possible spaces. By analyzing live television along these axes, I will demonstrate the manner in which each of these formal variations suggests differing spectatorial positions in relation to the events represented within the broadcast.

Categorical analysis will provide a great deal of insight into the range of formal presentations used in live broadcasting, but this is only useful insofar as it lays the groundwork for theorizing television's potential for engaging viewers with both the subject of a broadcast and each other.[6] Once the properties of particular televisual modes are defined, it will be necessary to examine them thoroughly in an effort to understand the specific qualities attributable to that form. As was the case in my earlier work on televised sporting events, these qualities will be examined both in a cultural context and in relation to individual viewers.[7] My desire is to better understand the spectator's relation to each mode of broadcasting as well as to its particular narrative strategy. Once an individual mode is defined as a category and analyzed in terms of spectatorial engagement, it will be possible to consider how these elements function in relation to the public sphere.

Categories of Liveness

Live television encompasses a range of programs operating along what I see as a continuum of liveness. At one end of the spectrum is the completely live program that airs as the event is happening without recourse to taped or prepared material. On the other end of the liveness continuum would be a program that is almost entirely taped but contains a few moments of live address. In between these poles lies the majority of television we generally refer to as live. In order to better understand the differences between programs along this continuum I distinguish between four categories of live broadcasting: (re)presentation, ceremony, unstructured event, and unscripted event. The classification of live programs according to these categories acknowledges the variety of programs operating along the continuum of liveness and is intended to allow for the discussion of all live programming.

(Re)presentation

Programming that is characterized by the (re)presentation of stories or events, such as the news, can be located at one end of the continuum of liveness, closest to taped or recorded material.

Programs in this category expend great effort creating the *appearance of happening*; for example, by emphasizing the present tense of the enunciation that is—or appears to be—"live," instantaneous with the viewer's reception. In (re)presentations, the use of language helps to mask the multiple and carefully interwoven temporalities as well as the spatial separations, or layers, within the broadcasts. In reality, both space and time within the program are separated/layered between the site or time of the broadcast, the events depicted, and the program's reception. As Margaret Morse demonstrates, whether segments or entire news programs are taped or live, the effect of the broadcast is the production of a *present tense*.[8]

Unlike other modes of "live television," (re)presentation incorporates both live and taped segments in an effort to give the feeling of *happening* to events that we know have *already* happened. In the case of television news broadcasts, the anchors and reporters are generally presented live while the subjects of their reports are taped. Although the entire show is scripted and composed in order to present what Paul Weaver has called "a single unified interpretation of the day," the live presentation by the anchors—and their live interactions with other reporters—give an overall feeling of "liveness" to an already prepared broadcast.[9]

The net result is that we feel we are participating in the world by being informed of events in the "present"—and yet this participation remains symbolic. Live television (re)presentations actually distance viewers from the events themselves by presenting them as discrete moments that have occurred in the recent past rather than as ongoing and dynamic events *in the present—and presence—*of the audience. By positioning the viewer in relation to the broadcaster—and only through the broadcaster to the event—and by presenting the event after the fact as happened, the viewer is separated from the events and occurrences in the world. This temporal and spatial distancing serves to spare the viewer— in a physical, emotional, and psychological sense—from both *response and responsibility* in relation to the tragedies and atrocities that take place in our world.[10] This may relieve the viewer of the pressures and anxieties associated with responsibility, but it also works to discourage the impulse toward action or intervention.

Ceremony

The category that I have designated "ceremony" has been discussed in great detail by Daniel Dayan and Elihu Katz in their book *Media Events*.[11] Unlike the (re)presented events depicted within the news program, ceremonial events are generally broadcast instantaneously with their occurrence. Yet these "media events" can be distinguished from other live forms because the events themselves are highly scripted and structured; and their course and outcome are common knowledge to viewers, broadcasters, and participants alike. For example, in England the press documented every detail of Prince Charles and Princess Diana's wedding (including pictures of the wedding dress) prior to the event. Similarly, days before the inauguration of President Clinton in 1992, a complete minute-by-minute schedule was released to the press. In these and other ceremonies, the meaning is not located within its narrative outcome; rather, the purpose is to unite a group in various forms of celebration (Charles and Diana's wedding) or loss (JFK's funeral) that function to structure and reinforce a sense of community and identity. On a temporal axis, the ceremonial events such as those discussed by Dayan and Katz—coronations, inaugurations, weddings, and funerals—are relatively "more live" (more instantaneous, and "less mediated") than the (re)presentational broadcasts—such as the news—that have dominated most discussions of "live TV."

Dayan and Katz's categorization demonstrates the overlap and the interweaving of live categories, and their analysis of viewer participation opens up numerous avenues of interrogation. Of particular significance within this category are relations of power between event organizers (for example, the president and his staff), broadcasters (networks), and viewers. Traditionally, we have accepted that if the president wants publicity he merely calls a press conference; if the networks show a political leader making a dramatic speech we will accept that it as an important event and watch it as news. Dayan and Katz demonstrate that viewers and broadcasters are far more discriminating, and they point to several examples of national and international events that viewers choose to ignore as well as instances where the networks simply decided not to televise. This category of live broadcasting then offers an excellent example of the ongoing and dynamic power relations that inform each live broadcast. The viewer is not a passive receptacle waiting to accept anything the network puts on the air.

Unstructured Events

In contrast to the highly planned narratives of live ceremonies, the live broadcasting of unstructured events is characterized by an absence of planning in terms of the timing, contents, and the outcome of the events; a lack of narrative containment; and ongoing and/or relatively spontaneous coverage. Examples of this type of broadcasting range from the assassination of President Kennedy, to the explosion of the space shuttle *Challenger,* to O. J. Simpson fleeing police in his white Ford Bronco. In this type of "live" broadcasting, the rules are discovered in relation to the event itself as its coverage develops. In this sense, the unstructured event is a transitional form that inevitably develops into one of the more structured and contained narrative forms as the event itself progresses—becoming predictable and (re)presentable. As the examples above illustrate, this transformation may be to any of the other three categories: (re)presentation (the *Challenger,* O. J. Simpson, JFK), ceremony (the JFK funeral), or even unscripted events (the O. J. Simpson trial). Most often, however, the way in which "unstructured events" are mediated (by network news teams) eventually leads to their containment in the form of a (re)presentational broadcast. The narrative engagements of "unstructured events," and the degree to which their form suggests involvement on the part of the viewer, varies according to the individual narrative and its handling by the broadcasters.

On one hand, the unknown and undetermined outcome—as well as the live and ongoing broadcasting—of "unstructured events" resemble the televisual presentation of unscripted events that I will discuss below. On the other hand, the form of mediation typical of "unstructured events" places the broadcasters (commentators/presenters) in between the viewers and the events in a discursive style borrowed from the (re)presentational form of news programming. In some cases, such as the O. J. Simpson chase, the event is in a process of developing, and in these cases the viewers are positioned as onlookers along with the broadcasters. In other situations, such as the *Challenger* explosion or JFK's assassination, the event is complete, but the story is not yet containable. In these instances, announcers are spatially situated between the viewers and the event as they struggle to give form to an unstructured narrative. While the spatial arrangement may vary depending on the event, the temporality is always immediate. The immediacy of the broadcast provides an opportunity to involve the viewer in the process of making meaning or making sense of a story of "great importance." Rather than the digested and packaged stories usually presented on TV news or the structured and rehearsed events that constitute ceremonies, the form of unstructured events suggests an involved viewer who is trying, along with the broadcaster, to piece narrative fragments into a whole.

Unscripted Events

Despite the fact that critical attention has primarily been focused upon what I call "live televisual (re)presentations" (such as the news)—with some recent work focusing on mediated ceremonial events and the broadcasting of "unstructured events" (crises and catastrophes)—the form of live broadcasting that I call unscripted events is clearly the more popular form.[12] The unscripted events category is comprised primarily of popular or "low cultural" genres—including live talk shows and sporting events—as well as the live (ongoing and instantaneous) broadcast of political events such as the U.S. presidential debates. The primary criteria for including a live broadcast within this category are temporal *and* structural: the unscripted event is happening at the same time that it is broadcast and received, and its unfolding constitutes an unfinished and undetermined narrative within a known structure. Despite the potential diversity in the contents of unscripted events, these structural elements tend to engage the viewers in a particular relation to the mediators, to the events, and to each other.

The use of the *present tense*—not only of the enunciation but also of the event—allows for more fluid and reversible relations of power and knowledge than is the case when events are presented as *having* happened. In fact, the televising of unscripted events seems not only to allow for but to expect and encourage an active spectator, who is addressed as *participating along with others* in the completion of the unfinished narrative. Further, this *temporal present tense* may also evoke a sense of *spatial presence*—a feeling of proximity to an event—as opposed to the formally and discursively distant position that characterizes "live (re)presentations."

What is most significant for this analysis is this possibility that the program may encourage the audience's (inter)activity and participation in actual, historical events—while other forms of broadcasting tend to discourage both symbolic and real responses on the part of viewers. This can be readily demonstrated by considering, for example, the function of announcers during unscripted events. Broadcasters of live unscripted events may in some cases narrate what is happening before our eyes. However, they do not—as the mediator of (re)presentation must—describe discrete and already-determined narratives. Rather, as Ava Rose and I argued in our paper "TV Sports as Mas(s)culine Cult of Distraction," the role of the com-

mentators in presenting an unscripted event is pivotal in engaging potentially distracted viewers; and functions to provide a discursive model for the
spectator's reading of the event.[13] While sports commentators are clearly
ideal readers—having access to historical and contextual information, statistics, and so on—the unscripted nature of the sporting event and the
simultaneity of its broadcast tend to relativize the privileged position of the
commentators. Thus, like us, the broadcasters of the unscripted event are
responding to a story that is unfolding in the present. They are reading *with*
us rather than to us. In this way, their reading provides a discursive model
that is interactive and participatory rather than unidirectional.

What I hope to suggest is that the televising of unscripted events works
to draw spectators into a discursively mediated involvement with the text
and ultimately with the events themselves—as well as into an interpersonal
involvement with other viewers, who are understood as co-participants in
events that are happening. In other words, the broadcasting of unscripted
events has the potential to encourage participation, discussion, and the formation of opinions among members of a "real"—and not merely "fictive"
or symbolic—community.

There are several formal elements of the unscripted event that contribute
to the construction of this participatory space: the present tense of the
broadcast, the unique role of mediators in the presentation of the live
event, and the unscripted nature of the events themselves. Unlike the "live"
(re)presentations that characterize the news, in the broadcasting of
unscripted events, both the broadcast and the event *are* happening, and the
use of the present tense has a different relation to the events and to the viewers. It is significant that the unscripted event unfolds before our eyes and the
eyes of the broadcasters at the same time. It is not only the enunciation of
the commentators that is in the present tense in this case: there is a physical
simultaneity between the event's occurrence and its broadcast. This puts the
broadcasters in a relation to the event that is more like our own: their discursive mediation of the event becomes an interpretive narrative overlay
rather than a (re)presentation of a story that is already known to—and
shaped by—them.

Because unscripted events are unfolding in the present and before our
own eyes, the role of the broadcasters is not so much descriptive—as in the
case of (re)presentations—as it is interpretive. While it is a reporter's job to
tell a story that has recently happened, the commentators at a live event (a
football game, a political debate, or even some talk shows) also work to
illuminate and anticipate the action that is unfolding before us.

A perfect illustration of this type of narration can be found in the coverage of the North Hollywood bank robbery that occurred in the Los Angeles
area during November 1997. This was an "unstructured" rather than

"unscripted event" because it was unplanned, it interrupted regular programming, and the broadcast was completely live and in process as it was
viewed around the world. During the first half-hour of the coverage, the
visuals were provided through a news helicopter circling over the scene. The
announcer in the studio conversed with the helicopter pilot (or cameraman), describing and attempting to understand what was transpiring below.
At one point early in the broadcast, the two announcers described and discussed a man standing beside a vehicle outside the bank. They repeatedly
referred to him as a police officer and speculated about what he was
attempting to accomplish. As they described what was taking place, it
became clear to viewers that the man was not an officer but one of the bank
robbers outside of the building. In this instance, the confusion on the broadcast mirrored the confusion on the ground, and relations of power and
knowledge—between broadcaster/viewer—were somewhat neutralized. As
this example illustrates, the reporters in this mode of live broadcasting—as
is the case with unscripted events—reads and relates *with us* rather than *to
us.*

Narrative Engagement

This phenomenon of live events unfolding in the present and "before our
very eyes" may help to explain the sense of "being there" that so many
viewers and theorists have associated with live TV. The event that is unfolding in present time is also in our presence—on our television screens, in our
living rooms. At the same time, the address of the live commentators seems
to make a discursive place for us, to invite our presence as witnesses.

In his 1979 article "Television News and the Social Contract," Ian Connell notes that television news—or what I refer to as "live" (re)presenta-
tional programming—positions spectators as "onlookers" to a reality that
is "in and through this visual mode made to seem *out there.*"[14] Connell further suggests that through this positioning, viewers are addressed by the
text as "uninvolved."[15] "The exposition and interpretation of those cast as
involved falls to the narrators, newsreaders, or specialist correspondents."[16]
The implication in Connell's model is that, if these dominant practices were
subverted through the elimination of current representational conventions,
the relations between the viewer, broadcaster, and event would be significantly altered.[17]

These conventions are certainly at play in the distancing of viewers from
the events or stories covered, but in order to theorize an "involved viewer,"
we must also address the ways in which temporal displacements effect the
possibilities of "interactivity" or "involvement." While Connell is correct to
describe the television audience as "onlookers" in relation to televised news

events, it would be more accurate to think of the viewer as involved with the broadcast itself, rather than with the (re)presented processes or events that constitute the subject of its coverage. In this sense, Connell seems to echo Jürgen Habermas in suggesting that we are drawn into a relation with the text (the discourse of the news) as a substitute for the real. In his book *The Structural Transformation of the Public Sphere,* Habermas discusses the qualities of contemporary society that serve to curtail the emergence of a functional public sphere. Specifically, Habermas targets current media practices that he feels inhibit the reactions of their recipients in a unique way. "They draw the eyes and ears of the public under their spell but at the same time, by taking away its distance, place it under 'tutelage,' which is to say they deprive it of the opportunity to say something and to disagree."[18] Habermas argues that in today's society, individual organizations and political parties engage in public relations so as to validate their actions and improve their image rather than to encourage or engage the public in a rational critical debate involving the issues at hand. In this sense, Habermas, like Connell, sees organizations as parading *before* the public body in an attempt to accumulate and display prestige rather than *in* the public sphere where debate may take place.

According to Habermas, the only way the public sphere could be realized today is "on an altered basis, as a rational reorganization of social and political power under the mutual control of rival organizations committed to the public sphere in their internal structure as well as in their relations with the state and each other."[19] By this, Habermas means organizations that are committed in their structure to the maintenance of an environment conducive to rational critical debate among private citizens while at the same time being publicly open in regards to their financial interest and the motivations surrounding interactions with similar organizations.

The inability to speak or disagree may not be a response endemic to the medium but rather one that is invited by particular forms of broadcasting. This is not to suggest that our response is formally determined, but rather that, as a relationship, the form of broadcast will have some effect upon the co-constituted meaning and reaction to the program. No longer involved or implicated in the events that transpire throughout the world, viewers instead enter a relationship with and view under the "tutelage" of the broadcast and broadcasters themselves.

In this way, we are not only freed from response and responsibility in relation to world events, we are also, as Robert Stam has noted, allowed to sit back as "armchair imperialists" and consume history.[20] We watch from a seemingly omnipotent perspective without being required to act; we take pleasure in the knowledge we obtain and in our sense of ourselves as knowledgeable. We are allowed comfort in our distance from events, and at the same time we're offered membership within a community of viewers that Stam appropriately calls "the regime of the 'fictive We.'"[21] Thus part of our attraction to the news may, as Stam has suggested, derive from a sort of epistemophilia.[22]

By capitalizing on its capacity for "liveness"—and by *advertising* itself as the place where the news is happening—television creates a self-perpetuating relationship with the desiring subject. In this way, the "live" (re)presentation of television news can be thought of as both generating and satisfying the acquisitive desire for knowledge. However, there is a price to be paid for this acquisition. In exchange for the privilege of responsibility-free knowledge, the consumer of the news takes up a passive position in relation to world events. While there is comfort and symbolic power in our "armchair imperialism," there is at the same time a literal disempowerment. The news "stories" are presented as taking place in a symbolic, spatially displaced "out there," in relation to which the viewer at home becomes a passive observer, unable to affect—and without cause to discuss, learn more, and debate—events which seem to transpire in another realm.

Interactions and the Public Sphere

In our consumption of the news for entertainment, information becomes an object to possess, and the viewer is driven to be aware—and in possession—of the ever-developing and evolving news. The commodification of world events and their use as lures to promote the news broadcast increasingly positions the show itself, rather then the information presented, as the product consumed. News is no longer geared towards informing, as in providing a basis for rational critical debate, but instead it has become an end it itself. News in the form of (re)presentation presents itself as a complete package ready for consumption, and therefore it additionally suggests that it is capable of providing for all our information needs.

It is significant that the packaged (re)presentation that we consume as the new serves as a substitute for, rather then in addition to other news sources. The news in the form of (re)presentation does nothing to encourage the gathering of further information outside the viewing of the next news segment and instead presents its accounts as adequate and complete. This can be contrasted to the "unscripted event," which by virtue of its unknown resolution and temporal simultaneity seems to encourage the search and acquisition of extratextual information so as to prepare the viewer for the potential events. A political debate does not foreclose or discourage the gathering of information either before or after the event (especially if there is going to be another debate). The same is true with sports: before the event we read to prepare, and after the game we read to evaluate our interpretations and begin to get ready for the next event. This process extends the event and encourages extratextual preparation and testing both in the form of reading and discussion.

In order to theorize the range of relations of power and knowledge that are involved in the witnessing of—and response to—televised unscripted events, we must examine the ways in which these broadcasts engage viewers. If we consider the broadcasts as narratives, it is clear that we are drawn to watch unscripted events—and take pleasure in witnessing them—precisely because of their unscriptedness. It is because the events are open ended and unfolding in real time that we are able to engage in a discourse of *anticipation* and *prediction* along with the broadcasters and other spectators, and it may be our ability to participate in the completion of these unwritten narratives that generates our primary attraction to this form. Furthermore, the unknown and unscripted outcome of the event has an equalizing effect on the relations of power and knowledge between witnesses.

While other theorizations of "liveness" have suggested that our attraction to the broadcasting of these events involves a desire to witness history in the making, I am suggesting that this witnessing also involves a kind of narrative in the making: we take pleasure in our own act of "reading" these events as they unfold, testing our knowledge by guessing the progression of events, and in some cases—such as elections—testing our ability to affect the outcomes.[23] In this way, the broadcasting of "unscripted events" allows us to test and sharpen our skills: our knowledge of world events, our intuition, and our ability to analyze, evaluate, and predict the events that are taking place in our world.

This narrative pleasure, then, cannot be understood as strictly symbolic: our viewing of unscripted events on television reflects and informs our real-life decision-making processes, shapes our knowledge of the world in which we live, and affects the ways in which we use that knowledge. Thus while the knowledge itself is an important commodity, acquiring and "possessing" information is not the only thing at stake in the viewing of mediated events. The formal properties of these televised events—their temporality, their narrative structures, and the different ways in which they are mediated—work to engage their audiences in a diverse range of relations of power, knowledge, and interaction.

Unlike the live (re)presentations of the news, the broadcast of an unscripted event presents itself to the viewer as an open text with difference at its foundation. In fact, the unscripted event on television can be seen as a celebration of differences in perspective, and the media's presentation of unscripted events unfolding in the present is a never-ending process of incorporating those different perspectives into a polyphonic metatext. The viewers are not merely offered a number of perspectives to choose from—

aligning themselves with one view of an event or another—the television spectators are themselves positioned as witnesses to the events, and the number of perspectives is potentially as great as the number of viewers. Multiple viewers can, for example, watch the same political debate and walk away with varied, even oppositional interpretations and valuations of what transpired. These interpretations then fuel discussion as well as preparation, on the part of viewers as well as participants, for future engagements. Perspective and interpretation are open, and the text not only invites but supports the inclusion of as many points of view as possible.

While existing analyses of "liveness" have attempted to account for our attraction to the live event, the significance of this form of broadcasting extends beyond the boundaries of television spectatorship. In addition to engaging viewers with specific texts, the presentation of live events on TV has the potential to engage the audience interactively with other spectators and in relation to the events themselves. Although unscripted events may comprise discrete texts (a single game, debate, or election), ultimately these narratives must be understood within the larger contexts and metanarratives of which they are a part. A game is always part of a season, the history of a given sport, the lives of its players, and so on. A political event is always part of a larger political process that is always unfolding. By positioning us as witnesses to particular events, live television engages us in an ongoing relation to the unfolding of events that (ideally) extends beyond our television viewing. While live, unscripted events are only broadcast periodically, the discussion of the events, the gathering of information, and the responses and actions that the events provoke can extend indefinitely. In this sense, the televisual event can be seen as a site for social interaction, with extratextual discussions of the issues or events informing and being informed by the narrative interactions that take place at—and surrounding—the event.

Our witnessing of mediated events in the present cannot and should not substitute for real participation in the world. But "live television" can position us as participants in world events and contribute to our sense of "being there." Significantly, this is not so much an individual as a collective process. Individual viewers need not simply be engaged in the solitary acquisition of knowledge or the private pleasure of consumption but can be explicitly addressed as part of a "collective witnessing." Unlike the passive consumption that characterizes the "fictive we" of network news, this collective witnessing involves us in a collectively experienced process. This "we" is not simply a fiction: when we witness events that take place in our world and impact on our experience, when we discuss these events with others, when we interact with others and are moved to participate in world events, we actualize that discursive community that would otherwise remain fictive.

NOTES

1. By this I simply mean that the taped program could be identical in every respect to the live telecast received in other parts of the country, but that would not change the fact that it is taped.

2. This is an ongoing issue for *Monday Night Football,* which not only affects West Coast viewers by asking them to be home by 6:00 P.M., but also impacts East Coast viewers, who must watch past midnight to catch the end of the game. As part of their ongoing effort to maximize the number of viewers, ABC and the NFL announced that beginning with the 1998 season, they would move the starting time of their Monday night game to 8:30 P.M. EST. This change creates more hardship on the West by making the live start time 5:30 P.M. but might increase East Coast viewing. Ironically, the East and West Coasts represent the most extreme time frames, are the largest viewing audiences, and are the hardest to accommodate. Throughout the discussions and debates over broadcast and game time, one thing has remained clear: the game must be televised live (except in Portland, Ore.).

3. For example, President Kennedy's funeral, the *Challenger* explosion, the Gulf War.

4. *Oxford English Dictionary,* 2d ed., s.v. "live."

5. This understanding of the diverse practices that comprise "live television" is not intended as a formula for the neat and tidy dissection of live broadcasting. Rather, my analysis is intended to stress the complexity and multiplicity of the forms of live television programming and to suggest the varied degrees and types of involvement related to these forms.

6. At no time do I plan to argue for the content of a given broadcast but rather for the possibility of a form. For Habermas, the journals provide the raw data that fuels the public debate. According to Habermas, financial and political influences eventually compromised the journals and severely curtailed their ability to function as a catalyst for the public sphere. This is an important argument in relation to television, and I will address it primarily in relation to my discussion of ceremonies. Dayan and Katz have begun a discussion regarding the relations among viewer, event, and broadcast that I will continue in relation to the public sphere. For Habermas the key point is equality. There was never "objective" material, but with the production of varied points of view, these subjective writings were in fact aimed at fostering rational critical debate. The commercialization of media marks its decline in relation to the public sphere. According to Habermas, the separation of the market and the public sphere is no longer visible. I would argue that it never was. Instead I would like to focus on relations of power between participants and whether or not the form of engagement seeks to encourage debate.

7. Ava Rose and James Friedman, "TV Sports as Mas(s)culine Cult of Distraction," *Screen* (Spring 1994): 22–35.

8. Margaret Morse, "The Television News Personality and Credibility: Reflections on the News in Transition," in *Studies in Entertainment,* ed. Tania Modleski (Bloomington: Indiana University Press, 1986), 62–63.

9. Paul Weaver, "Newspaper News and Television News," in *Television as a*

Social Force: New Approaches to TV Criticism, ed. Douglas Carter and Richard Adler (New York: Praeger, 1975). 84–85.

10. This term is borrowed from Vivian Sobchack, "The Passion of the Material: Prolegomenon to a Phenomenology of Interobjectivity" (unpublished paper, 1992).

11. Daniel Dayan and Elihu Katz, *Media Events: The Live Broadcasting of History* (Cambridge, Mass.: Harvard University Press, 1992).

12. By this I mean that sporting events and presidential debates on television rank among the highest rated programs of all time. The number of talk shows currently on the air attests to the popularity of this format.

13. Rose and Friedman, "TV Sports," 12.

14. Ian Connell, "Television News and the Social Contract," in *Culture, Media, Language,* ed. Stuart Hall et al. (London: Hutchinson, 1980), 155.

15. Ibid.

16. Ibid.

17. By focusing their analysis on the formal properties of the broadcasts and the effects of these forms on viewers, these theorists seem to imply that a change in formal properties would result in a change in viewer-broadcast relations. While this seems sensible enough, most scholars (including Connell, Feuer, Morse, Rath, and Stam) have primarily considered those formal properties of "live television" that relate to the *spatial* distancing of viewers while ignoring their *temporal* displacement. It is my contention that both the temporal and spatial displacement must be accounted for in order to theorize a participatory spectator.

18. Jürgen Habermas, *The Structural Transformation of the Public Sphere,* trans. Thomas Burger (Cambridge, Mass.: MIT Press, 1989), 171.

19. Jürgen Habermas, "The Public Sphere: An Encyclopedia Article (1964)," *New German Critique,* 1, 3 (1974): 55.

20. Robert Stam, "Television News and Its Spectator," in *Regarding Television,* ed. E. Ann Kaplan (Los Angeles: American Film Institute, 1983), 25.

21. Ibid., 39.

22. Ibid., 23–24.

23. See, for example, Mimi White, "Television: A Narrative—A History," *Cultural Studies* (October 1989): 282–300; and Claus-Dieter Rath, "Live Television and Its Audiences: Challenges of Media Reality," in *Remote Control,* ed. Ellen Seiter et al. (London: Routledge, 1989).

Cyborgs in Cyberspace

White Pride, Pedophilic Pornography, and Donna Haraway's Manifesto

DANIEL BERNARDI

In the traditions of "Western" science and politics—the tradition of racist, male-dominant capitalism; the tradition of progress; the tradition of the appropriation of nature as resource for the productions of culture; the tradition of reproduction of the self from the reflections of the other—the relation between organism and machine has been a border war.
—Donna Haraway

This epigraph from Donna Haraway, a paradigm-breaking theorist, concerns the ontology of the cyborg, "a hybrid of machine and organism, a creature of social reality as well as a creature of fiction."[1] Introduced to critical theory in "A Cyborg Manifesto: Science, Technology, and Socialist-Feminism in the Late Twentieth Century," Haraway's cyborg is a metaphor that has evolved into a methodology for critical intervention into the lagging conditions of modernism (figure 1). Of utmost concern to this method are the trajectories of natural history, particularly the onset of Homo cyberneticus, as well as techno-authoritarianism, the persistence of gender and racial hierarchies, and the politics of critical theory. Foreshadowing the rise in popularity and power of cyberspace, or the graphic-rich space-time of communication networks and multimedia computers, Haraway's manifesto asks activist-minded scholars to reevaluate and resist structuralizing paradigms—Freud, Marx, and so forth—in their attempts to break apart conditions of social and semiotic authority.[2] Her cyborg is a poetic vision and socialist plan for action, a manifesto of the highest signifying order.

Like the targeting beam that hangs precariously over the eye of each drone in the Borg collective, those cyborgs in the *Star Trek* universe that aspire to assimilate all species into their techno-oneness, Haraway's human-machine hybrid sheds a little Orwellian light on the proverbial fork in Bill Gates's road ahead. On the one hand, technological progress can usher in a new social reality—one with considerably less oppression. Divorced from

Donna J. Haraway

Simians, Cyborgs, and Women
The Reinvention of Nature

FIGURE 1

the structures of modernism, Homo cyberneticus becomes a multicultural and transgendered species. On the other hand, technological progress can end up monopolizing ideology and, in the process, relegate the future to history. Married to the structures of modernism, Homo cyberneticus leads us toward an even greater dependence on capitalism, technology, and white patriarchy. It is this contestation of possibilities, the new world order of the new millennium, that Haraway is concerned with, and she advocates critical consciousness as the guiding light. As she writes in the forward to *The Cyborg Handbook,* published ten years after her original manifesto: "Whatever else it is, the cyborg point of view is always about communication, infection, gender, genre, species, intercourse, information, and semiology."[3]

Haraway's cyborg is a blaspheming metaphor and an ironic thesis that confronts the dangers of a technological age that is forcing humanity to either insulate its dualistic tendencies—and thus its alienating, misogynist, racist base—or break from them with revolutionary evolution. "Blasphemy protects one from the moral majority within," the theorist writes, "while still insisting on the need for community." Irony, she continues, is a "rhetorical strategy and a political method." Blasphemy and irony comprise the metarhetoric that contextualizes the quasi-fictional notion of the cyborg: "creatures simultaneously animal and machine, who populate worlds ambiguously natural and crafted."[4] Kicking the Terminators of the world where it hurts the most, her cyborg leads us toward a post-human world that is, by definition, post-gender, post-race, rich in abstraction, fraught with socialistic aspirations.

A number of years and the theatrics of Y2K have passed since the publication of "A Cyborg Manifesto." Given this history, we might rightly ask: to what extent is the metaphor of the cyborg applicable to the social and textual realities that it critiqued and prophesized? Has the social reality of old given way to the more egalitarian world inspired by Haraway's manifesto? More modestly, is the metaphor of the cyborg still a useful method for activist-minded theorists in the early twenty-first century? These are reasonable questions to ask of a contemporary theory of praxis that relies as much on the past as it does the future.

Theorizing, Storytelling, and Morphing Identities

At the heart of Haraway's project is a challenge to the paradigms that comprise modern critical theory, mainly Freudian psychoanalysis and classic Marxism. For those of us who are theorists or use theory in our work, these structuralist approaches are out—turned inside out rather than on their heads. In today's cybernetically enhanced environment, principles of psychosexual individuality and advance capitalism are no longer able to fully describe, explain, or politicize the ongoing system of technological intradependence or the mutability of postmodern identity. Dependent on notions of original unity that, from the bottom up, automatically lead to either psychical repression or class alienation, psychoanalysis and Marxism become reductive and essentializing worldviews. Left out of their equations is human diversity. Haraway's evidence for the gaping lack in these preordained structures consists of women of color—living cyborgs that have been relegated to the periphery by Freud, Marx, and most of their disciples.[5] These cyborgs, she recognizes, "are the preferred labour force for the science-based industries, the real women for whom the worldwide sexual market, labour market, and politics of reproduction kaleidoscope into daily life."[6] The fathers, sons, and daughters of critical theory, irrespective of their hard-fought interests in psychical catharsis and class solidarity, end up fixing these colored Others in singular positions. In doing so, they ironically and almost hypocritically erect their own version of the haves and have-nots. To compensate for this paradigmatic dilemma, Haraway offers us a form of poststructuralism that critiques the beginning and end game of master narratives in an attempt to open the door to profound diversity.

Another key aspect of Haraway's theory is the incorporation of creative sensibilities into the mix of critical consciousness. Art and literature provide clues for critical theorists searching for ways out of codified criticism. Haraway's case study is science fiction (SF), a genre of literature and popular media that consistently engages issues of identity, domination, resistance, and society. SF chronotopes like aliens and time travel ask readers to revisit the disunity of difference and the plight of history in order to better understand the trajectory of the present. In this way, SF is art in the form of literature—and much of its work sees the colorful universe that is before us and aspires to rush toward it with open but skeptical arms. Haraway cites the work of Octavia Butler, but this trend is perhaps best illustrated by the father of cyberpunk, William Gibson. In *Neuromancer* (1986), a text now canonized in new media studies, Gibson introduces the world to the notion of cyberspace, a virtual reality that is facilitated by microchips and computer networks.[7] Bleeding into and back out of physical reality like a wave of electricity, Gibson's space-time is dystopic replete with urban decay and corporate rule. As both SF fans and political activists will attest, it also turns out to be strikingly prophetic.

Following Haraway, techno-theorists and social critics such as Allucquere Rosanne Stone and Sherry Turkle have proffered imaginative arguments about the multiplicity of identity and the morphing realities of cyborgs and cyberspace.[8] These theorists have shown us that, in the age of cyberspace, we have the ability to recreate our identities—with those creations producing as much meaning as the identity that is forced upon us in the "physical" world. I, for example, can go into a MUD or a chat room and construct an identity that is simultaneously female, lesbian, rich, and Native American. I can also be an animal or an alien or an animal/alien hybrid. Morphing identities like these are the apparent norm in our cybernetic world, a norm that is more than accepted, applauded, and encouraged to shift, differentiate, and ignore when appropriate. Somewhat like *The X-Files,* Stone and Turkle show us that the truth is not here but out there.

Clues that Homo cyberneticus is at our evolutionary doorstep are everywhere. Contemporary cyborgs range from grandparents with pacemakers to parents with transplanted animal organs to children who cannot leave the house without their cell phones and Palm Pilots. These are wired cyborgs as *Wired* tells us every month. Still others among us assume the embodied identity of the cyborg for artistic and political reasons. One of the more interesting examples is a French performance artist, Orlan, who has had numerous cosmetic operations in an effort to mold her phenotype into the man-made images of Venus, Mona Lisa, and other historic (and alien) models of beauty (figure 2). Embodying radical feminism, Orlan's goal seems to be a de(re)construction of the "female" subject in the new millennium. As the artist is quoted on one Web page: "Through my performances, I want to address the status of the body in our society and in future generations, since we must prepare ourselves to genetic engineering."[9]

FIGURE 2

To be sure, Haraway's metaphor is more socially applicable than medical, technophilic, and performing artist cyborgs might suggest. As I noted earlier, women of color are the political referent in the cyborg code, simultaneously signifying oppression and hope. They live the experience of fractured, binary identities. When seen in relation to white women, for example, these women are *all* color. Their feminine identity is neglected as they do not quite meet the standard of the pale paragon. When seen in relation to men of color, they are all woman. Their racial identity is neglected by the patriarchy of colorful men and nations. For Haraway, women of color are between and betwixt the dominant identities that fathered and mothered them. This is why they are the epistemological essence of the cyborg, revealing the possibilities of the future while simultaneously acknowledging the fractional, binary pressures of patriarchy, racism, and white feminism.

Yet, how free of dualism and its remnants can cyborgs of color be if their birthplace is the structures, strictures, and stratagems of modernism? After all, the idea for cybernetic organisms emerged in the 1960s when NASA scientists Manfred Clynes and Nathan Kline suggested that altering the human body with machines would be an advantage for space travel. It was these scientists who coined the term *cyborg,* and their goal was to support NASA's mission to colonize outer space. Moreover, the idea for the Internet was an outgrowth of the United States' Cold War budget battle with Evil Empire. The goal was to facilitate efficient and immediate communication between scientists and the military working on various government grants and projects. The Internet has since evolved into a mass medium known as cyberspace, a space-time that includes, as I will show later, violent sparks of white pride and an inferno of racialized and pedophilic pornography. And then there's GPS, or global positioning satellites. They direct not only our entertainment and personal information networks but also the "smart" bombs—the Tomahawk cruise missiles—that have hit Iraq, Afghanistan, Sudan, Eastern Europe, and at least one Chinese embassy.

Haraway's response to the question of origin is strikingly naïve and implicitly binary. It amounts to this: how many of us completely—obligingly—follow in Dad's footsteps? She writes, "Illegitimate offspring are often exceedingly unfaithful to their origins. Their fathers, after all, are inessential."[10] The paternal aspect of our gender system is key here, for it is the metaphor of the "father," or the social reality of patriarchy and all that it signifies, that becomes the locus of rejection. White feminism is also out but only the part that mirrors the racism of patriarchy. In the spirit of Mother Nature, socialist feminism provides us with the eggs we need to evolve beyond the current dystopian, color-lined order of things. Forget that, like a hive of killer bees, a queen controls *Star Trek*'s Borg collective (figure 3); we should reject Dad in the hope of becoming multicolored, transgendered, maternal cyborgs.

At the risk of appearing structuralist, I would argue that Gramscian hegemony—the stuff of history, culture, ideology, and the machinations of public intellectuals—is alive and kicking hard in contemporary cyberspace and cyborgs. The stuff of Hollywood films and television, not to mention the more disturbing texts of the pornography industry, are claming cyberspace as their own and bringing with them a history that still requires rigorous critical confrontation despite new paradigms. Indeed, what I want to do in the rest of this paper is politely, if only momentarily, turn Haraway inside out. For while I agree with the spirit of her manifesto—that we should let go of our dualistic tendencies as we walk up the mountain toward the Promised Land—I fear that, despite multiculturalism and new feminism, postmodernism, and poststructuralism, there is a growing number of us not making the journey. This is imminently clear when one considers cyborgs in cyberspace—particularly the expanding number of hateful and pornographic hybrids that, when actually analyzed, perpetuate all-too-familiar discourses, tropes, and stereotypes. What lies around and before us in cyberspace is a whitewashed consciousness speckled everywhere with bestial/exotic/childlike colors. While critiquing the past and the present, Haraway's theory runs the risk of bypassing this omniscient future.

White Pride in Real Time

It took about fifteen years, from 1969 to the mid-1980s, for the Internet to develop from a cumbersome communication platform for the scientific and military communities into a reliable post office for academic and corporate Netizens.[11] It took another ten years or so for this electronic post office to develop into the World Wide Web, a graphic and interactive network. As AOL's recent acquisition of Time-Warner suggests, today the Web is fast becoming an entertainment medium for the masses. And its popularity is

FIGURE 3

rising even if at the moment the NASDAQ is falling. Netizens can access Web entertainment from the office, home, car, cell phone, and handheld electronics. If the chip and manufacturing sectors have their way, let alone the corporate sponsors of "Bluetooth" technology, we will soon be able to surf cyberspace and engage stories from everyday appliances like the toaster and refrigerator.[12] The Web is ubiquitous.

In many ways, the network nature and ubiquity of the Web undermines the monopolistic plans of media conglomerates like AOL and Time-Warner. Even current market forces that seek to dominate Internet portals are fighting an uphill battle. This is partly due to the relatively inexpensive costs associated with both accessing the Web and serving up programming. While there are certainly communities that have been bypassed by Al Gore's information superhighway, the on-ramps and vehicles are not nearly as narrow or expensive as they are on the road to film and television production. All that is required is a Internet service provider (ISP), which are abundant, a multimedia computer, and a marketing strategy. You don't need expensive cameras, large production crews, celluloid, or megawatt transponders. Unlike public television, cyberspace is by the people for the people. It is, as technophiles like to point out, the most democratic form of mass communication in human history. But democracy, like polysemic television and postmodern "identity," doesn't always lead to emancipation and critical consciousness. Hate is democratic.

The federal government has paid attention to the mass power of cyberspace. Recent legislative activity has sought to develop laws and regulations to control and limit Web programming. Most of these efforts, including the Communications Decency Act (CDA), were directed at indecency, obscenity, and child pornography (which I will address later).[13] The question of on-line hate speech—speech that is patently racist, misogynist, anti-Semitic, or homophobic—is a more difficult discourse to regulate for several reasons, including determining the responsible party. As Roger Eatwell explains, it is legally unclear if the "publishers" of on-line hate, the Internet service providers, are "like a telephone line company, who is not legally responsible for what is said, or more like a publisher, who is."[14] Moreover, the Supreme Court protected hate speech in the last millennium, consistently ruling that the government in rare and exceptional circumstances can only limit it. As Eatwell continues, "Even the apparently inflammatory claim that the United States was run by ZOG [Zionist Occupied Government]" is protected, whereas a call to attack "a specific prominent Jew would fall foul of other laws."[15] The court's rationale is straightforward: citizens have the right, however offensive to the majority, to articulate hate outside the confines of violent threats to specific individuals.[16]

Cyberspace presents those of us who fear censorship more than the ugliness of hate speech with a mandate for critical study and intervention. It is on the Web that the articulators of hate find additional, global opportunities to both spread their words and recruit the young. As Don Black, one of the more notorious leaders of the white pride movement, has acknowledged, "The benefit is that we reach tens of thousands of people, potentially millions . . . It's almost like having a TV Network."[17] Or as the Simon Wiesenthal Center has reported, "In all these cases, the rhetoric and visuals [of on-line hate] are not new. What is new is the opportunity to cheaply, effectively and directly market hate to a coveted audience—the young, who are the heaviest users of cyberspace."[18]

Cyberspace is fast becoming an artery for fascists and hate mongers wishing to expand their network. While it is difficult to determine the exact number of hate sites or measure the social effects of their content—the Wiesenthal Center now tracks thousands of sites that they consider "extremist"—it is clear that there are many such sites and that the consequences are anything but virtual. Kim Wimpsett, who looked into the various cases of terrorism in the United States, including the Littleton, Colorado, high school massacre, notes, "Federal agents investigating at least 30 bombings and 4 attempted bombings between 1985 and June 1986 recovered bomb-making literature that the suspects had obtained from the Internet."[19]

Alarmist concerns notwithstanding, I am not sure that on-line hate is all that new to mass media. For example, the film and television industry has consistently engaged in hate speech, albeit under bright white lights and Hollywood realism. Relying on scholars from numerous disciplines, I have argued as much in my work on U.S. cinema and science fiction.[20] From *Chinese Laundry Scene* (1896) to *The Birth of Nation* (1915), *The Jazz Singer* (1927), *Gone With the Wind* (1939), *The Searchers* (1956), and the *Star Wars* series (1977, 1980, 1983, 1999), Hollywood, including its "classics," has perpetuated white ideals at the degrading, often-violent expense of colored Others. And this dirty little secret has definitely made its way into cyberspace as is demonstrated by the *Mr. Wong* ifilm (Internet film) series created by Pam Brady and Kyle McCulloch and featured on *Icebox.com*.[21] In the ongoing series, Mr. Wong comes across as a caricature reminiscent of the Oriental butler Mr. Yunioshi (Mickey Rooney) in *Breakfast at Tiffany's* (1961) (figure 4). Like Mr. Yunioshi, Mr. Wong is a condensed Oriental male, a hybrid of stereotypes, feminized in the traditions of Orientalism. He comes replete with buckteeth, a "choppy" accent, and a buffoonish nature. The fact that *Mr. Wong* is marketed as a postmodern parody does not make its racial characteristics any more palpable as he is part of a long history of Orientalism that has rationalized such practices as a joke.

What is remarkable is that the design and marketing characteristics of on-line racism seem as thoughtful, albeit nascent, as the stylistic innovations ushered in by Griffith. Indeed, while more rigorous critical work is required, the following cursory review of on-line hate reveals a level of sophistication and organization reminiscent of the "Joe Camel" ads that led the way to an increase in the number of young smokers. Stormfront.org, for example, provides a useful if unremarkable case study.[22] Taking up space since the birth of the Web, this site of white pride takes full advantage of basic interface design techniques and networking strategies to achieve its less-than-emancipatory goals. The site's Web master, Don Black, has become a sort of star, having been interviewed by the likes of *Nightline* and the BBC (which Black makes available on his site). Stormfront provides its viewers with a sampling of current news stories, an archive of past stories, a general store stocked with Ku Klux Klan (KKK) and neo-Nazi literature and music, among other commodities, and a place to chat with like-minded whites. It also provides enough on-line pride (fear) to make its worldwide aspirations meaningful and socially significant and thus worthy of sustained critical intervention.

When you bring up the Stormfront site, the first item to appear is the group's coat of arms: a Celtic Cross surrounded by a poetic manifesto,

FIGURE 4

"white pride, world wide." The Celtic Cross suggests that the designers of Stormfront have a sense of history and a global objective (figure 5). As Eatwell explains, "The Celtic Cross logo serves as a signal—for those familiar with neo-fascist iconography—that this is not simply an American 'nativist' site, concerned largely with American issues. The Cross was the emblem of the French Charlemagne Waffen-SS division and has frequently been used by European neo-fascist groups."[23] On the opening page, Stormfront refrains from articulating blatant hate or calling for outright violence. Like the cleverest forms of propaganda, the site camouflages its ideology with palpable code words programmed in saturated colors and gothic fonts. We see, for example, "Stormfront.org" centered just above the Celtic Cross and "White nationalist resource page" centered just below it. The symmetry, bright red colors of the text against the gray background, and simple but slick lingo reveal an understanding of the very basic principles of two-dimensional design. The site also reveals a sophisticated knowledge of how to market hate to a curious but unaffiliated network. In other words, the designers are adept at attracting Netizens who might be otherwise put off by overt racism and calls for violence. This is a site of pride not prejudice.

For those wishing an explicit understanding of Stormfront's goal, below the Celtic Cross, framed in black and lettered in white, is their mission statement:

> Stormfront is a resource for those courageous men and women fighting to preserve their White Western culture, ideals and freedom of speech and association—a forum for planning strategies and forming political and social groups to ensure victory.

There is only a subtle hint of violence, "fighting to preserve," and no mention of the enemy, people of color. Instead, we read about a struggle for unity that identifies ground zero as culture, speech, and free association. With a hint of political irony, this blasphemous embrace of the First Amendment beckons white surfers to join a community of likeminded folks in pur-

FIGURE 5

suit of a noble cause. Albeit motivated by less than the egalitarian goals of
either Marx or Haraway, this is a manifesto that is also about signification,
synthesis, and community—of symmetrical design, rhythmic rhetoric, calls
for solidarity, and a promise of victory in the future. Adolf Hitler, the failed
artist turned successful tyrant, would have been proud.

To the right of the Celtic Cross is a stable navigation array. It remains
stationary when you scroll down the page to see what lies beneath the mission statement. In this array, Stormfront takes full advantage of the network
characteristics and community-building potential of the Web. We see a link
to "Chat/Discuss," which takes you to a page facilitating white pride discussions in real time. We also see links that allow surfers to "Subscribe to
Maillists," to search for "Upcoming Events," and to find out about "Web
hosting Info" in case visitors wish to build their own white pride site. We
also see the first reference to hate: "What is racism?" Click the link and a
pop-up window replaces the Celtic Cross. In it, you can read about "The
'racist' double standard: how Whites are made to feel guilty and 'hateful'
for loving their own people and culture." This manifesto reads as a classic
doctrine of reverse discrimination reminiscent of new right and neoconserv-
ative projects from the 1980s and 1990s that sought to roll back bussing,
affirmative action, and other civil rights initiatives. As Michael Omi and
Howard Winant note, "The new right's use of 'code words' (non-racial
rhetoric used to disguise racial issues) was a classic example of rearticulation, geared to mobilize a mass base threatened by minority gains, but dis-
inclined to embrace overtly racist politics. Neoconservatism represented the
most sophisticated effort to rearticulate ideology."[24] In Stormfront's rearticulation of history, whites are the victims of racism—making their mission,
like that of Griffith's KKK, necessary and noble. Black's Web site is the
future written with lightning.

The Stormfront navigation array also provides users with the opportunity to join likeminded subcultures and thus serves as a recruiting tool tai-

lored to specific demographics. Like TV networks and advertisers, Black
targets specific identities. We see, for example, a "White Singles" page, a
"Women's Page" and a "Kids Page." The "White Singles" page maintains
the symbolic orthodoxy of a white god with a wink to eugenics and misce-
genation, offering an image of a beautiful butterfly suckling at a flower—
suggesting that whites dating whites is as natural as the birds and the bees,
the flowers and the trees (but not other forms of crossbreeding). Click on
the site for women and you see the following patriarchal admonishment in
bold font: "This is not a feminist page, but rather a page to celebrate and
honor white women." In looking at this page, I remembered the hundreds
of Griffith short films I watched at the Library of Congress that used lighting, cinematography, and narrative discourse to highlight white women as
paragons of beauty and purity—only to have them threatened by men in
blackface (or brown, red, yellow face) and subsequently saved by white
knights (often with white sheets on their heads).[25] To understand the history
behind Black's foregrounding of white women, one need only cut back to
the site's main page to review a carefully placed quote: "'Rape was an insur-
rectionary act. It delighted me that I was defying and trampling upon the
white man's law upon his system of values and that I was defiling his
women.' Eldridge Clever [sic], former Black Panther leader on why he raped
white women." Back on the "Woman's Page," toward the end of the scroll,
Stormfront offers a black-and-white picture, perhaps taken just before
World War II, of two women, one stern and the other playful, both dressed
formally, sitting on a blanket decorated with the swastika (figure 6). Like
white women in Griffith's *The Birth of a Nation,* Black's women, while
threatened by Others, will be saved by white knights in the service of a
white nation. This is the social realism of Black's fiction.

Like Hitler's youth, Don Black targets the underage demographic by
employing a child. Stormfront's "Kid's Page" is mastered by a little white
devil—Black's own son, Derek:

> Hello, welcome to my site, I can see by the fact that you have visited my page
> that you are interested in the subject of race. I will start by introducing myself,
> my name is Derek. I am eleven years old and I am the Webmaster of
> kids.stormfront.org. I used to be in public school, it is a shame how many
> white minds are wasted in that system. I am now in home school. I no longer
> get beat up by gangs of non-whites and I spend most of my day learning,
> instead of tutoring the slowest kids in my class. In addition to my school work,
> I am also learning pride in myself, my family and my people.
>   White people are taught in school to be ashamed of their heritage. Teachers
> cram as many politically correct ideas as they can, into your head in 180 days.
> All the great white accomplishments throughout history are diminished.
> Therefore, I think that now is the time that all of the white people across the

FIGURE 6

globe should rise above the lies and be proud of who we are. To take back our freedom and win for all to see our heritage in its greatest glory.

Spoken like a constructed cyborg, Derek has reconstructed his identity, with pride, through a concise articulation of history. He goes on to end his welcome message with the following plea: "If your thoughts towards me are as sick, and vile as some people, please keep them to yourself. After all, I am only eleven years old and I really do not need your hateful thoughts in my head." With touching irony, young Derek is aware of the hate that is out there. His father, however, seems unconcerned—willing to use his young son as bate to entice whites into supporting his perverse mission.

Stormfront embraces the marketing potential of the Web, complete with a banner ad for the "David Duke Online Report." With entrepreneurial sensibility, the site asks Netizens to "Help support Stormfront by ordering now! Flags, t-shirts, license plates, stickers, and Celtic jewelry also in stock, with many other items coming soon." There are links to a number of other sites that will also sell literature, flags, and music, among other white pride commodities. As I suggested earlier, Stormfront also encourages its Netizens to review coverage of its star, Don Black, on *Nightline,* the BBC, and *Rivera Live,* among other talk shows and in newspapers articles. In doing so, the site fosters the aura of legitimacy and gets its users to buy into the story of whiteness.

On-Line Pedophilic and Racialized Pornography

There is far more pornography in cyberspace than there is hate speech, although this division is problematic because a growing amount of pornography is explicitly misogynist and patently racist. The Web also serves up a disturbing amount of child and "teen" pornography, making it a mass medium that is also a tool for child abuse. Of course, not all pornography on the Web falls into these categories, and some texts that could be labeled as such also can be interpreted as remnants and actuators of an active, healthy imagination. Nonetheless, even a cursory analysis of on-line pornography, particularly texts that appeal to puerile and racial aesthetics and stories, evinces the point that children, gender, race, sex, and violence are intimately entangled in cyberculture.

According to Matt Rosoff, the number of pornographic sites ranges from 20,000 to 7 million.[26] Kim Wimpsett, quoting Nielson/NetRatings, offers a more meaningful statistic: "In January 2000 alone, 17.5 million surfers visited porn sites from their homes. To put it in perspective, the top adult site, PornCity.net, had more unique visitors than ESPN.com, CDNow, or barnesandnoble.com."[27] Pornographic texts are easily accessible from computer terminals with Internet connections, as even an innocent use of a Web search engine will bring up pornographic hits. For example, a search of the phrase "Black Women" I conducted on C/Net resulted in several sites, including *Ebony Teenies*, "The largest image collection of fucking young ebony bitches known to mankind."[28] A search of the word "Latinas" resulted in hits like *YoungLatina.com*, which offers "ultra hot pics of young Latina babes."[29] Finally, a search of the word "teens" resulted in such hits as: *The Original Amateurs Network, Teen Models* and *Cuteangels*.[30] Each link is programmed to attract search engine hits, and each link takes you to a site that includes graphic pictures and explicit language. As *Ebony and Interracial Paysites Reviewed* advertises for one of the sites it links to, "White teens blowing big black cocks and black women taking throbbing white cocks up their wet pussies." The aesthetics are unimaginatively denotative; interpretation is not required or necessary. Debased and banal, these dirty words can best be described as overdetermined. And, of course, that is the marketer's point.

Like the home video market, and thus both the VCR and commercial outlets that sell or rent X-rated videotapes, the growth of cyberspace was significantly inspired by pornographers and Netizens wishing to sell, trade, and experience X-rated works.[31] As Rosoff aptly points out, "If there is something successful and new happening on the Internet, there's probably somebody with an adult background heading it."[32] There are three factors that support this argument. First, the Web provides pornographers with a global market and thus a wider demographic of buyers. Much of this market is new to pornography, enabling the pornography industry to repackage its vast libraries into digital and distributed forms. Second, since the Web can be accessed from private spaces such as the home, and thus away from potential public embarrassment, it provides would-be spectators more anonymity than traditional outlets such as X-rated movie houses or video stores. Apparently, women are one of the fastest growing markets for on-line pornography. Correspondingly, traditional outlets such as X-rated movie houses are often in unsafe neighborhoods—particularly for women.[33] Finally, the Web and digital technologies make it much less expensive or cumbersome to produce and distribute pornography to national and global markets. The main reason for this is that these technologies are increasing less expensive to buy. As Frederick Lane summarizes, "As the costs of production and distribution have steadily fallen over the last 25 years, the financial attractiveness of the pornography business had steadily grown."[34]

The growth of on-line pornography has raised interesting legal and constitutional issues. Today, sexual material falls within three legal categories: socially valuable, indecent, and obscene. Socially valuable texts include nude or sexual tropes that are construed as neither indecent nor obscene, and thus are fully protected by the First Amendment. These texts might include Renaissance nude paintings or contemporary photographs of nude children taken by artists such as Jock Sturgis or Sally Mann. Indecent texts, on the other hand, are illegal in certain contexts or situations. Unlike art, the courts have generally ruled a text "indecent" if, in representing nudity, sexual activity, or "dirty words," it travels over public airways into private spaces at certain times of the day. These spaces, the argument goes, lack reasonable parental control.[35] A broadcast network such as ABC, NBC, or CBS runs the risk of government fines and civil lawsuits if it offers nudity or sexual activity in fiction works at certain hours of the television schedule. This is because they use the public airways in providing programming. It is legal, however, to broadcast the same text on cable television, which uses a commercial infrastructure and offers parents more options for control. Finally, obscene texts are illegal irrespective of the medium by which they are distributed. They are not protected by the Constitution. Depending on community standards, obscenity can range from bestiality to graphic heterosexual sex.

Justice John M. Harlan's famous remark, "One man's vulgarity is another's lyric," calls attention to the obvious problems in defining socially valuable, indecent, and obscene texts. This problem is exacerbated by on-line pornography. The current precedent for judging whether a text is legally obscene is the 1973 Supreme Court decision *Miller v. California*. In this decision, the court ruled that texts are "obscene" if they meet the following criteria:

(a) whether the average person, applying contemporary community standards would find the work, taken as a whole, appeals to the prurient interest; (b) whether the work depicts or describes, in patently offensive way, sexual conduct specifically defined by the applicable state law; and (c) whether the work, taken as a whole, lacks serious literary, artistic, political, or scientific value.[36]

The community standards test is the basis for much contemporary debate since the Web recognizes no borders—community or national. Indeed, a variety of technological advances have undermined the logic behind the Court's "community standards" criterion since X-rated texts can easily bypass a viewer's community by traveling over the phone lines, cable television, or the Internet. Conversely, it can be argued that because of its anarchistic, networked, and global structure, the Web encourages and facilitates absolute free speech.

Child pornography is illegal irrespective of community standards. Child pornography was defined in *New York v. Ferber*. The court's ruling is worth quoting at length:

> (a) The States are entitled to greater leeway in the regulation of pornographic depictions of children for the following reasons: (1) the legislative judgment that the use of children as subjects of pornographic materials is harmful to the physiological, emotional, and mental health of the child, easily passes muster under the First Amendment; (2) the standard of Miller v. California, 413 U.S. 15, for determining what is legally obscene is not a satisfactory solution to the child pornography problem; (3) the advertising and selling of child pornography provide an economic motive for and are thus an integral part of the production of such materials, an activity illegal throughout the Nation; (4) the value of permitting live performances and photographic reproductions of children engaged in lewd exhibitions is exceedingly modest, if not de minimis; and (5) recognizing and classifying child pornography as a category of material outside the First Amendment's protection is not incompatible with this Court's decisions dealing with what speech is unprotected. When a definable class of material, such as that covered by the New York statute, bears so heavily and pervasively on the welfare of children engaged in its production, the balance of competing interests is clearly struck, and it is permissible to consider these materials as without the First Amendment's protection.[37]

U.S. federal law also attempts to be explicit: "'child pornography' means any visual depiction, including any photograph, film, video, picture, or computer or computer-generated image or picture, whether made or produced by electronic, mechanical, or other means, of sexually explicit conduct."[38] Thus child pornography includes images of an actual child under the age of eighteen engaged in sexual conduct or that exhibits genitalia in a "lewd" fashion.[39]

The Web also throws most of these definitions and standards into crises. First, while indecent and obscene texts are restricted over public airways, children can easily access these works in cyberspace. Additionally, adults and children in any community in the United States, providing they are using a computer terminal without a filtering program such as CyberNanny, can view all forms of "obscene" texts—including child pornography.[40] Babes in cyberspace, represented or spectating, are subject to a profound degree of sexual violence. All Netizens young and old can be exposed to this material with a few clicks of the mouse. Web surfers who want to view pornography can use mainstream search engines and relatively innocuous search terms to find it; Netizens can also be exposed to it unintentionally thanks to push and click-through marketing techniques. Because of the anonymity of the Web, as well as the fact that that many problematic Internet service providers reside outside U.S. geographic borders, viewers can obtain forms of pornography that could not be legally sold in U.S. adult bookstores or theaters.

Peddlers of pedophilic texts have taken full advantage of the democratic structure of cyberspace and the availability of inexpensive recording and distributing technologies. As Anna Grant and her colleagues outline:

> The advent of personal videocameras and digital photography reduced the visibility of production, and the risk that illegal material might be called to the attention of law enforcement by commercial photo developers. Moreover, new digital technologies allow child pornography to be copied, stored, and transmitted quickly and unobtrusively, and with perfect accuracy. When posted in cyberspace, it is potentially available to anyone, anywhere in the world, who has access to a personal computer and a modem.[41]

In this new technological order, it is also exceedingly difficult to track and prosecute pedophiles and other cyber child abusers. As Grant et al. conclude, "The committed trafficker of child pornography who has not already exploited technologies of anonymity and privacy can seek refuge in more covert corners of cyberspace."[42]

Reflecting and refracting the waking world of capitalism, on-line child pornography fits within the much larger context of the exploitation of women and children for sex—particularly living cyborgs of color. As Phil Williams points out:

> The exploitation of children in the sex trade, however, goes well beyond their movement from one country to another, and includes other forms such as sex tourism in which the consumers visit countries such as Thailand or Sri Lanka where there is a permissive attitude toward sex with children. Rather than the children being brought to the consumer marker, the customers visit the markets that are promoted as part of the tourism industry. Another form of exploitation is the abuse of children for pornography, which is increasingly circulated among pedophiles using the Internet and the World Wide Web.[43]

The global dimension of colorized misogyny and child abuse is enhanced by new technologies like the Web. As Williams concludes: "The exploitation of women and children for pornography had become much easier and less costly with the capacity to reproduce and distribute digital images at very low cost."[44]

While child pornography is illegal, pornography that panders to puerile scopophelia is not necessarily illegal. There is an abundance of pornography that advertises children and teenagers as subjects of explicit and elicit fiction. A search of *Persiankitty.com*, a popular crossroads of pornographic Web pages, reveals the following: *Just Teens, Teen Steam, Slick Beaver, Baby Teen Pussy Galore*, as well as *Asian Heat, Dark Obsessions*, and *Latin Sex Party*.[45] Of the 529 links brought up on the day I searched, 103 (19.5 percent) were advertised as "teen" and 64 (12.1 percent) were marketed in some way as racial. If you entered any of the other 362 sites, you will likely be presented with a teen or racial option. Along with hard core, lesbian, and gay genres, among others, race and pedophilia are ways in which on-line pornography is marketed and narrativized.

Pornographers are also inventing creative but intrusive ways to "push" their texts out and onto Netizens, both the interested and the ignorant. Almost all of the amateur and all of the pay sites advertised on *Persiankitty* are programmed with banner ads and forced pop-up ads, often in separate browser windows, as well as basic design techniques directed at leading your eye through the page and to additional paid sites. Clicking on any of the advertised links takes you to additional banner ads and pop-up windows. In some sites, if you choose to exit, additional windows open and advertise increasingly "extreme" material such as "teens with animals." Even performing a controlled escape (simultaneously depressing the "ctrl," "alt," and "del" keys, normally used to unfreeze and close a stuck program) causes additional pornographic sites to reload and pop up. In case you made a mistake in leaving or want to come back for more later, one of these windows will offer you the opportunity to sign up to receive "The Hottest Hardcore Directly to Your E-Mail."

The *Teens2* site is fairly typical, offering explicit images of young women engaged in sexual activity.[46] All of the images, offered in collages or as thumbnails (small, quick-to-load versions linked to larger graphics), lead site visitors to scroll down the page, like a striptease, to see what lies beneath. At the bottom of the page there are additional banner ads and key words/links in deep blue: "Celebrity," "Teen," "Asian," "Gay," "Black," and "Fetish." Below this list of links is an ad where visitors can "Subscribe to Sexy Nineteen for FREE and Get Daily XXX Girls In Your E-mail!" Click on any of the key words, and up pops a separate window advertising "the Newest, Hottest Sites on the Net!! All for FREE!!" This window includes animations of young women engaging in explicit sex. The sex tour does not end here, however, as the original page links to yet another pay site for "Asian Pleasures." At each crossroad, users are asked to pay for services.

Web advertisers are adept at using children to sell products while seeming to maintain legal status. The designers of *lo-li-ta.com* offer static images of nude pubescent girls as if the site was for artists and its aficionados.[47] "You'll spend months watching it," a link advertises as it takes browsers to pay options. "Aren't they cute." "See thousands more," the site continues. Aware of the morphing boundaries of the Web, *lo-li-ta.com* also offers free thumbnails of pubescent "asians." Like blow-up dolls, a click on one of the thumbnails results in a life-size photo of a naked Asian child. Perhaps in an effort to protect itself from prosecution, the site includes a link to "legal info" that reads as follows:

> All art works presented on this site are legal according to US law. Our site opposed what is called child pornography and legally defined in Unties States Code Title 19 part 1 Chapter 100 Section 2256. The Government statute is provided as a link for the curious.
>
> Also, images displayed on this site can be purchased in bookstores all over the USA. Their authors—famous photo artists have made careers photographing adolescent females and males. Lo-li-ta.com is offering opportunity to see similarly similar art works at lower cost.

Included in this disclaimer is an actual link to the U.S. code that it references. Nonetheless, the drafters of the disclaimer are aware that most of their clients are uninterested in the artistic or legal merits of the site's offerings, concluding with a virtual wink and nod: "The question of the work's artistic value is left solely to the viewer." Although pretending to be about art, *lo-li-ta.com* self-reflexively acknowledges that a sizable share of its market is likely to be strictly interested in the pedophilic dimensions of their product. In this way, it functions similarly to the "must be 18 to enter" ads seen on most sites—as an enticement for young and old to enter. Like other pornographic sites, exiting *lo-li-ta.com* causes another pedophilic pay site to load, *Euro-lolitas.com*.[48]

Yet another apparently legal pedophilic site, *Lolita Land!!* uses the format of direct mail flyers for missing children to advertise its images and stories.[49] In one of these blasphemous ads, we see an African American girl sucking her finger, in black and white, with the caption: "Age 14, female, name, Katrina, 5'4", 103 lbs. Has habit of sticking things in mouth to suck." A second parody consists of a European American girl, presented in close-up with her mouth open, over the caption: "Age 15, female, name, Stacy, 5'5", 106 lbs. Will swallow anything!!" The pictures and captions are located under "MISSING" in bold and capital font, much like actual flyers and milk cartons. For the discreet, *Lolita Land!!* offers its users anonymity, claiming: "No one will know you joined Lolita Land! Your credit card will be billed by Lancelot!!" It also offers links to "14 and she swallows!!!" and to bestiality sites. Both links take you through an endless relay of pop-up windows, many with explicit images that are difficult to categorize as anything but legally obscene. In other sites like *Lolita Land!!* there is another advertising trend: a filmstrip consisting of one girl per frame, some clearly pubescent but not nude nor engaging in sex, and others "barely legal" and engaging in sex. In the tradition of associative montage, the "filmstrip" juxtaposes children and sex. This marketing of pedophilia has a clear goal: to entice the willing or unconscious Netizen to go further into the site to pay for its illicit services.

The sites themselves offer up a smorgasbord of explicit language and images, much of which is expressly violent. Not unlike Hollywood "R" rated films and their marketers, most child pornography sites use violence to sell subscriptions, hoping to attract paying Netizens with an array of brutal images in vivid color and motion. The following sites are among those that were downloaded into a new browser window after attempting to exit *Teens2*:

Fear & Torture
101% Rape, Bondage & Abuse
Youngest Schoolgirls Being Raped
Lolitas RAPED (13 y/o Lolitas Being Raped)
Forced Sex and Torture
Rape Mania
Rape Max
I.N.C.E.S.T..R.A.P.E.!.!.!
The Rape Site
Russian Cops Rape Teens in Prison
Brutally Raped Secretary
Lolitas Raped by Father-Real Incest
100% Free Extreme Rape
Monkeys Rape Young Girl

Thumbnails and banner ads of women with expressions of fear and pain accompany many of these links (figures 7–9). While these are advertisements designed to engage the Netizen's deepest fantasies, they are not just the expression of fantasy. They are electronic bits of textual practice that—articulated in bright colors and slick design, pushed on surfers though click-through strategies—require critical intervention, not least of which for the reason that they are available in a mass medium accessible in many offices and homes, to youth and adult alike.

FIGURES 7–9

When critiquing these pedophilic and misogynist texts, a striking feature is that much of it is racially bound and gagged. People of color, young and old, gay and straight, men and women are subject to torture in cyberspace. One site advertises Japanese school girls "abducted, abused!!! Raped and Tortured!!!"[50] In fact, on-line pornography includes many of the same old racist stereotypes found in Stormfront and the history of white supremacist media. Latinas are associated with animals and degraded as female dogs. *Dark Pussy* offers: "Links to the hottest Latin and Black women on the Net!"[51] At *Pure Bitch,* subtitled "sugar, spice and OHH so nice," a to-be-looked-at Latina is posed sitting, legs spread, with the chihuahua from the Taco Bell commercial in front of her crotch (figure 10). The graphic has been animated, so the dog shakes before our peering eyes as a dialogue bubble reads "yo quiero teen action?"[52] This ironic parody of the Taco Bell ad reveals not only the racism in on-line pornography but that on-line pornography takes advantage of the racism in traditional media to sell its texts—even if for a joke. This is a clear case of televisual reality seeping into cyberspace and extending its history of racism in explicit direction.

Black women and men are also constructed as dirty animals in need of taming. One site advertises: "Dirty black bitches humping white cock and

FIGURE 10

gulping gallons of cum!" The same site offers "Huge Black studs pumping horny white wives, amateurs and teens." In many cases, black women are featured enjoying rape—undoubtedly to maintain the viewer's perverse vision of slavery. There is a long history to this trope and its corresponding reality. As Patricia Hill Collins notes: "Pornography, prostitution, and rape as a specific tool of sexual violence have been key to the sexual politics of Black womanhood. Together they form three essential and interrelated components of the sex/gender hierarchy framing Black women's sexuality."[53] In cases of both gay and straight pornography, Black men are represented as out-of-control beasts. Not unlike a Robert Mapplethorp photo, though admittedly without the artistic merits, they are represented as having universally large penises. In many instances, graphic photos depict one or two black men, their penises in the foreground of the frame, violently penetrating either a white women or a white man. This is apparently what Don Black fears the most.

Asians are the largest group of women of color exploited in on-line pornography, a case that parallels the ways in which Asian women and children are treated in the sex-tour industry. Again, the stereotypes are all too common and frequently graphic, revealing a particular fascination with imagined Oriental phenotypes. Web works like these fetishize their "alien" body parts, as many thumbnails and collages focus on the subject's crotch (which is often shaved to further suggest childlike characteristics). Several have the woman or child contorted in such a way that you see both their eyes and their crotch. In most cases, the Asian females, teens and children, are represented as violated, submissive, but willing participants. They are also shown with expressions of fear and anguish on their faces. One site advertises: "See Horny Asian sluts taking huge cocks in all their tight little holes at once!" The same site continues, "Submissive Asian schoolgirls gulping cum for the first time!"[54] Adjacent to these advertisements are pictures of Asian women being penetrated from behind. In almost every case,

FIGURE 11

the designer makes sure that you see the woman's face—and thus her exotic Otherness. Another site, "Tied up Asian Girls," written in "chopstick" font to highlight the marketing of Orientalism, offers free pictures of young Japanese women in bondage (figure 11). The pictures, presented initially as thumbnails, surround a banner ad that reads: "Submissive Cum Suckers. Make Her Eat Your Load!"[55] Haraway's political referent is still being violated at light speed.

An Initial Conclusion

Cyberspace perpetuates the representational, discursive, and cultural exploitation of "cyborgs" of color. I am unconvinced, however, that censorship of on-line hate or pornography is the appropriate recourse to curb the exponential flow. For one thing, the prudish and puritanical dimensions of American society have arguably caused more social and psychical problems than either hate mongers or pornographers. Countless cultural historians have suggested that the latter thrives when the former stacks their side of the seesaw with the weight of the law. The stuff of cyberspace, including pornographic texts, facilitates adult fantasies, and all citizens have the right to fantasize in black and white. Besides, while it is exceedingly difficult to reconcile the positive dimensions of on-line pornography with pedophilic texts, it is difficult to imagine either the repercussions or the mechanism by which one might censor cyberspace given its ubiquity, anarchistic culture, and global dimensions.

Activist minded scholars must apply their tools, old or new, to a rigorous analysis of the expanding presence of hate and pornography in cyberspace if only because it is a mass medium ripe with social consequences. There is an unacceptable lack of critical intervention into the birth and growth of on-line racism and pornography despite the fact that these texts are clearly in line with the articulation of child abuse, misogyny, and whiteness in other media industries such as Hollywood. While there is nothing new to the content of hate and sex on the Web, cyberspace provides distinct design and aesthetic features, advanced marketing strategies, and global channels for inculcation. The prophets of white pride are skilled at building virtual communities and real networks, and pornographers are adept at forcing violent texts out and onto the physical world.

There are several reasons why critical and cultural studies scholars have yet to confront this emerging reality. One factor might be that cyberspace studies has yet to earn a place in most cultural studies and media departments in academia. I also suspect that far too many media scholars see the Web as merely a post office, a vehicle for e-mail and attachments, and thus not a mass medium capable of using aesthetics and storytelling techniques, let alone hypertext and interactivity, as tools of social realism. An additional critical factor stems from current critical methodologies, including branches of poststructuralism, that have overtheorized language, invested heavily in technotopia, underhistoricized polysemic texts, and concluded that identity is just an illusion. Polysemic texts, mutable identities, and "new" theory, like Hollywood realism and "old" theory, have failed to lead to a radical rearticulation. Homo cyberneticus is entrenched in a very old and powerful border war.

I would not put Haraway's work on the side of the enemy, as the theorist demonstrates a committed and passionate interest in challenging structuralizing ideologies and the many structural methodologies that have neglected the task. Her cyborgs manifesto opens the door to new forms of critical intervention. However, its tendency toward technotopia has resulted in the children of the method focusing on the emancipatory aspects of cyborgs and cyberspace rather than these other realities. Compounding the problem is the implicit binary between socialist feminism and white feminism, as well as between structuralism and poststructuralism, as neither politic or method has been successful in bringing about critical emancipation. This is obvious when one considers the racial dimensions of on-line hate and pornography. After all, Don Black and his son are cyborgs. So, too, are the numerous men, women, and children, white and colorful, embodied and disembodied in cyberworld. Constructed as human/machine/animal hybrids, they are creatures of fictions as well as creatures of social reality.

NOTES

1. Donna Haraway, *Simians, Cyborgs, and Women: The Re-invention of Nature* (London: Free Association, 1991), 149.

2. See also Donna Haraway, *Modest-Witness@Second-Millennium.Femaleman-Meets-Oncomouse: Feminism and Technoscience* (New York: Routledge, 1997).

3. Donna Haraway, "Cyborgs and Symbionts Living Together in the New World Order," in *The Cyborg Handbook,* ed. Chris Hables Gray, Steven Mentor, and Heidi Figueroa-Sarriera (New York: Routledge, 1995), xiv.

4. Haraway, *Simians, Cyborgs, and Women,* 149.

5. Haraway seems to be following bell hooks's lead in *Ain't I a Woman: Black Women and Feminism* (Boston: South End Press, 1981).

6. Haraway, *Simians, Cyborgs, and Women,* 174.

7. William Gibson, *Neuromancer* (West Bloomfield, Mich.: Phantasia Press, 1986).

8. See Allucquere Rosanne Stone, *The War of Desire and Technology at the Close of the Mechanical Age* (Cambridge, Mass.: MIT Press, 1995); and Sherry Turkle, *Life on the Screen: Identity in the Age of the Internet* (New York: Simon and Schuster, 1995).

9. http://www.caipirinha.com/Bodies/bodies.html

10. Haraway, *Simians, Cyborgs, and Women,* 151.

11. For a concise account of the development of the Internet, see Walt Howe, "A Brief History of the Internet," in *The Internet,* ed. Gray Young (New York: H. W. Wilson Company, 1998), 3–7.

12. Bluetooth refers to an effort by a consortium of technology companies, initiated by Ericsson, to create a wireless platform that will connect computers, cell phones, and handheld devices to each other and the Web. See http://www.bluetooth.com/.

13. While provisions of the CDA were overturned by the Supreme Court, the justices left standing the illegality of Internet obscenity, child pornography, and child predator provisions.

14. Roger Eatwell, "Surfing the Great White Wave: The Internet, Extremism, and the Problem of Control," *Patterns of Prejudice* 20, 1 (1996): 69.

15. Ibid., 68.

16. The alternative, of course, is the slippery slope of censorship, a discursive order that Orwell warned against in *1984* and that many scholars fear in 2001.

17. Don Black, quoted in "Poisoning the Web: Hatred Online," http//www.adl.org/frames/front_poisining.html (November 29, 2000).

18. Ibid.

19. Kim Wimpsett, "Net Vices: Sex, Violence, and Gambling," http://www.

cnet.com/techtrends/0-1544318-7-1956441.html?tag=st.sr.1544318.linksgp (May 31, 2000).

20. See Daniel Bernardi, ed., *The Birth of Whiteness: Race and the Emergence of U.S. Cinema* (New Brunswick, N.J.: Rutgers University Press, 1996), and Daniel Bernardi, ed., *Classic Hollywood/Classic Whiteness* (Minneapolis: University of Minnesota Press, 2001). Both collections contain bibliographies on the subject of race in popular culture, the latter compiled by Beretta Smith-Shomade.

21. http://icebox.com/index.asp (November 29, 2000).

22. http://www.stormfront.org/ (November 29, 2000).

23. Eatwell, "Surfing the Great White Wave."

24. Michael Omi and Howard Winant, *Racial Formation in the United States: From the 1960s to the 1990s,* 2d ed. (New York: Routledge, 1994), 118.

25. Daniel Bernardi, "The Voice of Whiteness: D. W. Griffith's Biograph Films (1908–1913)," in *The Birth of Whiteness,* 103–28. For a thorough critique of the white knight figure, see Gina Marchetti, *Romance and the "Yellow Peril": Race, Sex, and Discursive Strategies in Hollywood Fiction* (Berkeley: University of California Press, 1993).

26. Matt Rosoff, "Sex on the Web: An Inside Look at the Net Porn Industry," http://www.cnet.com/specialreports/0-3805-7-280110.html?tag=st.sr.1544318.linksgp (September 1999).

27. Wimpsett, "Net Vices."

28. http://www.ebonyteenies.com/ (November 29, 2000).

29. http://YoungLatina.com/ (November 29, 2000).

30. http://www.ssex.com/girls.html, http://www.trueblue.net.au/, http://www.cuteangels.com/ (November 29, 2000).

31. For a useful history of pornography and the Web, see Frederick Lane III, *Obscene Profits: The Entrepreneurs of Pornography in the Cyber Age* (New York: Routledge, 2000).

32. Matt Rosoff, "Sex on the Web."

33. The fact that the Web allows Netizens to view adult works without having to leave the house or office should not be undertheorized.

34. Lane, *Obscene Profits,* xix.

35. This standard was spelled out by the Supreme Court in *FCC v. Pacifica Foundation* as follows: "Indecent sexually oriented material, while not illegal if distributed on the open market strictly to adults, becomes illegal if broadcast over the telephone, radio or TV because it invades the privacy of the home and exposes children to harmful materials."

36. *Miller v. California* (413 U.S. 15).

37. *New York v. Ferber* (458 U.S. 747).

38. U.S.C. Title 18, Part 1, Chapter 10, Sec. 2256.

39. The New York statute, as quoted in the court's decision, "defines 'sexual performance' as any performance that includes sexual conduct by such a child, and 'sexual conduct' is in turn defined as actual or simulated sexual intercourse, deviate sexual intercourse, sexual bestiality, masturbation, sado-masochistic abuse, or lewd exhibition of the genitals." Ibid.

Cyborgs in Cyberspace   181

40. Programs that filter pornographic material are a useful resource for parents and schools where children actively engage the Web, but, like cigarette machines, there are many ways around them.

41. Anna Grant et al., "Child Pornography in the Digital Age," in *Illegal Immigration and Commercial Sex,* ed. Phil Williams (Portland, Ore.: Frank Cass, 1999), 176.

42. Ibid., 183.

43. Phil Williams, "Human Commodity Trafficking: An Overview," in *Illegal Immigration and Commercial Sex,* 4.

44. Ibid., 4.

45. http://Persiankitty.com/ (November 7, 2000).

46. http://super-sites.net/teens2.htm (November 7, 2000).

47. http://www.lo-li-ta.com/ (November 29, 2000).

48. http://www.euro-lolitas.com/ (November 29, 2000).

49. http://www.lolitaland.net/main.html (November 29, 2000).

50. The address for this ad is not listed in the pop-up window.

51. http://www.darkpussy.com/ (November 29, 2000).

52. http://www.purebitch.com/ (November 29, 2000).

53. Patricia Hill Collins, "Pornography and Black Women's Bodies," in *Gender, Race, and Class in Media: A Text Reader,* ed. Gail Dines and Jean M. Humez (Thousand Oaks, Calif.: Sage Publications, 1995), 281.

54. http://www/asiaporno.com/join.php?h (November 29, 2000).

55. http//www.japan-lolita.com/hardcore.htm (November 29, 2000).

THREE

Real Discourse

Television Vectors and the Making of a Media Event

The Helicopter, the Freeway Chase, and National Memory

MARITA STURKEN

The contemporary transnational media web, with satellite communications, multinational media conglomerates, all-news cable channels, international news services, and the dissemination of American popular culture throughout the world, has contributed to the view of the media as a global enterprise that unites audiences across national boundaries. Media viewers are imagined as global citizens, who can access via their remote control a vast array of programming from local news to national news, from endless all-news programming to brief headlines to global weather forecasts, and from conventional television viewing to countless Web sites and on-line news sources.

Within this globalized mediascape, television is often singled out as a primary element of an increasingly unboundaried world. Television, the story goes, is so easily transmitted across national boundaries, so emblematic of American cultural imperialism throughout the world, and so ubiquitous, that it has created a new global media consumer and homogenized the world audience as a global market for American popular culture. Television, it has been widely asserted, effaces national boundaries and empties the category of citizenship of meaning.

Yet characterizations of the global and hyperbole about the effects of globalization have tended to gloss over the ways that television remains at this moment of history a powerful force in the constitution of citizenship, significantly through the national experience of live television events. In both television's relentless everydayness and the moments of national trauma when people remember "where they were," Americans (as well as citizens of other countries) are incited to experience themselves as citizens through the technology of television. In the experience of watching the first moon walk, the Watergate hearings, the Challenger explosion, the Persian Gulf War, or the Los Angeles riots, or the terrorist attacks of September 11,

American viewers, regardless of the ways in which they are individually marked by difference, are addressed as members of a specifically national culture and as citizens (both literal and figurative). Similarly, it could be said that global events such as Princess Diana's funeral create simultaneously a global audience and a specifically national audience, speaking not only to the British citizenry but to all viewers as British citizens. The experience of the television viewer is an essential component in generating the sense that a national culture, a "people," exists, even as globalism imagines we have gone beyond the nation.

Hence, while television has been traditionally understood contradictorily in terms of both its potential capacity to create a global village and as a medium of isolation that can separate families and communities, it emerged ironically in the late twentieth century as a primary means through which participation in the nation takes place, in particular in times of national debate and trauma. Television is a pedagogical medium, one that instructs citizen-viewers about national culture and citizenship.[1] Sports events, advertising that sells the idea of America, news programs, TV movies, and tabloid talk shows are among the genres that reinforce viewership in terms of nationalism, speaking to an established set of codes about belonging to the nation. Sitting before the television screen, viewers are provided by television conventions with a sense of their fellow audience members, scattered throughout the country, watching along with them.

It is above all live television that aims to establish a national commonality among viewers. Live television events such as sports and awards ceremonies are used to promote television's claims to spontaneity and the unexpected. Indeed, the live television moment, while actually relatively rare in the many hours of programming shown every day, continues to be a defining part of television's meaning in American culture. A significant number of the conventions of television genres, such as the pseudo-spontaneity of talk show and newscast chatter, are about establishing codes of the live, and hence of television as immediate, in contexts in which often it is actually taped. The desire for the value of live television is the reason why many moments of television are live for no inherent reason, such as the convention of newscasters reporting live from sites where news events took place earlier in the day (but that are now without activity). The immediacy and urgency that such moments can produce is thus central to the definition of television.

This quality of liveness has often been seen by cultural critics as evidence of television's negation of memory and history, defined as it is by simultaneity, banality, distraction, flow, and catastrophe.[2] Yet it could be said that the presence of television as live marks events as historical precisely through television's capacity to interpellate viewers as citizens. Indeed, studies show that people often misremember where they first heard of national events by imagining themselves in retrospect as having seen the event first on television.[3] The events through which history is confirmed via television range from the crucial and the tragic to the trivial. In other words, live television can create a sense of the national in events of no apparent historical significance. This does not mean that history is increasingly trivial, but rather that the trivial can acquire meaning through its status as live television and its tele-historization.

This essay examines the intersections of television technology with the construction of national culture through an analysis of the ultimate all-American event of television of the mid-1990s: the televised freeway chase of O. J. Simpson in June 1994. What are we to do with the fact that one of the primary "television events" of the 1990s consisted of millions of viewers tracking the chase of a Ford Bronco driving on the (miraculously empty) Los Angeles freeways on a Friday afternoon, followed by twenty police cars? This event offers a means to examine the complexity of communication vectors that establish the contemporary media event and the role of active viewer participation in codifying television events as both newsworthy and nationally significant. This was simultaneously a global, national, and local event, through which the increasingly complex geography of television was revealed. The O. J. Simpson freeway chase demonstrated the rich mix of genres of contemporary media events in that it was at once a sports event, a crime drama, a car chase, and a moment of national trauma. This event demonstrates that within the global terrain of television, the national and the local are constantly in play—in other words, that the role of television at this historical moment is in part to reassert the national in a global context. This essay thus intends to capture this play by approaching this singular event through a number of different frames: the geography of global, national, and local media vectors, the role of the news helicopter and the freeway in the construction of a media event, the interplay of genres in television news events, and the role of television in the creation of cultural memory.

Media Vectors: The Geography of the Media Event

The space of television events is defined by the transmission of images through media vectors. Hence, the contemporary media event has a highly complex geography. Through the interconnections of satellite technology, portable broadcast video equipment, television news helicopters, cellular telephones, and radio simulcasts, media vectors create a geography into which television audiences are inserted. It has been argued that this renders the living room a virtual space, obliterating notions of public and private, and effacing national boundaries. For example, in his book *Virtual Geography,* McKenzie Wark notes:

> [Global media vectors] can make events that connect the most disparate sites of public action appear simultaneously as a private drama filled with familiar characters and moving stories. The vector blurs the thin line between political crisis and media sensation; it eclipses the geographical barriers separating distinct cultural and political entities; and it transgresses the borders between public and private spheres on both the home front and the front line.[4]

The global media event, defined by its instant transmission around the world, affirms both the powerful state of multinational media networks and some form of global unity through its establishment of the newsworthy. The Persian Gulf War of 1991, occurring ten years after the establishment of CNN (Cable News Network) and soon after the development of satellite phones and electronic news gathering equipment with the capacity for instant global transmission, marked the beginning of the instant global media event. Despite the fact that the American coverage of the war was highly restrictive and censored, it was seen as establishing the collective, live, global television audience. Since that time, there have been several events that have contributed to the live, global television experience, most recently, the spectacular television coverage of the tragic events of September 11. These events define a space of electronic transmission, a network of communication vectors crisscrossing the globe, to be shared by spectators unified in their act of watching. Each event is as much about the extended reach of televisual transmission as it is about the event itself.

The matrix of electronic, virtual, and televisual space can be seen as a global space; however the new geography of television also constructs national audiences, whether of wars fought on foreign terrains, relayed by satellite back to the national audience, or events of national importance that are transmitted live throughout the world. The television coverage of Diana's funeral, for instance, was designed to export a particularly ritualistic form of British national identity throughout the world as much as it was directed at a national audience. In addition, it could be argued that the global coverage of the Persian Gulf War by CNN served more to Americanize the war and produce nationalist sentiments than to obliterate concepts of the national.

While these events may have had a broader reach in the context of these expansive communication vectors, their coverage also underscores common assumptions about television viewing that long proceeded them. For instance, the idea that television coverage provides a "better" view of an event than the experience of being there, which forms much of the promotion of contemporary media events, has long been part of the discourse of television, in particular televised sports. David Morley and Kevin Robins have pointed out that there have even been cases where the trauma experienced by the television viewer of a tragic event, as opposed to the direct participant of that event, has been seen legally as more pronounced "by virtue of the camera's ability to bring into sharp focus events that might not be as clear to an observer of the real event."[5] It may be that the television view of an event provides more of an omniscient view that affords a sense of structure and explanation that one might not experience in person. Yet the fact that most audience members experience world events through television and not in person also has the effect of heightening the desire to actually be at a sports events, the scene of a catastrophe, or a freeway chase—to witness with one's body and perhaps become part of the event itself. In other words, television creates media events that then elicit the desire to participate beyond the screen itself.

The construction of a local, national, and global television event and the desire of viewers to place themselves within the frame are fundamental aspects of the most notorious television event in the United States in the 1990s, in June 1994 when O. J. Simpson and A. C. Cowlings attempted to flee law enforcement on the Los Angeles freeways. Driving a now-famous white Ford Bronco, Simpson and Cowlings were spotted by passing motorists after the Los Angeles police announced that Simpson had fled his home, where he was about to be arrested for the murder of his ex-wife Nicole Brown Simpson and her friend Ron Goldman.[6] While the actual murder had been a media story of phenomenal proportions, and the subsequent two trials of Simpson (and his acquittal in the criminal case and conviction in the civil trial) were to epitomize a 1990s media frenzy, the car chase was itself an extraordinary and unexpected event. The freeway chase was watched by 95 million viewers, including 68 percent of Los Angeles TV viewers.[7] Once the Bronco was spotted and police began pursuit, the media vectors of the event quickly took hold. Television news helicopters followed the car, transmitting the image live on several channels. The freeways were quickly closed ahead of the car, which, unlike most car chases, was travelling at a leisurely speed of 45 mph. This was because the police had been warned by Cowlings to keep their distance since O. J. had a loaded gun and was threatening suicide. It was a Friday afternoon, the highest traffic time of the week, and hundreds of thousands of motorists were either on or attempting to get on the roads. People began to call in to radio talk shows to discuss the events and to plead with O. J. to give up, presuming that O. J. and Cowlings were listening in the Bronco. At the same time, thousands of drivers pulled over on the freeway and lined the overpasses to witness the Bronco pass by as if it were a kind of sports marathon, holding signs and cheering the men on yelling "Go Juice Go!" and "The Juice is Loose!" O. J. and Cowlings had several conversations with the Los Angeles Police Department on a cell phone throughout the chase, and detective Tom Lange eventually persuaded Simpson to give up.[8] All of this was taped by news helicopters and cameras on the ground and broadcast live to millions of viewers, finally pushing the National Basketball Association (NBA) finals, a major sports event, off the screen. The chase ended a few hours later when the Bronco pulled into the driveway of Simpson's Brentwood home, and he turned himself into police after requesting and drinking, however absurd this may sound in retrospect, a glass of orange juice.[9]

O. J.'s flight from the police drew upon codes of the sports event and the genre of the cinematic car chase. What geography was defined by this event? Where did it really take place? On the freeway, where crowds stood by with signs (for both O. J. and the TV cameras)? On the radio, where callers presumed O. J. was listening to their pleas? Through the cellular phone on which O. J. spoke to the police? On television, where the tracking of the white Bronco (already linked to its fellow Bronco as evidence of the crime) pushed the NBA finals into a little box on the screen? The Simpson freeway chase was a media event of intersecting vectors in which the notion of national and local participation was reinscribed. Two aspects of this event deserve more discussion of how they created its geography of media vectors: the helicopter and the freeway.

Scanning the Urban Landscape: The Helicopter as Icon

Many communication vectors were at play in the Simpson car chase—cell phones, live television and radio transmission, and telephone calls to radio and television commentators. Not the least of these elements was the role played by television news helicopters. It was the capacity of the TV news helicopter to transmit the image of the Bronco driving on the freeway that made this a television event and alerted both television and radio audiences to the location of the vehicle. Indeed, it could be said that the "imagined community" of American culture often is facilitated through events that become national precisely because of the presence of news helicopters.

The helicopter's signification of American technological power is not incidental to its role in flying TV news cameras and audiences into new terrains. Furthermore, the use of the helicopter in American culture today, as a war machine, a police device, and a news mechanism, cannot be separated from its signification in the Vietnam War. The helicopter was the most important machine of the "theater" of the Vietnam War. The dense terrain of Vietnam made the helicopter an essential mode of transport, and it rapidly acquired both symbolic and mystical value. The helicopter was often the only means of rescue, support, and transportation for the troops. Helicopters were used almost exclusively by Americans in the war, thus symbolizing America's dominance in the air and weakness on the ground in a guerrilla war. Alasdair Spark writes, "The helicopter became the American touchstone, symbolising a transcendent American power incarnate in metal—the Vietcong were aware of it, and awarded high honours to soldiers who downed ships."[10]

Helicopters quickly acquired associations of both the cavalry and the Indians of the American West, no doubt aided, according to Spark, by the Army's policy of naming them after Indian tribes—Sioux, Iroquois, Chinook, Cheyenne, and so on. In the literature of the war, the helicopter is presented as the ship of rescue and release as well as a machine to be admired, if not loved. Michael Herr wrote of the Loache helicopters in his well-known book *Dispatches*, "It was incredible, those little ships were the most beautiful things flying in Vietnam (you had to stop once in a while and admire the machinery), they just hung out there above those bunkers like wasps outside a nest. 'That's sex,' the captain said. 'That's pure sex.'"[11] For Herr, the helicopter was the ultimate memory trope, a "collective metachopper," and "the sexiest thing going": "saver-destroyer, provider-waster, right hand–left hand, nimble, fluent, canny and human; hot steel, grease, jungle-saturated canvas webbing, sweat cooling and warming up again, cassette rock and roll in one ear and door-gun fire in the other, fuel, heat, vitality and death. . . ."[12]

In its constant rescripting in Hollywood Vietnam War films, the helicopter signifies both the haunting memory of the war as well as the power and failure of American technology. Films such as *Apocalypse Now* (1979) use the "thuk thuk" sounds of the helicopter rotors as a primary motif, and helicopter scenes of rescue (in the *Rambo* series) and abandonment (in *Platoon*) are recurring motifs. As Spark writes, "The helicopter, like the soldier, is a veteran of Vietnam."[13] When Saigon fell in 1975, Americans witnessed the evacuation of the city as huddled masses grabbing onto the rails of departing helicopters. The image of Americans pushing their helicopters off aircraft carriers into the sea was profoundly symbolic of the nation's political and technological defeat.

After this symbolic demise, the recuperation of the helicopter has taken place through its role as a machine of urban environments and television vectors, in other words, from *Apocalypse Now* to *Boys 'N the Hood*. Armed with its associations with both the cavalry (invading the frontier space) and the Indians (as warriors), the urban helicopter also carries its signification with the guerrilla war of Vietnam. In Los Angeles, the helicopter is a primary means by which the LAPD patrols neighborhoods and engages in chasing suspects. In this context, one can see the tangled traffic of Los

Angeles streets operating as a counterpart to the jungles of Vietnam—the helicopter provides the means to travel above it and awards power to those who do. In addition, the Los Angeles news media are hugely dependent on news helicopters for news events and traffic reporting. In the city of Los Angeles, the helicopter replays its role of charting the frontier—no traffic jam, no potential criminal, no neighborhood, no celebrity wedding is safe from its intrusion.

The helicopter is a conduit of geographic space that links the city through its images, marks the panopticism of the urban/suburban space, and extends the vector of the freeways to the rest of the country. The city is constantly surveyed from the air and increasingly defined by the aerial view of the helicopter lens. Los Angeles is haunted by the sound of helicopters; many Vietnam veterans in L.A. find themselves ambushed by memories with the constant refrain of the rotor blades. With thirteen media helicopters, Los Angeles defines the space of news from the air more than any other U.S. city.[14] Hence when O. J. Simpson and Al Cowlings drove through the Southern California freeways, it was the presence of television news helicopters as simultaneous mechanisms of urban surveillance, traffic monitors, and news generators that defined the media event.

The Freeway as Theater and Containment: Rewriting Traffic

The freeway has long been considered the primary symbol of Los Angeles, both in terms of its initial promise as a non-toll road that would pave the way to L.A.'s automobile-driven, mobile future but also as the dominant means through which the contemporary urban and suburban landscape of the city is conceived. The freeways are what distinguish Los Angeles from the modern urban environments of New York and Chicago or the boulevards of Paris. They allow, in many ways, for the analysis of the city as a postmodern landscape defined by velocity and transit and as a city of the future, teetering on the abyss. In 1973, Reynard Banham described Los Angeles as defined by four regional "ecologies": surfurbia (the beach cities), the foothills (Beverly Hills, Bel Air), the "plains of Id" (the central flatlands), and "autopia" (the freeways as a way of life).[15] Hence, the freeways are central to defining the geography of the city. The freeways both demarcate and divide the neighborhoods of Los Angeles and have long been implicated in the vast discrepancies of wealth between the rich and the poor as well as in the racial tensions of the city. Freeways cut through the neighborhoods of South Central and Inglewood; they traverse nowhere near the wealthy enclaves of Beverly Hills.

The freeway is both a means by which neighborhoods and trajectories are defined but also how daily life is organized. People refer to freeways as unique, calling them "the 10" or "the 405" as if each were an individual. Traffic is a constant in the life of most residents of Los Angeles. As the source of traffic congestion and the site of daily mobility and interaction of citizens, the freeway is a primary site of news in Los Angeles. It is as if every day the trials and tribulations of ordinary citizens—getting to work, doing their jobs, keeping it together—are enacted by the news of traffic and freeway events and given historical import. The lanes of the freeway are the most obvious shared symbolic space of the city, yet they are defined not as a place so much as a vector, a place to drive through rather than to be in. While communication vectors define the linkages of different media, the vector of the freeway is a line that signifies transit and is never a destination itself. Margaret Morse defines the freeway as nonspace, displacement, and a form of derealized space. "Channels of motion dedicated to one-way, high velocity travel," she writes, "freeways are largely experienced as 'in-betweens,' rather than enjoying the full reality of a point of departure or a destination."[16] Yet even as it is a space in between places, it could be argued that the L.A. freeway is also a central theatrical place in the city, established through the surveillance of the television news and traffic helicopter.

The freeway as a form of racial containment has also been a dominant narrative of Los Angeles. As a vector that inscribes the geography of L.A., the freeway has often been described as a means by which suburban and urban space is segregated, the roadways that drive over and render invisible the inner-city neighborhoods they traverse. While this sense of the freeway as a safe space removed from dangerous neighborhoods shifted in the early 1990s to the freeway as a potential site of danger because of road rage—specifically people shooting at cars that cut them off—the elevation of the freeway over the city remains a primary trope in its public representation. Yet the symbiosis of two central freeway events, the police chase of Rodney King and the freeway chase of O. J. Simpson, calls into question any simple analysis of the freeway's racial symbolism. It was inevitable that with Simpson and Cowlings, the image of two black men being chased by a flank of police cars (albeit at 45 miles per hour) would evoke the previous L.A. freeway chase of Rodney King, driving (apparently) in excess of 90 miles an hour before he was beaten by police under the watchful eye of an amateur video camera. Yet the Simpson freeway chase defied simple analysis of the freeway as a racially marked space. This was not the freeway through which white Angelenos drive their cars above and over poor black and Latino neighborhoods, the freeway as the vector that insures the invisibility of South Central. Here was a black man returning to the enclave of his wealthy white neighborhood under the buzz of the helicopter, with the police delicately giving him an escort, driving past the ghettos. That this was an escort, rather than a hostile chase, would seem to contradict Simpson's defense that he was framed by white police officers. That defense, which succeeded in the criminal trial, linked Simpson symbolically to the figure of Rodney King, a linkage facilitated by freeway stories.

Yet clearly Simpson's freeway chase was marked by race even as it rescripted the racial text of the freeway. The television news helicopters rendered Simpson either suspect or celebrity, and as a black male celebrity he was inevitably marked as the black sports hero. Television coverage of the freeway chase allowed the image of O. J. as the black male suspect to be replaced by O. J. the black male sports hero, running past the cheering crowds. Simpson's media representation was contingent on a limited group of stereotypes into which he could be inserted.

Cell Phones and Talk Shows: Talking the Nation

The space of the O. J. Simpson freeway chase was created not only through the vectors of the freeway and the surveillance of the television news helicopter but also through the newly embraced phenomenon of talk radio shows and cellular telephones. This was crucial not only to public participation in the event but also to the negotiations between the police and O. J. that eventually led to his peaceful surrender. It is probably safe to say that if O. J. had fled in a time before the cellular phone, his confrontation with the police could have been significantly different. Indeed, when Simpson arrived at his house but still refused to leave the Bronco, there was a temporary breakdown in communications with police because the battery on his cell phone had run out. Even though proximity would at that point have allowed him to speak to police in person, the negotiations were still happening only on the cell phone.

In November 1996, one year after Simpson was acquitted in the criminal trial and during the civil suit against him, the LAPD released a transcript of his conversation with police on his cellular phone. In the transcript, Detective Tom Lange asks O. J. to think of his children and tries to convince him to drop the gun with which he is threatening to commit suicide. At one point, in contrast to his later claims against the police, Simpson says, "Ah, just tell them I'm all sorry. You can tell them later on today and tomorrow that I was sorry and that I'm sorry that I did this to the police department."[17] The release of the transcript completed in a certain sense the public fantasy of the event, which included many rumors about what was actually said between O. J. and the police and speculation about Simpson's frame of mind when he attempted to flee.

At the same time, cellular phones and call-ins to radio and television stations during the freeway chase established an electronic space for the participation of the listening public. Listeners at home watching television and in their cars listening to the radio called in large numbers to radio talk shows and television stations to speak to O. J. These actions were predicated on the belief that Simpson and Cowlings were listening to the radio precisely because they were in a car. Simpson's first wife, Marguerite, was speaking to KNX Radio when she shouted out to O. J., "Run, go, run, keep going" and several members of the National Football League called radio stations asking him to give up.[18] That it is unknown and unlikely if Simpson heard any of the pleas on the radio does not diminish the public fantasy, facilitated by the technological vectors, that he could have heard them. This collective fantasy was acted out in the television movie *The O. J. Simpson Story,* made in 1995, in which O. J. listens to the radio call-in pleas and is heartened by the crowds. This is a national fantasy—the fantasy that the nation called out to O. J. to forgive him and to beg him to live, and that he heard these calls. It is the listener who authenticates the message of the radio talk show.

Radio talk shows, which are more dependent on call-ins than television talk shows, became central to concepts of public discourse in the 1990s. During the Simpson freeway chase, television newscasts interviewed experts such as psychiatrists and forensic pathologists and also took on the format of radio call-in shows, laying the sound of talk over the helicopter images of the Bronco. This occasionally placed celebrity television news anchors in the unscripted context of fielding unverified calls. In one particularly bizarre moment, ABC anchorman Peter Jennings took an on-air call from someone who had convinced his producers that he was a neighbor of Simpsons, near the scene of the action. When at the end of his statement he said in a strange accent, "Ba, ba, booey to you," a phrase that is a signature of radio bad boy and talk show host Howard Stern, they surmised that a fan of Stern's show was playing a joke on them.[19]

As a central element in the contemporary public sphere, the radio talk show is a means through which ordinary citizens can feel that they are speaking to each other and a national audience. So it could be argued that the explosion of participation and interest in radio and television talk shows at the end of the twentieth century has been fueled by a desire to feel that one can participate in some form of public debate. The genre of talk shows has also always been about allowing viewers to feel that they are witnessing the private lives and authentic selves of celebrities. The public fantasy of the talk show in the Simpson freeway chase combined both this desire to witness a celebrity in a private moment and the desire to speak to a national audience.

The Freeway Chase as Media Event

While the media event of the Simpson freeway chase took place through the complex intersections of television news helicopters, cellular phones, and radio call-ins, another primary element of the event was the participation of spectators alongside the freeway and on overpasses as the Bronco drove by. In what would later provide the strangest images of the event, people crowded the edge of the road shouting encouragement to Simpson and holding impromptu signs with phrases such as "Go Juice Go!" The technologically defined space of the event—from freeway vector to media vector—had also established the freeway as a particular space. This was not a space merely traveled through but a space of performance and audience participation in which people were prompted to place themselves bodily in the event (and before the television cameras).

Yet what could the codes of behavior at such an event be? The crowds that lined the overpasses stunned reporters by cheering on O. J. as if he were running for a touchdown instead of being a man pursued by police as a murder suspect. This was a national sports event in which simulcasting rendered those who had front-row seats (the spectators on the side of the road) the stand-in audience for the television viewers. That the goal of O. J.'s run was unclear, that the only obstacles he had to traverse were not defensive linebackers but betacam operators, did not lessen the crowd's enactment of sports fans' protocols.

The aspects of the chase that enacted the codes of a sports event were aided by its coincidence with the NBA finals. This posed a dilemma not only for the stations that were broadcasting the game, between the New York Knicks and the Houston Rockets, but also apparently for their fans. Some stations cut away entirely from the game, and others put the tense final minutes of play into a small box in the corner of the screen so that viewers could watch both. Hence the audience that was watching the incident when it began already included a large number of sports fans.[20]

O. J. was thus contained in the event within his role as black sports icon, so that his transgression—at this point, more of a transgression of lack of will and a display of weakness than anything else—was rescued by his quasi-touchdown run, his final run past the crowds. This was the endless reenactment of the O. J. run: O. J. the football player's run, O. J. the Hertz salesman's run through the airport, and O. J. the crime suspect's run. It was also the run of O. J. the celebrity held within the panoptic view of the television news helicopter, a machine whose role it is to invade celebrity enclaves.

Yet this event was, for many observers, really a story about traffic. For many people who live in Southern California, the shock of "O. J. is running away" was equaled by "My God, look how empty the 405 is on a Friday!" The Simpson freeway chase took place during the prime traffic time of a Friday evening, when people in Los Angeles are in the habit of scheduling their lives according to heavy traffic jams. The freeway chase produced significant traffic problems both because of the strategic shutting down of certain entry ramps to the 405 freeway to allow the Bronco to pass (a police strategy usually used for visiting dignitaries such as the president) and because of the crowds who went to line the freeway in order to see the spectacle themselves.

The iconography of the chase, from the legacy of the western, the road movie, and the television police drama, is specifically coded American, and there are certain ingredients necessary to its construction: an outlaw outnumbered by police/authorities, speed, obstacles, and the potential of the chasee to get away. Yet the Simpson chase took place at slow speeds that no self-respecting freeway driver would ever attempt, with Simpson and Cowlings feeling enough in control to order the police to keep their distance. There were no obstacles in their way. In the endless rehashing of the Simpson chase on national tabloid shows, which took about a week to be completely milked, I saw one revealing rendition, a replaying (perhaps on *Hard Copy*) that laid over the image of the Bronco the soundtrack of none other than *Thelma & Louise*. Suddenly it all made sense—O. J. and A. C. as Thelma and Louise, the chase, the pan back from the car to reveal twenty police cars in pursuit. And the final moment when Thelma and Louise know they are doomed because what rises up before them from the Grand Canyon but a helicopter.

Yet cognizance of the media event as an event in itself prompted reporters and participants to see it as "history in the making." Many observers standing along the highway or on overpasses told the press that they felt the event was both historic and sad. One told CNN, "I just wanted to be part of history." News commentary, as usual, attempted to instantly establish the event as historical, comparing it both to the Kennedy assassination and the Persian Gulf War. These comparisons were not because it was an event of consequence but because it was an event with a huge television audience, one through which national unity was supposedly created. At the same time, the news media was clearly in thrall of the entertainment drama of the event, in which real life appeared to trump Hollywood. For instance, NBC news anchor Tom Brokaw described the chase as "a scene that is playing out that no scriptwriter, no dramatist, could possibly conceive." Rumors that O. J. was holding a gun that was a prop from the ill-fated Warner Brothers pilot *Frogman,* in which Simpson had starred, demonstrated the permeable boundaries between social arenas that characterized the media event.[21]

The freeway chase as sports event and the heir apparent to the western chase is also crucially tied to the freeway as the primary site of theater in Los Angeles, both as a "theater" of war and as the stage from which Los Angelenos speak to the city at large. Freeway chases are an increasing staple of the evening news in Los Angeles, so much so that one occasionally wonders if the LAPD and local news stations are not working together to produce them. One outcome of this phenomenon, beside the recent proliferation of TV shows such as *The World's Scariest Police Chases,* is the use of the freeway by citizens to make statements to a national news audience. This happened most violently and tragically in Los Angeles in May 1998 when Daniel Jones pulled over on the ramp between two major freeways, the Harbor Freeway (the 110) and the Century Freeway (the 105), unfurled a banner making a statement against HMOs, set himself and his truck on fire (with his dog inside) and shot himself on camera. Motorists had called the police when Jones began pointing his shotgun at passing cars, and both freeways were closed. As the police closed in and television news helicopters monitored his actions, local television shows cut away from children's programming to show the event live. Estimates are that more than 900,000 households saw the suicide live on camera, including large numbers of children. (One station, KTTV, which cut away from children's programming, ran a warning that asked children to go get their parents.)[22]

This event prompted an immediate outcry against the tactics of television news to cut away from regular programming in order to turn freeway incidents into media events. There was much hand-wringing and apologies from the media, which prompted some rethinking of live coverage policies (including instituting a seven-second delay), but for the most part the public debate was short-lived.[23] Two months later, the *Los Angeles Times* ran a story about how a construction company employee who was run over and severely injured by a piece of heavy equipment only survived because his boss, who was caught in the immense traffic jam resulting from Jones's suicide, decided to make an unscheduled visit to the work site. This kind of redemptive story about fate and the freeway proliferates in Los Angeles and adds to the mythic and symbolic status of the freeway.[24]

Clearly the Jones suicide could become a media event because of the presence of television news helicopters, and Jones presumably chose this site as the place from which to speak to the media—a place of guaranteed media coverage. This instant media coverage is the result not only of the visibility of the freeway from the air but also because all traffic stories are news stories. One of the major aspects of the Jones suicide was that it closed two major freeways in the city for several hours, thus creating a huge traffic jam that lasted well into the evening. It was thus primarily a traffic event. As one LAPD sergeant put it at the time, "the whole city is at a standstill."[25] Whether enacted in the codes of a sports event, as most car chases including the Simpson chase are, or in the codes of a public forum, freeway incidents such as these form a symbiosis between the television news helicopter and the traffic story.

The freeway chase or incident is also centrally about the process of witnessing. With the constant repackaging of freeway chases into TV shows, the genre of the freeway chase has taken its place among crime and disaster coverage. It is now possible for addicts of freeway chases to join the Pursuit Watch Network, which for $9.99 for three months will page them whenever a freeway chase is being covered by a television news helicopter.[26] In each case, the aerial news camera functions as a means through which viewers are allowed to feel they are witnessing as viewer/citizens and hence as members of a larger audience.

Television Memory: Reenactments

As the Simpson saga, from freeway chase to courtroom drama, emerged as the national story of the 1990s, it claimed national and global attention to an extraordinary degree over a period of several years. It can be credited in retrospect not only with establishing Court TV as a staple of cable channels but also with invigorating radio talk shows and aiding in the more recent proliferation of all-news cable channels. The case also functioned as a primary forum through which the general public learned about the legal process. This is a source of concern for many legal experts, who feel that the difference between this trial and most criminal trials, both in terms of legal tactics and the effects of media coverage, made it an unfortunate site of legal pedagogy. However, it could be argued that one of the effects of the trial is that most Americans now understand the concept of "reasonable doubt."

Certainly this was in all its aspects a made-for-television event, both with its inception in the freeway chase and its televised courtroom dramas. The Simpson saga fed into the ontology of television, which is defined by repetition, reenactment, and docudrama. Each phase, be it freeway chase or courtroom spat, was endlessly replayed, endlessly reenacted, endlessly analyzed. Indeed, the freeway chase was both reenacted in the TV movie and was actually perversely predicted in popular culture with the film *Speed,* which was released just prior to it. It was also uncannily replayed when O. J. was released from jail upon acquittal and was driven home in a white van at slow speed, followed by a phalanx of police cars under the gaze of many television news helicopters. He was greeted at his house by A. C. Cowlings. At the time, news reports stated that O. J. was deliriously happy to see, above all else, the freeway. ABC news anchor Peter Jennings, remarking upon the strange symmetry of the events, paraphrased Yogi Berra in stating, "Does this seem like déjà vu all over again, folks?"[27]

The media event of the freeway chase is thus not simply defined by the virtual geography of its media vectors, it is also defined through its reenactment. Its meaning is constantly rescripted, narrativized, replayed. This, in essence, is how television operates as a site of cultural memory. Many cultural critics, such as Stephen Heath and Fredric Jameson among others, have written about television as a force of anti-memory, the endlessly postmodern repetition of events that makes no history. However, I would argue that this interpretation does not allow for the role of repetition and reenactment in memory. Indeed, television's reenactment is much closer to the fluid ways in which memory operates not as a stable force but as a constantly rewritten script. Renarratization is essential to memory; indeed, it is its defining quality. We remember events by retelling them, rethinking them, and, according to Freud, by reconstructing their narratives in light of new stories in our lives. Television repetition, either in the form of repackaged footage or the dramatic reenactment of television movies, is thus a memory-making process rather than a negation of cultural memory. It is a contemporary making and remaking of the historical.

So, the story of Simpson's freeway chase played out its trajectory through cultural memory as a continuously replayed television script, inseparable from the TV images it generated. Ironically, participation in the national television audience rendered citizens suspect for the task of jury duty, one of the few tasks that Americans are actually called upon to do as citizens. Prospective jurors in the Simpson case were grilled about their participation as viewers of the media spectacle, and the jury itself was sequestered for the duration of the trial in order to keep them away from media coverage. (From the prosecutors' point of view, this decision clearly had negative consequences, since many of the jurors were understandably very unhappy about being sequestered.) At the same time, the idea that the media coverage of the freeway chase and the murders created a national audience also worked to render suspect those who had not participated in it. One prospective juror later made headlines, and was clearly regarded as a kind of freak, when she professed to not know who Simpson was or what had happened.[28] Media citizenship can thus be seen as taking over the category of traditional citizenship. Participation in witnessing the Simpson freeway chase was understood as the work of citizen-viewers, an activity that produced an important commonality in its audience.

Television, in its capacity to render all events as both simultaneously legitimate and suspect, made this event, continuously rescripted, one of national memory. The Simpson freeway chase was witnessed by a global audience, for whom the event was characterized as a specifically (and perhaps perversely) American one; by a national audience, for whom the chase was a witnessing of a celebrity hero; and a local one, in which the theater of the freeway was reaffirmed. Television operated in this event to affirm both the national and the local as primary sites and in turn to construct O. J.'s sad story as one of American tragedy. The nation is also a continuously rewritten script, a mediated concept that is reasserted, refigured, produced through tension and conflict. It is not a stable but rather a shifting and fluid terrain. In this sense, television is a species of pedagogy not only about what it means to participate in the nation but about the instability of the category "nation" itself.

NOTES

This essay was funded by the James Irvine Foundation through the Southern California Studies Center of the University of California. Thanks to Sarah Banet-Weiser and Dana Polan for helpful comments.

1. See Lauren Berlant, "The Theory of Infantile Citizenship," *Public Culture* 5 (1993), 395–410.

2. See, for instance, the essays in Patricia Mellencamp, ed., *Logics of Television: Essays in Cultural Criticism* (Bloomington: Indiana University Press, 1990).

3. See Ulric Neisser and Nicole Harsch, "Phantom Flashbulbs," in *Affect and Accuracy in Recall,* ed. Eugene Winograd and Ulric Neisser (Cambridge: Cambridge University Press, 1992); and my discussion of the *Challenger* explosion in *Tangled Memories: The Vietnam War, the AIDS Epidemic, and the Politics of Remembering* (Berkeley: University of California Press, 1997), chap. 1.

4. McKenzie Wark, *Virtual Geography* (Bloomington: Indiana University Press, 1994), 15–16.

5. David Morley and Kevin Robins, *Spaces of Identity: Global Media, Electronic Landscapes, and Cultural Boundaries* (New York: Routledge, 1995), 131.

6. According to the California Highway Patrol, Chris Thomas and Kathy Ferrigno, a young couple who were on their way to go camping, called in the first verified sighting of the Bronco. Minutes later it was spotted by an Orange County sheriff's deputy. The car was spotted at 6:25 and the chase lasted until after 8 P.M. Jim Newton, "'I'm Sorry for Putting You Guys Out,'" *Los Angeles Times,* June 19, 1994, A1.

7. Karen Heller, "Simpson Case Seems to Stain All It Touches: A Year Later, No End to O. J." *Arizona Republic,* June 11, 1995, A1; Associated Press, "L.A. Eyes Glued to O. J. Ride," *Daily Variety,* June 20, 1994, 1.

8. Christopher Reed, "Transcript of Calls Reveals Desperate Man," *Guardian* (London), November 28, 1996, 22.

9. Cable News Network (CNN) News, June 18, 1994.

10. Alasdair Spark, "Flight Controls: The Social History of the Helicopter as Symbol of Vietnam," in *Vietnam Images: War and Representation,* ed. Jeffrey Walsh and James Aulich (London: Macmillan, 1989), 89.

11. Michael Herr, *Dispatches* (New York: Avon, 1978), 160.

12. Ibid., 9.

13. Spark, "Flight Controls," 102. Because the sandy desert terrain in the Middle East is destructive to helicopters, they were used less in the Persian Gulf War. Hence their iconography in the United States remains tied to the Vietnam War.

14. These helicopters are now priced at $100,000, whereas several years ago they cost $1 million. They carry "high-powered gyrostablized cameras" that can

magnify up to seventy-two times. Kathy Haley and Rich Churchill, "Chopper Wars Heat Up the Sky," *Broadcasting and Cable*, September 21, 1998.

15. As quoted in Greg Hise, Michael Dear, and H. Eric Schockman, "Rethinking Los Angeles," in *Rethinking Los Angeles*, ed. Michael Dear, H. Eric Schockman, and Greg Hise (Thousand Oaks, Calif.: Sage Publications, 1996), 2. See Reynard Banham, *Los Angeles: The Architecture of Four Ecologies* (Harmondsworth, England: Penguin, 1973).

16. Margaret Morse, "An Ontology of Everyday Distraction: The Freeway, the Mall, and Television," in *Logics of Television*, 199. Morse is drawing here in part on the work of David Brodsly, *L.A. Freeway: An Appreciative Essay* (Berkeley: University of California Press, 1981).

17. Reed, "Transcript of Calls," 22.

18. Geordie Greig, "Run, Run! Nation Joins in the OJ Murder Sensation," *Sunday Times* (London), June 19, 1994.

19. Tom Kiska, "How TV Covered the Simpson Chase," *Detroit News*, June 18, 1994.

20. Gregory Gross, "Sports Fans Strain to See Twin Bill," *San Diego Union-Tribune*, June 18, 1994, A1.

21. Associated Press, "L.A. Eyes," A1.

22. Greg Braxton and Brian Lowry, "TV Stations Reconsider Live Coverage Policies," *Los Angeles Times*, May 2, 1998, A19.

23. Ibid.

24. Mike Downey, "A Life-and-Death Tale of Freeways and Fate," *Los Angeles Times*, July 8, 1998, A3.

25. Alan Abrahamson and Miles Corwin, "Man Kills Self as City Watches," *Los Angeles Times*, May 1, 1998, A1.

26. Deanne Stillman, "Cops on the Freeway in Pursuit. Who Can Turn It Off?" *New York Times*, February 28, 1999, 43.

27. Robert Laurence, "Media Saturated Ending Bring the Public Spectacle Full Circle," *San Diego Union-Tribune*, October 4, 1995, A3.

28. Tribune News Services, "Potential Juror in Simpson Trial Truly Uninformed," *Chicago Tribune*, October 1, 1996, 13.

Tomorrow Will Be . . . Risky and Disciplined

TOBY MILLER

24-hour programming on the Weather Channel has a wonderful narcotic effect.
Not only is its focus so narrow as to exclude 98 percent of all human excitements,
but we've spent an entire evolution trying to insure our safety from the elements.
So what could be more soothing than the contemplation of huge climatic events
reduced to a pixeled 19-inch image, rendered in cartoon symbols and schematic
maps and narrated by preoccupied "weather hosts."
—*Daniel Menaker, "My Favorite Show"*

Weather comes to us in a state of culture. It is tempting to get metaphysical
about the weather by stressing the elemental humanness that supposedly
emerges as we battle it.[1] And its spiritual significance has been testified to by
almost a century of fights between physicists and theologians over whether
heaven or hell is hotter, given the Bible's ambivalent calculation of these
matters.[2] But the weather is equally to do with the mundanity of the quotidian. And our mediated ways of knowing the weather derive not from a dis-
interested search after truth but from the "demands of specific clients": the
informational needs of rural producers, airlines, and the military, and the
commodity needs of advertisers. Their preparedness to pay large sums to
satisfy those desires grants the weather exchange value.

Weather also comes to us in a governed form. U.S. presidents have long
invested in creating a human-run climate, back from the time when Thomas
Jefferson maintained that "rain follows the plow."[3] Clearing land westward
would make rain for the plains in time for cultivation—a miraculous homology between expansion and the nationing of weather. The gamut of modern
attempts to control weather runs from firing cannon and rockets and ringing
bells to inserting dry ice in supercooled clouds, including the splendidly
named "Soviet hail suppression scheme."[4] In 1961, John F. Kennedy pro-
posed that the General Assembly of the United Nations embrace the project
of modernity in a thoroughly technological way—weather was to be mastered, brought under human domination so that populations would no
longer be susceptible to its caprices. He called for "cooperative efforts
between all nations in weather prediction and eventually in weather control."[5] This "cooperation" took many different forms, of course, notably the

CIA's weather terrorism, which sought to undermine Cuba's sugar by seeding clouds before they hit the island, and the Department of Defense's attempt to make the Ho Chi Minh trail impassable.[6] The CIA continues to invest in climate change. It promises that mastery over the weather, which the agency refers to as the country's "greatest single challenge," will reward the United States with "the primacy in world affairs it had in the immediate post–World War II era," as climatic change affects agriculture in other countries.[7]

In keeping with that history, and the recent turn to neoliberalism, it took a century for the federal government to give the weather autonomy from the army and departments of agriculture and commerce. Today, however, we confront the privatization of meteorology.[8] In short, the historical and contemporary field of weather knowledge is sodden with governmentality and commodification. Meteorology is supplemented by economics, to assess the value of a public good; psychology, to evaluate individual and collective conduct; statistics, to plot trends and probabilities; and management studies, to control organizations.[9]

Sometimes this corporate/state history takes bizarre form. In the 1960s, Guy Lombardo complained to the Federal Communications Commission that New York TV forecasts were diminishing crowds for his outdoor summer shows at Jones Beach, while the Car Wash Institute lobbied the commission to require meteorologists to replace the expression "partly cloudy" with "partly sunny" in order to assist summer business.[10] After the devolution of self-government to Wales and Scotland in the late 1990s, the BBC instructed its announcers not to refer to "national weather" anymore.[11] The story can also be more seriously conspiratorial. Svetlana Boym notes that watching TV in the Soviet Union during the attempted 1991 coup was only possible via the satellite signal of CNN, so Muscovites saw footage of the revolt interspersed with Hurricane Bob's progress across New England. The flow between these stories produced intertextual slippage, with some viewers believing that the hurricane was on its way to Siberia and would wreak inordinate havoc. Of the three events, two real and one mythic, Radio Beijing found space to cover only the major storm season in the United States.[12] In China, it took until 1999 for the news media to be granted the freedom to report temperatures in excess of the human body's own norm.[13]

The weather resists political reading, even when climate change is the outcome of industrialization. Consider the moment in 1988 when Republicans drew breath as NASA scientist James Hansen testified to Congress that it was "time to stop waffling so much. We should say that the evidence is pretty strong that the greenhouse effect is here." The nation's lengthy drought and heat wave drew all the major networks to cover his testimony.[14] This was a high-water mark in news and current affairs' coverage of ecological issues, but it did not turn the weather report into an environmental watch, for all the flurry of intergovernmental scientific congresses that followed, precisely because of that technologization and an ideological counteroffensive. *Forbes* magazine offered a conspiracy theory, that "just as Marxism is giving way to markets, the political 'greens' seem determined to put the world economy back into the red, using the greenhouse effect."[15] The Republicans' "wise use coalition" protested that environmentalists were "putting rats ahead of family wage jobs."[16] Some Third Worldists saw U.S. media and governmental concern as crypto-colonialism, with climate change an alibi for shutting down development in the South. And segments of the domestic left feared that eco-panic might be a last, desperate, post–Cold War lunge for money by the remnants of "big science."[17] This "conspiracy," whether it was the creature of big business, big science, big neocolonialism, or big leftists, did not retain governmental or media interest—Al Gore left the Senate for veepish pastures and a series of key journalists resigned.[18] Content analysis of the *New York Times* and the *Washington Post* between 1980 and 1995 reveals a movement from coverage of global warning as a potential disaster to a topic of intramural scientific controversy.[19] Nor was the slack taken up by TV meteorology. The seeming reality—that carbon dioxide from gaseous emissions permits the sun to penetrate the atmosphere and stay there, rending the ozone layer asunder—was not tied in to television weather's daily policing of life, as might be the case if the latter were seriously concerned with explaining climatic relations of cause and effect.[20]

TV meteorology does not describe the corporations, governments, technologies, and techniques that help to make weather happen. Instead, the weather on television exemplifies vicarious living—you could look outside, consult a temperature gauge, or open a window to examine the sky, the heat, or the wind. But no, you turn to TV. So it's easy to see television weather as the epitome of all that is wrong with the medium in general— that it makes for passive spectatorship and defers us from direct experience of life, distracting viewers from both autotelic pleasures and the great tasks of history. It has been suggested that people accept what is given them as irrational precisely because it is beyond human control.[21] For the location of weather in traditional news formats—after politics and sports—positions it on the cusp of entertainment. It brackets commercials and politics, neither one nor the other: "a kind of bridge from news of a very serious nature to something at least a little lighter."[22] The weather simply happens and is reported well or ill. There seems to be no politics to its "immobilizing power."[23] Critics point to the gimmicky absurdity of TV weather reports from cookouts.[24] This almost jocular banality is exacerbated when presenters become celebrities (as when the Weather Channel's Cheryl Lempke featured in a 1999 *Mirabella* fashion shoot).[25] So PBS maven Susan Murphy refers to the weather as "extraneous" and "fluffy" in explaining to viewers why they should support *The News Hour* and *BBC World News* rather than commercial bulletins. As she put it (on WLIW, March 8, 1999): "Only special people watch *BBC News* . . . I know you're a responsible citizen."

This essay examines some of the history of covering weather on television both as a component of the news and as programming in its own right, as well as considering how meteorologists signify in popular culture more generally. The fact that the thirty on-air staff at the Weather Channel (1998)— the classic case of the genre that became a medium—are neatly divided between those with college degrees in meteorology versus communications captures the dynamic of science and performance that is characteristic of the field. The absence of environmental deduction or induction in their presentations illustrates the genre's decontextualized, apolitical blend of empiricism and prediction (its source of appeal to many viewers).[26]

I seek to follow Bruno Latour's proposal that we allow equal significance to natural phenomena, social forces, and textualization in the analysis of contemporary life.[27] For just as the objects of science only come to us in hybrid forms affected by power and meaning, so the latter two domains are themselves affected by nature. The mix of faith and skepticism in technology and the media, added to the pervasive military, corporate, and environmental politics underpinning and overhanging weather forecasting, make it very much tomorrow's topic. Meteorology encapsulates the notion of a "risk society," characterized by "institutions of monitoring and protection" that watch over threats to people and institutions from "social, political, economic and individual risks" in the service of the time discipline required by capitalism. Rather than risk being occasional and/or manageable, weather is now a constitutive component of being and social organization.[28] Advanced industrial/postindustrial societies induce massively increased feelings of risk in their populations by admitting and even promoting the irrationality of the economy. This is evident in TV meteorology, which serves as an icon of displaced concerns that also helps in disciplining the workforce and the stock market. In fact, the latter's first innovation of the new century was to sell weather derivatives, with a utility-industry benchmark of 18.3 degrees centigrade.[29] Anyone for weather?

History and Narrative

We Americans can and do keep track almost instantaneously of events the world over. Because we know and care about what is going on, we are perhaps better citizens.
—*Bob Siller, Ted White, and Hal Terkel,* Television and Radio News

Very quickly, the TV weather forecast turned out to be a very saleable commodity.
There were always sponsors for it. It always made money.
—*Frank Field*, Dr. Frank Field's Weather Book

Australia has a magnificent TV weather service. In the US, weather is showbiz.
—*Australian Director of Meteorology John Zillman*

After the U.S. Civil War, signals officers sought a justification for their continued employment and found it in reporting on the weather. President Ulysses Grant signed a congressional resolution mandating such a service in 1870.[30] Fifty years later, a newer technology took over the task. Weather was a major programming feature of college radio in the early twentieth century, with Morse code transmitting forecasts before the first news breaks. This should come as no surprise since physicists were key people in the technical management of the stations. Among audiences, there was competition to pick up the most-distant signals in the face of both geography and climate. As one of these self-styled "radio maniacs" put it, the search for a perfect apparatus and reception proudly pitted self-reliance against "the endless perversity of the elements."[31] The new medium was both a carrier of weather information and a sign of "man's" capacity to succeed in spite of it. By 1921, the University of Wisconsin's 9XM aired full forecasts. The new medium was soon embraced by the U.S. Department of Agriculture, which supplied stations with market and weather information in the interests of farmers. This grew into part of rural-extension distance education.[32] The first full-time weather presenter was hired by Cincinnati's WLW in 1940.[33] American broadcast weather's early days saw a direct radio link to what was then called the U.S. Weather Bureau, where stolid bureaucrats would give brief synopses.

After World War II and the televisualization of America, the weather report was positioned as an entertaining forum for stations to "help" audiences plan their work and leisure. There were personality-driven segments, the first being NBC's "Wooly Lamb," an animated sheep that pronounced on the weather in the 1940s. "Wooly" quickly ran into competition from women in bikinis and Jan Crockett playing the ukulele—CBS held that "[w]omen sell more." NBC countered with a singing weather presenter and puppeteers through the 1960s, though there were also spots for returning GIs who had worked in meteorology during World War II. (This populist past lives on. Willard Scott's former occupation was as Bozo the Clown before he graduated to being the first Ronald McDonald.) The Midwest held out against comedy routines—its storms were deemed too dangerous to permit such levity—and weather forecasts featured the redoubtable Clint Youle, inventor of a cattle gate that permitted vehicles and people free passage but smacked cows in the head. In the 1960s, interest in space and science, plus the advent of satellite photography, encouraged the networks to look for presenters who could offer a blend of fun (through beauty or gimmickry) and accreditation (via study in college or the military).[34]

In Australia, by contrast, the process functioned in reverse: all presenters came from the Weather Bureau on a rostered basis until one of their number, Alan Wilkie, appeared umbrella in hand to signify rain. This indexically inclined official became the country's first star performer, subsequently leaving the bureau and public television for a career on the networks.[35]

The first professionally qualified and nationally prominent U.S. weather forecaster was NBC's Frank Field in the 1980s (father of the wonderfully named Storm Field, who *had* to follow Frank's lead into TV). In addition to the diet book *Take It Off with Frank!* (truly), he wrote *Dr. Frank Field's Weather Book* (1981). It catches the dynamic of science as prophecy and fun that characterizes the profession. Dr. Frank records moments when he was aided by a pet dog or greeted by anchors with a hail of snowballs and accusations of personally devising the weather.[36] This combination of expertise and jollity continues to be deemed crucial to ratings, especially in the morning, when industry lore holds that people tune in for the weather above all other segments of breakfast TV.[37]

As Western Europe was transformed in the 1990s via deregulation and technology from a sphere of highly controlled media systems dedicated to a comprehensive service into wild TV markets, the weather came to loom large. British station L!ve TV, for instance, marked out its early days with a woman in a bikini reading late-night forecasts of U.K. weather in Norwegian (with English subtitles) and forecasts of Norwegian weather in English (with Norwegian subtitles). A similar program with nude weather reporters is produced in Canada by nakednews.com.

This requirement to give pleasure in delivering the weather has inevitably led to a narrative form. In 1963, NBC evening news executive producer Reuven Frank instructed his staff that with the expansion of their program from fifteen minutes to a half hour, each story must "display the attributes of fiction, of drama. It should have structure and conflict, problem and denouement, rising action and falling action. . . . These are not only the essentials of drama; they are the essentials of narrative."[38] And they remorselessly emphasize risk. John Langer deploys narratology to understand disasters on TV, arguing that coverage mimics fiction.[39] A state of equilibrium is assumed, where life is ordinary and manageable; a problem occurs, which sets disequilibrium in play; then normalcy is restored. Of course at times of dire emergency, the weather forecaster is more than a teller of tales. The Oklahoma City residents who survived tornadoes in the spring of 1999 attributed their escape to information from the television that pinpointed the path of the hazard.[40]

This reminds us of sociological functionalism, where an organic condition of consensual harmony is disrupted, but systems from within that consensus deal with the disturbance and offer renewal through governmentalized time discipline. Examples of such occasions and responses would be hurricane devastation followed by weather forecasts and related stories about overseas aid, emergency services, martial law, insurance, and so on. Official responses to natural disasters within the United States started as components of Franklin D. Roosevelt's welfare state (see, for example, Pare Lorentz's documentary film *The River* of 1937).[41] Disaster policies and programs are among the few unchallenged "relics" of that fabric of care, so inured to their benefits are key Republican and Democratic constituencies and funding sources.

Outside such extreme cases, Justin Lewis doubts the relevance of narratology to understanding news on television.[42] He argues that the genre is not organized via narrative codes: no equilibrium is established, disrupted, and restored. Rather, viewers are greeted in media res. A wild and wooly program provides only limited information about the background of stories and a structure that is fundamentally disjointed (albeit hinged to other programs by sports and weather). Lewis notes that empirical audience research suggests recollection of the news is minimal compared to other genres that are driven by eteological narrativity. The news lacks historicity, which minimizes spectatorial recall in contrast with soap opera or situation comedy. The absence of historical context and the chaotic interpretations this induces are not celebrated by Lewis as forms of resistance, however. He identifies a repetition of various orientations that are all about sustaining the status quo of politics. In this sense, TV weather is a nation-binding technique that acknowledges difference but ultimately contains it within averaged norms and reassurances of predictable change.

As Lewis notes, while the weather can form the basis of headline stories about chaos, it equally serves the function of demarcating the end of the news from the next program or break, reassuring viewers through the rhythms of climate and the materiality of geography. In this sense, it redresses the inchoate form of the news genre. The forecast also represents a crucial part of TV's star system—the scientific aura of weather presenters is matched by a humanizing one. Unlike experts who are interviewed on air, forecasters can represent themselves by opening and closing their segments and directly addressing the camera. The combination makes meteorology accessible, for TV weather is characterized by an essential stability in its order and reach. The same population centers are mentioned each night, located in the same spatial relation to one another. This helps to fix the otherwise asymptotic quandary of the weather as a component of time and space—infinitely knowable via the expansive reach and measurement of technology; but infinitely willful, frustrating all efforts to control it and sucking up the detritus of industrialization, generating unintended tomorrows.

In 1982 the Weather Channel began broadcasting to a potential cable audience of 2.5 million sets—now extended to 76 million in the United States alone, or 93 percent of cabled households. This rate of growth easily outstrips the average for cable networks and delivers numbers to advertisers that are far beyond MTV's performance. Cable operators themselves are key viewers, preferring it above all other stations apart from CNN.[43] Merrill Lynch dubs the network "a cash machine," with 1998 revenue of $200 million and operating profit of $100 million and reported 1999 revenues of $235 million.[44] Its average rating in 1999 was 0.4 of cable viewers (or 269,000 people), up 33 percent from the previous year, while Hurricane Floyd (September 1999) drew an average of 1.7 million spectators each hour and on one occasion 2.5 million, in addition to making it into sports bars![45] The company has developed El Canal del Tiempo and the Weather-Channel-Brasil for Latin America and the Caribbean, with locations in Miami, the new entrepôt for Latin/U.S. cultural production. In 2001, the Weather Channel is available to 95 million sets worldwide.[46] The network's one failure was a 1995 move into Europe, where the cable world was already filled to bursting.[47]

It has Web sites in English (attracting over 3 million hits per day and 23 million during Floyd, it is routinely ranked first in surveys of content-based addresses and was the twenty-first most-visited site in January 1999) as well as Spanish and Portuguese, a phone card call-in service, e-mail lists with personalized forecasts, direct presence in 250 U.S. radio markets, sale of weather information to over fifty newspapers and many company Web sites (despite serious Web competition from CNN, Yahoo, Accu-Weather, and *USA Today*), and customized wireless content covering 44,000 locations through pagers, cellular phones, and personal digital assistants.[48] As the network puts it: "If hell freezes over, you'll hear it first," a claim taken up by the 2 million viewers who tuned in over a fifteen-minute period during Hurricane Fran in 1996.[49] When a number of storms lashed the Eastern seaboard in January 2000, Weather.com received 63,976 e-mail messages over the month, including 4,331 on one day—evidence for its boast that the service gives "designer weather," a fine oxymoron standing for total commodification.[50] It also engages the Internet weather fan via chat rooms, archives, and special events, such as the splendidly named "Severe Tuesday."[51]

Clearly, the channel has worked out how to commodify its service in synchronization with new technology, unlike most other TV businesses.

This is partly due to the nature of its textuality. At once international and highly specific, the weather can be shuttled between macro- and micro-settings with great ease, thanks to its *toujours déjà* dependence on technology and a vast network of governmental and amateur workers who provide information that can be sold by the company: the National Weather Service (NWS) divides the United States alone into over four thousand zones, which have quickly been turned from purely governmental into commercial sites. Returning to Lewis' provocation, the network is said to encapsulate " 'detextualized' television." It lacks clear markers delineating one program from another, with the entire signal based on repetition and updates.[52] This specialization generates anxiety over the potential for "[a]udiences addicted to information pertaining only to their own special interests"[53] and led the network at one point to represent its viewers as sports fans cheering for cold versus hot and presenters to refer privately to their employer as "The Map Channel." The station's contemporary research divides its viewers between the "deeply serious" and "weather-involved" (who will watch anything and make up 20 percent of the viewers), "busy planners" and "instant users" (pragmatists in search of immediate information), the "weather-concerned" (cosmopolitans who look to see where they used to live or where they have relatives and friends), and "weather enjoyers" (who like the network's apolitical style of "television wallpaper").[54] It refers to the regular viewer as a "weather weenie."[55] And when the new century brought competition from the Discovery Channel's "Tornado Week" and "Hurricane Week" documentary festivals, plus a direct rival via WeatherPlus, the network responded with a 10 percent increase in expenditure on training, clothing, and new program segments.[56] In Australia, the locally owned Weather Channel introduced interactive advertising in 2000 and announced that 2001 would see telephone-connected set-top boxes for direct purchase of advertised commodities via an infrared keyboard.[57]

Weather Metatexts

[I]nformation about the weather has value only insofar as it affects human behavior.
—*Richard W. Katz and Allen H. Murphy,* Economic Value of Weather and Climate Forecasts

One out of three people in a recent American survey said they believed that astrology was "sort of" scientific. In a similar survey of Britons, only 63 per cent knew whether the Earth went around the Sun and fewer than a third knew that antibiotics do not kill viruses.
—*Lynda Birke, "Selling Science to the Public"*

I am chairman of the department of Hitler studies at the College-on-the-Hill. I
invented Hitler studies in North America in March of 1968. It was a cold bright
day with intermittent winds out of the east.
—*Don DeLillo,* White Noise

As the 1998 storm season saw Hurricane Georges sweep along the
Caribbean and Floridian coasts, New Orleans's WWL-TV took a call from
Nash Charles Roberts Jr., an eighty-year-old ex-weathercaster for the station known for deriding NWS forecasts as "house thinking." Roberts
alerted the news director that "[i]t's time for me to go on." His televised
message, conveyed via ink markers on a white board in place of the usual
presenter's Doppler computer technology, was that the National Hurricane
Center had got it wrong. New Orleans would *not* be the next landfall. He
was proven correct. Roberts based this counterprediction on a combination
of NWS data and information from oil rigs in the Gulf Coast, for whom he
was doing private work.[58] This story references three interconnected tendencies: residual media Luddism, the use of corporate resources to supplement
governmental ones (or alternatively, the fact that meteorology is part of corporate welfare), and a sense of the weather presenter as a magician, connected to the "specialist of the occult arts" who divined daily conduct for
absolutist European monarchs and Nancy Reagan.[59]

   This alchemical quality is a key theme in the mid-1990s mass-market
novel *The Weatherman*.[60] Dixon Bell is a bizarrely accurate forecaster at a
Minnesota television station (he predicts a tornado that slips past NWS
radar, and refers to officials of the service as "clowns").[61] Bell is ultimately
convicted of misogynistic serial killings, confirming the book's early prediction: "It took a special kind of animal to read the weather."[62] His quixotic
and uncanny forecasts are made all the clearer in the novel through graphic
descriptions of the state's weather extremes. There is a clear analogy
between Bell's insight, the climate, and the killings, all of them other-
worldly.

   A complex homology to violence is also part of the mystique surrounding the Weatherman/Weather Underground terrorist groups of the late
1960s and early 1970s. They drew their name from a Bob Dylan lyric, predisposed to argue for a need to go beyond mechanistic applications of
Marxism-Leninism in order to foment revolution against U.S. imperialism.
Here, the weather itself was enlisted over didacticism, with meteorology a
model of official knowledge whose intellectual and moral authority must be
swept away.[63] This is the riposte to Steve Martin's TV forecaster Harris K.
Telemacher in *L.A. Story* (Mitch Jackson, 1991), who insists, "I have to
maintain some dignity. People have to respect me so they'll believe what I'm
telling them."

It is interesting that the Weather Channel's Web site features some on-camera meteorologists' "Top Ten List[s] of favorite weather events." Rather than spectacular summer swimming or mild autumnal walks, these are dominated by violence: "The Blizzard of '79" and "Hurricane Agnes in 1972" (preferred by Rich Johnson), "Hurricane Andrew of 1992" (Marny Stanier), Georgia's "Governor's Tornado" (Terri Smith), Cincinnati's 1974 F5 "tornado event" (Kim Perez), and East Coast snowstorms in general (Mike Bono). Mike shares with us that his "favorite weather event is a good snowstorm," and he also enjoys severe thunderstorms, "when they're not threatening property." Ah ha. Good to know the latter. Must keep that property secure.

The fact that these folks highlight disastrous occasions yet never speak of human suffering in their accounts combines a mystical regard for weather power with a compulsion to "know" it, to bring natural phenomena within their understanding, if not their control. The autobiographical myths instantiated on the Web by their employer emphasize these aspects in ways that match the mysticism of anti-computer New Orleans ink-pen users and fictional Minnesota serial killers—the drive to comprehend is paramount.

In *Groundhog Day* (Harold Ramis, 1993), meteorologist Phil Connors (Bill Murray) loses all sense of time discipline during his February 2 stay in Punxsutawney, Pennsylvania, to report on the groundhog (also named Phil), which mythically finds its own shadow each year on that day in prediction of an enduring winter. Groundhog Phil is deemed a meteorologist nonpareil. Sent to perform his dubious duty for the fourth year in a row, Connors is caught in both a blizzard and an individual time warp that makes it impossible for him to leave. He is the true victim of time discipline—unable to transcend the specific date that has brought him to the land of the Northeastern rube. Sadly, the film turns this into an allegory along the lines of Scrooge from *A Christmas Carol.* At first, the sardonic city humor of Phil Connors turns unwanted repetition into daredevil arrogance. Realizing that there is no tomorrow because today will always recur, he vows, "I'm not going to live by their rules anymore." But then Connors goes through a form of redemption. Instead of playing his transcendence for all it's worth, he turns civic.[64] The part of Connors that accepts the diurnal tedium of weather merges with the character caught in the warp. Rather than continuing to abuse nerds, mock the repressive state apparatus, and be sexually straightforward/a jerk, he embraces normativity. The will to know is reinforced as part of bourgeois subjectivity even as it is achieved via a mystic experience. We could, of course, view this more positively, as the weather man ultimately foregoing the will to power of his profession, modeling in the process the emptiness of a consumer's "perfect knowledge."

Gus Van Sant's *To Die For* (1995) is some distance from this fairy tale, yet it too stresses the wildness of TV meteorology via Suzanne Stone Maretto (Nicole Kidman). Her weather forecasting is such a turn-on for Jimmy Emmett (Joaquin Phoenix) that he masturbates when she announces severe weather on the rise. Seduced by her and encouraged to kill her husband, he eventually does so in front of her live alibi, the nightly report, translating this into a sexual fantasy that both excites him and encourages deliverance from her alleged history of domestic violence. At the other end of the spectrum, the demonic Sir August de Wynter (Sean Connery) uses secret British government techniques for controlling the weather to destroy the world's climate in *The Avengers* (Jeremiah Chechik, 1998). Here, the desire for domination over the skies crystallizes his mania—from epistophilia to epistomania. The Brain in Steven Spielberg's *Pinky and the Brain* Tiny Toon animation series is compelled by similar ambitions, as is the evil Karl Stromberg (Curt Jurgens) in *The Spy Who Loved Me* (Lewis Gilbert, 1977). He intends to flood the globe in order to "change the face of history," introducing "a new and beautiful world." A milder obsessive form, afflicting his love life, troubles Leo, the meteorological protagonist of Robyn Ferrell's novel *The Weather and Other Gods.*[65] He fears ignorance of *"things like Flaubert, Althusser and leverage leasing,"* but remains comfortable with his profession.[66] (The academic literature addressing the impact of the weather on human conduct is voluminous.[67] Leo could have filed away potential smart-set conversation from plowing through it.) In *Twister* (Jan De Bont, 1996), the desire of storm chasers to penetrate tornadoes drives them to disaster; conversely, *Mr. and Mrs. Bridge* (James Ivory, 1990) illustrates Paul Newman's stubborn certainty in himself in a dramatic sequence when he avows that a twister he and his wife can actually feel will nevertheless not touch down to interfere with their dining. Newman and Joanne Woodward stoically sip their drinks as chaos envelops the country club. Mr. Bridge will not bend to nature or cultural change. He inhabits a different Kansas from the one Dorothy imaginatively flees courtesy of a tornado ride in *The Wizard of Oz* (Victor Fleming, 1939). Where she takes a risk, he favors discipline.

Risk-Discipline

Fortune returns when the weatherman's voice calms the airwaves.
—*Tom Conley, "Le quotidien météorologique"*

For me, the weather has always been the most reliable witness that the world would soon change.
—*Andrew Ross*, Strange Weather: Culture, Science, and Technology in the Age of Limits

When the weather wreaks havoc, it turns the world upside down. Objects and processes once considered straightforward and benign (spark plugs, drainage, commuting, or sitting by the window) are transformed into sites of great peril. An "other" side to domestic and professional life emerges as monstrous under altered conditions of existence, with the very weather itself anthropomorphized as willful.[68] No wonder meteorology performs the same structural task as superstition (a.k.a. religion): explaining forms of life that are outside the control of those experiencing them. This is crucial to the mythology of the Old Testament/Hebrew Bible. In Genesis, God manifests his omniscience via a flood to punish the world for its wickedness. His narrowcast to Noah predicts the torrent and enables redemption and continuation of life.[69] There are counterparts in Babylonia's Gilgamesh epic, ancient Rome, India, Burma, and Papua New Guinea.[70] The Kaguru people explain the existence of baboons as an unworthy evolution from humans—when newly circumcised boys and novice girls were permitted to consort after the rains had come, they turned into beasts. This serves as a taboo.[71] The personification of natural phenomena helps people make sense of what confronts them. At the same time, the drive towards sensationalism that impels weather today, where ratings are so critical in a fractured world of television, sees unnecessary hysteria. So the *Miami New Times* (1998) foregrounds the institutionalized anxiety of WFOR-TV's Bryan Norcross, referring to him as "South Florida's favorite weatherman-in-catastrophe" and deriding his "breathless, panic-mongering hyperbole."

Don't I know it. I well recall my first week as a cabled subject. I had been in New York a fortnight. At last, TV was mine. I turned it on, planning to take myself off shortly to a movie and dinner. But I was confronted by local news, specifically the forecast: "Whatever you do, don't go out. No matter what happens, do not go out. Stay home, stay tuned to . . ."; and so it went. I stayed home and stayed tuned while the city below stayed dry. The same thing happened the weekend before I finally drafted this chapter. Five years on, and the Weather Channel announced dire storms for the New York area. Same result—no storms, lots of TV watching, and much anxiety about turning on the word processor to write, given the risk of a lightning strike. This time I knew what was up—viewer security.

The time discipline inscribed by weather organizes key social institutions and their personnel around risk—get to work on time by allowing for nature so that the sale of your labor power is not interrupted, dress your children appropriately so they can turn up and obey the dictates of school as preparation for work, and plan your renovation to allow for climatic variations and safety costs. TV weather is politically conservative. It is part of what Thomas Mathiesen calls "the synopticon," which trains viewers to regard and emulate a small number of iconic figures (presenters) who serve as symbols of self-discipline and achievement.[72] It is the recto-verso of the panopticon, where the many are overseen by the few; here, discipline is instilled through simultaneous scrutiny of performers by audiences. This identification is assisted by the fact that weather presenters are frequently less attuned to conventional beauty telegenics than other front-of-camera news staff. Male anchors appear ruggedly intellectual, female anchors look attractive without being glamorous, and sports presenters seem as though they could once have done what they report on. But weather people need not resemble *Vogue* models, athletes, or clouds. They could be from next door, admittedly spruced up. Their achievement in getting to work each day is ordinary, like that of their viewers, and both do so through weather conditions. The forecaster encapsulates the midpoint between technology and nature, a handservant to contradictory masters who performs the parable of the dutiful worker.

For all this functionalism, of course, weather is about something more than norms and routines. The dogged time discipline of working life under capitalism must equally deal with difference—the diverse U.S. population parallels our climatic variations, occasioned by the absence of horizontal mountain ranges despite an immense land mass. This is matched in turn by regional identifications that buttress states' rights with the fabric of climatic specificity—a crucial part of anti-centralism.[73] And blue-collar workers may broker inclement climatic norms into improved wages and conditions. Difference can rapidly turn into crisis, with meteorology bleeding into disaster services and "the Feds" (suddenly) far from inclement in the eyes of good ol' boy bigots and their libertarian confrères. Unlike the psychology and victimology of crime and illness, the weather's capacity to destroy can engulf an entire news program, permitting the closing calm of the forecast to stand in for crisis management of suburbs, cities, regions, and nations. At this point, the forecast becomes a local, national, or international technique for binding communities together. More than information, it is an article of faith in empathy and sympathy.[74] It is governmentality.

When news editors select disasters for coverage, this is critical to public policy and civil society. For the Third World, First World largesse depends on Western media organizations defining a disaster as newsworthy and as related to conditions supposedly beyond human agency—the *"sudden, elemental"* kind occasioned by weather and geology. Of course, it is ludicrous to understand these events as apolitical. For example, the very notion of there *being* a sovereign state of the Republic of the Maldives relies on its not being consumed by the sea, while Bangladesh necessarily experiences floods and tidal waves because of where its people must live.[75] Like environmental despoliation, this *should* lead to the development of *"social meteorology,"* a form of knowledge that makes sense of the weather at the intersection of "social life, natural life, and economic life."[76] That can happen, as when Washington, D.C., forecaster Bob Ryan stood on Capitol Hill at the 1990 Earth Day rally and shouted in the direction of the White House: "This is what clean air looks like. This is the kind of sky we want."[77] Such a mixture of passion about nature with the "scientific" endorsement of media personalities is dangerous for capital, because it portends a potential populist critique of social relations.[78]

Technological knowledge of a natural phenomenon, the stretching and calibration of a key component of everyday life, is more than it appears. Televisual representations of the weather derive from and inform an economy of work and control, of time disciplined and described by institutions of capital and education that operate from the workplace and the department store to the school and college. At the same time, TV weather embodies the desire of modernity to know and control, that quirky combination of respectfulness, struggle, and destruction that characterizes industrial approaches to climate. This allegory of domination pits applied science against forces of nature. It establishes cause-and-effect relations between people and climate that are one-way, via models that set naturally occurring norms and breach conditions *against* human activity—so when we are given average temperatures for July, these are just "up" on the norm. No conclusion about global warming as a consequence of pollution is drawn from the fact that the 1990s were the hottest decade on record. The generic distinction that puts the Rio convention on climate control into the main body of news reportage, hermetically sealed in politics and kept separate from its indexical corollary at the end of the same program, is a crucial one. It defines the risky living engendered by economic modernity as a natural form, thus permitting a radical break between green politics and how to dress the children that morning. Tomorrow will be . . . risky and disciplined.

NOTES

Thanks to James Friedman, Marie Leger, Randy Martin, and this volume's copyeditor for their insightful comments and Marita Sturken, Ken Sweeney, Andrew Ross, Natalie Hirniak, Ed Buscombe, and Diane Zimmerman for references.

1. Lance Morrow, "The Religion of Big Weather," *Time*, January 22, 1996, 72.

2. Geoff Shandler, "Weather Report," *New Yorker*, July 30–31, 1999.

3. Andrew Ross, *Strange Weather: Culture, Science, and Technology in the Age of Limits* (London: Verso, 1991), 224.

4. William R. Cotton and Roger A. Pielke, *Human Impacts on Weather and Climate* (Cambridge: Cambridge University Press, 1995), 3–10, 48.

5. Matthew Paterson, *Global Warming and Global Politics* (London: Routledge, 1996), 24.

6. Ross, *Strange Weather*, 203.

7. Ibid., 202.

8. See Stanley R. Johnson and Matthew T. Holt, "The Value of Weather Information," in *Economic Value of Weather and Climate Forecasts,* ed. Richard W. Katz and Allan H. Murphy (Cambridge: Cambridge University Press, 1997), 75; Ross, *Strange Weather,* 226.

9. Richard W. Katz and Allan H. Murphy, eds., *Economic Value of Weather and Climate Forecasts,* ix.

10. Frank Field, *Dr. Frank Field's Weather Book* (New York: G. P. Putnam's Sons, 1981), 34.

11. Walter Bagehot, "Sunshine and Showers," *Economist,* April 10, 1999, 58.

12. Svetlana Boym, "Power Shortages: The Soviet Coup and Hurricane Bob," in *Media Spectacles,* ed. Marjorie Garber, Jann Matlock, and Rebecca L. Walkowitz (New York: Routledge, 1993), 118, 120–21.

13. Johnson and Holt, "The Value of Weather Information."

14. Allan Mazur, "Global Environmental Change in the News: 1987–90 vs. 1992," *International Sociology* 13, 4 (1998): 462.

15. Paterson, *Global Warming,* 1.

16. Konrad Von Moltke and Atiq Rahman, "External Perspectives on Climate Change: A View from the United States and the Third World," in *Politics of Climate Change: A European Perspective,* ed. Tim O'Riordan and Jill Jäger (London: Routledge, 1996), 336.

17. Paterson, *Global Warming,* 2.

18. Mazur, "Global Environmental Change," 467–69.

19. Katherine McComas and James Shanahan, "Telling Stories about Global Climate Change," *Communications Research* 26, 1 (1999).

20. Alison Anderson, *Media, Culture, and the Environment* (New Brunswick, N.J.: Rutgers University Press, 1997), 2.

21. I. C. Jarvie, "The Problem of the Ethnographic Real," *Current Anthropology* 24, 3 (1983): 317.

22. Field, *Weather Book,* 23.

23. Tom Conley, "Le quotidien météorologique," *Yale French Studies* 73 (1987): 218.

24. Bill Flick, "Weather Channel: Now It's Even Getting Competition?" *Pantagraph,* August 20, 2000.

25. Geraldine Fabrikant, "The Weather Channel's High-Profit Center: Low Costs and Loyal Viewers Create One of Cable TV's Success Stories," *New York Times,* March 15, 1999, C9.

26. Morrow, "The Religion of Big Weather."

27. Bruno Latour, *We Have Never Been Modern,* trans. Catherine Porter (Cambridge, Mass.: Harvard University Press, 1993), 5–6.

28. Ulrich Beck, Anthony Giddens, and Scott Lash, *Reflexive Modernization: Politics, Tradition, and Aesthetics in the Modern Social Order* (Stanford, Calif.: Stanford University Press, 1994), 5.

29. "Cold Comfort Farm," *Economist,* January 22, 2000, 73–74.

30. Erik D. Craft, "Private Weather Organizations and the Founding of the United States Weather Bureau," *Journal of Economic History* 59, 4 (1999): 1063–1071.

, 31. Susan J. Douglas, *Inventing American Broadcasting 1899–1922* (Baltimore: Johns Hopkins University Press, 1987), 308.

32. Susan Smulyan, *Selling Radio: The Commercialization of American Broadcasting 1920–1934* (Washington, D.C.: Smithsonian Institution Press, 1994), 21–22.

33. Edward Bliss Jr., *Now the News: The Story of Broadcast Journalism* (New York: Columbia University Press, 1991), 14, 458.

34. Field, *Weather Book,* 12–14, 25; Nick Ravo, "Clint Youle, 83, Early Weatherman on TV," *New York Times,* July 31, 1999, B7.

35. Brian Davies, *Those Fabulous TV Years* (Sydney: Cassell Australia, 1981), 54.

36. Field, *Weather Book,* 11.

37. Neil Postman and Steve Powers, *How to Watch TV News* (New York: Penguin, 1992), 37.

38. Doris A. Graber, "The Infotainment Quotient in Routine Television News: A Director's Perspective," *Discourse and Society* 5, 4 (1994): 483.

39. John Langer, *Tabloid Television: Popular Journalism and the "Other News"* (London: Routledge, 1998), 104–33.

40. Rick Lyman, "Residents Watched on TV as the Tornadoes Neared," *New York Times,* May 6, 1999, A31.

41. William James Burroughs, *Does the Weather Really Matter? The Social Implications of Climate Change* (Cambridge: Cambridge University Press, 1997), 47–48.

42. Justin Lewis, "The Absence of Narrative: Boredom and the Residual Power of Television News," *Journal of Narrative and Life History* 4, 1 and 2 (1994): 25–40.

43. Mike Reynolds, "Sports and Weather Are Ops Favorite Viewing," *Cable World,* February 1, 1999; Jim McConville, "A Revised Forecast," *Electronic Media* 19, 6 (2000); Johnson and Holt, "The Value of Weather Information."

44. Fabrikant, "The Weather Channel's High-Profit Center"; Johnson and Holt, "The Value of Weather Information."

45. McConville, "A Revised Forecast"; Associated Press, "Channel Weathers High Pressure Role," *Florida Times-Union,* February 14, 2000; Andrew C. Revkin, "Gaze Deeply into My Eye," *New York Times,* September 17, 1999, B1, B9.

46. The Weather Channel, http://www.weather.com/aboutus/.

47. Fabrikant, "The Weather Channel's High-Profit Center."

48. The Weather Channel, http://www.weather.com/aboutus/; Fabrikant, "The Weather Channel's High-Profit Center"; "The Weather Channel reigns; the all-weather network reaches 98% of all U.S. cable households," *Business Wire,* March 30, 1998; "The Weather Channel reaches growing Spanish-speaking internet community throughout Latin America with Weather.Com/Espanol," *Business Wire,* January 24, 1999; "The Weather Channel puts the weather in your pocket," *Business Wire,* August 14, 2000.

49. Brian Lowry, "Stormy Weather Brings Bright Ratings to Network; TV: Atlanta-based Cable Outfit Gets Its Best Response from Viewers When Events Like Hurricane Bonnie Dominate the News," *Los Angeles Times,* August 26, 1998, A8.

50. Kirk Laughlin, "Weathering the E-storm," *Teleprofessional* 13, 5: 51–53.

51. The Weather Channel, http://www.weather.com/interact/chat/.

52. Robert C. Allen, "Introduction: More Talk about TV," in *Channels of Discourse, Reassembled: Television and Contemporary Criticism,* ed. Robert C. Allen, 2d ed. (Chapel Hill: University of North Carolina Press, 1992), 12.

53. Bliss, *Now the News,* 459.

54. National Public Radio, "Who Watches the Weather Channel and Why?" *Morning Edition,* September 7, 1995.

55. Fabrikant, "The Weather Channel's High-Profit Center."

56. McConville, "A Revised Forecast"; and Johnson and Holt, "The Value of Weather Information."

57. Paul McIntyre, "Hot Stuff at the Weather Channel," *Australian,* July 20, 2000, M12.

58. Corey Kilgannon, "Forecaster Is Right On after Gulf Storms," *New York Times,* October 4, 1998, 26.

59. Conley, "Le quotidien météorologique."

60. Stephen Thayer, *The Weatherman* (New York: Viking, 1995).

61. Ibid., 14.

62. Ibid., 4.

63. Harold Jacobs, ed., *Weatherman* (New York: Ramparts Books, 1970).

64. For another view welcoming this as a quasi-Jungian crisis of masculinity, see Suzanne M. Daughton, "The Spiritual Power of Repetitive Form: Steps toward Transcendence in *Groundhog Day,*" *Critical Studies in Mass Communication* 13, 2 (1996): 138–54; and Davies, *Those Fabulous TV Years.*

65. Robyn Ferrell, *The Weather and Other Gods* (Sydney: Frances Allen, 1990).

66. Ibid., 31.

67. Philip M. Parker, *Climate Effects on Individual, Social, and Economic Behavior: A Physioeconomic Review of Research across Disciplines* (Westport, Conn.: Greenwood Press, 1995).

68. Langer, *Tabloid Television,* 115, 117.

69. Genesis 6:17–18.

70. *Brewer's Dictionary of Phase & Fable* (centennial ed., 1970), 310–11.

71. T. O. Beidelman, *The Cool Knife: Imagery of Gender, Sexuality, and Moral Education in Kaguru Initiation Ritual* (Washington, D.C.: Smithsonian Institution Press, 1997), 121, 124.

72. Thomas Mathiesen, "The Viewer Society: Michel Foucault's 'Panopticon' Revisited," *Theoretical Criminology* 1, 2 (1997): 215–34.

73. Ross, *Strange Weather,* 197, 215.

74. Langer, *Tabloid Television,* 111.

75. Jonathan Benthall, *Disasters, Relief, and the Media* (London: I. B. Tauris, 1995), 11–13.

76. Ross, *Strange Weather,* 13.

77. Ibid., 196.

78. Anderson, *Media, Culture, and the Environment,* 55.

Neighbours from Hell

Producing Incivilities

GARETH PALMER

In August 1997, Britain's ITV network screened the first *Neighbours from Hell*. The program was an hour-long special at prime time and featured a range of stories concerning the behavior of people caught in disputes with their neighbors. To considerable surprise, the program attracted 11.5 million viewers, a very healthy figure at any time and an astonishing one for a documentary however loosely defined. The success of the show was such that both ITV and BBC ordered more of the same resulting in a scheduling war in 1998 more suited to the launch of a new soap opera then factual programming. *Neighbours from Hell* has inspired quite a debate with John Mulholland arguing that the program marked a sort of watershed for serious program making in the U.K.[1]

In the following essay *Neighbours from Hell* will be considered in the context of those changing documentary forms and practices sometimes grouped under the banner of "reality TV." First the new context in which communities and citizenship exist is discussed. The second section will consider how the style and language of the program are in many ways typical of the new broadcast climate in which sensationalism married to a fascination with surveillance is increasingly seen as acceptable. The third section shows how the discussions around *Neighbours from Hell* are expressive of some deeper concerns about the identity and function of the documentary-making community as they struggle to survive in a new climate.

The New Context

Neighbours from Hell is ostensibly about the extraordinary disputes that arise amongst neighbors, but the program is also necessarily about citizenship and the ways in which civility is not a natural condition but one that has to be fought for. As it provides a snapshot of Britain's community life, it is important to put the series in its political perspective.

The ideal of the neighborhood as a space where families can develop in relative safety has long been ideologically central to Tory and Labour governments. But the political climate changed substantially when Margaret Thatcher came to power in 1979, and these changes have altered the meaning of neighborhood.

Although first given legislative expression by the Labour administration of 1945–50, the welfare state was accepted by the Tory party and not substantially changed in any way during the following thirty years. The welfare state was part of a mixed economy in which the operations of the state worked with the market. What developed was a climate in which the state, working more or less hand in hand with local government via experts, planned ideal environments for its people. Although paternalistic and patronizing to the needs of those people, the plan was to create neighborhoods where organic communities could develop and provide the sort of intimate care impossible to legislate. It is only by understanding the depth of this consensus that the impact of the first Thatcher administration can be understood. When Mrs. Thatcher famously said, "There is no such thing as society, only individuals and their families" she was seeking to "restore the family and its rights to autonomy and privacy, to reconstruct its legal status as a domain outside the powers of the law, and to decolonize the immediate environment."[2]

The Tory governments of 1979–97 put a focus on law and order that stressed the importance of the neighborhood. The family was specifically addressed in anti-crime campaigns such as "Together we'll crack it." Crime was depicted as something that hurt not communities but neighborhoods composed of families. This depiction of crime as something threatening to the family was to feature in government campaigns but soon migrated into television programs such as *Crimewatch UK*. The Neighbourhood Watch program, which took its inspiration from a similar program in America, stressed the importance of organic communities composed of home-owning families. Very soon the widening gap between rich and poor found expression in the ways in which neighborhoods were maintained. The affluent suburbs are now patrolled by private security firms with an imprecise relationship to the police. Working class districts have become increasingly remote neglected spaces where urban decay has put new pressures on families. Here we witness the fragility of public order as a result of the "harsh policies of economic adjustment in the 1980's; a widespread crisis of political legitimacy, and the exclusionary impact of the space of flows over the space of places . . . took their toll on social life and organization in poor local communities."[3] The poor are sometimes patrolled by local gangs monitoring their territories in return for protection money. Like the private security firms, these individuals are also known to the police, a relationship that brings an uneasy calm to these troubled districts.[4]

It was formerly the case that the local authorities had a considerable degree of autonomy in dealing with their districts, towns, and cities, but another innovation of the new right in the United Kingdom was the "systematic dismantling of the local authorities by the state." When combined with the privatization of many services, it is not hard to see why the local authority had little role to play in the formulation of neighborhoods. As Hughes has written, "There now exists a profound democratic deficit . . . in the arena of local democracy,"[5] which is a direct result of Margaret Thatcher's "fanatical" dislike of local government.

Into the void created by the retreat of the police from the city centers has come new technology. England and Wales have more closed-circuit television (CCTV) systems than any other countries, making them the most viewed countries on the planet. These moves toward increased surveillance had the backing of the Tory government who gave out over twenty million pounds for the City Challenge for local centers to set up CCTV in city centers. The current Labour administration is funding similar schemes. This policy has the virtue of reducing the cost of law and order and is said to have the backing of the public (although actual responses to CCTV are far more ambivalent than we are commonly lead to believe).[6] It is because they are a popular and economic way of deterring crime that these systems are being extended to the neighborhoods where it is hoped they can bring cost-effective order. In 1995 Newcastle was the first English city in which CCTV cameras were deployed in a working class suburb to be monitored by the police. Other English cities are monitoring this scheme before developing their own programs. The CCTV camera stands as a sign of order and regulation, the advance guard of the coming technological invasion that will order us all more effectively.[7]

In a mirror to this panoptic vision, the populace are subscribing to the new technology of seeing. Two rationales have inspired this change. Some homeowners have taken to using videophones and externally mounted CCTV cameras to monitor their properties. Over the years, there has been an exponential rise in the advertising and selling of these devices for security purposes. Such cameras are seen as a boon in security and are considered assets when selling a home. However, the vast expansion in the ownership of home video equipment has been in the form of the camcorder, which has in turn become an important element in the new programming formats such as reality TV. Indeed, the impetus to film all aspects of domestic life is an untutored mass observation project in which edited highlights pop up in a variety of formats.

Neighbours from Hell can be seen as a haphazard contribution to the debate on citizenship. What it presents is a series of crises with which the traditional apparatus of the law seems unable to cope. The series' heroes are those individual families acting autonomously but with an innate sense of decency to restore order to the neighborhood. One need hardly add that such a perspective has a high degree of fit with both the Tory and Labour governments' shared ideological project to promote the family as a central meaning making unit in society. After shattering the consensus in her early years, Thatcher's reforms have lead to the creation of a new consensus in which the family has been restored to pride of place for both Tory and Labour parties.

In 1979, it was Thatcher's avowed intention to challenge the duopoly of BBC and ITV and their associated unions, which she saw as the last bastion of restrictive practices. The introduction of Channel 4 in 1982 was in some ways the last hurrah for public service television. What followed was the opening up of the market. The independent television companies had to make their bids for their franchises in sealed envelopes. They were to establish a desire to maintain quality broadcasting while also promising financial benefits to their shareholders. Not a few writers have seen the failure of some companies to have their bids renewed as a punishment for their production of shows that criticized the government (such as Thames Television and *Death on the Rock*). The government also welcomed entrepreneurs such as Rupert Murdoch who extended his control over British media by setting up Sky satellite television. More channels were soon followed by the introduction of cable television. The BBC has not been able to remain idle while the competition around it has increased and has had to adapt its own programming leading to management innovations such as Producer Choice. These changes have not all been welcomed, and the BBC has come in for increasing scrutiny as the public wonder to what extent the many repeats and the vastly increased provision of light entertainment formats still constitute "public service."

Neighbours from Hell developed in this new and aggressive broadcasting climate. Documentary is not the protected space it once was where it used to represent some of the best traditions of public service television and helped to fashion a public sphere. By the 1990s, important documentary programs such as *World in Action* and *First Tuesday* were cancelled because they were no longer able to garner the sort of ratings necessary for survival in the new broadcasting climate. This is not to suggest that documentary is dead, but it has had to adopt new strategies and use techniques it would not have considered in the past. New forms of documentary are all more accessible and less challenging than the old. Thus we see the rise of docu-soaps, which bring a documentary style to the investigation of inner workings of public institutions such as *Jailbirds, Health Farm,* and *Airport.* Another new trend is represented by the mini-documentaries such as *3-D,* which take eight minutes to provide a snappy portrayal of a situation that might previously have merited an hour.

The debate over the question of quality is still conducted in earnest by television professionals such as the Campaign for Quality Television who argue that certain "light" forms of documentary such as the docu-soaps have their place but that they are significantly different from the quality documentary. This debate has been complicated by the revelation of fakes in recent "serious" documentaries. Carlton Television recently incurred a substantial fine for the faking of scenes in a documentary on drug trafficking. Another prestigious company has been investigated for alleged fakery in a documentary on Manchester's infamous Moss Side.

Given the proliferation of new subgenres it may not be surprising that the critical reception to *Neighbours from Hell* has been mixed. Some have seen merit in the revelation of injustices while others have been negative— partly because the series fits neatly the "dumbing down of television" thesis and partly because it is a hybrid. Indeed, what both critics and documentary traditionalists are keenly aware of is this mix of styles.

The Series

Hybrids are designed to maximize the audience by combining a range of generic pleasures. *Neighbours from Hell* offers many: the immediacy of local TV stories, aspects of access television, legal cases so we may play at being judge and jury, the work of the video vigilante in the use of grainy camcorder footage capturing dangerous and often illegal acts, and the emotional thrills of the docu-soap and new police reality series (although most of the officers are not in action). All of this is presented in an ironic voice, which occasionally conflicts with sober documentary purpose. What unites the stories is a voyeuristic gawping at people who, like us, live in neighborhoods but whose world, unlike ours, appears to be out of control. We are bound to ask what sort of citizenship this is.

In the series screened in January and February of 1999, a total of fifteen stories were featured. Two-thirds of the participants could be identified as the "economically and spatially disadvantaged," that is, working class living in rented accommodation or council estates. The problems were all concerned with neighbors but more specifically the infringement of aural or spatial borders. The police were involved in half of the incidents although mostly as commentators rather than as active participants. This is important, for the series is not about the official forces of law and order but presents a situation where the people have tried to negotiate the legal system themselves. It asks what happens when the law is not enough; how do people order themselves; why has the system broken down? The focus is on people moving in (and out) of neighborhoods where they do not seem to fit. How does the ordering system of our culture work before the police are called in? Can we survive without them?

Each story begins in the same way—with a general view of the city, town, or village in question—and then gradually focuses on the actual location of the incident. Of course, this is a very traditional approach. But given that the program is all about a nexus of looking in a new climate of surveillance, this opening sequence might be read as that of a spy satellite scouring the country for signs of disorder. The narrator introduces us to the participants who all define the way they see the problem. These interviews are often followed by a reconstruction of the incident that sparked the trouble. Sometimes the subject's own camcorder footage is integrated into the narrative. If a legal decision has been made against an individual then this changes the representation: the criminal is shown in slow motion or in mug shot, the classic signifier of criminal guilt, and the program's duty to impartiality can be abandoned. The validity of the judgement is "proven" by the suffering of the family. If a case is ongoing, then both sides of an argument are portrayed so that we might decide for ourselves on guilt or innocence.

It is interesting to note that the criminal has no recourse to law if he has been found guilty of a crime before the moment of broadcast. Thus what might have been local punishment and shame are now turned into national spectacles. In other words, the criminal has lost the right to invisibility. Once the show has aired, the individual can now be branded a criminal; it is fair to "name and shame" them. This is itself reflective of new policies being adopted in some American states and in Australia where, as part of their punishment, young criminals are named and shamed before the entire community. It is also symptomatic of the times that producers of these shows are unashamedly concerned with catching criminals. In a survey conducted for *Broadcast,* an industry magazine, it was revealed that one of the goals of producers is to aid the police via the programs. A simple equation operates. The police can provide exciting "real" footage. This cuts costs and provides the *frisson* of the real. In a new economic climate this makes sense. But the attitude adopted by these new producers represents a paradigm shift of some distance from the traditional documentary codes of objectivity. New reality TV series represent an unquestioned obedience to the forces of the law and not to the searching inquiry that is necessary to create an informed citizenry. The rise of this form of television does not deepen or balance the viewers' understanding of law and order.

The visual language adopted in *Neighbours from Hell* is that of the tabloids. When a window is said to have been broken, we get a close-up of exactly that. When we hear of shadowy figures, this is precisely what we see. The show is unashamedly sensationalist, focusing on human interest stories and using all available methods to maximize an emotional response. This is not to claim that documentary has always shied away from adopting dramatic emotional appeals. However when it does resort to such tactics, it does so within a more formally structured enquiry into a social problem. In *Neighbours from Hell,* the social and political context is stripped away so that the gaze can focus on the pitiful object of attention. Music is often used to highlight the emotional qualities of the scene.

The segment featuring the Sumners is typical of this emotional approach. The story begins with a slow-motion drive-by tracking shot of a "dangerous estate" where youths, their faces digitally disguised, lurk on corners. We then cut to an interior where the young couple tell of their struggle. What follows is a catalogue of disasters in which they recount (and we see dramatized) break-ins, window smashing, and so on. The culminating incident involves their baby, who was almost hit by a stone thrown by one of the youths. As a result of this, the Sumners decided to inform the police. Making such a decision only meant that their troubles escalated. The gangs stepped up the level of harassment, and the couple were forced to abandon the home thereby falling from the housing ladder and losing over six thousand pounds. The final shot is of the couple leaving the ransacked home, all their possessions in a van. In a country where home ownership has been an important dream and a fundamental tenet of government policy with obvious ideological connections to the family, this scene is sure to have a powerful resonance.

Stark contrasts are drawn between the good nuclear family with the young baby as a symbol of innocence and the literally faceless youths. The former are always photographed in daylight, seated together on a settee together in a home. The gangs are only seen via infrared cameras at night speaking in the shadows. After the tearful testimony of the victim, we hear the street code of the shadowed gangs speaking of the "respect" the couple should have shown them. The traditional forces of law and order have proven ineffective: in the end all the Sumners can do is to sell up and move.

The series represents a comment on the perpetual questions of social order. Disputes arise because people have conflicting rules. However the program is not about exploring the background to the situation. Beyond an interview with a shadowy gang member (who may or may not have been connected to the Sumners), the program is depthless. The gang is uninvestigated and all the more sinister because of this. When faced with such terror and an impotent police force, what else is there to do but propagandize on behalf of surveillance technologies? The series develops a perception of incivilities in a lawless otherworld, thus increasing fear of crime. Increased surveillance is suggested as one of the answers. Such technology hardly fosters friendly relations, and as a result, suspicion breeds a frightened neighborliness. Television has a vested interest in these domestic dramas along with other private security forces whose existence depends on a strictly policed form of order.

And yet *Neighbours from Hell* does not only focus on the shadowy underworld of the working class. It also features stories demonstrating how the "respectable" suburbs are having problems. In another episode we encounter the Smith family, who live in a building converted into flats. Their neighbor, Mr. Hope, offered to give them free access to satellite television and connected them up to his own system. All participants were happy with this scheme until one day Mr. Smith noted a tiny camera looking out at him from the side of the screen. Mr. Hope had been filming the couple secretly and had amassed a huge collection of tapes. The voyeuristic interest in the story was justified by the fact that the legal system had failed to prosecute Mr. Hope because he had not broken any law. He was charged only with unlawfully filming a minor and given a three-month sentence.

This story focuses on one of the principal themes of the series—the sanctity of the family space. The invader was an unmarried middle-aged man, already, according to the ideals of the series, a dysfunctional creature. He was filmed in slow motion, his criminality sealed in the use of local newspaper headlines. In its outrage at this story, the series measured its own boundaries about the limits of the acceptable. And yet another unintended consequence of the show was that it played to our fears that we are being surveilled, that the private space of the family has been exposed as never before. A whole technological system is at work interrogating the private domestic sphere and seeking to regulate the functions of the family. Indeed we are encouraged to become more self-aware as we operate what Rose calls the unceasing reflexive gaze of our own self-scrutiny. What made Mr. Hope's interventions unwelcome was that they were hidden. *Neighbours from Hell* seeks to define the limits of acceptable surveillance, which are to protect the family.

The vast majority of the series's stories show the ordinary nuclear family unit trying to live next to strange individuals, some of whom lived alone and sought to pursue their own lifestyles. The widow who tried to get back her land, the old lady who looked after her many dogs: these people were pictured as oddballs at once part of Britain's rich heritage of eccentrics and yet also people who are out of step with the traditional family. It was made clear that without the intervention of the law, war would break out between neighbors because incivility is an ever-present threat.

In championing the family as victim, the series adopts an authoritarian populism and cultural traditionalism. Such an approach adopts the perspective of the new right whereby the public's, and in particular the victim's, view of crime is the principal determinant in designing policy objectives. It makes criminals "other" by portraying most of them as minorities and dismisses the idea of dialogue as ridiculous. It features a view of crime that is hardly conducive to a productive or open public life.

Thus far we have seen that the sensational treatment allocated these neighbors from hell is part of the drive to maximize audience in a new broadcasting environment. The series focus on victims and the role of surveillance technologies make it a typical product of the era. However, in some cases, the program appears to have a sort of an access function in which people have the opportunity to tell their stories. Thus *Neighbours from Hell* brings us stories from the front line of an uncivil nation.

What is of interest here are the ways in which these situations are presented as problems for governance, that of self-governing families and only secondarily that of the police. The last episode of the series features the problems of those who live on the Cranhill estate in Glasgow, a drug-riddled stereotype of urban squalor. The telling of the story brings together many of the themes that have featured in the series.

What we learn from the Cranhill is the process by which democracy emerges, partly as a defensive identity but principally as a voluntary association developed through "informal practices that foster the norms of participation co-operation and civic responsibility."[8] Despite the signs of neglect caused by unseen others, it is families coming together voluntarily who do the work of self-government and, in doing so, aid the police by policing themselves.

The Cranhill estate is first described as one of the most dangerous places in Glasgow by one of the police officers whose "patch" it is. The story then moves on to the inhabitants who tell of how drug dealers and their clients make life unbearable. People are afraid to carry money for fear of being mugged, others are afraid to go out because of the very real possibility of being burgled. The situation climaxes in the death of a thirteen-year-old from a heroin overdose. As Councillor McCann recalls, "the priest said we were all to blame." The first half of the program concludes with photographs of the funeral.

The second half of the show chronicles the way in which the inhabitants fought back against these conditions. They began with a candle-lit vigil in which twenty people were anticipated. Five hundred joined them. Thus ensured of support, they decided to tell the police what they knew, in other words "grassing" for the sake of their families like the previous couple. They set up a residents' association to vet anyone planning to live in their block. As a result, the number of known dealers in the block is down to two. The story ends with the police praising the bravery of these women and recounting the increased number of arrests.

What we note in this story is how the communities are spurred on to act because they are frustrated at not being able to perform family duties such as attending christenings or looking after their children outside. What seems remarkable here is their dedication to the community when the reaction of many viewers will have been to leave the area as soon as humanly possible. The program thus demonstrates what can be done when people are working together. Community can only be restored by making a hard choice, to side with the forces of law and order rather than giving in to the drug dealers—"the participation of the governed in the elaboration of the law constitutes the most effective system of governmental economy."[9] The very idea of dialogue when faced with such extraordinary conditions seems laughable. The criminals are inhuman, beyond the pale. The environmental determinism that might be used as an excuse for such behavior is not countenanced. This is not a program about plans and policies. It is about the human consequences of such policies and how people deal with the situation. Sidestepping tricky political questions of blame enables the producers to focus on what is immediately understandable. By learning to empathize with other families, we reject the criminal as an alien other beyond thinking. Efficient government should not make them our problem. Our focus is the family.

We are offered three sets of reactions to such television—a pleasure at not being there, a fright at the incivility of others and a concern that the law be updated and the police given more powers to act swiftly and decisively. Such reactions help to foster increased calls for more policing and the need for self-government because the law is not always enough. While waiting for it to catch up, we continue to police ourselves.

The Decline of Expertise

If we return to the original objections to the series from critics and program makers, we see that *Neighbours from Hell* was attacked because it failed to do what "serious" documentary does—contextualize the problem, address the wider issues, interview the ministers/officials responsible—in short, to enroll levels of expertise. Its apparent willingness to flit from one scene to another looks frivolous against a historical background of sober and focused enquiry. The citizens it presents to us belong not to any group but are united only by a want of good neighbors. Citizenship is reduced to being something as simple as "Why can't we just get along?" Other possible reasons for the state of the neighborhood such as the neglect of urban planning, misguided policy directives, and new socially divisive policing strategies are literally no longer in the frame. To include them might draw our eyes away from the drama with unnecessary complications.

But when detractors complain about such programming, what they are implicitly discussing is the changing role of "serious television" in the public arena. The fundamental change that the series represents indicates a declining role for the expertise of documentary with concomitant shifts in the role of governance and therefore citizenship vis-à-vis documentary. In Foucault's sense, governmentality "has come to depend in crucial respects upon the intellectual technologies, practical activities and social authority associated with expertise. It argues that the self-regulating capacities of subjects, shaped and normalized through expertise, are key resources for governing in a liberal-democratic way."[10] It is suggested that documentary programs are part of the work of experts. Documentary has been both the *product* of expertise in terms of carefully honed skills in journalism, directing, editing and as a legitimate space for the *illustration* of expertise in terms of accredited sources, academics, and other authorities. In being presented with this range of views citizens have had the opportunity to make up their own minds. But series such as *Neighbours from Hell* eschew this type of expertise on the grounds that it is expensive and "dull television." However this change should force us to reconsider the role of documentary in a new climate where the work of governance is still going on.

One of the legitimizing narratives that propelled documentary was that it arose as a response to what John Grierson believed was a crisis of understanding. In his original formulation, Grierson believed that in order for democracy to work people need to feel they have a role to play, a connection beyond themselves. Citizenship was to be "sold" via documentary. In this classic formulation, documentary celebrated workers' activities and then illustrated their connections to the wider economy. The project then might be described as one of explaining order. The first documentary makers, educated middle-class fellows, leftish but not entirely unhappy with the status quo, became explorers of the unknown other world of the working class in the "jungles of the Clyde" and so on. But despite Grierson's desire to speak to this class for mutual celebration, the documentaries of the thirties gained their audiences in schools, museums, and cinema clubs. Distributors and exhibitors were less than keen to take the films because they didn't attract audiences. Thus the working class became objects of attention to a middle-class group of schoolchildren, cineastes, and administrators.[11]

It was in the mid-thirties that groups from the left of the Conservative party and the right of the Labour party formed alliances in organizations such as the Next Five Years Group and Political and Economic Planning. The intention of these groups was to apply scientific solution to society's ills. It was their belief that an intellectual strata fully supplied with all the relevant facts could redesign society more efficiently. The documentaries produced by the British Documentary Movement, particularly in the later half of the thirties, can be seen as informing this new scientific ethos. In documentaries now considered classics such as *Children at School* and *Housing Problems,* social ills were revealed alongside the ideal and practical solution. As such they became part of the matrix of expertise that would eventually lead to the creation of the welfare state in 1945. "What might be called a natural-social demand for order or for mechanisms to integrate individuals into appropriate schemes of behaviors and activity is met by an expertise licensed by the state but formally independent of it; medicine, psychiatry, psychology, criminology, pedagogy."[12] Documentary was taken up by the BBC in the 1950s when it soon became the province of middle-class university-educated men. In appointing Paul Rotha the first head of documentaries, the ethos (if not the personnel or films) of the former movement found a new and powerful means of reaching that class that had eluded it for so long. Despite the appearance of a few mavericks, documentaries were made by men institutionalized in the BBC. Documentary soon settled into a series of established forms. One of its early pioneers recalled seeing *Housing Problems* at school and was determined to emulate its style and content. Documentary performed the function of bringing unknown issues to the light and was very much at home in the public broadcasting institution where it lived in a protected space and sometimes served as its conscience. (In this sense it was and is very different from film documentary whose irregular appearance, uncertain financial base, and infrequent screenings serve to give it a more radical, less comfortable edge.) Indeed it may well be argued that documentary was an important element in keeping the concept of a public sphere alive.

When ITV began in 1955, it also looked to make documentaries. It followed a similar pattern to the BBC with thirty-minute or one-hour programs that followed a social rather than a political agenda. This is not to dismiss them or the impact they caused but to stress how they were fired by the social conscience of their personnel rather than a particular political agenda.

As is inevitable in institutions, documentary makers developed their own practices, codes, and working ethos. As a result of this, documentary took a number of relatively fixed forms. A documentary lexicon arose, a certain way of telling a story became dominant. "All government depends on a particular mode of representation: the elaboration of a language for depicting the domain in question that claims both to grasp the nature of the reality represented and literally to represent the form in a form amenable to political argument and scheming."[13] Documentary went through a range of innovations in the sixties and seventies, such as drama-doc, which extended the appeal of the genre and became a staple part of the lexicon. Yet these documentaries remained connected to Grierson in that they demonstrated a continuity of purpose and a celebration of expertise both behind and in front of the camera. Documentary's status and function to inform the body politic was not substantially challenged.

Neighbours from Hell represents a problem for documentary makers because it uses the language of the genre but does not demonstrate the same sober continuity of purpose. Rather than locating itself as one of the discourses of sobriety, it flits from one issue to another refusing depth and the expert recommendation. Indeed it seems free of expertise and abandons the notion of balance that is integral to reasoned argument and debate. This betrayal of expertise is justified in that it speaks to the democratization of knowledge and the rise of populism. But perhaps it also points to a more disturbing trend towards the flattening out of the world.

The disappearance of the expert is taking part in a range of programming types from the talk show to new legal series such as *Judge Judy* and *America's Dumbest Criminals*. In these latter formats, the legal representatives face us not as members of a profession, for this is merely their uniform, their license for being there in the first place. What the legal expert is expressing is common sense, the sort of judgment that eschews expertise as other worldly and academic and celebrates instead the unarticulated wisdom of the "man-in-the-street." It is an important question for media researchers amongst others to learn how this common sense is generated. Yet what is hard to ignore is the growth of TV opportunities for common sense to be articulated in place of expertise. This is itself part of a trend to simplify law and order policies such as "three strikes and you're out," which are said to be the desire of the common man but which are crude and hopelessly ineffective ways of dealing with the complexity of crime.

Neighbours from Hell is keen to let "the people" speak for themselves but presents that voice in a way that is emotionally manipulative. It is symptomatic of a time when documentary expertise may no longer be appropriate. When the documentary makers complain about this exploitative style, they are also expressing a fear of disorder and the demise of their historical function.

With the changes that have come to broadcasting, we see how difficult it is for expertise to find a new footing in the market where the entire public service ethos is in doubt. This is not merely a funding crisis but a situation that fundamentally destabilizes the traditional documentary project. As a result, we are now seeing hybrid forms that seem to cross boundaries. A terrible beauty is being born somewhere between the old ideals where knowledge has a place and the looser still forming ideals of a quasi-liberal era where "the people" know best.

In its presentation of victims who fight back, *Neighbours from Hell* provides a fascinating glimpse of government in action. That fight is an expression of governmental power that "constructs individuals who are capable of choice and action, shapes them as active subjects and seeks to align their choices with the objectives of governing authorities."[14] At the center of this is the crucial work of the family as the way forward—for social change and in elaborating the work of the law. As Dean put it, "demands of the rights of individuals against the state necessarily require the development of new forms of governmental practice to secure, defend, protect and foster these rights . . . the state thrives through demands both for liberties and rights and for order, provision and welfare."[15] Series such as *Neighbours from Hell* make a pretense to social understanding, but the model of citizenship implied is based solely on the family, a family whose main project is to make itself secure and electronically remote from all signs of dangerous difference. What sort of community can be built on such feeble foundations? The state can develop strategies of increased surveillance because the evidence to which the public respond helps to bind them with insecurity and fear.

Neighbours from Hell closes down rather than opens up the democratic project. Citizenship becomes a matter of the consumer in the home and not individuals in public space. As documentary material, such work contributes to the debate on privacy but in a way that fuels the call of experts for more surveillance and more disciplinary technology. It offers us a very limited understanding of public life. In short, this is a sort of anti-documentary but it does not critique or create solutions. This is documentary that actively participates in the divides between citizens, that defines people into categories good and bad, black and white, rather than offering an alternative at a time when we need a critical voice more than ever. And yet it is also symptomatic of the era. The documentary language and the experts who have spoken through it are no longer firmly in place in large institutions. A different style is not only a sign of its tired currency but evidence that it has become empty and uncertain in the age of the fake.

These changes in documentary form are not merely a sideshow for an industry that loves to talk about itself.[16] Documentary's central place in the public sphere and its role in the process of governmentality are mutating in a way that affects public knowledge of the world beyond and ourselves. These changes have to be linked to other policy directives that affect the way we are governed and govern ourselves. There is a pressing need for media academics to examine how governmentality works through television and how it links to other developments in the public realm.

NOTES

1. John Mulholland, "What's up, Docs?" *Manchester Guardian*, January 26, 1998, 7.

2. Nikolas Rose, *Governing the Soul* (London: Routledge, 1989).

3. Manuel Castells, *The Power of Identity* (Oxford: Blackwell, 1997), 63.

4. Sandra Walklate, "Excavating the Fear of Crime: Fear, Anxiety, or Trust?" *Theoretical Criminology* 2, 4 (1998).

5. Graham Hughes, "Communitarianism and Law and Order," *Critical Social Policy* 16 (1996): 17–41.

6. Elaine Short and Jason Ditton, "Seen and Now Heard: Talking to the Targets of Open Street CCTV," *British Journal of Criminology* 38, 3 (1998).

7. Jock Young, "The Tasks of a Realist Criminology," *Contemporary Crises* 2 (1998): 337–56.

8. Bill Jordan and John Arnold, "Democracy and Criminal Justice," *Critical Social Policy* 15 (1995): 170–82.

9. Mitchell Dean, *Critical and Effective Histories: Foucault's Methods and Historical Sociology* (London: Routledge, 1994), 187.

10. Paul Miller and Nikolas Rose, "Governing Economic Life," in *Foucault's New Domains,* ed. Mike Gane and Terry Johnson (London: Routledge, 1993), 75.

11. P. Swann, *The British Documentary Movement 1929–1945* (Cambridge: Cambridge University Press, 1979).

12. Graham Burchell, "Peculiar Interests: Civil Society and Governing the System of Natural Liberty," in *The Foucault Effect: Studies in Governmentality,* ed. Graham Burchell, Colin Gordon, and Paul Miller (Hemel Hempstead: Harvester Wheatsheaf, 1991), 142.

13. Miller and Rose, "Governing Economic Life," 80.

14. David Garland, "Governmentality and the Problem of Crime," *Theoretical Criminology* 1 (1997): 173–211.

15. Dean, *Critical and Effective Histories,* 186.

16. Mike Carter, "Time for a Reality Check," *Broadcast,* September 18, 1998, 38–40.

The Court of Last Resort

Making Race, Crime, and Nation on America's Most Wanted

MARGARET DEROSIA

I can't help but see how each piece of the drama fits neatly into the other: one
woman's misery is another man's pleasure; one man's pleasure is another man's
crime; one man's crime is another man's beat; one man's beat is another man's TV
show. And all of these pieces of the drama become one big paycheck for the
executive producer.
—*Debra Seagal*

We're in the business of tricking people into thinking that spending hundreds of
millions for new prisons will make them safer.
—*Daniel O'Brien, assistant to Minnesota's Commissioner of Corrections*

America's Most Wanted premiered on the Fox network in 1988 and quickly
became the network's number one show. Like others in the genre of reality-
based crime shows, it cost much less than a standard television sit-com to
produce and drew $5 million in profits in 1997 alone. Although nearly can-
celed in 1996, viewer and law enforcement protests reinstated it as *America's Most Wanted: America Fights Back*. As its former executive producer
Michael Linder notes, *America's Most Wanted* has become "a national
neighborhood watch program," fitting given that the trailer for the 1996
season's premiere enticed viewers with the line *"America's Most Wanted* is
Fox's *own* brand of justice."[1]

The program follows a standard format. John Walsh, father of a child
who was murdered, hosts an hour of profiled true-crime scenarios and their
presumed criminals turned fugitives. Typically each show features from
three to ten profiles; some reenactments feature the real-life victims as
actors. Walsh's commentary frames interviews with victims, their families,
witnesses, and law enforcement officials in order to abet the fugitives' capture. Throughout the show, a hotline—1-800-CRIMETV—is broadcast that
people may use to report information about people or crimes profiled. In

addition, the show also sponsors a Web site at which people may provide information, join listservs or discussion forums on both new and old cases, and even purchase clothing and coffee mugs with the *America's Most Wanted* logo.

America's Most Wanted has come to occupy a stable place in law enforcement in spite of its origins as a tabloid television program. The show's sensationalist and titillating qualities increasingly have been overlooked as its links to more official channels of law enforcement have been developed and strengthened. As a means of moving into my analysis I appropriate the punctuated vignette-style representations seen on *America's Most Wanted* in order to consider the following four instances in which either *America's Most Wanted* or John Walsh as its chief representative have appeared to both the public and government as a branch or extension of law enforcement:

- At the FBI building in Washington, D.C., a display plaque lists the various means by which top-ten fugitives have been captured; for example, through law enforcement efforts, citizen reports, or fugitives turning themselves in voluntarily. Now included on the plaque is a list of fugitives caught through *America's Most Wanted*.
- In an Associated Press article on the discovery of what was presumed to be the body of multiple murderer Andrew Cunanan, John Walsh was one of two people initially cited as an authority on the identification of the body and cause of death: a gunshot wound to the head. John Walsh possesses no medical or forensics training, but, apparently, his authority is indisputable given his familiarity as a television personality.
- The near cancellation of *America's Most Wanted* in 1996 prompted the following national response: "Word of *America's Most Wanted*'s demise spread quickly. Letters from over 100,000 viewers, 35 governors, 40 congressmen and many state attorneys general pleaded for the show's reinstatement. Nevada Governor Bob Miller, chairman of the National Governors' Association, issued the following statement to Fox: 'Strong legislation and committed law enforcement officials cannot stop crime alone. It takes programming such as *America's Most Wanted* to involve the public and lead to arrests and convictions.'"[2]
- The July 18, 1998, tenth anniversary episode began with John Walsh stating: "Ten years ago, we decided to use television as a nationwide crime-fighting tool, to deputize everyone in America as members of an electronic, interactive posse." The episode concluded with a taped message of support for the show from one of those deputized, self-proclaimed fans: President Bill Clinton.

What does it mean that "strong legislation" and "committed law enforcement" are insufficient tools for the combating of violent crime? The sentiment is especially troubling given that the 1995 crime bill rendered law enforcement and more broadly the criminal justice system better equipped legally, financially, and materially, in terms of personnel and technology, than any other period in the nation's history. Indeed, what is the cultural significance of the intensified development of television programming as an extension of law enforcement? As *America's Most Wanted* commences its eleventh season with an endorsement from the president, such an inquiry is more urgent than ever before.

The conflation of law enforcement and entertainment that *America's Most Wanted* enacts is troubling for many reasons, but this essay focuses on one in particular: such a conflation capitalizes on false, racist conceptions of criminality and helps construct a national climate of unwarranted fear and paranoia. The essay interrogates *America's Most Wanted* as "Fox's own brand of justice," and turns the show's investigative gaze back on itself. In particular, I take Dave Shiflett's characterization of the show as "the Court of Last Resort" seriously but with a more skeptical attitude than his original—and heroic—invocation implies.[3] Two interrelated aspects of *America's Most Wanted* will be examined, concentrating primarily on the 1996–97 and 1997–98 seasons. First, the show's reliance on racialized constructions of crime serves to legitimate a broader political economy of surveillance. Surveillance technologies are employed on *America's Most Wanted* extensively, but more broadly, the show actively promotes a suspicion of community members that demands surveillance by its viewers. Second, the fetishism of the physical, racially marked body on *America's Most Wanted* serves as evidence for the national body's assumed vulnerability to crime. The show traffics in familiar racist tropes and representations as the visual field from which crime itself may be signified.

America's Most Wanted engenders a climate of fear through specific televisual constructions of crime and evidence. Upon delineating the overarching aims of the show as well as how these aims may be interpreted, this essay analyzes a typical reenactment involving three African American male suspects from the summer of 1996. This particular reenactment is emblematic of the overall character, limits, and dangers of the show. Ultimately, the economy of surveillance promoted by *America's Most Wanted* constructs the very threat of crime it supposedly seeks to dispel, a threat mediated by racist imagery and motivated by oxymoronic notions of community: that is, communities constructed through and, ultimately, undone by paranoia.

Although this analysis concentrates on the national effects of *America's Most Wanted*, the show needs to be seen within its broader international and historical context. The televisual antecedents that inform *America's*

Most Wanted's genealogy stretch back to a set of European reality-based television programs beginning in the late sixties. The earliest example of this tendency was the program *Aktenzeichen XY . . . Ungelöst* (*Case XY . . . Unsolved*), which first aired in October of 1967 to Swiss and Austrian audiences but was produced in the Federal Republic of Germany. It focused on perpetrators of political not, as in later U.S. and European programs, violent crime.[4] Nevertheless, the success of this program influenced the production of similar programs across Europe. Instigating a turn toward concentrating more on violent than political crimes, the Dutch show *Opsporing Verzocht* (the words are taken from police lingo that loosely means "request information on the whereabouts of . . .") aired initially in 1984 and, despite declining ratings, has continued to air through the 1999–2000 season.[5] A more direct predecessor of *America's Most Wanted* would be the U.K.'s *Crimewatch,* which began in 1985 and which also has continued to air up to the present; currently the show is the BBC's top-rated factual program.[6] Though analogous to *America's Most Wanted,* Stuart Cosgrove argues that, in contrast to *America's Most Wanted,* murder is not the most profiled and reenacted crime on *Crimewatch* (which focuses on car theft, burglaries, and deceitful con men as often as murders).[7] The European influence on late eighties and early nineties U.S. reality-based television production inverts in 1993, as *America's Most Wanted,* among similar European programs, influences the creation of the French show *Témoin No. 1 (Prime Witness)*.[8] Finally, Crime Stoppers International, which originated in Albuquerque, New Mexico, in 1976, started the practice of making *Crimestoppers* vignettes, often produced and aired locally. The spots expanded beyond local and even national contexts: by 1988, there were 700 programs in U.S. cities, 29 programs in Canadian cities, and similar programs in Australia, England, and Sweden.[9] According to *America's Most Wanted* publicist Jack Breslin, the original creators of *America's Most Wanted* in 1988 "were familiar with the British and European predecessors, and wanted to Americanize them."[10]

American reality-based television programs about crime have drawn on a long tradition across print, radio, film, and television media invested in documenting and exploring, often through titillating modes of representation, the presence and effects of violent "true" crime.[11] While it is beyond the scope of this essay to document this history fully, *America's Most Wanted* has developed in the United States as a result of a particular nexus of national, political, and televisual programming factors. Within the United States, and beyond the already mentioned *Crimestoppers,* the most obvious televisual influence was the series of television specials on NBC in 1987, *Unsolved Mysteries,* which became a series on the same network the following season (reruns now air almost nightly on the cable channel Lifetime—"Television for Women"). Beyond the televisual domain, *America's Most Wanted* emerged from and responded to the conservative national political climate of the Reagan and Bush years. In fact, the show premiered only a year after the infamous and highly successful Willie Horton ads in then–Vice President George Bush's presidential campaign. During this period, social services were dramatically slashed, and the nation fixated on crime as omnipresent threat of modern American life. Also in this period, television news became more graphic in its representations of violence, much of which disproportionately represented violent crime as occurring in urban, predominantly African American or Latino neighborhoods. Increased televisual representations of racialized crime deflected attention from how law enforcement concurrently targeted these communities for increased surveillance and monitoring.[12] Throughout this period, passage of federal anti-crime and pro-incarceration legislation has proven increasingly popular; witness the easy passage of the 1995 Crime Bill, despite its problematic provisions of eroded or diminished civil rights, especially in racial and class equity in sentencing and appeals practices.

America's Most Wanted, like the above reality-based crime programs, emerged in this climate and represented itself as a tool to combat the rising tide of "real" crime. However, such programs, and *America's Most Wanted* in particular, actively encourage and in part construct this kind of an anxious and defensive political economy. By embodying the signifier "crime" with images and stories, they facilitate belief in the imagined inevitability of it. Indeed, as Anna Williams states, *America's Most Wanted* "constructs the criminal as the embodiment of his own guilt. Crime is 'explained' as the irrational violence of dangerous individuals and, therefore, as something which can only be responded to and not anticipated or prevented."[13] Such rhetoric then constructs, by extension, the implied national body as vulnerable and weak from within and therefore in need of greater discipline, tougher legal penalties, and more freedoms for law enforcement. But strengthening the national body by these measures sets up a vicious cycle: it ultimately translates into the production of greater systems of surveillance both at the level of the individual citizen and the state. As a result, suspicion becomes that which defines but ultimately unravels notions of local and national community.

Indeed, why has fear of violent crime and programming on the topic intensified in the last ten years when FBI statistics consistently have demonstrated a steady if slow decrease in actual criminal acts for the past twenty years? Why do opinion polls regularly contend that crime needs to be stopped no matter what or how? Such a climate of opinion is disturbing and leads me to ask several questions about the specific role *America's Most Wanted*—this "Court of Last Resort"—plays in this economy of ever more necessary systems of surveillance, incarceration, and punishment. First, are there really such inadequacies in our current justice system that we must resort to unconstitutional and sensationalist measures in order to fight crime? Second, is tabloid television, an exclusively profit-based and ratings-driven form of programming that distorts more than it objectively represents current events, a fair and reasonable way to counter these supposed inadequacies? Third, what sort of safeguards are being destroyed in order to assuage the intense fears produced by weekly exposure to lurid reenactments or surveillance footage of violent crimes? Fourth, what are the consequences of a rigid moral opposition between, on one side, law enforcement officials and institutions (portrayed as unequivocally beneficial individuals) and, on the other side, the often not yet tried and sentenced criminal figures (presumed guilty before proven innocent)? In terms of this last point, what or who is really on trial in this production of a collective national paranoia about rampant crime?

One of the primary mechanisms with which this economy of surveillance perpetuates and intensifies itself is through representations of racially marked forms of criminality. *America's Most Wanted* clearly contributes to the impression of a vulnerable national body by capitalizing on an extended historical association between criminality and people of color. Indeed, *America's Most Wanted* perfects the synthesis of associational and rhetorical forms of documentary representation as a means of persuading its audience of this supposed connection. Robin Anderson discusses this synthesis in reality-based television:

> A narrative discourse examining the multiple factors responsible for the situation [of violent crime in contemporary life], one that intends to explain, is replaced by images evoking waves of revulsion that wash over the audience. *Drugs, criminality, young black men*—the words go together like a media mantra. The fragmented associational narratives are divorced from the economic and social dynamics that explain them. . . . In an era driven by the influences of advertising, associational language has become the language of non-fiction programming as well.[14]

Such associations efface the myriad ways in which an intensified economy of surveillance has had and continues to have the most damaging effects on these same people of color it repeatedly targets.

My argument is not about the sheer numbers of specific racial identities on *America's Most Wanted*, but I do draw from a content analysis by Mary Beth Oliver of this show and other reality-based crime programs. She offers a set of statistics that demonstrate a pattern of how routinely these shows overrepresent white people as law enforcement officials and people of color as criminals.[15] According to FBI statistics of the period she examines, only 13 percent of crimes committed overall are violent ones. By contrast, on the television programs she examines, 80 percent of crimes depicted are violent.[16]

The emotional stakes are arguably higher in violent crime than political, corporate, or white collar crime, for example, and the U.S. violent crime rate is greater than most others, but there are obvious problems with the almost exclusive focus on representations of violent crime on reality-based television programs. First, the definition of what constitutes "violent" crime is generally held to fairly narrow standards. That is, the violence done to whole communities as a result of irresponsible and often premeditated forms of social, political, or corporate acts of crime does not receive the same critical treatment that isolated incidences of individual violent crimes do—if represented by the media at all. To treat both corporate and individual actions as similar signifiers of crime would undermine a central emphasis of contemporary media coverage of crime: that crime is always a problem of unprincipled or purely evil individuals, not a social problem or indicator of broader socioeconomic crises. Second and more pertinent to *America's Most Wanted* specifically, reality-based television programs frequently represent random rather than premeditated acts of violent crime. This tendency, as Oliver's analysis demonstrates, intersects with the show's frequent representations of people of color as suspects for these random acts of violent crime. As a result, reality-based television programs give a false impression of the extent of the threat of random violent crime in contemporary life and especially target white viewers' fears of people of color as the most likely perpetrators of that violence.[17]

The skewed numbers of white law enforcement officials and people of color as criminals that Oliver cites thus magnifies the above problems occurring as a result of *America's Most Wanted*'s representations of crime as predominantly violent crime. Because of the broader racist imaginary that serves as the backdrop to intensified fears of violent crime, people of color will be represented and viewed by white viewers on *America's Most Wanted* as more menacing than whites. Many episodes of the show confirm this mode of viewing, but an especially clear example can be seen on an episode from the spring of 1998, in which only two out of twelve people represented as criminal suspects were white. In sharp contrast to how people of color's acts of violence were represented on the episode, both of the white individuals' capacity for violence was characterized as inexplicable and shocking; interviewed (white) subjects referred to them as "not the type to do this sort of thing." By contrast on this episode and beyond, not only are people of color portrayed as perpetrators of violence more often, but when they are, they often are labeled explicitly as "the type to do this sort of thing." The perpetual return to the racialized body as a "naturally" violent one ultimately staves off fears of white criminality and promotes the image of the criminal as intrinsically threatening, alien, and other. The show thus relies on this dialectic of the racialized elsewhere threatening to encroach on the whiteness of *America's Most Wanted*'s viewers' homes, where the domestic, suburban living room functions as metonymic of the nation.[18]

Televisual vigilantism becomes an almost instinctual spectator response to this dialectic, especially given the show's extensive reliance on second person and direct address. Rarely employed on contemporary television as consistently and forcefully as on *America's Most Wanted*, Walsh frequently points his finger at the camera with a dead-serious glance and asks "you" the viewer to call in and provide information that will bring this criminal/ punk/scumbag/animal—all interchangeable terms, apparently—into custody. Keeping Oliver's analysis in mind, "the criminal," in opposition to Walsh's "you," continues to be represented implicitly or explicitly as a poor, drug-addicted person of color and gang member, usually male, whose body and actions evidence a presumed propensity to violence. Given this racialized opposition, then, the show's primary thesis casts a menacing tone: you're not going to be one of "them" if you're part of America fighting back.

The urgency of this opposition is underscored by the show's "live" broadcast. I qualify "live" because a majority of *America's Most Wanted* is prerecorded and assembled into a package of pseudo-liveness reminiscent of "live" television in the forties. Although television of that period was taped, it often promoted itself in opposition to cinema as a "live" medium in which anything could happen. The self-reflexive nature of many programs could be seen in frequent juxtapositions of the on-screen image and behind-the-scenes shots of camera operators and crew, direct address to the audience/camera (especially in variety shows like *Texaco Star Theater*), and narrative or generic content that encouraged or required audience participation (that is, quiz shows). Direct, live address and the call for audience participation on *America's Most Wanted* echoes this televisual past and acts as a barometer of authenticity within and for a shared community of viewers. However, this construction of authenticity ultimately derives from advanced visual technologies of editing and visual design that represent both "evidence" and its imagined community of viewers in highly selective and often racist ways.

As Jane Feuer attests, "live" television is not unique to the medium's inception but has been modified and updated over time in order to become television's governing ideology:

> As television in fact becomes less and less a "live" medium in the sense of an equivalence between time of event and time of transmission, the medium in its own practices seems to insist more and more upon an ideology of the live, the immediate, the direct, the spontaneous, the real.[19]

The delay between the time of event—the crime—and transmission—the broadcast on the show—is precisely that which gives *America's Most Wanted* its urgency: it represents an anxious prolongation of fugitives' escapes and, therefore, promotes spectator vulnerability, not mastery. That is, by invoking a participatory dimension to televisual viewing, Walsh's concluding proviso—"And remember, you *can* make a difference"—disavows the show's role in actively engendering fear and vulnerability in its spectators. The sense of spectator vulnerability engendered by viewing *America's Most Wanted* also positions the program as an extension of the legacy of "live" television in another manner. Many theoretical discussions of contemporary televisual "liveness" discuss a single emergency or "catastrophic" event that is out of the ordinary, such as O. J.'s Ford Bronco chase or the police brutality trial replays of the Rodney King video on network news.[20] *America's Most Wanted,* by broadcasting live and performing taped reenactments of violent crimes as if they were live, takes the logic of live television's fascination with catastrophe and death a step further. It makes the conception of live television's implied state of emergency a weekly norm, as "America" is seen under siege and infiltrated by dangerous criminals who are simultaneously both like and unlike "us," the supposedly law-abiding citizens watching at home.[21] In particular, *America's Most Wanted* demonstrates that this state of emergency traffics in specifically racially marked representations of the uncontainable threat of crime. "Liveness" highlights this threat by signifying race in specific, menacing ways, and by giving these acts of signification a veneer of the real; if the event being described is represented as a live one, audiences are more likely to view it as an unmediated representation, a window onto things as they really are. Like O. J.'s darkened face on the cover of *Time* magazine, however, *America's Most Wanted* doctors reality in subtle and not-so-subtle ways in order to promote the racist hypervisibility of "race" itself.[22]

In *America's Most Wanted*'s construction of criminality, and especially racialized criminality, evidence appears primarily as an elaborate network of images. Unlike other branches of law enforcement, *America's Most Wanted* does not need to provide proof of its accusations because it is "just" entertainment. Moreover, a shift toward more objective modes of representing evidence would disrupt the program's necessarily affirmative image of law enforcement itself. I say "necessarily" because *America's Most Wanted* could not sustain its source of material if a more skeptical or critical attitude were deployed; that is, local, regional, national, and sometimes international law enforcement agencies provide the content for the show and legitimate it culturally as authoritative and true. To introduce questions about law enforcement in turn would introduce moral, ethical, and, as I have been arguing, racial ambiguities about guilt, innocence, and the criminal justice system that reality-based television about crime cannot negotiate.[23]

As Paul Gewirtz states, "Most things about [a] trial refute the idea that 'I feel, therefore I judge.'"[24] By contrast, the Court of Last Resort not only demands but actively produces a view of evidence premised on "I feel, therefore I judge." In order to promote specific kinds of feeling, the show employs a highly cinematic style and advanced visual technologies that mask how biased its seamless scenarios of guilt are. Evidence is interpreted by Walsh and his "experts" through a series of techniques: rapid MTV-style editing that blurs temporality and spatiality; synthesized, nondiegetic sounds, voices, and music that amplify emotional response; brief snippets of infrared night filming (sometimes stock footage from other crimes) of police undercover or suspects under surveillance; intensive use of computer-generated imagery, particularly of DNA models; stock footage of DNA lab testing facilities, employees, and procedures; and finally, intricate forensic illustrations and sculptures of victims' and criminals' imagined aging, body composition, and disguises. Apart from Walsh's pithy commentary and voice-overs, these high-tech visual narratives are punctuated only by interviews with victims' tearful families or dedicated law enforcement officials. The images and testimonials thus perform a kind of reciprocity: the testimonials give the technologies of representing evidence emotional immediacy, and in turn, the technologies suggest scientifically and juridically viable forms of material evidence that authenticate the testimonials. Finally, the hamstrung (by laws that ostensibly favor criminals over victims), beleaguered, and dedicated detectives function in this exchange as both protagonist and witness, a point of identification as well as information.

But this montage ultimately evinces a lack of materiality. Two key questions are never asked: what evidence is being *omitted* from these reenactments, such as evidence that might presume innocence, or what evidence is being *constructed* in them in order to promote guilt? Indeed, the word "evidence" is spoken so many times on *America's Most Wanted* and concretely identified so selectively that it takes on a fetishistic status. Given the victims', families', and detectives' testimonials of grief and vengeance, it becomes almost crude and insensitive to press for more concrete renditions of what really might have happened.

Such representations of evidence have dangerous racial repercussions. As stressed above, racially marked representations of criminal bodies in this media(ted) context cannot be neutral and most likely will promote racist "feelings" about the guilt or innocence of a suspect who is not white. This racist subtext of *America's Most Wanted* can be seen in a set of images that recurred on the Washington, D.C., episodes in the 1996–98 seasons.

Between reenactments, Walsh narrates at a setting he calls the "Washington Crime Center": seated or walking behind him are phone attendants who take calls and monitor computer screens in a dimly lit studio setting reminiscent of a police station. Behind these attendants, thirty television screens show the following images: mug shots, most of which are of people of color; police at supposedly "live" crime scenes; blurry lists of "most wanted" fact sheets; and most ominously, shadowy hooded figures being led to and from police cars. These hooded figures clearly encode African American gang members, images that represent in the white imaginary the very symbol of crime—and people—out of control. Juxtaposed to these signifiers of crime is the background wall image and key part of the program's opening credits: a large aerial shot of the Capitol building and White House taken by helicopter at night.

The multiple images suggest racialized criminals as the broader, threatening specter of crime infiltrating the national body. By juxtaposing the images of the White House with the implied dark gang members especially, *America's Most Wanted* appears to flesh the invisibility of the criminal out of this shadowy wilderness through an elaborate circular network of surveillance: hidden camera or property surveillance film; police photos, videos, and reports; stock footage of real or fictional images of crime and supposed criminals; and most importantly, the viewer as the subject who will perform her or his own acts of surveillance within the community because of the suspicion engendered by the images and technologies to which she or he responds. In terms of the implied gang members shuffling to and from police cars as a guiding image behind Walsh and the show's proclaimed objectives, *America's Most Wanted* clearly demonstrates not only the need for but also the success of multiple levels of surveillance; success, however, that has been mediated by the captured and contained racially marked dark male body "caught" on tape.[25]

America's Most Wanted's reenactments, however, are the most telling examples of its racial prejudice. Here we witness tales of danger that law enforcement no longer can contain legally. All motivations are known in advance, guilt is presupposed, and the suspect's perspective is offered rarely (and if it is, the perspective is so brief and decontextualized that it supports any claims of his or her subhumanity). Ostensibly these reenactments are shown to help viewers identify criminals, but they generally are more titillating than informative, especially when the case involves endangered children or women. In terms of this argument, the reenactments regularly promote highly stereotypical views of people of color—both as suspects and as victims. The reenactments generally portray an exoticized and othered urban culture usually seen at night and set to rock or rap music against which Walsh's stern voice intervenes as the very symbol of an oppositional white rationality.

America's Most Wanted is in certain respects more dangerous than, for example, *Cops,* given the former's comparatively more revered status; the president, after all, counts himself among the show's most supportive fans. Indeed, the programming of *Cops* right before *America's Most Wanted* every Saturday night generates a feedback loop: the criminal is caught in the act and taken to jail on *Cops,* but escapes or evades sentencing due to slack crime laws and an overburdened justice system, which is where *America's Most Wanted* and the viewer at home step in and take over, beginning the cycle anew each week.

A reenactment from an episode set in Phoenix in the summer of 1996 is typical. The episode's first section is a profile of Michael Lawrence, the leader of three men apparently involved in a string of robberies. The episode opens with Walsh introducing the episode and reenactment from inside an airborne police helicopter above Phoenix. This shot seamlessly cuts to a series of aerial shots of Phoenix set against instrumental rap music while Walsh's voice-over says that the city had been "plagued by a string of daring and violent robberies for over a year." Then there are a series of close-ups of the three African American male suspects (played by actors) as Walsh introduces them, with Lawrence being last; these close-ups of actors' faces and upper bodies suggest not only violent (according to Walsh) tendencies but also visually encode a highly sexualized, even fetishistic representation of the black male body. After these close-ups, there is a shot of the Kmart that the men will target—with a white store manager and all white customers inside. The men enter the store and in a series of slow-motion close-ups, take their guns out of their jeans and aim them at the manager and various customers while their voices are slowed down and synthesized to sound more menacing and animalistic. The action is intercut with an interview with the chief detective of the case, a middle-aged white man. He describes the dangerous character of the suspects—concluding with a comment on Lawrence being "in complete command"—while there is a cut to a low-angle, slow-motion shot of Lawrence and one of his partners striding through the doors of the Kmart.

After the robbery, there is a high-speed chase between the suspects and a young white male police officer on the ground and more police in a helicopter. As Lawrence fires at the cop on the ground, the helicopter is forced to "take evasive maneuvers," and the suspects split up: one drives away while two others, including Lawrence, run into a suburban neighborhood. This segment is intercut with an interview with the cop who chased the suspects by car, his testimony echoing and validating the preceding detective's.

The next segment of the reenactment shifts to the interior of a white family's home, with a young boy up late watching television alone. Threatening, pounding music implies that he and the family will be the next target of these violent and unpredictable men's actions. The image of the family is intercut with interviews of the real family narrating the moment, as well as with long shots and Walsh's voice-over describing a widespread evacuation of the neighborhood on account of these escaped and dangerous men: again, all of the people shown being evacuated from their homes are white, as are the police officers going door to door. The entire sequence of the family prior to and during the evacuation uses cinematic conventions of horror films. The camera follows the boy and family throughout the house from behind and therefore suggests the perspective of a perpetrator of violence even though ultimately we realize the suspect is not even inside the house: he went into the kitchen to steal the car keys, not to terrorize the family or take them hostage. Ultimately the older sister recognizes one of the suspects hiding in the back of their car, and after she screams for help, he is apprehended.

The segment concludes with the fictional reenactment of the other suspects' arrests, each of which feature the men on their knees, being tackled and violently handcuffed, or in a similarly degrading position (Lawrence climbs up a tree, but is surrounded by cops on the ground). Lawrence escapes after bail is posted, and we learn that he is the chief target of this reenactment as his partners are in jail. While Walsh speaks, an image of Lawrence dissolves between a black-and-white mug shot and a color photo of Lawrence. Walsh describes him as "a very nice dresser with a Black Panther tattooed on his chest," and says that "he likes to rent expensive hotel rooms and throw parties there." Walsh concludes by warning, "Lawrence comes across as very polite, but don't forget how dangerous he really is." The sequence concludes with the show's standard conclusion to reenactments: a computer-generated skeletal head that dissolves into the suspect's real head (in this case, Lawrence) and a written description of Lawrence's age, race, height, and weight. Against this image Walsh issues his familiar command: "If you've seen this man, call 1–800–CRIMETV."

Clearly this reenactment represents multiple connotations: crime as endemic to both public and private (white) spheres, its embodiment in racially marked bodies and stereotypical racist representations, and the production of the necessity for surveillance, here literally embodied by Walsh as the eye in the sky and later by the helicopter with its blinding white spotlight. The opening close-ups are telling in their connotation of the black male body as embodying uncontrollable, sexualized violence. The men seem clearly out of place in and dangerous to the Kmart with its white customers and workers. The synthesized, distorted voices are set against low-angle, slow-motion shots and an almost loving focus on their guns as an extension of their bodies, thus further confirming their guilt and brutality. Conversely, the white female store manager is clearly coded as an innocent victim. Her racism is evident; one doubts she would have approached a white customer who enters the store with the snidely spoken comment that she extends to these men: "I'm the store manager. Can I help you with something?" The men's subsequent attack, however, validates her and, by extension, the implied racism of the viewers.

The stylized slow-motion opening contrasts with the hectic, cinema verité chase scene that follows, with the presence of the helicopter echoing Walsh's introduction. As the suspect fires the gun at the camera, it is as if we the viewers are his target, stand-ins for the vulnerable whites—police officers on the street and in the sky, white child and nuclear family in their home. The narrative moves from a public space of whiteness to a private one at the opposite side of the city: innocent white families are evacuated and forced out onto the street by these three always out-of-place black men. Because of the men's dangerous presence and mobility (and Lawrence's invisibility), however, no place in the city or nation is safe for "ordinary"—read white—Americans. Indeed, the reenactment almost parodies the notion of "white flight" to the suburbs as a means of avoiding racialized urban criminality.

Lastly, this segment's concluding "success"—shown by images of two black men confined on the ground by white officers—is offset by the lingering threat of the third man still at large. Lawrence's Black Panther tattoo marks him as a dangerous criminal element—the vestigial results of sixties black radical politics. Furthermore, the concluding comment that "Lawrence comes across as polite, but don't forget how dangerous he really is" reminds us that we cannot trust anyone, and that appearances of polite behavior and nice clothes on this black man are, in fact, the very symbol of his deviant violence. One wonders if Lawrence would have agreed with this assessment or with the initial detective's statement that he was "in total command." Indeed, the reenactment makes painfully clear who is in total command of *this* narrative. The final image instills an almost soap operatic connection between viewer and show: tune in next week to see if you are safe, but even if *he* is caught, you can be sure that there will be others to take his place. If they are not visible to you from where you are now, *America's Most Wanted* will construct that visibility—and fear—for you.

Conclusion

As the year 2000 come to a close, *America's Most Wanted* sustains its position within and effects on local, regional, national, and, increasingly, global surveillance. On November 19, 2000, the show broadcast a special live episode entitled "50 States, 50 Fugitives." The format was altered slightly for this special episode: from the Washington Crime Center (now called the

America's Most Wanted Crime Center) Walsh is shown in dialogue with "reporters" from a number of "regional crime centers" headquartered in vulnerable urban centers—New York City, Miami, New Orleans, Detroit, and Los Angeles. Each regional host mimicked Walsh's characteristic hand gestures, diction, and direct address to the camera. Through their exchanges with and performances of Walsh, the regional crime centers' reporters reconstructed and heightened the intimacy Walsh constructs weekly on the show with viewers. Indeed, just as the program has "deputized everyone in America as members of an electronic, interactive posse" nationally, the "50 States, 50 Fugitives" episode authorizes, encourages, and, indeed, deputizes regional "posses" to form as an extension of that national body of vigilant viewers. If, on the standard episode of *America's Most Wanted,* one could take some comfort in seeing the threatening criminal figure at least occasionally far from one's own home state, this special "live" episode, with its proliferating regional crime centers, localized Walsh surrogates, and a fugitive from every state, renders such safety illusory and precarious.

At the same time that *America's Most Wanted* constructs its turn toward regional deputization, localized law enforcers, and endangered viewers, Walsh alluded several times to the need for cooperative relationships between U.S. and international law enforcement bodies and viewers. The latter reference especially marks how the audience for "America's" most wanted no longer can be, strictly speaking, an exclusively American one. As a result, the national not only contracts to support the demands of the regional and the local but also expands to encompass the transnational, bringing the international impetus and influences of the program's creation back to now-transnational viewers. Moreover, the extension beyond and within national borders occurs through links at the *America's Most Wanted* official Web site. A search at Yahoo for Web sites and pages using the key words "America's Most Wanted" provides hundreds of links, not only back to the program's official site but to similar, interactive multimedia sites about crime, including ones that range from "The World's Most Wanted" (which can be translated from English into Spanish) to the Nashville Police Department's "Rate Your Risk," which invites the visitor to take tests in order to determine whether she or he will be "raped, robbed, shot, beaten, or murdered."[26] The simultaneous worlding and personalizing of *America's Most Wanted* thus renders the television series as one link in a multimedia chain that encloses as it represents criminality's seemingly infinite scope and range.

The kinds of dangerous interpretations that can result from this milieu premised largely on racialized fear echoes Judith Butler's interpretation of Rodney King as constructed by defense testimony at the infamous police brutality trial of 1992. She writes:

Consider that it *was* possible to draw an inference from the black male body
motionless and beaten on the street to the conclusion that this very body was
in "total control," rife with "dangerous intention." The visual field is not neutral to the question of race; it is itself a racial formation, an episteme, hegemonic and forceful.[27]

The visual regime of *America's Most Wanted* clearly relies on a racism
that masquerades as objective and necessary. This allusion to verisimilitude
is why *America's Most Wanted* is ultimately more dangerous than beneficial: it promotes racist conceptions of criminality and a national economy
of surveillance and fear that fractures community even as it purports to
build connections and empower its viewers. Thus I dispute Walsh's statement that *America's Most Wanted* has deputized "everyone in America as
members of an interactive, electronic posse," for the show, like the national
body from which it emerges and in turn constructs, does not treat every
American equally when it comes to representing criminality. And the word
"posse" has dangerous historical overtones to those Americans who have
been and continue to be targeted by groups of whites, even and perhaps
especially by groups of white law enforcement officials.

Surprisingly few people criticize *America's Most Wanted* because insofar
as its primary objective is concerned, it works: it catches criminals and locks
them up, supposedly rendering the rest of us "safe." But what is the larger
cost of this "safety"? When a constant threat of violent crime is being sys-
tematically—and largely falsely—promoted, and as a result people live in
fear and surveillance of each other, what sort of safety and citizenship can
"we" as a nation really have? Ultimately, as *America's Most Wanted* produces its own body of evidence for the national threat of crime and encourages a widespread economy of surveillance in response, its viewers may
increasingly find the gaze they once trained on dangerous racialized others
turned back on themselves in ways they had never imagined.

NOTES

1. Scott Nelson, "Crime-Time Television," *FBI Law Enforcement Bulletin*
58, 8 (1989): 8.

2. Dave Shiflett, "America's Most Wanted Manhunter," *Reader's Digest*
(May 1997): 55.

3. Shiflett writes, "*America's Most Wanted* has become a major asset for
law-enforcement authorities. For more than ten million viewers, meanwhile, the
show has become a kind of interactive entertainment that also serves an important
public good. And for victims and their families, *America's Most Wanted* has grown
into the Court of Last Resort" (53).

4. Gray Cavender and Mark Fishman, "Television Reality Crime Programs:
Context and History," in *Entertaining Crime: Television Reality Programs*, ed.

Gray Cavender and Mark Fishman (New York: Aldine De Gruyter Press, 1998), 9.

5. Chris Brants, "Crime Fighting by Television in the Netherlands," in *Entertaining Crime*, 175–91.

6. http://bbc.org (December 6, 2000).

7. Stuart Cosgrove, "Borderlines," *New Statesmen and Society* 3, 130 (December 7, 1990): 32. For a thoughtful analysis of how women viewers in particular interpret *Crimewatch*, see R. Emerson Dobash, Philip Schlesinger, Russell Dobash, and C. Kay Weaver, "*Crimewatch UK*: Women's Interpretations of Televised Violence," in *Entertaining Crime*, 37–58.

8. Hugh Dauncey, "*Témoin No. 1*: Crime Shows on French Television," in *Entertaining Crime*, 193–209.

9. Cavender and Fishman, "Television Reality Crime Programs," in *Entertaining Crime*, 9.

10. Ibid., 10.

11. Ibid., 8–10.

12. S.ee Robin Anderson, *Consumer Culture and TV Programming*, (Boulder, Colo.: Westview Press, 1995), 174–210, for a detailed critique of reality-based American television programs. She highlights how the rise in this kind of television programming connects with historical events like the Bush administration's "war on drugs" policy—a policy that specifically targeted communities of color. This policy and reality-based shows on crime make connections about drugs, race, and crime that deliberately ignore how, as Anderson states, "the largest segment of drug users are the ones least talked about—the affluent white users of powdered cocaine" (191).

13. Anna Williams, "Domestic Violence and the Aetiology of Crime in *America's Most Wanted*," *Camera Obscura* 31 (January–May 1993): 102.

14. Anderson, *Consumer Culture*, 184.

15. Mary Beth Oliver, "Portrayals of Crime, Race, and Aggression in 'Reality-Based' Police Shows: A Content Analysis," *Journal of Broadcasting and Electronic Media* 38, 2 (1994): 179–91. Oliver's analysis covers five shows from the 1991–92 network television season: *America's Most Wanted*; *Cops*; *Top Cops*; *FBI, The Untold Story*; and *American Detective*. According to FBI statistics for the period of Oliver's analysis, 54.3 percent of all criminal suspects were white, 29.9 percent were black, and 15.8 percent were Hispanic. On the television shows Oliver examined, however, only 38.4 percent of the criminal suspects were white, whereas 77.0 percent were black and 85.9 percent were Hispanic. Disproportionate representation of law enforcement officials also occurred: FBI statistics stated that 88.3 percent of officers are white, 9.0 percent are black and 2.6 percent are Hispanic. On the television shows, 61.6 percent are white, 23.0 percent are black and 14.1 percent are Hispanic. Although these shows represented greater percentages of people of color in law enforcement than in reality, the substantially higher representation of people of color as criminal suspects ultimately encourages belief in people of color's presumed propensity toward criminal behavior.

16. Ibid., 185.

17. For media effects and sociological analyses of this phenomenon beyond

America's Most Wanted, see the following: Gertrude Moeller, "Fear of Criminal Victimization: The Effect of Neighborhood Racial Composition," *Sociological Inquiry* 59 (1989): 208–21; Mary Beth Oliver and G. Blake Armstrong, "The Color of Crime: Perceptions of Caucasians' and African-Americans' Involvement in Crime," in *Entertaining Crime,* 19–35; Mary Beth Oliver, "Influences of Authoritarianism and Portrayals of Race on Caucasian Viewers' Responses to Reality-Based Crime Dramas," *Communication Reports* 9 (1996): 141–50; Craig St. John and Tamara Heald-Moore, "Racial Prejudice and Fear of Criminal Victimization by Strangers in Public Settings," *Sociological Inquiry* 66 (1996): 267–84.

18. The construction of whiteness on *America's Most Wanted* would be another essay unto itself. Briefly, there is an elision between white criminality and lower-class status (among both men and women), and in the case of women suspects, homosexuality or bisexuality are invoked as symptoms of violent tendencies. The most frequent representations of white criminals on the show are scenes of child molestation, kidnapping, and/or murder. These domestic and largely "white" crimes sharply contrast with representations of racialized stranger street crime. Put another way, people of color tend to be shown engaging in random acts of street violence, but premeditated crimes within and against the family more often are represented as occurring in white homes. In this way, *America's Most Wanted* portrays a double threat: in addition to the dangers of racialized street crime, corollary dangers form within the space of the white family and home with secrets to be exposed. The show not only induces fears of crime occurring at both sites but represents itself as the only authority that may distinguish between normal and "abnormal" white families. Given the show's investment in maintaining a pervasive fear of crime, and given its racist assumptions about crime in general, the presence of white intrafamilial criminality on the show does not assuage or counter racism so much as it confirms it. In other words, racialized criminality appears to have contaminated the white familial sphere.

My analysis thus differs even as it draws from Williams's "Domestic Violence," 97–119. The mid- to late-nineties images of crime do not conform to Williams's assessment that *America's Most Wanted* "depicts crimes which do not take as their objects random members of the population" (108) and that "crime is always situated within the family" (109). I would argue that the focus of Williams's analysis—that on *America's Most Wanted,* the white middle-class nuclear family is presented as one under siege with a casualty list composed of women and children—is still firmly in place, but it has been supplemented and informed fundamentally by broader racist fears of the threat as one coming from people of color. In turn, people of color generally are represented as outside of the supposedly protective spaces of the familial, domestic, and suburban in favor of a menacing urban and always visible public space. As Williams wisely observes, however, the familial, domestic, and suburban spaces are hardly protective for women. Moreover, in her reading she identifies a crucial and "paradoxical task" of *America's Most Wanted*: "the depiction of the normalized nuclear family as the primary locus of crime at the same time that it constructs that same family, in the form of John

Walsh, as the antithesis and active opponent of crime" ("Domestic Violence," 115).

19. Jane Feuer, "The Concept of Live Television: Ontology as Ideology," in *Regarding Television: Critical Approaches—An Anthology,* ed. E. Ann Kaplan (Frederick, Md.: University Publications of America, 1983), 14.

20. In addition to Feuer, see the following texts for other discussions of the relationship between liveness and television: Mary Ann Doane, "Information, Crisis, Catastrophe," in *Logics of Television: Essays in Cultural Criticism,* ed. Patricia Mellencamp (Bloomington: Indiana University Press, 1990), 222–39; Stephen Heath, "Representing Television," in *Logics of Television,* 267–302; Stephen Heath and Gillian Skirrow, "Television: A World in Action," *Screen* 18, 2 (1977): 7–59; and Sasha Torres, "King TV," in *Living Color: Race and Television in the United States,* ed. Sasha Torres (Durham: Duke University Press, 1998), 140–60. Doane and Torres make the important and provocative point that the object of live "catastrophe" television's rhetoric is, ironically, death. Death as live television's essential corollary is crucial to *America's Most Wanted,* as the show constantly restages the event of murder especially in order to eradicate the murderer's presence in the public sphere. But like any repetition compulsion, no single resolution can allay the fears inspired by the broader threat posed by the replayed visible image.

21. For a related discussion of how American citizenship functions through multiple sites (popular movies, television sit-coms, music videos, and *Time* magazine covers of an immigrant-laden America), see Lauren Berlant's chapter, "The Face of America and the State of Emergency," in her *The Queen of America Goes to Washington City: Essays on Sex and Citizenship* (Durham: Duke University Press, 1997), 175–220. The above sites intersect to produce the view that the contemporary conception of (white, normative) American national identity is under siege from immigrants, people of color, and queers, resulting in a citizenship always emerging within and against a "state of emergency."

22. See the front cover of *Time* 144 (July 4, 1994).

23. For more extended discussions of the reasons for and effects of this affirmative, even symbiotic relationship between law enforcement agencies and reality-based television programs on crime, see Pamela Donovan, "Armed with the Power of Television: Reality Crime Programming and the Reconstruction of Law and Order in the United States," in *Entertaining Crime,* 117–37; and Aaron Doyle, "*Cops*: Television Policing as Policing Reality," in *Entertaining Crime,* 95–116.

24. Paul Gewirtz, "Some Stories about Confessions and Confessions about Stories," in *Law's Stories: Narrative and Rhetoric about the Law,* ed. Peter Brooks and Paul Gewirtz (New Haven: Yale University Press, 1996), 152.

25. In the fall of 1997, Fox broadcast a series of one-hour specials loosely based on footage of law enforcement officials engaged in "real" situations like car chases or prison riots. One of these specials was called *Criminals Caught on Tape* and was an hour of "success" stories of the uses of surveillance tape in abetting criminal suspects' captures. *America's Most Wanted* in particular constantly focuses on surveillance tapes in its reenactments, usually as a means of identifying

suspected criminals after the crime has been committed. However, I have noticed a disturbing trend in the 1997–98 seasons of not only replaying images of the suspected criminal but also of the violent crime act itself, even murders, as both images are caught on surveillance tape.

26. http://www.amw.com, http://www.mostwanted.com, and http://Nashville Net/~police/risk/ (all examined December 6, 2000).

27. Judith Butler, "Endangered/Endangering: Schematic Racism and White Paranoia," in *Reading Rodney King, Reading Urban Uprising,* ed. Robert Gooding-Williams (New York: Routledge, 1993), 17.

FOUR

Real Fiction

Prime-Time Fiction Theorizes the Docu-Real

JOHN CALDWELL

Long before various new waves complicated the antagonism between narrative and reality in big screen cinema, television, on the small screen, had made the split a fundamental part of its viewer's consciousness. And while the entertainment/drama versus news/reality worlds represent entrenched institutional differences in broadcasting—produced as they are by different production communities, for different day parts, and different audiences—the segregation of these worlds is far from total. Whereas the dramatization and stylization of news and public affairs television has caused hand-wringing from journalists, producers, and academics alike, far less concern has greeted reality overhauls of *narrative* on television. Docudramas and re-creations have, after all, been a staple of movies of the week (MOWs, or what have conventionally been castigated as "disease of the week" telefilms) and episodic TV from early on, an unremarkable status that tends to earn them the respect of neither historians or critics and proponents of "quality television." But docudramas and MOWs are actually far less ambitious or knowing in their ontological manipulations than another, more acute narrative meditation on the real.

I hope in this chapter to consider what is now, arguably, a recognizable genre in episodic television: something I will refer to as the "docu-stunt" or "docu-real" fiction. By these terms I refer to episodes in entertainment programs that self-consciously showcase documentary units or modes as part of their narrative and plot and/or documentary looks and imaging as part of their mise-en-scène. Considering this ploy merely as a plot premise—even a hybrid one, following traditional genre theory—helps elucidate a number of commonalties among widely divergent shows. But a closer examination of the shows suggests that far more may be at work in this kind of television than the internal, structural relations of episodic and serial "texts." Docu-stunts do work to complicate genre through mixage and hybridity and complicate television narrative by "discursifying" the telling.[1] But docu-fictions also invariably appear as programming "stunts"—special episodes aimed at eliciting coverage and viewership during sweeps weeks and season premieres or critical prestige for Emmy consideration. The genre, then, invokes marketing and programming strategies as well as aesthetic forms. It is in these extratextual relations and logics that I hope to find what might be termed an "institutional theory" of docu-real fictions.

Beyond textual and institutional intrigues, however, docu-real fictions also provide an extensive set of critical-theoretical meditations on fundamental aspects and definitions of television, the televisual apparatus, and the television experience. Docu-real fictions, that is, function not just as "low theory" or "lay theory," but are rich examples of "distributed" or "situated cognition" and "critical-theoretical production practices."[2] Analytic-critical ability, and facility with what has been termed "grand theorization," are pervasive aspects not just of academic media theory and cultural studies but of industrial culture, as well.[3] The range of critical-theoretical "framings" in docu-stunts—*on screen,* in front of large television audiences— offer extended meditations on the nature of television; relations between fiction and documentary; tensions among entertainment, art, and reality; phenomenological issues of television experience; and aesthetic questions of program quality. These public critical interventions, in fact, frequently provide a level of complexity and depth far greater than that offered by standard-fare TV critics in the print media. This is perhaps not surprising if one considers the fact that the creative communities in Hollywood that produce episodic television now typically have a deeper grounding in cultural histories and aesthetics, and certainly a much more extensive time investment in series and individual episode development, than the overtaxed print critics spinning critical improvisations to meet daily deadlines. Looking closely at docu-real fiction also means recognizing the importance broadcast institutions give critical production practice.

Examining the genre, as I will do next, through a range of docu-real permutations suggests that the resilient form delivers to broadcasters both textual and institutional benefits. What follows, then, is a kind of formal-historical map of the genre from "archaic" prototypes in the fifties, to classical and postmodern forms in the seventies and eighties, to poststructuralist hybrids in the nineties. By describing a taxonomy of ways that prime time performed, masqueraded, and stunted as documentary, I hope, finally, to consider how the docu-real developed into a generic caste system—one that provides therapeutic functions for the production ensemble and institutional leverage for broadcasters.

Archaic Live-Real and the Coming of Tape

Precursors to the contemporary docu-stunt can be found in widely popular shows in the fifties and early sixties. Although such shows were not fully developed docu-stunts per se, as prime-time meditations on new television technologies that produced the "live" and the "real," many of the terms favored in mature docu-real fictions were at work in these "archaic" forms of the genre as well. In a strange 1954 episode of *Father Knows Best* entitled "Formula for Happiness" (strange because domestic sit-coms, or dom-coms, are usually thought of as formulaic vehicles with muted style and production values), both the father and family face a psychological torment that intrudes into the episode's fiction in the guise of live and "recorded" television. In an early scene, father Jim is haunted by the ambiguous status of this reality, and remarks, "the strange thing about this dream . . . is that it was so real." A recollection in flashback shows his family traumatized in front of live TV lights when an enigmatic intruder interrupts during the telecast. A wise psychiatrist later responds over coffee to Jim's malaise with a paradigm unavailable to Freud when he wrote *On the Interpretation of Dreams*: "the mind is like a tape recorder . . . sometimes it plays back." Jim takes the bait, and fills in the gaps of the analysis. Of course, "my brain subconsciously recorded it all; and played it back as a dream." In rapid succession, Jim painfully puts the pieces of his indifference and insensitivity together. "His" missing formula was actually a simple gift from his young daughter—whom he had unwisely ignored—conceptually glommed onto fragments of an evening newscast. Having realized his failure as a distracted parent, Jim's retrospective road back to psychological health links his child's adage about treating everyone fairly to universal notions of the golden rule to the truism that "if everyone followed this advice, there'd be no wars." The moral: world peace starts at home; be a good father. Thematically, then, being a good father was also posed as a key to international diplomacy; no small insight given ongoing military tensions in Korea at the time. Structurally, however, the entire episode serves the function of an analyst's couch, with Jim's flashbacks posing as a psychotherapeutic "session." Jim's distraction while watching live TV becomes a moment of acute mental condensation that demands analysis.

So fictional characters dream in the form of live television even as live broadcasters attempt to invade the world of the sit-com—invade, that is, the "real" parts of fiction. So a big reversal unfolds here. Live "recorded" TV is posed as an altered psychic state while the sit-com's fiction is framed as a form of naturalism—a place where the truly real is available, and morality stands as proof of authenticity. Moral solutions in the domestic sit-com, that is, appear more truthful and "real" than the live/news apparatus. Jim replays his private daily confusion as a live television broadcast to millions, creating a crisis of the "real" and of his realization. In this archaic stunt, the "live" instigates crisis, and recorded tape solves it. Both actions allow fictional characters to dream and to solve life's problems by mastering television's emerging technologies of the real.

Another domestic sit-com, *Leave It to Beaver,* also incorporated dramatized depictions of live and taped television.[4] By following the show's child stars to adolescence, the show also implicitly traced the period during which television became the dominant vehicle for the transmission of American culture. In the episode "Beaver on TV," the "Beave" is invited to share his views on a local show entitled "Teenage Forum."[5] More than simply an obligatory situational predicament for the series star, the entire episode can be seen as an extended meditation on modern electronic telecommunications.

This sit-com narrative starts with a family debate over appropriate access to telephones by teens, moves to scenes setting up daytime public affairs programming, then climaxes when Beaver has what appears to be an out-of-body experience when attempting to understand and negotiate the complexity of "live" versus taped live television. Like Jim Anderson in *Father Knows Best* before him, Beaver's best intentions in *Leave It to Beaver* are frustrated by the traumas of live broadcasting. Like Jim, Beaver hallucinates with nagging questions about the nature of time, perceptual turmoil, and the television series *The Twilight Zone.* His buddy brings home the genre logic of Beave's predicament: "That's that program where people keep seeing things that aren't there. And doin' stuff that never happened. I think they call it psychic phenomenon or something." As in *Father Knows Best,* the crisis of this sit-com episode is finally mediated through the ideology and agency of expertise. Unlike *Father Knows Best,* however, the expert "therapist" here is no longer a psychotherapist, but is rather the floor director at a local television station. He lays out the key to grasping the new television culture: "Our new facilities are in and starting last week this show is being taped in advance. That means this show will be not seen today, but will be seen a week from today. That'll give you all an opportunity to see yourself on TV." This (psycho) broadcaster does not, like his clinical precedent, describe for the mind of the television viewer the complex workings of the "brain recorder" but rather the complex workings of the newly invented and recently installed video recorder.

"Beaver on TV," then, does not simply develop the main character's persona through another weekly way station on his road to adolescence. The episode also stands as an overdetermined attempt to teach the audience at home how to think about fundamental aspects of television. First, it questions the nature of live versus taped programming and simultaneous versus delayed transmission. Beaver, his classmates, teacher, and parents trouble over his apparent disappearance from both the classroom and the very airwaves he was slated to appear on. "You say you were on. You saw the show and you weren't on. She says you won't be on till next week. Gee, this sounds like a mess." Second, the episode steps through arguments for and against public service versus entertainment programming. During a first viewing, an educator sees only a mindless western telefilm on the classroom set, rather than the public service discussion she anticipated. Third, the show weds the sixties science and technology of the space race (invoked in ads for Bic pens and the NASA-developed Tang drink) with the promotion of one of the post-wasteland's most utopian and earnest antidotes: educational television. Beaver's classroom is replete with the newly dispersed TV sets that came with the promotion of national educational television in America in the mid-1960s. Even as he smiles on as America's everyboy, a slurry of aggressive rebukes and jokes about his awkward early pubescent body underscore Beaver's dramatic, anxious, even painful need to understand the new technoculture of television. For concerned programmers and broadcasters who wanted to cultivate the now lucrative teen demographic in American consumer culture, teen angst had as much to do with mastering transistor radios and television usage as anything else. An added benefit for these particular producers was that unlike the on-screen Warner telefilm western deprecated in this episode, the episode as a whole also posed *Leave It to Beaver* as a "public service." Viewing the sit-com rather than the news as a public "forum" was not a small symbolic accomplishment in the seasons immediately following Newton Minnow's denigration of "mindless" entertainment television.

Public perceptions of docu-reality and liveness, then, did not simply emerge in TV's news and public affairs divisions. These early shows suggest that docu-reality was publicly exploited both as a fictional problem and as a way to heighten a programming "moment." Such shows did not masquerade as documentaries, but they did create tactical anxieties by self-consciously juggling live and taped actualities.

Classical Docu-Real Fictions (1970s)

"The following is in black-and-white."
—*anonymous narrator to audience in* M*A*S*H

"Some of the saltier comments have been deleted."
—*on-screen reporter to audience of* M*A*S*H

The episode that did as much to define the docu-real fiction as any other was surely the highly lauded episode of *M*A*S*H* entitled "The Interview."[6] The critical success of this sweeps-week stunt also suggests a change in expectations for "quality" in seventies programming. The diegetic presence of an on-screen documentary newsreel crew in the *M*A*S*H* unit gave the producers the opportunity to alter the very look of the show. "Quality television" during this time had been defined by its recognizable ability to evoke contemporary social and political topics (in the Tandem/TAT productions of Norman Lear) and social lifestyle issues (in the serious relevance comedies of MTM).

Larry Gelbart's M*A*S*H, on the other hand, began to use plot events to motivate changes not just in script dialogue but in visual style as well. The interview episode used a mode of filming easily recognizable as documentary: direct address interviews (rather than the oblique glances that typified the show's classical film style), the presence of microphones and interviewers, and black-and-white film stock (rather than the color stock associated with this highly rated series).

Not only did the episode use documentary technology, but it showed off historical emulation as well. Evoking the celebrated Edward R. Murrow report from the Korean War front, each camera set-up was static; compositions were rigidly bilateral and symmetrical; and interviews were all centered in safe-zone obsessed, medium shot. This fifties documentary mode, however, did allow the quality of acting to change for an episode. Compared to Hawkeye's weekly demeanor in prime time, the character in this episode, facing the newsreel unit, is both more brutally honest, jaded, and pessimistic. When asked about fear, Hawkeye also offers one of a number of direct allegories to the power of the show itself, as well as a blueprint of this episode in particular. "Terror—you know—it's like a car accident when everything goes into slow motion. And then you suddenly see things for the way they really are." The black-and-white, static, staring newsreel gaze—rather than slow-motion—provided in this stunt an altered, perceptual state of the same dimension.

In another instance, Hawkeye lays out the logic, arc, and dramatic purpose of his narrative character. "It's like an overcoat I take out every once in a while and put on. See, what I do is provoke other people into disbelief . . . then I see that disbelief in their eyes . . . Otherwise it's like looking into a mirror and not seeing anything . . . because everybody's got that self-involved glaze in their eyes." Even as he acts, Hawkeye, the ensemble provocateur, provides an on-screen analysis of his acting method for the prime-time audience. His logic is one of survival. The method: deadpan sarcasm that keeps everyone else off balance—skewering defenses to animate survival instinct.

After years of episodes in the series, the documentary stunt cuts through to provide the psychological "B-line" (or subtext) and backstory for each character in the ensemble. Crying, cursing, sighing, sadness, and remorse ensue. The documentary unit not only cuts through the stoic group's surface, it instigates deeper introspection on the part of the characters and provides a metacommentary on the complex world of the series and its cosmology. These are also metacritical comments on the series by the actors. Together, their metacriticisms stand as a kind of de facto bible that screenwriters might use to produce stories for the show. The producers know the backstory, the players know the character motivations, and the audience celebrates this analytical knowingness along with the production culture.

This was, then, a highly special episode, one that focused on stripping away the guarded barriers that participants in a war zone (and by implication, a production ensemble) erect around themselves. In describing the insanity of the war almost to a man, the episode evokes footage of the Tet offensive at Hue in 1968; when fatalistic oaths by on-camera U.S. marines under attack in prime time shattered any illusion that the war effort was sane in the minds of ground troops.

Nonfiction emerges, then, as a direct intervention into the world and lives of the fictional characters by offering psychological back story that deepens the intensity of the depictions. Docu-real back story gives the cynical, jaded, and dark humor of the participants even more pathos. As visible evidence, the docu-real camera "proves" the lengths to which these noble but fatalistic *M*A*S*H* doctors have gone to buffer the reprehensible pain of war-torn trauma. Late in the Vietnam era, "The Interview" episode reanchored the snappy thirty-minute sit-com as a highly deflected and condensed attempt to deal with the horrors of real destruction and violence. The docu-real mode here, that is, does not let the comedy's fiction erase the importance of pain as an originating source. Rather—in contrast to the flat and affectless delivery of the show's dialogue—this documentary masquerade dramatizes the depth and sensitivity of both the show's characters and the production company's creative personnel. It is comedy, yes; but the production cadre celebrates its own existential import in the stunt as well.

The series finale of *M*A*S*H*—an unusual two-hour offering—became the most watched episode in American prime-time television.[7] For the highly hyped culmination of this long running series, the producers chose to set the episode within the psychotherapeutic interview setting. And while this premise does not depict a documentary unit per se, it does allocate substantial screen time to static interview shots of Hawkeye being questioned by a psychiatrist. The narrative begins in a locked psychiatric ward when Hawkeye responds to the question "So how are you feeling?" By this point, then, what was only a subtext in archaic docu-stunts became an explicit spin on this episode's "interview." As a textual engine in the genre, the filmed documentary interview has regularly had a psychological function within the narrative economy of prime-time fiction. Whereas the "Interview" episode used a faux-professional documentary unit as an episodic foil, "Goodbye, Farewell" simply cut to the chase and showed the device for what it was: a painful stripping away of one person's torment, recollection, and regret. In this classical variation, the docu-stunt stands as a psychoanalytic intervention: one that explains the mega-text of the long-running show's narrative in pained and reflective retrospective terms.

Coming to grips with the historical significance of the show's fiction, therefore, was also directly tied to two other historic registers—the history of the Korean (and implicitly Vietnam) conflict(s) and the history of American television programming. Placing the finale in a tortured interview setting allowed the writers and producers to overdetermine or "over-produce" the historical importance of the series.[8] Even as his textual character free associated in a locked ward, star Alan Alda was lauded in the press as the cocreator of both "The Interview" and the "Goodbye, Farewell" episodes. In this way, the most private, intimate act of personal disclosure in the text (by clinical definition) worked in programming terms to fuel and spin in the final installment a form of "historical exhibitionism."[9] The documentary interview in this case clearly functioned to underline and exploit "real" world importance for its dramatic show as a programming event.

St. Elsewhere continued invoking the docu-real as part of its weekly showcase for "quality" television.[10] Produced by Joshua Brand and John Falsey, the show became known for its liberties with conventional dramatic TV form, and docu-motifs appeared in a number of guises. The show's repertoire of docu-flourishes ranged from documentary ecstasies to very basic kinds of actuality tactics. Making the documentary gaze a part of the show's look, characters in one episode ("Down and Out on Beacon Hill"), remark about a video surveillance camera being installed in the ward.[11] Establishing shots in the same episode code time/day info into their images even as they pan rotely in the manner of a security camera; evidence that asserts, "this is happening now and here, and it is happening to all of these people simultaneously." Underlining simultaneity in this way enables complicated ensemble dramas—with their extensive networks of characters—to hold together and maintain coherence.

Another episode, "Weigh-in, Weigh-out," opens with a video image framed within a frame.[12] Monochromatic and grainy, the images that follow prove that this is an invasive camcorder depiction of the attempted delivery of a baby, followed by an anguished episiotomy and a near stillbirth. The voice of an obnoxious father behind the camera claims ownership of the image as he complains about having "shelled out the big bucks for this camcorder." The image and the voice is callous, opportunistic, and self-centered. At the moment of crisis, the camcorder malfunctions, the image breaks up, and the picture turns to snow. The pushy, invasive quality of the "home" docu-unit falters in the sight, and touching bedside manner, of these humble and highly competent professionals.

A third episode moves beyond mere apparatus referents (the ensemble as surveilled) and the docu-stunt as an invasive plot element (the home-movie conceit) to structure its entire televisual discourse around a frame that is closer to PBS than to prime time. Entitled "Their Town," the episode plays off of Thornton Wilder's home-spun existential model of American literary pathos but works at the same time like an episode from This Old House or one of the many other on-camera "host" documentaries that carpet public broadcasting.[13] Each of the major acts starts with the main ensemble character narrating the story of his town and life, on location and in direct address to the camera. The viewer hears the plain language and wise common sense of a reflective everyman. Walking towards the camera as he narrates, thereby sealing an empathic relationship with the audience, the host verbally choreographs depictions with steady interjections in voice-over. "Well, you can imagine what happens next. . . . So let's just skip that." The stunt here does not involve the simple overhaul of scenes to mimic a documentary gaze. Rather, the eye-to-eye address—typical of the host-style docugenre on public television—provides the down-home empathy needed to weather the text's ensuing traumas of late-life crises and broken marriages.

St. Elsewhere worked the ground of the real and elaborated subtle permutations of the docu-real enterprise. Like *M*A*S*H* before it and *China Beach* and *ER* after it, *St. Elsewhere* was an ensemble drama placed in the hectic and anxious world of crisis medicine. The dramatic world depicted in this narratologically complicated genre seemed to benefit from the periodic ontological anchoring that docu-real fictions offered.

Later in the 1980s, *China Beach* updated the same kind of mixed-genre mode to focus its vision of wartime anxiety.[14] This time, however, the docu-stunt modalities shifted by a decade or so. The war was Vietnam not Korea, the issues eighties feminism and not sixties antiwar rhetoric, and the look was the "oral history" pose of *The Good Fight* and *Seeing Red* rather than Morrow's black-and-white newsreel. Couched as a realistic remake of the earlier conflict, the series *China Beach* was actually an unabashed docudrama fueled in weekly doses by Motown and pop culture nostalgia. The show used Diana Ross and the Supremes' "Reflections" as a theme song and featured, in one episode, rock interludes like Nancy Sinatra singing "These Boots Are Made for Walking." In *China Beach*'s docu-stunt, the "documentarist's" questions are kept off camera and edited out.[15] While soft, side-lit painter's light set the stage for intimate disclosure, "real" women vets who had served tours in Vietnam reminisce in emotional and articulate hindsight.

This episode and the series in general was posed as an intricate play of female subjectivity, and the documentary segment showed that those most sensitive to world might also be the most moving indexes of traumas in the world: the hard-strapped medical community and the women who loved the dying and maimed men. Studio and network marketers pitched the notion to critics and viewers that producer John Sacret Young's version of Vietnam would be both more accurate and more compelling given his first-person experience in the war. Episodes of *China Beach* suggest that this show succeeded where male Vietnam shows at the same time like CBS's

Tour of Duty failed because *China Beach* set in motion and exploited intimacy and melodrama more typical of soap opera than the war pic.[16] Whereas the show's mise-en-scène won raves from the production community, that is, the secret to its loyal but narrow audience appeared to be its reflective touch; the documentary episode positioned the interview as the most direct portal to the inner life of the show's nurses, female officers, and prostitutes. Even as dramatized reporter Wayloo Holmes sutured the sense of documentary witness into the very presentational fabric of the show during the first season, on-camera interviews in the 1989 docu-stunt allowed the producers of *China Beach* to make hand-wringing observation a part of anxious characterization and spectatorship as well.

The Docu-Real Look: Fictional House Style

The taxonomy of docu-real permutations mapped here includes not just one-time programming events but also a set of series fictions that mimic documentary "experience" for the viewer. That is, while docu-stunts invoke or invent the one-time presence of a documentary unit to infiltrate the "secrets" of a show's narrative regime built over weeks and months, other series appropriate some experiential part of documentary for their series look. Spatio-temporal perspectives associated with documentary, for example, informed the camera work and lighting of *Hill Street Blues*.[17] A "neurotic" documentary filmmaker, and in episode the long-take aesthetic, drove both the series and one sweeps-week episode of *Mad About You*.[18] The docu-real, that is, can be invoked not just as a matter of some "plot-event" that spikes a standard series screenplay template. The docu-real can also be tied, more simply, to some observational or experiential quality of the "real" as well.

In an art historical sense, classicism has been identified as an aesthetic that values unity of form and content. *Hill Street Blues* was arguably a classic in this sense, for although it did not invent a documentary unit within the diegesis of its ensemble drama, it appropriated the look of direct cinema as the "house style" of the series. Jerky handheld 35mm cinematography and the use of lighting practicals defined the show in gritty terms from the premiere episode's first roll call until the end of the series six years later. Critics lauded the naturalism of the concept and execution, making this initial ratings struggler the poster child for visionary writer-producers who wanted to be given the same latitude that the networks had shown Steven Bochco in letting the initially low rated show develop a loyal audience over an extended period of time. In *Hill Street Blues,* the docu-real was not simply a "stunt" allowing the fiction to masquerade for one episode as something else. Rather, *Hill Street Blues* used a verité gaze to position the audience of the series in explicit documentary terms.

In the aesthetic pantheon of filmic "taste cultures," the nonfiction look that typifies the higher taste castes of PBS and documentary film fit well the complex ensemble dilemmas churning each week on *Hill Street Blues*.[19] Whip pans and rack focusing show a film crew—and by substitution, the audience—struggling to keep up with volatile on-screen actions. Social realities and contradictions in the urban jungle of *Hill Street Blues* fit comfortably within the celebrated—but limited—omniscience of the direct cinema gaze. Reality is complicated and fleeting, film theorists and aesthetes have murmured. The workaday verité gaze in *Hill Street Blues* underscored and rewarded this existential ambivalence for the audience in prime time as well.

By the 1997 season, *Mad About You* was consistently rated as one of the top sit-coms on television, and lead actress Helen Hunt had won an Emmy for best actress. The series as a whole offered a number of docu-real permutations. The character played by Paul Reiser was, for example, portrayed as a neurotic documentary filmmaker in the fictional world of the show. In a heavily promoted installment in December 1997, the *Mad About You* duo "performed" the entire episode in a single take. The network underscored the risks taken by selling enlightened economic effacement: "now NBC presents a special episode of *Mad About You* in one act. Shown with no commercial interruptions." Interestingly enough, this premise invokes not the accidental quality of nonfiction film, but rather the supreme mastery of body and voice by actors. The paradigm of long-take/wide-shot, then, while borrowed from documentary, actually helps the comedy cross over to an even higher aesthetic caste: stage drama.

This episode would be performed in one take, broadcast in real time, and would demand the kind of skill and facility long associated with the Golden Age of live television and hour-long dramas in the 1950s. The stunt, then, was actually about the integrity of a long-shot, long-take look that would work to document the Reiser/Hunt performance as "real." The traditional notion of, and need for, a willing suspension of disbelief was no longer an issue in a series that had achieved this stature. These were, after all, recognizable actor/stars performing in an event not a fiction. Like the other docu-stunts, this was a docu-real intervention in the series by the producers. By aiming to authenticate theatricality—rather than any extradramatic reality—for audiences, the show exploited television's historic tendency to define realism not by any photographic quality but by its "mise-en-abyme" (or frame within a frame),[20] and by its ability convince an audience that they were witnessing an authentic act of theatricality. The artifice of the docu-gaze is used here to "prove" the hyperrealist status of this drama.

Counter Docu-Real Fictions/Postmodernism

Hill Street Blues and *Mad About You* merely appropriated and "quoted" space-time qualities of documentary to focus attention—in a unified way— on dramatic issues and performance. A very different sort of attitude had already begun to rule the docu-real perch since the mid and late 1980s, however, one that clearly aimed to strip television's "real" of any remaining credibility.

Max Headroom was imported to prime time by ABC based on its cult-series status in the UK.[21] The show's premise: a computer-generated intelligence and an electronically appended male reporter struggled to make sense of a postapocalyptic, postindustrial, post–*Blade Runner* dystopia. Depictions of the video-documentary apparatus were everywhere in the diegetic world of *Max Headroom*. It is important to note that most of the docu-stunts cited so far were shot and depicted as, or on, a form of film stock. *Max Headroom* was one of the first prime-time shows to show and exploit the docu-real as a product of video-electronic origination. Recognizing qualitative differences between electronic and filmed gazes would become an important distinction in many of the docu-real fictions that followed.

Following the wave of shows that made postmodernism an orthodoxy in the 1980s *(Max Headroom, Moonlighting, Twin Peaks, Pee-Wee's Play-house),* animation reappeared in prime time as a multidemographic entertainment product. The new fourth network Fox built much of its success around the continuing popularity of the animated series *The Simpsons.*[22] Much of what makes the series popular is not only its reflexivity and deconstruction of animation as part of the entertainment experience but the show's sharp, unending critical references to other and related media forms. *The Simpsons* created metacritical episodes about film, film festivals, film and TV criticism, advertising, consumerism, television, television producing, tabloid television, video, and broadcasting.

The series as a whole offers one of the most extensive models of, and most comprehensive critical articulations about, reality television. There are musings, for example, on the technical apparatus that makes TV's live-reality axis possible. An episode of *The Simpsons* focusing on Sideshow Bob's election considered the political menace of talk television and radio and conflated the *Larry King Live* and *Rush Limbaugh* shows ("we *are* the fourth estate") with right-wing political conspiracies, coercion, and even vampirism.[23] But the show's critique does not just target conventional politics. It targets internetwork rivalries and market jockeying as well. An on-camera Larry King warns his talk show audience, "Even though we are being broadcast on Fox [rather than King's more respected CNN] there's no reason for hooting and hollering." At which point the quintessentially anarchic Fox audience hoots and howls.

In an episode about televised executions, the producers build the show's dramatic plot around a trial demonstration of an electric chair ("televised live") by the mayor at the Springfield prison.[24] The mayor grabs both microphone and screen time with calm bravado as he summarily teaches and warns the audience about capital punishment and live television. "Now as I mime the convulsions of a condemned criminal, I must remind my staff not to come to my assistance, no matter how realistic my performance may be." The notion of "live" actuality as "performance" is an accepted truism here, but because of a mishap, the mayor accidentally takes a real jolt and begins to fry before the televised audience. They respond in appreciation to the cloud above his head: "That was really entertaining. How did you make that smoke?" This is indeed a very dark vision of the circuslike nature of actuality television that issues from news divisions. In Simpson theory, "live" is not more ontologically real. It is, rather, a product of staging and orchestration.

In the docu-stunt about television reporting, the entire episode is constructed around an invitation to Bart and Lisa to become local, on-air reporters who find and air documentary stories.[25] A station executive betrays the institutional logic of (the otherwise despised) nonfiction programming and moans, "Our licensing renewal is on the bubble. We need educational programming, fast." Lisa and then Bart find prominent roles as on-camera reporters in the youth-oriented news show that results. Although Lisa goes with content, Bart is lauded for his "zazz" and on-camera cool. He somehow gets the coanchor nod but defies his doubters by showing that he too can do "serious" documentary work. In introducing his first actuality breakthrough, Bart counters his critics with a stalwart, camera-never-lies truism: "No, I went out with a camera, and did a different kind of story . . . It's about one man, a simple man, he's one of . . . 'Bart's people.' . . ."

In a stoic, static, wide shot, Bart uses the camera to document a simple reality (a lonely man), but then develops the lone shot into an interpretation of absurdly existential and earthshaking proportions. The sequence as a whole is a thoroughgoing attack on the inability of television news to interpret—or even recognize—visible evidence. Actuality—the "reality" of the field camera image—evaporates under the onslaught of voice-over narration. The audience and crew, however, weep at Bart's profound ability to strip-mine emotion from a simple on-location videotape.

Perhaps because animation is a neither/nor medium (not really film or television), it is a rich middle ground from which to lob critical incindiaries into and onto any allied media form within its proximity or beyond. That *The Simpsons* exploited its critical media knowingness comes as little surprise given the show's reputation around Los Angeles as a haven for Ivy League screenwriters and alums of the *Harvard Lampoon*. It could be that the very "flatness" and artifice of these postmodern series—*Max Headroom* and *The Simpsons*—allowed them to critically engage the docu-real in ways that filmed series simply could not. That is, the dramatic telefilms examined thus far were forced to actually mimic or recreate their shows as credible documentaries, whereas the graphics-rich *Max* and the cartoon animation of the *Simpsons* could simply caricature, cite, and rip the duplicities of documentary from the safe confines of complete artifice and two-dimensionality. Even as Brecht might argue for the progressive potential of "flat" characters, animation and effects-inclined producers make the docu-real an issue of engaged quotation, not mimicry.

Fictive Docu-Realisms

Most of the examples thus far have clearly fallen within the purview of the docu-stunt genre, involving as they do fictional shows that become or incorporate documentary units or components. Another set of shows navigate the fiction/documentary split but do so from the other side: programmed "reality shows" that are in fact staged fictions but that also involve documentary units inside their on-screen worlds. By the late 1990s, some networks like Fox committed almost half of their program development efforts to reality-based series of one sort or another. Cable giant MTV even overhauled its stylized music network in order to showcase and feature "innovative" strips that worked as extended meditations on the real. Even though such shows sometimes unspooled during weekend and daytime slots, MTV also hyped shows such as *Road Rules* and *The Real World* in their "10-Spot"—the prized 10 P.M. programming spot in prime time on weeknights. Both shows evolved from essentially the same premise: gather an ensemble of young and attractive people, place them in an enclosed living or travel space, document them on small format video, and watch as they disclose things about themselves that "professional actors" never would or could.

Road Rules allowed Viacom to break the premise out of its narrow American setting in two ways: the show sent its reality ensemble on the road internationally (to Europe, Asia, Australia), and it added members to the touring group from the host country (the Netherlands, France, and Australia). *Road Rules* throws any number of stylistic elements together in a steady stream of disruptive montage, keyed and matted graphic images, on-camera focus groups that critique the "performance" of the documented ensemble, and direct address docu-style interviews by ensemble members to the camera.[26]

Unlike the "docu-real fictions" on special episodes of *M*A*S*H, St. Elsewhere, China Beach, ER,* and *Homicide,* "fictive docu-realisms" have, in some ways, a more extensive textual burden. Their producers must fill not a single half-hour or hour episode during a season but hours and hours of successive programming time with new elaborations of the original docu-real premise. Screenwriting in this vein, then, becomes less of a literary one-shot showcase and more like a very schematic, but daily, travel guide. Since the real-world people that inhabit the ensemble are beautiful but clueless late adolescents, there would be nothing to document if it weren't for the script blueprints that send them packing to another foreign land in search of tasks and clues dispensed to them by producers. Along the way, participants attempt to reflect on the experiences of their young lives to the documentary video crew. Questions, however, tend to turn to concerns and motives about suspect on-camera behavior and dysfunctional interpersonal relations: jealousies, competitions, PMS.

In this fictive docu-realism subgenre, then, documentary's "fly on the wall" apparatus can only effectively document the fundamental constructedness of the enterprise. First, these real people are always necessarily "scripted" by producer treatments and "clues" announced on-screen. Second, without any apparent dramatic goals themselves—a requisite form of structured desire in traditional narratives—ensemble members are made acutely aware that their narrative "goals" are being fabricated for them by external producers, lobbed down upon them from some Viacom Olympus. This is Homer's *Odyssey* in the age of cable—but without the hero quest, motives, stakes, or crises that typify classical narrative. So the most authentic direct-cinema mode—following a group of real people through their daily lives as a microcosm of some bigger truth—on *Road Rules* becomes a stylized testament that such persons are actually in someone else's fictive test tube, in this case, the producer's. Even this most real-promising cable endeavor, then, can only truly document that it is a producer's artifice. *Road Rules* turns out to be more of a prime-time "storyboard" than any traditional—or credible—unfolding of actuality.

Certainly one of the most influential of the fictive docu-realisms is MTV's *The Real World.* In the seventh year of its long-running life, the series moved its new late pubescent ensemble to the dark and evocative wharfs of Seattle, Washington, there to learn the ins and outs of young adulthood, coupling, sexuality, and identity.[27] *The Real World* was greeted in its early years by acknowledgement that the show was tilling creative ground otherwise impossible on network television and film: almost limitless coverage over long periods of time as people lived and found lives in the real urban settings (New York; Venice, California; and so forth). By the time of the Seattle installment, the series had almost become a parody of itself. The "home" for this group now appears as rehabbed light industrial space, with the hardwood floors, partially sided rooms, functional and expressive lighting, and set treatments that all communicate one thing: this "real world" is actually a real television set and soundstage, not an apartment complex, suite, or condominium.

And if the practical need to "block" the action and camera work dictated the soundstage layout of this particular "living room," the requisite dramatic "arcs" of real characters proved the most extreme evidence of narrativization. By the August 1, 1998, episode, the ellipical parallel actions and permutations of ensemble pairs were being intercut regularly with the regular disappearance of "David," who became a kind of charismatic and empathic "missing man." The group pondered. Why did he need time away? Was he gay? Were there problems with the group or with him? Surveilling him in the dark night on a wharf, the crew tapes him in anguished talk to some faraway lover, a device that fills both the phone booth and his on-screen persona with the tragedy of an impossible love. Eventually he comes clean, and at the climax of an episode, the audience learns from producer-generated voice-over that David has committed the unforgivable sin—he has fallen in love with one of the show's staff members. This development, however, is not just an acute example of metaconscious or modernist "reflexivity" on the part of the show. This actor-of-the-real has been "caught" in the love web of the producers. The audience is warned with David that to continue pursuing this love may cost David his chance for continued on-air stardom and his lover the chance for continued employment with the production company. Having gone docu-style wall to wall, the episode at this point provides a heightened visual-aural summa, foreshadowing the possible doom David's lust will bring upon the players, the show, and the world of the real. A montage predicts ensuing travel; David's reunion with his mystery lover (the show's [now] ex-casting director); the severe "talking-to" and threat the producers give David (he may have to be "terminated"); and what looks fleetingly, and nauseatingly, like a "Dear John" send-off by the woman in question. Even though the "story time" of the love-won/love-lost melodrama lasts but minutes, the "historical time" packed into the foreshadowing summa is impossible to discern. Will this tragedy happen now, next week, over the course of the remaining television season, never?

In 16:9 widescreen and expressive lighting, David confesses in angry direct address, "And I will never, ever take anything back. It's not gonna fuck up the process. Because this is real life. It's another human being loving someone. This'll make it more real than anything you fuckin' have! And don't ever be scared of that. Alright?" David's cathartic, tearful, and angry direct address to the camera seems clearly aimed at his producers as much as anyone else, for it refers to what they "have" on tape, what David has tragically sacrificed to give them.

This episode shows how MTV's fictive docu-realisms work by managing an economy, a textual heap, of possible narrative-discursive chunks. Even though the show itself is pitched as the real and about real time, each episode frames the actual with rapid-fire discursive hooks, set-ups, summas, and preview montages. *The Real World* works year in and year out because it narrativizes its participants in acute and excessive ways. In doing so, it manages narrativity in much more demanding ways than thirty-, sixty-, or ninety-minute television series or films. These *Real World* narrative arcs, needs, conflicts, and climaxes must be managed over a long period of time and a long series of installments. This form of the docu-real clearly fulfills the continuing serial demands that Flitterman-Lewis has explicated in soaps and Feuer has theorized in narrative television in general—factors that justify the current genre designation, "reality soaps."[28] The most real world, then, is also by definition the most textually managed and dramatically orchestrated. The fictive docu-real functions in these shows as a machine for long-form televisual dramaturgy.

Because contemporary television frequently works by quoting and citing contemporary television, it is no surprise that the docu-real has become itself a subject of other prime-time shows. An episode of the sit-com *Jenny* introduces to NBC's network audience a crew from cable TV's *The Real World* to complicate and exacerbate the lives of Jenny's episodic cohorts.[29] This enterprising stunt, therefore, combines in a single episode both a fictive docu-realism and a docu-real fiction. This particular episode of the sit-com ostensibly slams the artifice and duplicity of *The Real World* by schematizing the caricatured "types" that populate its "actuality": the African American "no-nonsense feminist from Michigan with guts and toot," the leather-clad "handsome Brit," the "house virgin," and so on. The episode also depicts Jenny (packaged with small-town naïveté and plenty of cleavage to work a medium shot) being exploited by what appears to be the most sensitive and working class guy in the *Real World* house. Using the now commonplace George Halliday/Rodney King camcorder trap, Jenny ultimately nails the egotistical Bruce Springsteen wanna-be by secretly taping him as he boasts: "I fooled the show's public. I fooled the show's producers. And I fooled those slack-jawed morons that I live with." Even the mindless and youthful sit-com deconstructs the duplicities of fictive docu-realisms.

By 1998, apparently, cable offerings were no longer ignored or avoided out-of-hand as program content by network producers. As part of commercial popular culture, viewer knowledge of MTV could be stroked and exploited even on the venerable networks as ways to increase audience share. Because Jenny was produced "in association with MTV Productions," one can no longer even talk about competition between the networks and cable in terms of two discrete and opposing camps. Now contractual business alliances have complicated the very notion of contestory network and program supplier interests. In the age of mergers and deregulation, the permeability of those boundaries makes it possible to exploit the corporate "other" from the inside, as well.

High Theory Docu-Real Fictions

Leading off UPN's attempts to become a fifth major network in September 1995, the very premise and originating concept of *Live Shot* was an extended meditation and critique of live television news and its documentary coverage.[30] Scene after scene folded fragments of the documentary and televisual apparatus into the passionate, personal, and professional lives of reporters and production personnel. This was television's own answer to Wexler's cynical critique in *Medium Cool* (1969) and Cheyevsky's angry prophecy against TV in *Network* (1976). But whereas *Medium Cool* and *Network* aimed their broadsides at television from the safe distance of the cinema screen, UPN appeared to rip itself and its cohort networks even as it tried to convince the new season's audience to discover the UPN network. The premiere of *Live Shot* is replete with self-denigrations: a depressed middle-aged anchor contemplating suicide is told by a security guard not to worry, "nobody really takes you seriously anyway." The postproduction staff crowds around the editing bay to watch the abundant, jiggling breasts of an assault-rifle-wielding women who is decimating a convenience store. As cutting and operatic as Oliver Stone's slam of tabloid news in *Natural Born Killers*, *Live Shot* rips the stylization and morals of tabloid documentary. While gazing at a preview monitor, a reporter comments on how much money they could make with the tape of the buxom convenience store killer as "an investment." A videotape editor responds that they could advertise it "in the back of men's magazines." Another fleshes out the subtext of the ad hoc story session: "yeah, right next to the penis enlargement ads." Finally, a postproduction staffer defends the dialogue to a producer who wants the unit to deal with something of more importance. Don't worry so much; this is "weekend news. Nothing happens on weekends." Belying this bored production chatter—and betraying *Live Shot*'s underlying cynicism about TV in general—the show then cuts to a massive "live" fire preparing to destroy a neighborhood near Los Angeles.

This kind of cynical positioning is all the more earnest when one sees it in relation to the Brechtian flatness and relative disinterest of *Max Headroom* and *The Simpsons*. But *Live Shot*'s fixation on the many flaws of television's news gaze perhaps makes sense institutionally. This new network, after all, is defined not by the kind of venerable and legitimizing news divisions that gave CBS and NBC their cultural patinas, but by the back lot at Paramount Studios (with its cash-cow *Star Trek* franchise in particular). As a studio entity, UPN would have none of the ambivalence toward TV analysis that the majors might have. Docu-real fiction helped during the network's inauguration to differentiate UPN's products and to individuate UPN's new network presence.

Two Emmy winning series in particular gave the docu-real stunt marquee status during the 1997–98 season: the premiere episode of *ER* entitled (significantly) "The Ambush"; and an episode of *Homicide,* directed by Academy Award winning documentary filmmaker Barbara Kopple.[31] The *ER* episode was heavily promoted in the weeks preceding its season premiere as the *ER* "live" episode—despite the fact that it was also advertised during its airing as available on home video. In this pose, "live" is something to hold and own—a document prepackaged for archiving and storage.

The *ER* docu-stunt opens with a semiotic one-two punch that foreshadows two opposing camps locked in an on-camera struggle. The standard dramatic opening for this episode condenses jacked-up visual fragments (clips of passionate and violent actions by its principals) into a frenetic, music-driven montage. This cinematic surge abruptly stops after a few seconds. White titles follow over black, and a simple audio sequence lays out the austere and minimal world of the documentary crew without visual or stylistic padding of any kind. The crew talks about recording tape, charging batteries, and the new location's smell. Hyped, gyrating, prime-time stars in montage give way, then, to meticulous, detail-obsessed documentary technicians. This affective-technical binary turns into a far more aggressive, extrasemiotic screen contest in the scenes that follow.

Like the *Homicide* docu-stunt, this episode of *ER* uses an extensive set of defining docu-signs: camera bumps, in-shot rack focusing, the removal of a lens cap during a take, and so on. With as much as 60 percent of the show normally filmed on Steadicam, and with scores of actors choreographed and blocked in complicated ways, the defining house look of *ER* has always predisposed itself to the documentary format. Being broadcast "live" to the nation merely underscored the notion that those who were choreographed were operating "without a net": made the producers devise even more elaborate continuity schemes to cover gaps and made the sound designers invent diegetic events that could justify audio track elements. At one point, viewers discover that a rhythmic percussive track emanates from a wacko drumming on-camera. Prerecorded music is slipped in under the "live" drumming, thereby enabling the percussive sequence to function as a much needed temporal interlude for the actors.

But the episode also clearly portrays a plot about a battle over the "stakes" in documentary representation. In the first act, the viewer learns that the documentary crew actually wants a cutting and intrusive personal exposé, not a document. The hospital, on the other hand, hopes the coverage will be helpful as consciousness raising and public relations. The medical staff tries to shield its identity and protect its reputation even as it plays along. "If I don't sign [the release form]," one doctor taunts the documentary cameraman, "you've wasted your time." As if to say "fine—you're not worth it anyway," the docu-cameraman fires back smugly: "It's tape, it's cheap; we'll shoot around you." The message? Make my day; you're in the way, anyway. But the doctors take their shots at the docu-unit as well, cynically acknowledging the artifice of the "reality" exercise: "Oh, so you want me to assist Dr. Welby?" What this sort of constant contentious interchange does is dramatize the dance of S and M that typifies the documentary "release" protocol in general. That is, the chief assumption is not whether there will be exploitation from the docu-gaze but to whom and how bad. To the *ER* ensemble, documentary is exploitation by definition.

As an extended meditation on how documentary takes advantage of and exploits its subjects, "The Ambush" episode also clearly functions as a performance of programming status and a form of institutional positioning. When an on-camera subject asks the documentarists, "Is this going to be on TV?" the crew replies, "Yes, it's presold to PBS." The subject naïvely wonders, "Is that a network?" The documentarists cynically and disingenuously respond, "No," and then walk off. NBC's *ER*, that is, involves a put-down of public broadcasting and its pretenses. But the show also slams the syndicated tabloid programming. When a new resident in the ward finally agrees to sign the release, she taunts the docu-crew: "Yeah, but keep this off of *Hard Copy.*" *ER*'s Hollywood television culture postures itself as far above the shallowness of tabloid reality programs, above the inflated pretense of PBS, and above even the opportunism of the independent documentarists filming the *ER*. This stunt is, then, a taxonomy and guidebook to the reality pecking order in television, with *ER*'s Steadicam-covered, fictionalized, prime-time, ensemble docu-drama at the top of the heap. Although the docu-stunt crew does linger on some things the fiction does not attend to (the sense of "inner circles, and girl talk around the water cooler), *ER*'s fiction underscores bigger theoretical points. This episode makes the points that documentary is directed, that documentary is a form that couches even reality as a "take" that directors need to "wrap" a scene: "O.K., that was great"; now get lost.

Textually this moral superiority by the Hollywood culture, represented by the regular characters of *ER,* comes after a repeated set of anxiety and "humiliation rituals" initiated by the docu-realists. The documentarists demean the critically noted actor-stars of the show: "don't look into the camera," and "our boom will pick you up, so act naturally." Of course *ER*'s stars cannot do either under the pressure of the docu-gaze. The docu-camera is always probing and prying: at one point trapping a doctor with a question about his violent personal past; at another, catching a medical team in the very act of malpractice. So *ER* does not simply offer a critique of documentary myths. It uses, or needs to use the volatile anxiety and humiliation potential that the docu-gaze brings to the world of *ER* and to its characters. As "quality television" of the highest order, *ER* uses the docu-real to unmask its stars, to bring its stellar pantheon down to earth, to ground its spectacle in the everyday. This dynamic allows the characters to exist in a double register at once tied to stardom and at another tied to the world of chance and humiliation recognizable to audiences. Stylistically, this cycle of elevation, being-looked-at anxiousness, and deprecation through exposure fuel the sense that a domineering spotlight is on the production cadre in prime time as well.

Where *ER* opens with binary semiotic clues to foreshadow the docustunt that followed, *Homicide* simply keys Barbara Kopple's director's credit over a prominently displayed U.S. flag in the episode's opening title sequence. The choice of Kopple, who had won the Academy Award for her labor/poverty documentary *Harlan County* in 1976, was provocative, given that her "independent" films are fundamentally tied to and lauded because of their outsider status. This *Homicide* venue, however, critically tangled with its target inside network prime time.

Homicide's docu-unit enters the narrative from a lowly rather than lofty position. Brody, the crime unit's assistant (essentially office help), produces a videotape on a dead New Year's Eve night and asks if the bored group of detectives wants to see it. Over pizza and cheap champagne ("from a gas station"), the unit pulls up chairs to view and analyze Brody's production. In what approximates a focus group or seminar, *Homicide*'s cast of characters proceed to interrogate the footage. In response to Brody's aesthetic pretension and titles about Baltimore's "mean streets," one cop retorts, "what are you, trying to rip off Scorsese?" At another point, the group does a shot-by-shot analysis more typical of film school: "ooh, montage; very surreal." Later the discussion mimics a postproduction session for a work in progress, complete with jaded protests that Brody's on-screen shots linger too long without providing useful information. This *Homicide* docu-stunt cycles through various media-critical rituals: focus group, critical seminar, and editing session.

There is a major temporal reversal at work here, one that makes the episode far different than many other docu-real fictions. Unlike the "real-time" pretense of *ER*'s "live" docu-stunt, *Homicide*'s is clearly retrospective. The cast critically analyzes and deconstructs an already completed documentary. Whereas *ER* and *M*A*S*H* place their fictions in the past and the docu-real in the present, *Homicide* places its diegetic fiction in the present and uses the dramatic world of *Homicide* to deconstruct the past-tense world of a completed documentary. This represents a major shift in critical competence in the genre. Rather than setting up the fictional unit as a "target" for an intrusive documentary unit and its gaze, the tables are turned. *Homicide*'s unit sits down to do a critical reading of the docu-unit's scenes. They are not, that is, simply locked in battle with an on-camera docu-unit. *Homicide*'s dramatic unit is given clear advantage over the docu-real in terms of critical-theoretical superiority.

This on-screen concern with critical-theoretical advantage in *Homicide* again suggests an institutional as well as textual logic. On the one hand, numerous ploys make the episode a primer in modernist and postmodernist forms of reflexivity. References in Brody's documentary to the unit's "home page" on the Web, to film aesthetics, to the "art versus reality" conundrum and to the pantheon of documentary filmmakers—the Maysles brothers, Pennebaker, and Ken Burns ("the only person who could make something more boring than baseball: a documentary about baseball")—might simply provide cachet for a series designed to stroke and reward viewer media savvy. But such ruptures are also a form of sociological and cultural marking. The episode is loaded with intense direct address shots of detectives talking to the camera as if threatening an incarcerated suspect. While this provides ample script fodder, the monologues are actually "what if" exercises with no real suspects present. The barrage of direct addresses, then, are really improvisational exercises meant to showcase actors' abilities. In this guise, *Homicide*'s docu-stunt is really a kind of "actor's workshop": not a causal kernel in a narrative plot but a platform for the show's critically acclaimed cast.

With spotlit performance the frame, even the most Godardian of flourishes in *Homicide* can be seen as institutional posturing. As two detectives pursue a suspect around the block and into an alley, they stumble into a large camera crew attempting to shoot a scene. Disrupting the take, everyone pauses, puzzled at the levels of filmic reality that have collided at this point. The *Homicide* characters turn to confront the "real" Barry Levinson (*Homicide*'s producer) and his large coalition of gaffers, grips, and production assistants fronted by production lights, diffusion, and c-stands. Brody's docu-real unit (inside of the "fiction") shakes hands with *Homicide*'s (extrafictional) personnel. As detectives correct filmmakers about appropriate slang and chatter about Baltimore and high school together, they dumbfound the disoriented criminal with displays of cross-textual, cross-register collegiality.

The reversal here relates as much to status as to time. *Homicide*'s stars grovel slack-jawed in the shadow of auteur Levinson and his troops. *Homicide*'s docu-stunt, therefore, is not just about reflexivity. The direct-address, "what if" sequences functioned as improv scenes and demo reels for the series stars; similarly the reflexive, cross-register ruptures like the one in Levinson's alley clearly demarcate cultural positions and elevated status for the show's production community. The docu-real in *Homicide*, that is, provides occasion for an extended meditation on the nature of the real and on the critical and cultural abilities of the producing coalition.

Structured Culture Lessons

Discerning the logic of a genre with the historic sweep of the docu-stunt means considering a series of questions. Where does the docu-real come from? What does the docu-real threaten in the established narratives of the genre? How does the intrusion of the docu-real change the narrative after it enters? Answering these questions provides a coded map of popular culture and a working caste schema for television programming. By constructing the real as an intrusion from somewhere else, these shows become as much articulations about those "other" places as about the internal world of prime-time fiction. For example, *Father Knows Best, M*A*S*H,* and *Max Headroom* all depict the docu-real as a force from network news divisions. *Leave It to Beaver, The Simpsons,* and *Live Shot* all pose the docu-real as an opportunistic practice by local broadcasters. The docu-stunts on *St. Elsewhere, The Real World,* and *Jenny,* on the other hand, construct the docu-real as a camcorder trap; one set to spring from the private world of the home and consumer. Since these institutional origins color the kinds of "disruption" that inevitably ensues in the docu-stunt, a summary of them as threats also stands as a critical judgement on various types of programming.

Table 1 suggests that prime time provides a graded taxonomy of docu-real modes—from legitimate, "insider" forms (including network news) to "outsider" and illegitimate modes (including independents who sell to PBS and camcorder consumers). The genre, in each of the iterations examined, also construes the docu-real as a force that enters and intrudes upon the normative and "natural" world of the fiction. This invasive quality presents "the real" as a problem that each docu-stunt text needs to solve. Legitimate variants of the docu-real in the "high castes" ("real" oral histories in *China Beach* and network newsreel in *M*A*S*H*) pretend to heal through a kind of reflective "talk therapy." Illegitimate, lower-caste modes (home cam-

TABLE 1. An Institutional-Therapeutic Genre System

Institutional Origins/Castes	Series with Docu-Stunts	Jeapordized by Docu-Real	Effects and Logic	Position
*"Real" Documentary	China Beach	• Regressive class and sexual values; excess nostalgia of popular media	• Life histories, 12-step healing; • "Memories-Anonymous" (M.A.)	"INSIDE" (Most BENIGN & THERAPEUTIC) ↑
*Network News	Father Knows Best	• Complacency, business as usual	• Dream condensation	• Psychoanalysis
	M*A*S*H	• Decorum, facade of normalcy & control	• Id management	• Psychoanalysis
	Max Headroom	• Structural oppression; status quo; conspiracies	• Scopophilia, unruly exhibitionism	• Men's Movement
*Local News	Live Shot	• Media power and control over image	• Analysis of voyeurism and fetishism	• Case study of sociological dysfunction
	The Simpsons	• Simple, common sense	• Diagnostic abstracts	• Brechtian DSM/TV diagnostic manual

*Cable TV/MTV	*The Real World*	•Secret personal lives and loves	•Forces characters to confess secrets	•The talking cure
	Road Rules	•Directionless adolescents	•Forces cast to confront each other	•Group therapy, transactional analysis
	Jenny	•Guarded naivete; female innocence	•Forces cast into artificial behavior	•Role playing, ego boundary defenses
*PBS/Independents	*ER*	•Complicated weekly production choreography	•Exposes malpractice; interviews vent at camera	•High dramas flaunt loss of control under "crisis" of the real
	Homicide	•White-collar crime; cutting corners; ability to manipulate	•Exposes workplace crime. Direct address vents anger at viewer	•Displays of anger at duplicities of PBS's docu-real pretense
*Camcorder Home Video	*St. Elsewhere*	•The patience of dedicated professionals	•Brute fact of tape threatens stillbirth	→ "OUTSIDE"
	Jenny	•The deceptive, pumped-up arrogance of cable TV	•Brute fact of tape destroys star career of poseur •Break-downs	(Most DISRUPTIVE & CATHARTIC

corder video in *Jenny* and *St. Elsewhere* and independent filmmakers in *ER* and *Homicide*) can only deliver brute and stupid facts—evidence intended to bring down liars, induce stillbirth, expose white-collar office crime, and document malpractice.

Such structural patterns also involve the audience in a kind of textual therapy—a filmic "acting out" of what Mimi White might term "therapeutic discourse."[32] For example, the extensive direct address sequences in *ER* and *Homicide* allow fictional characters to vent their anger directly to the viewer through the probing gaze of the documentarist's camera. In both shows, scores of shots are jostled by shoves and physical threats. The actor-improv sequences in *Homicide* also provide a barrage of taunts to both the docu-cam and viewer suggesting that "this kind of prime-time production is hell; you'll never understand it; be thankful you're not here." Ascending the caste system, cable docu-stunts like the reality soap *The Real World* stick their docu-lenses into ensembles to prove that their subjects cannot hide secrets—to prove, in fact, that those who do hide will be caught and humiliated in front of the international MTV audience. When David confesses in direct address to producers, he challenges the audience to individuate—financial penalties notwithstanding—and risk all for true love as he has done.

The higher docu-castes move beyond simple truisms about local news (fast and dirty reportage that sensationalizes and exploits) to muse on the roles that serious network news and real documentaries play in personal discovery. In *M*A*S*H* and *Father Knows Best,* network news takes the audience face-to-face with its sensitive characters. The docu-real in these episodes provides heightened moments of reflection as seasoned series characters "come clean" with the network audience.

The genre's highest caste, the "real documentary" pose, is intercut in *China Beach* to force viewers themselves to provide the psychoanalysis, to fill in the gaps between cinematic swoons and "real" memories. The message: "be troubled; come clean; come back next week. You, the anxious viewer, can work through post-traumatic stress memories." *China Beach's* mixed-mode real, then, idealizes and positions the viewer not in the maternal-reader role theorized in soaps but as both an emotional survivor and a conflict-weathered empath.[33]

Patterns emerge in this generic schema that reflect on the docu-types represented. "High" docu-forms (oral histories, network interviews) are injected into the narrative worlds of prime-time series to show the tragic flaws of idealized and celebrated characters/stars. The lofty are brought low in these one-time stunt lessons but in a way that celebrates the distance that such characters have actually risen. "Low" docu-forms (home video, naïve-but-idealistic independents who hope for PBS airings), on the other hand, merely provide a textual foil to demonstrate that series characters, by contrast, have enough common sense in prime time to see some normally ignored truth. As a problem-solving operation, the genre as a whole repeats a number of "lessons" celebrated during each of these stunts: (1) the docu-real is constructed and artificial (ultimately no different than the fiction of the show); (2) the docu-real effects crisis in individual character; (3) the docu-real provokes critical dialogue about meanings and difference and initiates attempts at mediating those differences; and (4) the docu-real exposes in the world of prime-time-series characters a fundamental fear of unmasking. Everyone in these texts is somehow involved in hand-wringing over potential disclosure and exposure. This stance—a defensive, reactive posture by a series under the glare of the real—is significant because it presupposes that (for one night at least) guarding and managing secrets is more pressing than a desire- or goal-driven structure—more pressing, that is, than enabling characters to seek goals or follow dramatic arcs as they typically do in offensive or proactive forms of episodic television. Because they open up fictions to provocations by, and dialogues with, the real, docu-stunts provide what might be called "liminal" textual rituals for prime-time series.[34] At heightened moments in programming time, these series texts stop to reflect upon and rework their established identities. In this way, docu-stunts are also moments of critical-textual performance and redefinition.

The Docu-Real as Theory in Practice

Docu-real fictions highlight their slips and slides across the divide between narrative and reality, they change over time, and they show a particular facility for "institutional reference" and "contestation."[35] As such, they are not profitably viewed within the constraints of structuralist genre theory, which assumes a set of "discrete, self-evident, and constellated categories."[36] Rather, docu-real fictions work in practice to articulate and highlight the very concept of genre on television. Docu-stunts make genre distinctions, hierarchies, and tendencies part and parcel of the viewer's interpretive activity in these episodes. In this way, docu-stunts stand as working theorizations about genre as a programming category and as a method of audience interpretation. This essay began by suggesting that docu-real fictions work as "critical television practices" or industrial theorizations about television. It is worth considering, furthermore, how docu-stunts are more than self-conscious discourses about genre in prime time.

Docu-real practice also aligns in provocative ways with how documentary itself has been theorized. At first glance, docu-stunts don't fit well within the purview of traditional, "prescriptive" theories of documentary.[37]

Because the genre cycles through a number of varied permutations rather than requiring a single presentational orthodoxy or look, docu-real fictions follow more closely in the spirit of theorists and historians that have created "taxonomies" of documentary forms or "modes."[38] Prescriptive and taxonomic accounts tend to presuppose, however, recognizable formal or structural properties that define static types. Docu-real fictions, on the other hand, are metareflections not on properties or structures but on the very *processes* of the documentary enterprise. They dramatize on-screen the trajectory, impact, and underlying significance of various documentary "interventions." In this way, the genre does work as a whole very much like Barnouw's lexicon of tactical strategies (*Homicide*'s Brody as "poet," *M*A*S*H*'s faux-Murrow as "reporter," *Max Headroom* as "guerrilla," and so forth).[39] Docu-real fictions, that is, do not just define or evaluate documentary types from a philosophical or structural point of view. They also show the docu-real actively engaging on-screen social subjects in a continuum of possible relationships from covert and illicit to engaged and direct.

Docu-real fictions are not simply analogous, then, to classical formulations of the documentary project. Because of the complex variations and uses of the documentary gaze in narrative and expository discourses on television, however, docu-real fictions do engage in the same kind of "apparatus" deconstructions that revisionist theorists have most recently brought to contemporary debates about documentary.[40] In the most comprehensive contemporary theorization about documentary, Bill Nichols has argued that the fundamental characteristic defining documentary is not any ontological, observational, or referential trait—nor is it based on a narrative versus nonnarrative distinction.[41] Rather, all documentaries (unlike fictions) share two tendencies. First, they make what he characterizes as "propositional" or "rhetorical" engagements with the audience by working as "arguments." Second, they make these arguments about "history" or the "historical world" or do so in a way that generates historical consciousness.[42] Following Nichols's revisionist historical framework, then, docu-real fictions on TV, strangely enough, can also be defined as documentaries per se. This seeming fit, however, is a difficult one to accept. Docu-real fictions seem far more capable of working within more recent "performance" theories of documentary and the real since they are works that perform the categories, guises, and styles of documentary and the real.[43]

The docu-real fictions examined thus far (reminiscent of celebrated outsider works like Jill Godmillow's *Far from Poland*) are, first of all, selfconscious masquerades or performances of the real. Yet they are typically spotlighted by corporate network publicity departments (not film festivals or "independent" film distributors or critics). Second, docu-real fictions in

TV (evoking Errol Morris's *Thin Blue Line*) work by processing argumentation (setting up dialectical oppositions, sequences of cause and effect, and evidence to support a discursive point of view). Third, docu-real fictions invariably work to produce historical consciousness within the stunt, if not of the topical issues represented in the diegesis, then especially of the institutional posturing that goes on as part of a docu-stunt (by producers, production company, and broadcasters). In this way, the institutional parrying between NBC and Viacom/MTV in *Jenny's Real World* stunt is not unlike Michael Moore's celebrated interinstitutional skirmishing in *Roger and Me*.

As "theory," the most complicated critical-theoretical articulations of the documentary predicament occur in *Live Shot, ER,* and *Homicide*. Because the docu-premise is more integrated in each of these one-hour episodes, their "theorizations" are far less binary, or reductive, than those of classical docu-stunts (as in the polar docu versus fiction yin-yang in *M*A*S*H* and *St. Elsewhere*). The fictional ensembles in the three nineties shows all get to master the tropes, signs, and devices of documentary even as they (like Trinh Minh-ha in *Reassemblage* and *Surname Viet, Given Name Nam*) knowingly and simultaneously expose and critique the contradictions, duplicities, and epistemophilia of the documentary pretense. Rather than the pitched genre battle (between naturalistic drama on the one hand and intrusive documentary on the other) that typifies *M*A*S*H, St. Elsewhere,* and *Jenny,* the casts on the *Live Shot, ER,* and *Homicide* episodes actually—in the grand participatory and interactive manner of documentary patriarch Jean Rouch's *Jaguar*—sit down and reflect back upon the documentary footage in question. These casts do not simply enact reality versus fiction conundrums; they provide street-hip Socratic dialogues about art and reality, the usefulness of montage form in exposition, and the traps of surrealism and poetic, self-indulgent filmmaking. At times their critical comparisons of Scorsese and a documentary pantheon of auteurs mimics cineastic critical posturing. At other times, their shot-by-shot analyses evoke the day-to-day world of postproduction staffs: the notion of an editing session driven by play-by-play evaluation, cohort feedback, and producer notes.

Logics of the Docu-Real

The docu-real text has historically proven a resilient vehicle for the institutional interests of programmers. In the logic of classical narrative, the docu-real provides a heightened textual moment to display acts of concealment, disclosure, catharsis, and therapy. The docu-real provides a discursive moment for reflection, crisis, and recognition. This "epiphany of the real," however, does far more. In the logic of production, the docu-real serves four ends among others. First, it functions to spotlight performance, depicting capable series actors under the "pressure" of live-recorded surveillance. This performative pose provides another opportunity—in a prime-time textual economy always linked to formulaic standardization—for guarded, but requisite, variation. Second, as a metareflection that elaborates distinctions about casts and characters, docu-real events highlight the aura of a show's Hollywood talent "pipeline." This kind of selling has always been important for broadcasters who use Hollywood talent and product to forge alliances with affiliate and independent stations. Third, docu-real stunts function simultaneously as primary and secondary texts—serving both as an episode of a series and as a "making of," with all of the value-added potential that the behind-the-scenes "making of" genre typically provides for series and films. Fourth, the docu-real can function as a very smart cover for a "clip show": for an episode late in a season composed mainly of clips from previous episodes. The docu-real, that is, gives the production entity a commercial incentive as well. Such episodes look like an exercise in refined deconstruction but can actually also justify reusing spent product.

The docu-real also rewards in several ways another kind of logic: that of broadcasters, who manage transmission strategies above production's textual community in TVs food chain. First, the glare of the docu-real ratchets up the very technological-perceptual qualities that many have seen as the key to network effectiveness: newness, nowness, liveness.[44] Second, the docu-real as a stunt attempts to amass an audience by pitching one episode as if it had event status. Even if such stunts fail (in an age where the mass audience may no longer exist), such efforts persist, if only to attract bullet points and expanded blurbs in *TV Guide*. Such is the nature of the event in the age of diminishing audience expectations. Third, docu-stunts can be tied to other programs in an evening's flow, providing local newscasts an opportunity to spin their own stories around the stunt. NBC-4 in Los Angeles hyped their 11:00 P.M. newscast throughout the evening of the *Homicide* docu-stunt because it contained a news story about how the episode was based on a "real" criminal apprehended by the crew shooting the show.

Finally—higher up still in the interconnected hierarchy of TV—the docu-real serves the logic of corporate media conglomerates. First, the docu-real serves to highlight prestige drama at a time of diminishing market share, a decline widely seen as a network identity crisis. Second, as conceptual reflections involving audience interaction, the docu-real tends to upend conventional taste-culture hierarchies that normally assign documentary to the higher, but smaller, taste cultures of PBS and entertainment to the lower, but far broader, middle taste cultures.[45] Third, the docu-real allows corporations to highlight "crossovers" within multinationals. Jenny's exploitation of MTV on NBC is far less exclusionist when one sees in the production credits at the end that the sit-com is produced by Viacom's MTV Productions *for* NBC. In this case, even if Viacom and NBC have no shared corporate identity, they do have mutually exploitable contractual relationships. This financial status allows NBC and Viacom to be both cable and network at the same time. This is to say that even apparent critiques of one side or the other in series texts can provide "win-win" opportunities for media corporations.

As "theorization" in practice, the docu-real offers a dense, complicated, responsive meditation on viewership, programming, and cultural taste. This critical engagement should come as little surprise given that practitioners are not unaware of antagonistic attitudes, theories, and criticisms leveled at television. Historically, the docu-real also provides something independent filmmakers have been celebrated for by academic theorists: an extended critique of the limitations of the real. The television industry, however, has provided this same basic critique of the real as part of its workaday world for almost three decades. Critical positioning goes beyond mere textual deconstruction and even positions industrial theoretical competencies above academic ones. In the *Homicide* docu-stunt, the show's prime-time cadre mocks the ambivalent existential ironies of its resident crusading documentary "analyst" Brody. It's as if the Hollywood community is saying of independent documentary: "Oh yeah. We know that. Next."

Therefore, docu-real fiction is not merely a genre, using fiction's "other" as a dramatic force to "conflict" its drama. Rather, docu-real fictions typically emerge as calculated and profitable performances by the production culture, as critical-industrial theorizations, and as corporate-institutional interventions. The psychic benefits the fiction earns from such performance mirrors the benefits programmers earn in an electronic culture that awards public posture and mastery of the real. Docu-real fictions are critical-historical articulations about television. But docu-fictions do in some ways document: they document an actual institutional performance by producers and broadcasters.

So the philosophical question of "what is real," is part of prime time's discourse as well. Who has more authority to address the question and explain an answer: prime time or documentary? Unlike documentary or news divisions—which are still generally locked into actuality myths—prime time flaunts its superior critical ability. Like Chris Marker in *Sans Soleil*, prime time flaunts its ability to step outside of narrative confines and break fictional constraints; it flaunts its ability to indulge in, meditate on, and deconstruct the real. In retrospect, then, the litany of recent "insights" in academic documentary theory seem like unexceptional and naïve platitudes. "One cannot accurately represent the 'other.'" "Documentaries are no more real than fictions." "The only thing that one can truly document is one's self; one's own subjectivity." We marvel at the guarded, calculated ambivalence of such academic breakthroughs. Yet docu-real fictions have made the same predictable points for decades in prime-time television.

FILMS CITED

Jaguar, directed by Jean Rouch, 1971.
Far from Poland, directed by Jill Godmillow, 1984.
Reassemblage, directed by Trinh Minh-ha, 1982.
Roger and Me, directed by Michael Moore, 1989.
Sans Soleil, directed by Chris Marker, 1982.
Surname Viet, Given Name Nam, directed by Trinh Minh-ha, 1989.
Thin Blue Line, directed by Errol Morris, 1987.

NOTES

1. See Todd Gitlin, *Inside Primetime* (New York: Pantheon, 1983); and Nick Browne, *Refiguring American Film Genres* (Berkeley: University of California Press, 1998), xi, xiii.

2. See John Caldwell, "Televisuality as a Semiotic Machine: Emerging Paradigms in Low Theory," *Cinema Journal* 33 (1993); Ellen Seiter, *Television and New Media Audiences* (Oxford: Oxford University Press, 1999); and William J. Clancey, *Situated Cognition: On Human Knowledge and Computer Representations* (Cambridge: Cambridge University Press, 1997).

3. Quentin Skinner, ed., *The Return of Grand Theory to the Human Sciences* Cambridge: Cambridge University Press, 1985).

4. Whenever possible, original airdates for shows referred to in this study are listed below. If airdates are not available, series episode numbers are listed. Given the incomplete and transient nature of the historical record and television program artifacts, archive record numbers for the episodes, when available, are indicated from the UCLA Film and Television Archives (usually designated "PVA-" followed by a three- to five-digit number). The series *Leave It to Beaver* aired from 1957 to 1963.

5. "Teenage Forum" aired on February 2, 1963. The archive number for the episode is PVA-8660t.

6. May 25, 1976, PVA-780t.

7. The series finale of *M*A*S*H* aired in May 1983.

8. James Schwoch, Mimi White, and Susan Riley, *Media Knowledge: Readings in Popular Culture* (Albany: State University of New York Press, 1990).

9. John Caldwell, *Televisuality: Style, Crisis, and Authority in American Television* (New Brunswick, N.J.: Rutgers University Press, 1995), 166.

10. *St. Elsewhere* (1982–88).

11. PVA-3248.

12. PVA-3233.

13. PVA-3249.

14. *China Beach* aired on ABC from 1988 to 1991.

15. Aired March 15, 1989.

16. CBS's *Tour of Duty* aired 1987–90.

17. *Hill Street Blues* aired on NBC from 1981 to 1987.

18. *Mad About You,* NBC, 1992–2000.

19. See Herbert Gans, *Popular Culture and High Culture: An Analysis and Evaluation of Taste* (New York: Basic Books, 1974); Pierre Bourdieau, *Distinction: A Social Critique of the Judgement of Taste* (Cambridge: Harvard University Press, 1984).

20. Lynn Spigel, "Installing the Television Set," in *Private Screenings,* ed. Lynn Spigel and Denise Mann (Minneapolis: University of Minnesota Press, 1992), 18–19.

21. *Max Headroom,* ABC, 1986.

22. *The Simpsons,* Fox, 1989– .

23. Syndicated airing, July 1998.

24. *The Simpsons,* episode, #5F13, syndicated airing, 1998.

25. Aired on Fox on April 19, 1998.

26. *Road Rules,* MTV, episode aired on August 1, 1998.

27. *The Real World,* MTV, episode aired on August 1, 1998.

28. See Sandy Flitterman-Lewis, "All That's Well Doesn't End—Soap Opera and the Marriage Motif," in *Private Screenings: Television and the Female Consumer,* ed. Lynn Spigel and Denise Mann (Minneapolis: University of Minnesota Press, 1992); Jane Feuer, "Melodrama, Serial Form, and Television Today," *Screen* 25, 1 (1984), reprinted in *The Media Reader,* ed. Manual Alvarado and John O. Thompson (London: British Film Institute Press, 1990). 253–64.

29. *Jenny,* NBC, episode aired November 16, 1996.

30. *Live Shot,* UPN, premiere episode, September 5, 1995.

31. *ER*'s "The Ambush" was aired in September 1997, and Kopple's *Homicide* episode aired in January 1997.

32. Mimi White, *Tele-Advising: Therapeutic Discourse in American Television* (Chapel Hill: University of North Carolina Press, 1992).

33. Tania Modleski, *Loving with a Vengeance: Mass Produced Fantasies for Women* (London: Methuen, 1982).

34. Victor Turner and Edward Bruner, *The Anthropology of Experience* (Urbana: University of Illinois Press, 1986).

35. Browne, *Refiguring American Film Genres,* xi-xii.

36. Northrop Frye, *Anatomy of Criticism* (Princeton: Princeton University Press, 1957); John Cawelti, *Adventure, Mystery, and Romance* (Chicago: University of Chicago Press, 1976); Will Wright, *Six Guns and Society* (Berkeley: University of California Press, 1976).

37. Paul Rotha, *Documentary Film* (London: Faber, 1935); John Grierson, *Grierson on Documentary,* ed. Forsythe Hardy (London: Faber, 1979).

38. Jack Ellis, *The Documentary Idea: A Critical History of English Language Documentary Film and Video* (Englewood Cliffs, N.J.: Prentice-Hall, 1989).

39. See Eric Barnouw, *Documentary: A History of Non-fiction Film* (New York: Oxford University Press, 1974).

40. Brian Winston, *Claiming the Real: The Documentary Film Re-visited* (London: BFI, 1995).

41. Bill Nichols, *Representing Reality* (Bloomington: Indiana University Press, 1991).

42. Ibid., 19, 27, 111–12.

43. From John Caldwell, "Television Negotiates the Gaze: The Televisual Documentary," paper presented at the Ohio University Film Conference, November 1990. See also Bill Nichols, *Blurred Boundaries: Questions of Meaning in Contemporary Culture* (Bloomington: Indiana University Press, 1994).

44. See Marshal McLuhan, *Understanding Media: The Extensions of Man* (New York: McGraw-Hill, 1964); Jack Ellis, *Visible Fictions: Cinema, Television, Video* (London: Routledge, 1982); and Jeffrey Sconce, "The Outer Limits of Oblivion," in *The Revolution Wasn't Televised: Sixties Television and Social Conflict,* ed. Lynn Spigel and Michael Curtin (London: Routledge, 1997).

45. See Gans, *Popular Culture,* and Bourdieu, *Distinction.*

Uncertainty, Conspiracy, Abduction

JODI DEAN

"The Future Is Here: All Bets Are Off"

The sixth season of *The X-Files* coincided with the House of Representatives' debate over Kenneth Starr's investigation of Bill Clinton and the resulting impeachment trial. The emptiness that followed the President's acquittal, the decline in Net chatter, and the editorial listlessness on the part of the e-zines and media commentariat was reiterated in the curious lack that accompanied the two-part "reveal all" centerpiece to the sixth season: there was evidence without satisfaction, truth without meaning, and information without action. During these episodes, entitled "Two Fathers" and "One Son," FBI agents Fox Mulder and Dana Scully discover the truth, but their discovery is not an activating one. People don't take to the streets. Politicians don't restructure the FBI. That Mulder and Scully can link together a conspiracy that involves the exchange of human families for alien DNA in the interests of the engineering of a hybrid alien-human race capable of surviving the extraterrestrial colonization of Earth doesn't affect the actual struggle between alien colonists and rebels. The galactic struggle of the aliens—some of whom fans call oiliens since they take the form of an infectious black oil—seems relatively independent of what Mulder and Scully know.

To be sure, in these centerpiece episodes, the alien plan to colonize Earth is temporarily thwarted and the conspiratorial syndicate implicated in the plan is burned alive by faceless alien rebels. But life goes on: the shadowy Cigarette Smoking Man (CSM) and seductive Agent Diana Fowley both get away. More specifically, despite having given over his wife, Cassandra, to an experimental program that infected her with alien DNA and turned her into a human-alien hybrid, and despite shooting his son, Agent Jeffrey Spender, the CSM escapes punishment. Neither vindicated in nor condemned for the choices he makes to save himself and sacrifice the planet, his betrayal of his wife and child is inconsequential. Similarly, Diana Fowley double-crosses Agent Mulder, with whom she had earlier worked and, presumably, had a romantic relationship. In "One Son," she thwarts Mulder's and Scully's efforts to protect Cassandra Spender by having them quarantined. There are also hints that Fowley may be allied with the CSM as they escape together the conflagration that destroys the syndicate. She, too, avoids giving an account of herself or her actions.

The initial run of *The X-Files* overlaps with the Clinton presidency, an administration haunted by conspiracy from the allegations around the death of Vincent Foster to the "vast right-wing conspiracy" invoked by the First Lady on national television.[1] Like the political events surrounding the Lewinsky affair, moreover, the conspiracies in the mythology that gives body to the series, that set its atmosphere, characters, and themes, reached an initial point of consolidation that was disappointing given all the energy expended in the search for truth (I say initial because, like the affairs surrounding Bill Clinton, the conspiracies in *The X-Files* are so murky and interconnected that they never really end). The "truth" of the alien conspiracy seemed less than the sum of its parts. After watching a five-year search for the secret behind UFO sightings, alien abductions, and the alleged crash of a flying saucer in Roswell, New Mexico, we already knew that there had been a deal made with the aliens over fifty years ago. The "reveal all" episodes were as revelatory as the House hearings and Senate trial in the Lewinsky affair; we had heard it all before.

We had also talked about, accessed, and clicked on it all before. Like the Starr investigation, which relied on the Internet for disseminating leaks and allegations (via the Drudge Report, in particular) and as the dumping ground for its voluminous, mildly pornographic report, *The X-Files* has flourished because of the Web. *X-Files* fans have set up scores of Web sites, trading episode summaries, interpretations, and reviews, posting photographs of and paeans to the series's stars, and leaking secrets about forthcoming scripts and imminent deaths. Not only is the best critical commentary on the series available on the Web (from Autumn Tysko and Sarah Stegall), but the series persists in an afterlife of fan fiction and conspiracy theories conjured up out of covert pathways in the American cultural imaginary and inspired by fantasies of Scully, Mulder, and others from the series.

Despite the unsatisfying quality of its revelations, then, *The X-Files* is effective because of its links to the interconnected insinuations and allegations of Net culture. This essay explains why, situating the series in the context of an American culture of technology and doubt that renders answers, like truth, perpetually open, unreliable, and suspect. My argument is that *The X-Files* enacts a condensed version of contemporary anxieties around truth and trust, that it depicts not a sci-fi realm of fantasy but the familiarity of strangeness in globally-networked media-entertainment culture. The never quite clear conspiracy that haunts the series's mythology invokes the never quite certain claims contradictorily clashing on the Net and in the unauthorized discourses of popular paranoia. "The future is here. All bets are off," as Mulder says in "One Son." *The X-Files* accesses this future of linked suspicions, these uncertain days when crashes and crime remain unexplained, when solutions seem unsettlingly inadequate.

"Jose Chung's *From Outer Space*"

We're a long way from flying saucers and Cold War science fiction. The episode opens with an alien abduction. A bright light paralyzes a couple of teenagers driving along a dark and lonely road. But then the aliens carrying out the abduction are themselves abducted by a larger, scarier alien. (UFO literature, familiar to at least some *X-Files* fans, identifies it as a Reptilian.) At this point, narrative coherence has been thrown to the wind: the search for truth makes links that associate a New Age cult version of a Hollow Earth enthusiast (that is, one who believes that UFOs originate from within the Earth itself, a view that preceded the extraterrestrial hypothesis), a burned out and lonely Dungeons and Dragons player aching to make contact with a UFO, and a challenge to Agent Scully's and Mulder's gender identities. Scully is taken for a man in drag (a nice bit of intertextual irony given that David Duchovny played a transvestite FBI agent on *Twin Peaks*). Mulder emits a girly and uncharacteristic scream upon discovering an alien body. Later, as Scully performs an autopsy on the body—an autopsy video-taped, cut, and remade in a parody of the alien autopsy broadcast by Fox Network during its previous season—she discovers that what looked like an alien is actually a human in disguise.

The motif of the conspiratorial human underpinnings of alien abduction repeats itself when one of the teenagers is hypnotized. Although in her first hypnotic regression she claims to have been examined and probed by aliens, when hypnotized a second time the girl instead recalls men in military uniforms. By the end of the show, truth itself has been abducted. When Mulder interviews an Air Force pilot, the pilot cannot confirm even his own existence.

In this episode, no one seems to know who he, she, or anyone else is. Or, if someone knows, he or she can't be sure. *Jeopardy*'s Alex Trebek shows up as an MIB (man in black). The conventions of the alien abduction narrative, as well as our expectations of a "normal" episode of *The X-Files*, have been pushed out of joint. And as these conventions have been twisted, so have the subject positions embedded within them. The military is alien. Women are mistaken for men. Videotapes link action within the episode to the network that broadcasts the series. Uncertainty reigns.

"Jose Chung's *From Outer Space*" comments satirically on *The X-Files*'s mythology of a conspiracy involving aliens, cover-ups, and a secret internal government, the syndicate.[2] It takes to a wild extreme the twists and tangles, the elaborate deceptions and implausible truths, that emerge in the series as the inchoate suspicion that everything is connected.[3] But it does more than this. By letting the audience know that it is fully aware of its own entanglement in the lunatic fringes of conspiracy culture, *The X-Files* gives a nod of complicity. It knows that we know, too. It knows that we are enmeshed in the same stories, the same fears and pleasures that inform its dark, conspiratorial world. This attitude of knowing reaches out into the audience, establishing the sense that "we"—the audience and the show—are coconspirators enjoying a secret awareness of the undercurrents of American culture that even as they appear in the mainstream remain, nonetheless, undercurrents.

More than commenting on the series itself, then, "Jose Chung's *From Outer Space*" acknowledges the cultural archive of the show's viewers. It recognizes that 80 percent of Americans believe that the U.S. government is covering up its knowledge of the existence of aliens, that growing numbers of people claim to have been abducted and forced to undergo sexual experiments.[4] It understands that conspiracy, connection, and layered uncertainty are not only part of the series' appeal, but that they are part of its appeal precisely because they correspond to the predominant experience of multiply interconnected pathways that haunts contemporary technoculture. As Kathleen Stewart writes, "Piles of information; it's hard to keep up; you can get paranoid trying. Who can tell the truth from the mistake, the inaccuracy, the flight of fancy, the lie, the cover-up, the manipulation, the disinformation?"[5] In the Information Age, strangeness is familiar, disruption as common as a 404, a broken link, and the virtual ghost towns of abandoned sites. *The X-Files* accesses these uncertainties, these suspicions that in a virtual age we can't tell who and what we should trust.

From Outer Space to Cyberspace

To understand the conspiratorial evocations of *The X-Files* in terms of the series's installation in Information Age technoculture, I draw from Lynn Spigel's compelling account of the familiality of strangeness in the fantastic family sit-com of the 1960s.[6] Two aspects of her analysis are helpful for thinking about *The X-Files*: its reading of the technological context of the sixties in terms of the space program and its conceptualization of the moment of doubt.

Viewing the fantastic family sit-com as hybrid combination of domestic themes and space-age imagery, Spigel situates it in a more general merging of space and domesticity in the 1950s and 1960s. Such a merging, she explains, was a result of efforts to provide Americans with a friendly, familiar sense of the technologies that would realize the utopian promise of

Kennedy's New Frontier. It begins with *Sputnik*. The success of the Soviets' 1957 satellite launch signified to many observers that there was a malaise in America. Americans were too consumption oriented; the domesticity of the postwar years had made them soft, complacent. Content with their barbecues and labor-saving appliances, they were unprepared to meet the Soviet threat, now made real by the possibility that Communists would control the skies. The Kennedy administration's packaging of technological progress and national freedom responded to both problems. Spigel writes: "The forthright do-gooder citizen to whom Kennedy appealed was given the promise of a new beginning in abstract terms. Ideas like freedom need an image, and the ride into space proved to be the most vivid concretization of such abstractions, promising a newfound national allegiance through which we would not only diffuse the Soviet threat, but also shake ourselves out of the doldrums that 1950s life had come to symbolize."[7]

Spigel explains that television had its own incentives for featuring the space race. Criticized as a low-brow wasteland, on the one hand, and reeling from the quiz-show scandals, on the other, the networks were looking to reorient their programming around more worthy and responsible issues. The space race was just the ticket: "Kennedy's promise to land on the moon before the end of the decade became television's promise as well. The space race gave television something to shoot for. It presented a whole new repertoire of images and created a whole new reason for looking at the living room console."[8] Indeed, television responded to the space race not only with reality-based documentary programs and news reports, but by reinscribing space imagery in a variety of contexts so as to make them new, exciting, and relevant. Conversely, it used everyday and familial imagery to connect space to viewers. Relevance, in other words, worked in two directions. Domesticity made the techno-scientific complexity of space travel warm and inviting even as space gave home life an aura of transcendent futurity.

Spigel's conceptualization of the moment of doubt follows from her analysis of the technocultural context of the fantastic family sit com. Drawing from the work of Tzvetan Todorov, she argues that "the fantastic often occurs at the point at which the hero or heroine doubts the credibility of the situation."[9] In series like *Bewitched* and *I Dream of Jeannie*, for example, this doubt rarely accompanies the outrageous dimensions of the shows. Their extra-worldly dimensions are not questioned; witches remain witches, and genies remain genies. The moment when a skeptical character confronts the outlandishness of an event, Spigel observes, "takes place in the realm of the natural."[10] So situated, this doubt calls into question the "naturalness" of suburban life—not the unnaturalness of magic. Spigel argues, "We are asked to hesitate in our beliefs about the normative roles of gender, class, and race that so pervade the era's suburban lifestyles. In this sense, the fantastic unmasks the conventionality of the everyday."[11]

My argument is that if the fantastic family sit-coms of the sixties mark a defamiliarization of the everyday, then *The X-Files* needs to be understood as an expression of the familiarization of a different kind of experience of the everyday, the everydayness of the strange. On *The X-Files,* doubt, rather than calling into question the norms of conventional, suburban domesticity, confirms the unknowability of experience. It attests to the already contested status of claims to truth and rightness. On any given episode, Scully will perform an autopsy or carry out a scientific test in order to find proof—of genetic connection, cause of death, or extraterrestrial life—the particulars vary with the case. Yet, no matter what the result of the test is, doubt remains. Not only is Mulder rarely convinced, but Scully herself sees her inability to provide conclusive evidence as a failure of science. Likewise, the rightness of any given FBI directive or decision is never clear. Scully and Mulder can't trust the motives of their superiors: is Assistant Director Skinner allied with them or the CSM? Unable to be certain of the source of their orders, of the origins and purposes of the instructions handed down to them by and within the FBI, they don't know whether what is happening *should* be happening. Whose interests are they serving? Whose side are they on—if the spatial connotations of sides even make sense? In contrast to the fantastic familial sit-com, then, doubt on *The X-Files* is not fantastic. It does not provide a moment of hesitation in which the narrative situation is called into question. Rather, doubt is inscribed within the everyday as an overarching—or undermining—hesitance that questions everything.

This hesitance is an attribute of the technocultural context of the 1990s, the first decade of the Information Age. Some culture theorists might characterize the nineties in terms of biotechnology, noting the prominence of the Human Genome Project, the emergence of cloning, and the new industries around genetic engineering. With cloning and hybridity as key themes in the series mythology and DNA tests as a prominent feature in numerous standalone episodes, *The X-Files* certainly notes this feature of the decade. Nonetheless, biotechnology does not set the mood of the series. The Internet—that technology of interconnection, proliferation, transgression, and access—does. This is not because the series is high-tech. Far from it—only a handful of episodes have been built around computers. No, the unescapeable sense of not knowing even when one should know, the unshakable possibility of a conspiracy, of a set of links and connections that cannot yet be expressed, is what marks *The X-Files* as a series for technocultural America. "Like 'The Twilight Zone,'" James Wolcott observes, "'The X-Files' expresses a national unease, which helps explain its hold on our nerves."[12]

This unease is best understood as the suspicious sense of linked uncertainties haunting America in the Information Age.

The X-Files first aired in September 1993 on Fox. By 1994 the series had acquired a substantial cult following, Emmy nominations, and the attention of media critics. By 1995 it was appearing regularly on television's top-ten weekly rankings lists. The convergence of three components of the 1990s technocultural context help make sense of this success: decentralization, tabloidization, and interconnection.

First, the success of *The X-Files* was in part a product of a shift in television from broadcasting to narrowcasting. By the mid-nineties, the three major networks that had dominated the earlier years of television were threatened by expansions in cable programming and the popularity of the VCR. With their audience decreasing to about 60 percent, the networks changed their programming strategy. They opted to target not the largest general or mass audience, which they were already losing, but select demographic subgroups, aiming to deliver specific viewers to advertisers. Fox, the "fourth" network created in the eighties, was particularly adept at this strategy. In fact, Jimmie Reeves, Mark Rodgers, and Michael Epstein argue that *The X-Files*'s popularity was in large part a result of its placement on the "fourth" network.[13] Because Fox was less established than the three major networks, its shows could succeed with lesser ratings; the network's goals simply weren't as high. Instead of a quantity of viewers, Fox aimed for avid fans, of the kind that followed *Star Trek*. Once it had them, the network capitalized on their dedication, licensing *X-Files* products and thereby generating the cultural buzz or mindshare that made the cult hit into a popular one.

Indeed, the complexities of the series's conspiracy mythology rewarded intense engagement and contributed to *The X-Files*'s transmutation into other media. Loyal fans videotaped episodes, implicitly reenacting Scully and Mulder's search for truth as they dug for hidden clues and meanings. Early discussions on the on-line service Delphi were followed by fan and then an official Web site, novelizations, comic books, trading cards, action figures, T-shirts, mugs, mouse pads, posters, and a full-length motion picture in 1998. *The X-Files*, then, was the product of the sense that there was no generally inclusive "we" of the American television audience. It targeted instead more particular and active networks of heightened involvement.[14]

Second, a major effect of television's decentralization, of the shift from three major networks to alternative media offered by cable, VCRs, and the Web, has been tabloidization, or a blurring of the lines between news and entertainment that the networks had sought to establish in the 1960s.[15] Examples of such tabloidization are reality-based shows that rely on videotapes of crimes, crashes, and disasters; confessional talk shows like Jerry Springer's that feature guests plagued by sexual and relational problems; and newsmagazine shows that rely on exposés of corporate negligence and political corruption. *The X-Files*'s pilot also fits in this category: the episode was preceded by the statement that "the following is inspired by actual documented events."[16]

Although the distinction between news and entertainment has never been an absolute one (both forms of programming, for example, depend on ratings and advertising), it makes sense to flag such key events in the shift as television's deregulation in 1987 and the corresponding rise in daytime talk shows; the emergence of CNN and the appearance on television of the "all news, all the time" format more familiar to radio; and the O. J. Simpson car chase and trial that dominated the media from 1994 through 1996.[17] These events put a premium on spectacle and immediacy, heightening the incentive to air not simply those real moments of spontaneity when *"anything might happen"* but all moments in case anything did.[18] Media tabloidization, in other words, relies on surveillance, on hidden cameras that can find "the real" out there beyond the televised spectacle. Since reality-based television privileges shock, however, what ends up being broadcast as real is often configured in terms of danger, violence, and death; it is often invested in bodies that seem monstrous, other.[19] And, of course, stretching the boundaries of programming tends to transform the very terms of the real. Alien abductions and UFOs, for example, are standard reality-based fare.

Finally, and most importantly, the technocultural context of *The X-Files* is that shaped by networked computers. The rise of the series has coincided with the rise of the Internet, flourishing with a medium that privileges the links and arcana *The X-Files* features. Like the explanations Mulder offers for the paranormal events he investigates, on the Web any one site or link is as plausible as any other. Authority is flattened out. If news on the Web is as likely to be found at disinformation.com as it is at CNN.com, then knowledge on *The X-Files* is as likely to stem from the conspiratorial theorizing of the Lone Gunmen (the hackers and conspiracy theorists who publish a newsletter entitled "The Grassy Knoll" and seem to be Mulder's only friends) as it is from Scully's scientific tests.

Indeed, *The X-Files* is invested by precisely those suspicions linked to the Internet, the uncertainty about what is true and who can be trusted. Although the Internet began the nineties as the information superhighway, by the middle of the decade it was denounced as the domain of pornography, pedophiles, and paranoia.[20] From the infamous *Time* magazine cover on cyber-porn (July 3, 1995) to Pierre Salinger's allegations of a conspiracy behind the crash of TWA flight 800 (November 1996) to the mass suicide of the Heaven's Gate UFO cult (April 1997), the more settled the cyber-frontier became, the more dangerous it seemed. Ester Dyson calls the Net a "medium for conspiracy."[21] Howard Fineman worries that it equalizes every unchecked "fact" (his scare quotes) and opinion.[22] And Amy Harmon writes: "The amorphous network often fosters the nagging hope that if only all the data on it could adequately be sorted, truth would finally emerge. This is all coupled with the utter certainty that such nirvana can never be attained, and thus the peculiarly comforting suspicion that something important is being hidden."[23]

As the Web has insinuated itself into the everyday lives of ever more people, *The X-Files* has seemed ever more prescient: both couple a mistrustful attitude toward experts and politicians with a sense that, even if one doesn't know what it is, the truth is still available. The possibility that the truth is out there invests the series with its lingering paranoia. Paranoia tells us that something is true, we just don't know what it is or how to recognize it. Mulder, because he wants to believe but isn't sure in what or why, gives *The X-Files* its paranoid dimension. He wants to believe even when he can't tell the difference between truth and a lie, even when he has no idea what method, procedure, or person can give him access to the truth. Indeed, not only are both Mulder and Scully haunted by the possibility of truth, but on both this haunting appears in the proliferation of forms and visions and approaches to truth. Scully relies on visions, ghosts, recovered memories, and psychic connections just as much as she does on autopsies and lab reports. Mulder learns from tabloids and conspiracy theorists. In the series, as on the Net, science and pseudo-science, skepticism and faith, hope and fear interconnect. Scully, the scientist, is a devout Catholic. Mulder, nicknamed "Spooky," weighs evidence of the existence of extraterrestrial life. There are a variety of ways to access information, to produce knowledge. Because the world is so strange, both Scully and Mulder's approaches are necessary and necessarily mutable. And this is why doubt, within the series, confirms rather than questions the everyday: when there are multiple, uncertain truths, doubt can only point to the possibility of a different point of access, another mode of analysis. Alternative explanations are only just that, alternatives.

Thanks to the Internet, we have access to information, opinions, fantasies, and facts that are virtually indiscernible from one another. Credible and incredible claims and sources intermingle. Computer-generated special effects, now available to anyone who can afford or pirate software such as Photoshop, make it difficult if not impossible to tell "real" from "altered" images. With twenty-four-hour news as entertainment available on television and the Web, we confront competing experts daily. Is mad cow disease a threat? Did the U.S. military use nerve gas in Laos during the Vietnam War? Has the American government conducted secret experiments on unknowing civilians? Was a vast right-wing conspiracy at work to destroy Bill Clinton? Faced with gigabytes of indigestible information, computer-generated special effects, competing expert testimonies, and the undeniable presence of power, corruption, racism, and violence throughout science and law, voters, consumers, viewers, and witnesses don't know what to believe or whom to trust. As Kathleen Stewart writes, "The Internet was made for conspiracy theory: it is a conspiracy theory: one thing leads to another, always another link leading you deeper into no thing and no place, floating through self-dividing and transmogrifying sites until you are awash in the sheer evidence that the Internet exists."[24] *The X-Files* opens a window to this experience of the contemporary world. The conspiracies it invokes are those configuring cyberia.

I use "cyberia" not simply to denote computer-mediated interaction but to evoke the broader expanse of virtuality producing the contemporary mediascape.[25] Cyberia is the sprawl of screens where surveillance and security interface with spectacle, consumption, and the viral spread of transnational corporate entertainment culture. In cyberia, as Joseba Gabilondo writes, "Everything left outside, repressed, comes back not as symptoms of a deep interior unconscious—as in modernity—but rather as exterior ghosts/monsters that haunt the interior and its cyborgs: computer-hackers, gangs, drug dealers, serial killers, serial rapists, homeless armies, illegal immigrants, mad third-world leaders who only yesterday were collaborators of the CIA (Noriega) and the Pentagon (Hussein)."[26] Cyberia's ghosts and monsters, in other words, are incorporations of the myriad exclusions thought necessary for a safety left further behind with every effort made to realize it. There are unintended consequences: super bacteria immune to antibiotics, ideas lost to crashed hard drives, privacies available for manipulation and extortion.[27]

Controvertible Evidence

How can I disprove lies that are stamped with an official seal? You can deny all the things I've seen, all the things I've discovered, but not for much longer, because too many other people know what's happening out there. And no one, no government agency, has jurisdiction over the truth.
—Fox Mulder ("Fallen Angel")

The mythology of *The X-Files* is based on Mulder's search for truth. Like Kenneth Starr's search, one that started as an investigation of possibly corrupt Whitewater land deals and ultimately produced the soft-porn longings and insecurities of a former White House aide, so too has Mulder's search morphed beyond its original directive. When those claiming the authority to designate truth cannot be trusted, when their motives are suspect and their interests are malign, what can count as evidence changes. Anything could be relevant. Unshackled from the strict presumptions of what truth might be and how one might find it, Mulder's search, again like Starr's, highlights evidence over plot and connection over coherence. Truth becomes an assemblage of information rather than a context for action. Like the fugitive truths of the Information Age, truth on *The X-Files* combats paranoia with excessive facticity, linking esoterica, minutae, and cabalistic significance in an effort to ward off pervasive, haunting doubt.

An Oxford graduate and accomplished profiler, Mulder investigates unsolved cases with paranormal flavorings for the FBI. He collects information, amassing evidence in files. His cases often remain unsolved, evidence accumulated but to no effect. In the first season, this was Scully's task as well. In the series's pilot, Scully, an M.D. recruited by the FBI, is partnered with Mulder and instructed to report to the bureau on Mulder's work. Most of the first season episodes end with her compiling these reports, typing on her laptop information that will be stored away.

The sinister doubt that accumulates with the amassing of vast quantities of information is made visually powerful in the last scene of the pilot episode. In this episode, Mulder and Scully investigate the murders of four teenagers. Mulder thinks they are linked to alien abductions, an explanation supported by evidence retrieved from an exhumed corpse—a metallic cylinder that had been implanted in the nasal cavity. An unexplained fire destroys the corpse, but Scully keeps the implant. She gives it to the bureau. The episode ends with the Cigarette Smoking Man filing the device in a bin in an enormous Pentagon storage room, a room filled with rows of shelving arrayed with uncountable brown boxes.[28] The truth is out there, but, in the context of so much information, it doesn't matter. Stewart describes this context as the world that conspiracy theory makes possible: "Events and phenomena call to us as haunting specters lodged somewhere within the endless proliferation of images and reports. The more you know, the less you know."[29] I see it as cyberia.

In the mythology episodes, the information Scully and Mulder accumulate starts to fold back on itself, casting doubt on what they thought they knew. Of course, some fans see these redoublings as inconsistencies resulting from careless writing and the lack of a master plan behind the series. The presence of bees in some episodes (as a delivery system for the alien DNA that will turn the human race into hybrids?) and clones in others (the new slave race) makes them mistrust series creator Chris Carter. For me, this criticism misses the point: the inconsistencies iterate precisely that reconfiguration of truth that the series enacts. As with the Internet, there is no master plan, no mainframe running a preinstalled program.

In "Gethsemane," the fourth season cliff-hanger, Mulder seems finally to have found undeniable proof of extraterrestrial life: an intact body, frozen in the ice. As he works to recover the body and submit it to various scientific tests, Scully encounters a mysterious Pentagon employee, Michael Kritschgau. Kritschgau has information regarding the inoperable brain cancer that developed in Scully following her abduction in the second season. He knows, moreover, about the alien Mulder found in the ice. It isn't evidence at all; it's part of an elaborately orchestrated hoax. Suspicious, Mulder asks him how he got his information. Kritschgau answers, "Working for the DOD. Watching a military-industrial complex that operated unbridled and unchecked during the Cold War create a diversion of attention from itself and its continued misdeeds by confabulating enough believable evidence to convince adepts like yourself that it could really be true." He tells Mulder, "The lies are so deep. The only way to cover them is to create something more incredible. They invented you. Your regression hypnosis; the story of your sister's abduction; the lies they fed your father. You want to believe so badly—and who could have blamed you?" Mulder refuses to believe Kritschgau. He is furious that Scully seems so easily to discount all that they've been through together. "What the hell did that guy say to you to make you believe his story?" She answers, "He said the men behind this hoax, behind these lies, gave me this disease to make you believe."

The next season, with Scully in remission, Mulder is just about the only person who doesn't believe in extraterrestrial life and alien abduction. Evidence of the reality of the alien presence accumulates undeniably, but Mulder continues to remain convinced that it is a hoax. Even after large numbers of abductees gather on Skyland Mountain (where Scully was originally abducted) and on a bridge at Ruskin Dam only to be torched by faceless aliens (their eyes and mouths are sewn shut), even after he has observed Scully go through regression hypnosis to recover her memories of the events on the bridge, and even after he learns of the alien colonization plan, Mulder suspects that all evidence is planted, orchestrated in an elaborate cover-up.

The facticity of evidence on *The X-Files* invokes the fugitivity of truth in the Information Age. Details can be reconfigured, reinstalled in settings to produce any number of virtual realities. Statistics can be offered to support most anything we like. Preoccupation with evidence marks our insecurity, our search for answers that elude us because our very search fills up the files. Although some cultural theorists read conspiracy thinking as informed by an obsession with plots, by an effort to map, narrativize, or make comprehensible the schemes behind the scenes, I think conspiracy is characterized by its excessive facticity, by its drive for information.[30] This makes sense when one recalls that precisely what the conspiracy is is never clear.

From Kennedy assassination conspiracies to those invoking the machinations of Freemasons and Illuminati to those spreading the AIDS virus in African American communities, conspiracy theories do not provide narratable plots. The plot takes a back seat to evidence, evidence that can be resituated and reinterpreted in(to) a variety of explanations. Derrida's thinking about the specter evokes this indeterminacy that I find in conspiracy:

> One does not know what it is, what it is presently. *It is* something that one does not know, precisely, and one does not know if precisely it *is,* if it exists, if it responds to a name and corresponds to an essence. One does not know: not out of ignorance, but because this non-object, this non-present present, this being-there of an absent or departed one no longer belongs to knowledge. At least no longer to that which one thinks one knows by the name of knowledge.[31]

Conspiracy haunts the Information Age because we don't know, but this not knowing is not the result of lack. We have an excess of evidence. Our data always exceeds any available plot; there is always something that eludes explanation, that remains unspeakable.[32] As Deep Throat tells Mulder at a time when, once again, the proof he thought he had is lost, "There are limits to my knowledge, Mr. Mulder. Inside the intelligence community, there are so-called 'black organizations.' Groups within groups conducting covert activities, unknown at the highest levels of power" ("The Erlenmeyer Flask").

It's All Connected

Everything is linked on *The X-Files*. Networks of kinship, computers, DNA, information, and paranoia inform and intersect with one another. Humans and EBEs (extraterrestrial biological entities) are genetically compatible. A child receives coded satellite transmissions from the snow on a television screen. A convict transmits messages from the dead. The CSM knew Mulder's father and may himself be the father of Mulder's sister. Scully is the biological mother of a dead woman's adoptive daughter, something Scully discovers following a phone call from her dead sister. Scully and Mulder don't simply investigate conspiracies; they are inscribed within them. Who they are, their histories, families, and how they see the world, are products of multiply interlinked networks.

The presumption of interconnection motivates the search for truth on *The X-Files*. What makes any bit of information evidence, what gives it meaning and significance, is its connection with something else. In "Blood," for example, the ubiquity of the LED interface becomes ominous, suggestive. In the episode, Scully and Mulder uncover a government operation involving the transmission of violent images; someone is behind the messages. In cyberia, we, too, receive messages every day that look the same—the read-outs on clocks, radios, ATMs. The similarity of these messages suggests an underlying connection. How they might be connected is unclear. That they are connected is certain. The fact of connection, in other words, establishes the primary criterion for accepting a claim to truth.

Interconnection is key to thinking in and about the Information Age. Freeways and flight patterns have replaced borders and boundaries. We've been told that a butterfly in Missouri can create thunderstorms in China, that a sports shoe fad in America contributes to the exploitation of children in Indonesia. Proprietary systems are tied. The same characters and images appear in film, on television, on the Web, on clothing, as toys, in a network of vertical integration. With constant, immediate media and telecommunications, we're all always connected. Like the Net, messages about ecology and the global environment transmit the message of connection.[33] This is the premise of the Human Genome Project, our genetic interconnection.

In conjunction with excessive facticity, pervasive interconnection installs a paranoid uncertainty in cyberia. Warnings circulate daily of viruses threatening to wipe out hard drives, to make our work, our information, meaningless with a few clicks and keystrokes. We've watched as an independent prosecutor's search for truth has created links between fellatio and the obstruction of justice in a story more outrageous than anything on *The X-Files*. Can it be a coincidence that Bill Clinton was caught in an illicit relationship with a White House intern or is it part of a vast right-wing conspiracy?

The X-Files clicks on the sense that coincidence is inadequate as an explanation, that it can't account for everything. The episode "War of the Coprophages," a humorous stand-alone episode about roaches, mocks the series's presumption of interconnection. The deaths Mulder is investigating turn out not to be connected; it really is a coincidence that several people in the same town end up in deaths that seem to have something to do with cockroaches. After each event, Mulder, who is investigating the case alone, calls Scully who has a compelling explanation for each specific event: allergic reaction, drug abuse, heart attack. The connections, in other words, are Mulder's. He is making them; they aren't already there.

In the Information Age, the tension between making and discovering connections induces a Mulder-like paranoia. If we can make them, they must be already there. But does this mean that someone is behind them? That one entity is behind all the connections that we make? On *The X-Files,* this is a dangerous assumption, one that misconstrues the complexities of power in age of global interconnection. Although the syndicate seems to be behind the abductions and cloning experiments Scully and Mulder investigate, who they are is unclear: we are told that they represent a consortium of global interests, but various members are killed over the course of the series. The relationship of the syndicate to the FBI and to operatives such as the CSM and the perennially deceptive Agent Alex Krycek is also unclear. The syndicate is not able to control the actions of those it employs. It does not have an iron grip on the FBI. Finally, Mulder's observations affect what happens. The links he makes are never merely discoveries but associations that influence to a certain degree the events he observes. The point is that the multiple connections on *The X-Files* are not hierarchically configured. They are not indications of a central control or plot. Rather, like the networked interactions of the Information Age, they have a branching, rhizomatic structure. They stop and start, existing coterminously like so many windows on a screen. These connections are unplanned, fortuitous, but suspicious nonetheless.

In his analysis of the grammar of hypertext, Steven Johnson highlights the interfacial element of the link as "a way of drawing connections between things, a way of forging semantic relationships."[34] For Johnson, the link is a haunting affiliation of half-glimpsed resemblance, an evocative device that remains partial, suggestive. On the Web, information is assembled through open-ended links of association. New paths may be traced, yielding different assemblages. New sites may be accessed, reconfiguring one's previous sense of how things are connected. *The X-Files*'s theme of conspiracy also operates through links of association. Its explanations are rarely satisfying, and this is why it succeeds as a series for the Information Age, for a time when the available evidence exceeds the coherence of the available plots. In the age of global technoculture, our connections may be products of a system, integrating us like so many PCs. They may be as insignificant or potentially significant as Internet links. We may be interconnected through proximity, inhabiting contiguous spaces in apartment buildings, shelters, or neighborhoods. We may be connected face to face. Traditions may link us. So may MTV or our choice of footwear.

Trust No One

Like "the truth is out there," the other catchphrase of *The X-Files* clicks on an Information Age meme, "trust no one." On the Net, the promise of interconnection has been paid for with intersubjectivity. Put somewhat differently, interconnections between people in no way presuppose or bring with them connotations of mutuality, responsibility, or support. That we are linked tells us nothing about how we are linked or the character of our linkages. Indeed, the fact of interconnection, the evocative force of myriad associative paths, reconfigures relationality. The rapid shifts and controls of networked interaction do not build trust.

That relation has been reconfigured as connection in cyberia is not the predominant mode of thinking about networked interaction. Some cyber-theorists have celebrated computer-mediated communication as a vehicle for new forms of community, for a realization of human ties capable of leaving behind the sexism and racism of embodied, face-to-face interactions.[35] In the early days of the Internet, this was theorized in terms of MOOs and MUDs, that is, as spaces where identities were mutable, where avatars could present themselves as whomever they wanted to be at any moment.[36] Critics worried that the indeterminacy of identity created a "springtime for schizophrenia."[37] Supporters applauded the new freedoms for expression, freedoms that seemed to break the hold of unitary accounts of subjectivity.[38] As more people have moved onto the Web, as it has become more commercialized, this debate has been replaced by concerns with the infectious seductions of conspiracy and pornography.[39] The consumer, usually configured as feminine and childlike, is naive, gullible, and in need of protection. The challenge of the Web in this incarnation of Net criticism is a challenge of regulation and legality. A focus on easy shifts in identity has morphed into a focus on easy shifts in desire, both made possible by the ease of interconnection. Connection seems so obvious that we need not even comment on it.

Those to whom one is connected go unnoticed. We are linked to different others, to strangers, to aliens, and the complexity within and difference among these relations is reduced, digitalized into fiber-optic cables. Put somewhat differently, the sense of total interconnection whereby anything can be connected to and exchanged with any other thing displaces attention from the ways in which relations between entities in cyberia are relations between people whose identities and desires do not simply shift and morph willy-nilly. Indeed, such a commodity account of cyberian subjectivity fails to acknowledge how those with whom one comes into virtual contact remain real others—that is to say, people embedded in histories, practices, and traditions that are not the same. That some people are wired does not mean everyone is, or is in the same way. Militia members, eBay auctioneers, tourist bureaus for Arab nations, and Disney-obsessed prepubescents come into contact on the Net, their previously separate domiciles and mind-sets now intersecting. We don't know who we will meet online.

These are the uncertain connections of *The X-Files*. It thematizes the clash of traditions and experiences made possible through the networked interactions of the Information Age. What happens when illegal immigrants contract diseases from complex insecticides? What happens when those initiated into the secrets of voodoo, exorcism, and cabala become part of cell-phoned, gated, surveilled, and digitalized suburbia? What happens when subgroups like the Amish or those from rural Appalachia interface with contemporary cultures of desire and perfection? These connections are more difficult than the globalist visions of cyberia allow.

The series does not presume that everyone is a conspiring double agent, hybridized genetic anomaly, or implant-controlled pawn, but that anyone could be. Those closest to us can betray us: Scully and Mulder reassert their doubts and insecurities in almost every episode. From the outset, Scully and Mulder have a connection based on incompatible ideologies and the possibility of deception. She was assigned to *The X-Files* so that her scientific training might enable her to debunk his UFO investigations and report back to the bureau. It shouldn't be surprising, then, that they don't always trust each other. In "Wetwired," for example, Scully fears that Mulder is conspiring with the Cigarette Smoking Man. She shoots at Mulder until her mother convinces her that he is not the enemy, that she is a victim of a mind-control experiment.

The "shippies" on the Internet, those fans who support a romance between the agents, would like us to think that if anything is certain on *The X-Files* then it must be the relationship between Scully and Mulder. In their fan fiction, episode readings, and online discussions, shippies emphasize the agents' close personal connection. They look for sexual tension between the two, sometimes writing it themselves in stories or photo captions. They often find such tension in the hints provided by the series. In "Small Potatoes," Scully seems to enjoy an evening of wine and intimate conversation with Mulder. She even seems amenable to the possibility of a sexual relationship—until the real Mulder bursts through the door, exposing the Mulder on the couch as a shape-shifting genetic anomaly. Scully wasn't paranoid enough. Even the partner she presumed to know was not who he seemed.

Like the uncertain subjectivities *The X-Files* thematizes—and again, these are uncertain not because the Net provides for performative explorations of multiplicity but because it provides the interface through which multiple subjects come into contact—memories on the series morph as easily as those in cyberia. Contents change as they are accessed through regression hypnosis, the technique that recovers Mulder's "memory" of his sister's abduction and Scully's "memory" of the mass abduction on the bridge. From different sites, however, these memories point in other directions: that Mulder's sister was kidnapped by a child-molesting serial killer and that Scully is implicated in a complex folie à deux and coming to share in Mulder's delusions. The contradictions that traverse the Information Age become inscribed in how we think of ourselves. The certainty of the secure

subject of modernity has been displaced by the insecurity of the paranoid
subjectivities of the Information Age.

Access Granted

The X-Files highlights the networked suspicions and uncertainties of contemporary technoculture. Like the World Wide Web, its preoccupations
with facticity, interconnection, and embedded subjectivities are unsettling,
opening up seductive paths into conspiracy and paranoia.

Like the Internet, the series' conspiracy theory challenges the presumptions of secrecy with the promise of information. And, like the Internet, the
series never really tells us what we want to know. It tells us everything, del-
uging us with details that escape meaning but make us want to believe.

NOTES

1. Hillary Clinton made this claim on NBC's *Today* on January 27, 1998. See
also Philip Weiss, "The Clinton Haters," *New York Times Magazine,* February 23,
1997.

2. As Matthew Debord explains, the series features three basic episode types:
those contributing to the conspiracy mythology, those standing alone and involving scary paranormal themes, and those satirizing the other two. See "The Truth
Isn't In Here," http://www.feedmag.com/html/assembler/98.07debord_linear.html.

3. See the discussion of the episode in the introduction to *"Deny All Knowledge": Reading* The X-Files, ed. David Lavery, Angela Hague, and Marla
Cartwright (Syracuse: Syracuse University Press, 1996), 13–20. See also the
reviews from Sarah Stegall at http://www.munchkyn.com/xf-rvws/x-files.html and
Autumn Tysko at http://www.geocities.com/Area51/Vault/1411/main_rev.html.

4. "Poll: U.S. Hiding Knowledge of Aliens," CNN Interactive http://www.
cnn.com/US/9706/15/ufo.poll/index.html (June 15, 1997). For a longer discussion,
see my *Aliens in America: Conspiracy Cultures from Outerspace to Cyberspace*
(Ithaca, N.Y.: Cornell University Press, 1998). The link between *The X-Files* and
the rise in media attention to claims of alien abduction is explicit. Chris Carter
credits his ideas for the series to learning about Harvard professor John Mack's
research on alien abduction and to the Roper Organization survey suggesting
that approximately 3 percent of the U.S. population thinks they may have
been abducted. See Brian Lowry, *The Truth Is Out There* (New York: Harper-
Collins, 1995), 11; and Lavery, Hague, and Cartwright, *"Deny All Knowledge,"*
7.

5. Kathleen Stewart, "Conspiracy Theory's Worlds," in *Paranoia Within Reason,* ed. George Marcus (Chicago: University of Chicago Press, 1999), 14.

6. Lynn Spigel, "From Domestic Space to Outer Space: The 1960s Fantastic
Family Sit-Com," in *Close Encounters: Film, Feminism, and Science Fiction,* ed.
Constance Penley, Elisabeth Lyon, Lynn Spigel, and Janet Bergstrom (Minnesota:
University of Minnesota Press, 1991), 205–35.

7. Ibid., 210.

8. Ibid., 212.

9. Ibid., 219.

10. Ibid.

11. Ibid.

12. James Wolcott, "'X' Factor," *New Yorker,* April 18, 1994, 98. Lavery, Hague, and Cartwright also note the link between *The X-Files* and the cultural moment of millennial America, noting that the show "reflects the mindset of its era" ("Deny All Knowledge," 2).

13. Jimmie L. Reeves, Mark C. Rodgers, and Michael Epstein, "Rewriting Popularity," in *"Deny All Knowledge,"* 22–35.

14. I am not assuming, however, that television ever was a monolithic totality determining its own reception. Rather, I agree with Elayne Rapping's point that up until the 1990s, television has been relatively successful "in hailing us a citizens with interests in common and in embodying a version of public debate on matters of common concern that has credibility and authority—in spite of questions about the quality of its mediation or its actual effects in terms of viewer behavior." *The Movie of the Week: Private Stories/Public Lives* (Minneapolis: University of Minnesota Press, 1992), xxxi.

15. Laura Grindstaff provides an overview of this tabloidization and includes a useful bibliography of traditional media's condemnation of the shift toward reality-based television. See "Trashy or Transgressive? 'Reality TV' and the Politics of Social Control," *Thresholds: Viewing Culture* 9. At http://www.arts.ucsb.edu/~tvc/vo9/index.html.

16. Lowry, *The Truth Is Out There,* 101.

17. For an analysis of the consolidation of television news and an account of media "newsification," see Michael Schudson, "National News Culture and the Rise of the Informational Citizen," in *America at Century's End,* ed. Alan Wolfe (Berkeley: University of California Press, 1991), 265–82.

18. Joshua Gamson provides a provocative analysis of the "moments of truth" in tabloid talk shows. See *Freaks Talk Back* (Chicago: University of Chicago Press, 1998), esp. 90–95.

19. For a nuanced account of the racist components of surveillance and tabloidization, see John Fiske, *Media Matters,* rev. ed. (Minneapolis: University of Minnesota Press, 1996).

20. See my analysis in "Virtually Citizens," *Constellations* 4, 2 (October 1997): 264–82.

21. Ester Dyson, "The End of the Official Story," *Brill's Content* (July/August 1998): 50–51.

22. Howard Fineman, "Who Needs Washington?" *Newsweek,* January 27, 1997, 52.

23. Amy Harmon, "NASA Flew to Mars for Rocks? Sure," *New York Times,* July 20, 1997, 4E.

24. Stewart, "Conspiracy Theory's Worlds," 18.

25. I take the term from Arturo Escobar, "Welcome to Cyberia: Notes on an

Anthropology of Cyberculture," in *Cyberfutures: Culture and Politics on the Information Superhighway,* ed. Ziauddin Sardar and Jerome R. Ravitz (New York: New York University Press, 1996), 111–37.

26. Joseba Gabilondo, "Postcolonial Cyborgs: Subjectivity in the Age of Cybernetic Reproduction," in *The Cyborg Handbook,* ed. Chris Hables Gray (New York: Routledge, 1995), 425.

27. See Edward Tenner, *Why Things Bite Back: Technology and the Revenge of Unintended Consequences* (New York: Alfred Knopf, 1996).

28. The room resembles the one where the ark of the covenant ends up in *Raiders of the Lost Ark.*

29. Stewart, "Conspiracy Theory's Worlds," 13.

30. In arguing that conspiracy is marked by evidence over plot, I'm taking issue with Stewart ("the founding practice of conspiratorial thinking is the search for the missing plot" [16]) and with S. Paige Baty, *American Monroe* (Berkeley: University of California Press, 1995), chap. 4. See my argument in *Aliens in America*, chap. 4.

31. Jacques Derrida, *Specters of Marx*, trans. Peggy Kamuf (New York: Routledge, 1994).

32. Michael Fortun talks about this unspeakablity in terms of "the willies" in a remarkable essay on teleportation. See "Entangled States: Quantum Teleportation and the 'Willies,'" in *Paranoia Within Reason*, 65–109.

33. See Nigel Clark, "Earthing the Ether," in *Cyberfutures*, 90–110.

34. Steven Johnson, *Interface Culture* (New York: HarperCollins, 1997), 111.

35. John Perry Barlow of the Electronic Frontier Foundation is one of the best-known of such thinkers. His writing is available at http://www2.eff.org/pub/Publications/John_Perry_Barlow.

36. Although his essay was itself an intervention in cyberthinking that marked_ a shift away from a utopian preoccupation with performativity on the Net, Julian Dibbell's evocation of the diverse characters in LambdaMOO gives a sense of the mutability that accompanied early experiments in virtual community. See his "Rape in Cyberspace; or, How an Evil Clown, a Haitian Trickster Spirit, Two Wizards, and a Cast of Dozens Turned a Database into a Society" in *Flame Wars,* ed. Mark Dery (Durham: Duke University Press, 1994), 237–62.

37. Mark Slouka, *War of the Worlds* (New York: Basic Books, 1995).

38. See Allucquere Rosanne Stone, *The War of Desire and Technology at the Close of the Mechanical Age* (Cambridge, Mass.: MIT Press, 1996).

39. See my "Virtual Fears" in the symposium "Virtually Regulated," *Signs* 24, 4 (summer 1999).

Television, Therapy, and the Social Subject; or, The TV Therapy Machine

MIMI WHITE

As an integral apparatus of post–World War II American consumer culture, television is centrally implicated in confessional and therapeutic strategies. Contemporary media technologies—broadcast television, cable, long-distance phone service, digital communications, and so on—are brought together, multiplying the opportunities and outlets for confessional and therapeutic relations. The new therapeutic dynamics of consumer culture embrace a wide range of strategies, encouraging people to manage problems, emotions, and fantasies. In conjunction with new technologies, a new sense of social subjectivity begins to emerge. In this context, basic conceptions of the therapeutic process are redefined. Therapeutic discourse involves negotiating and working through social subjectivity and does not necessarily involve achieving a specific transformation or effecting a "cure."

This conception of the therapeutic process emerges from Michel Foucault's discussion of confession as the discursive procedure at the heart of therapeutic practices. In *The History of Sexuality,* Foucault describes the central role of confession as an agency of truth and power in Western society.

> The confession is a ritual of discourse in which the speaking subject is also the subject of the statement; it is also a ritual that unfolds within a power relationship, for one does not confess without the presence (or virtual presence) of a partner who is not simply the interlocutor but the authority who requires the confession, prescribes and appreciates it, and intervenes in order to judge, punish, forgive, console, and reconcile; . . . a ritual in which the expression alone, independently of its external consequences, produces intrinsic modifications in the person who articulates it: it exonerates, redeems, and purifies him; it unburdens him of his wrongs, liberates him, and promises his salvation.[1]

For Foucault, then, confession in itself constitutes a therapeutic process, promoting expiation, a release of tension, or the narrative constructions of the psychoanalytic talking cure. This grounds the association of confessional discourse, therapeutic discourse, and therapeutic processes: the very act of speaking in confessional terms is necessarily transformative.

Yet television initiates a significant shift in the terms of the confessional transaction described by Foucault. The positions of confessor and interlocutor undergo substantial revision as they proliferate and create multiple possibilities for engaging viewers. This also involves heightened mobility, transience, and relativity of authority. Through these reconstructions, television offers new formations of individual and social subjectivity, displacing the modernist therapeutic project, recasting conventions of social decorum, and transforming conventional distinctions between private and public spheres. It transforms and mutes the importance of traditional transference—indeed of the psyche. What emerges instead is a networked subjectivity with identity construed in mediated performative terms.

All of this occurs in a wide array of television modes and genres, crossing boundaries between reality programming formats and dramatic fictions. In a variety of contexts, television reformulates ideas about the therapeutic process and how it works. Foucault's analysis of confession links the therapeutic process with a particular structure of speech that enacts self-identity and produces knowledge within relations of power. This is because confession involves a specific mode of enunciation, "where the speaking subject is also the subject of the statement."[2] The confessional "I" immediately implicates an interlocutor, the "you" to whom the statement is addressed, the authority who requires the confession, even if this is an internalized authoritative "other" (which is not the case in the institutional contexts privileged by Foucault—the church confessional and traditional psychoanalysis). Confession and its attendant "intrinsic modifications" is a sanctioned procedure conjoining truth and sexuality under the aegis of an interlocutor. Participation in the therapeutic process in these terms, either as confessing subject or as authoritative interlocutor, is integral to the production of a proper social subjectivity.

On television, confessional and therapeutic strategies figure centrally in a range of reality genres. In particular, a variety of fringe and daytime programming genres in the United States rely heavily on the participation of all sorts of ordinary people as guests, contestants, studio audiences, and home viewers. Many programs require the willing participation of real people who readily speak in a confessional voice. Despite substantial generic and programmatic differences, these programs engage a plethora of individuals who consent to perform on television in confessional terms. Talk shows, home shopping services, therapy/advice shows, and various couples-oriented game shows are prominent examples.[3] The sex advice show is a subgenre that blatantly exemplifies while also reformulating Foucault's ideas about confession, technologies of the body, and social subjectivity. In the 1980s, a number of programs (first on cable, then in broadcast syndication) featured sexologist Dr. Ruth Westheimer, who also had a radio show and frequently appeared on late-night talk shows as a celebrity guest.

Dr. Ruth came to be known as the person who brought frank sex talk into mainstream U.S. media in the 1980s, with persistent and patient discussion of such topics as masturbation, foreplay, and responsible sex. *Good Sex! with Dr. Ruth Westheimer* showed on Lifetime in the mid-1980s, a cable service aimed primarily at women. Because the program was so clearly designed to offer advice, it can serve as a prototype for examining the therapeutic dynamics of television. Because the program drew so heavily on the participation of ordinary people dealing with "real life" problems, it helps clarify what happens when television's versions of the therapeutic process at once implicate and redefine the very terms of what it means to be a "real" social subject.

During the course of the show, Dr. Ruth takes phone calls from around the country, verbally responds to letters, engages in dramatized therapy sessions, and chats with celebrity guests who also participate in conversations with viewers who call in. Dr. Ruth shares the stage with cohost Larry Angelo. Expertise and authority are redefined as *Good Sex* regularly offers multiple interlocutors, including people who do not possess Dr. Ruth's professional credentials. At the same time, Dr. Ruth is promoted as a celebrity television personality in her own right. Her value as a television therapist hinges on professional expertise conferred both by her advanced degree and her status as a media star. Callers frequently comment on how much they like Dr. Ruth and her show, clearly enjoying the ability to converse with a media celebrity as well as benefiting from her professional expertise. As a result, transference in the traditional psychoanalytic sense is reformulated in terms of media celebrity and fan culture.

This is exacerbated in the dramatized therapy sessions included in the program as actors perform the role of Dr. Ruth's "patients" while Dr. Ruth herself assumes the role of the sex therapist in these scripted scenes. The scenes provide the most familiar and conventional form of "therapy" offered on the show—the encounter between a patient and a doctor in the privacy of an office. But they are frankly presented as dramatized sessions, relatively brief (no more than five to ten minutes), and the patients in the scenes are explicitly identified as actors. The most traditional rendition of therapy is thus immediately identified with docudramatic mediation, distinct from the everyday viewers who phone in with their real problems, who are regularly reminded that Dr. Ruth cannot actually "do therapy" over the air.

The participatory confessional voice of real viewers emerges more directly in the phone calls and letters that comprise the bulk of the program. In the course of the calls, Dr. Ruth combines expert knowledge in the domain of techniques of the body with moral authority. Dr. Ruth is the expert professional and the star, and as such she controls the terms of discourse most of the time. Yet her position is decentered in a number of ways. Most obviously, she is subject to the structural and institutional demands of commercial television programming. Lengthy phone conversations are cut short, advertising breaks influence the pace of discussion, and dramatized therapy sessions fit into the time available between two commercial breaks. Cohost Larry Angelo's role becomes prominent in this regard as he signals transitions, impending commercial breaks, and upcoming segments. In this capacity, he speaks with the authority of the medium itself, at once containing Dr. Ruth and promoting her as a star persona.

In her visits with celebrity guests—such as TV weatherman Willard Scott, comedians Robert Klein, Al Franken, and Tom Davis, and science fiction author Isaac Asimov—Dr. Ruth calls on their expertise to address issues at the heart of the program, sex and relationships. The program implies that media celebrity, medical authority, and dramatic talent are permeable and mutually supporting positions. Even those who call seeking advice may be seen as educators and authorities for others, a position reinforced when Dr. Ruth compliments a caller for posing such a good question and indicates that their problem is shared by countless others. The caller is momentarily elevated to the level of "expert" by virtue of a willingness to speak; televisual confession slides into authority. At the same time, talking with Dr. Ruth on television affiliates the caller with media celebrity.

Expertise is further redistributed as Dr. Ruth routinely runs through the various additional interlocutors callers can consult to deal with their problems: a social worker, therapist, minister, doctor, mother, aunt, and so on. The necessity of talking with others, and of continuing to talk, is frequently underscored, a process that only starts with a call to Dr. Ruth. The inaugural confession to Dr. Ruth and a national television audience becomes the first step in a larger, ongoing process. Finally, Dr. Ruth's authority and expertise is tempered when she is unable to adequately address the problems raised by a caller, failing as both educator and therapist. Thus confessional and therapeutic discourse—and their contribution to star image and celebrity value—involve an ongoing circulation of discourse. An indeterminate group of people can move in and out of the positions of confessor and interlocutor instead of sustaining a more stable exchange between two people fixed in positions of patient and therapist. Television viewers may in turn identify with someone posing questions or with any number of interlocutors, including one who provides some sort of response; they can accept the expert authority, such as it is, or recognize its limitation. The apparatus itself provides the terms for the therapeutic relationship initiated by a confessional transaction that becomes the appeal of the medium—the appeal to watch TV in the first place. The multiple performative roles highlighted by the program serves to emphasize this.

Through the course of even one episode Dr. Ruth assumes a range of performative positions highlighted by shifts in setting and in how she addresses the camera. Letters and phone calls are received and discussed in one setting while the celebrity chats take place in another; the dramatized scenes involve yet another shift in staging. Each scene involves a distinctive televisual style, which can incorporate a display of the production apparatus. During phone calls, the speaker phone is initially visible, and Dr. Ruth's reply includes direct address to the camera in medium shot, visually implicating all program viewers as the addressee for any question, issue, or problem. In contrast to this, the unacknowledged third person point of view of the camera in the dramatized therapy sessions is clearly marked as a stylistic variation, especially since Dr. Ruth is involved in the "role playing." Through the permutations of visual style, scripts, live phone calls, self-conscious chitchat, and so on, distinctions between live and prerecorded events, and real and fictional scenarios, are crisscrossed and blurred to the point of nondistinction. What emerges instead is a larger concern for social identity that is defined through the multiple aesthetic and stylistic options offered by the program—an emergent reality of a social subject of therapeutic discourse. This subject is networked through television, real-time transmission, pretaped video, videotape reruns of previously aired episodes, and/or telephones.

Because the program relies on real people to call, willing to discuss personal sexual issues, it also caters to voyeuristic pleasures. One initial lure for viewers is the promise of overhearing and watching as others speak about problems in their sex lives and interpersonal relationships. The confessional revelations, requiring the presence of an interlocutor, initially authorize this voyeurism at the same time that they introduce a therapeutic transaction. And while the "first place" of the interlocutor is initially focused on the therapist-star—in this case Dr. Ruth—the program goes on to make this position relative and multiple, mobilizing the viewer (among others) as an essential participant within the therapeutic discourse. As interlocutors, even viewers who do not speak are implicated in this process. The tables may turn, however, when Dr. Ruth directly addresses the camera in medium close-up to answer a caller, and all viewers suddenly find themselves positioned, via the performative linguistic and visual address of the apparatus, as the "you" who initiated the call. The apparatus itself thereby claims a significant role, claiming the therapeutic relation as its own.

The result is a new therapeutic dynamics defined by a relational transaction enabled by televisual mediations in technological, stylistic, and performative terms. Real social subjects emerge only in this context. The medium and the modes of performativity it encourages provide a structure within which one can always appeal for help even while listening to others' confessions. Therapeutic discourse provides the grounds for understanding the appeal of the sex advice and counseling programs, even if neither the programs nor the viewers officially "do therapy" in traditional terms. Indeed, as I have tried to suggest, counseling programs supplant the terms of traditional therapy in favor of mediated, performative confessional practices that begin to redefine popular therapeutic processes and social subjectivity.

There are proliferating contexts in which these new confessional exchanges occur. Most prominently, talk shows and couples game shows (*The Dating Game, The Newlywed Game*) provide positions for contestants and viewers in terms of this reformulated conception of therapeutic discourse. Engaging these programs—as participant, regular viewer, or channel surfer—is facilitated by the availability of multiple and mobile positions for speaking and listening and by the performative opportunities afforded. None of this requires probing the sources of one's own individual subjectivity or the origins of one's own psychic formation and inclinations. Instead it involves continuous, serialized implication within a regime of performative, televisual confession. This produces social subjectivity as the product of discursive negotiation and management via technologically mediated confessional processes rather than through anything like individual analysis focused on any one person; real people are construed as technological and discursive networked entities of these new therapeutic procedures.

During the 1980s, Dr. Ruth appeared on television on Lifetime cable and then in syndication (usually in a late-night time slot). In both venues, the program was variously aimed at older and/or specifically gendered audiences. Within this context, it maintained some degree of decorum and restraint. Yet the program's basic procedures for confession set a standard that is reproduced in exacerbated forms on a more recent sex/advice show, *Loveline*. *Loveline* is shown on MTV, offering a substantial shift in the preponderant audience demographics along with significant innovations in visual style and technological apparatuses. These occur along the lines that one might expect based on differences between MTV and Lifetime cable services and the program's emergence in the mid-1990s. Like Dr. Ruth, the *Loveline* hosts also have a nationally syndicated radio show.

The individuals who participate in the program (men and women, usually between eighteen and twenty-five years old) pose questions by telephone, e-mail, and regular post; they can address the hosts from remote locations in the Los Angeles area (beaches, nightclubs, and so on) via the so-called pictel system that combines video and telephone in an on-screen image that looks like a computer screen; they can also ask questions from the studio audience. Even those asking questions from the studio have a number of options as they can face the camera or use a phone booth to hide their appearance. Large multiscreen video walls frame the hosts and their celebrity guests, variously displaying the program title, hosts, the individuals posing questions, or members of the studio audience. Because of the scale of the video wall, these images loom over the hosts, casting all who appear on it (including the hosts and studio audience) as integral components of the mediated, performative mise-en-scène. The program exploits rapid cutting, handheld cameras, extreme canted angles, and other stylistic devices typical of music videos and other MTV programs (such as *The Real World, Singled Out*, and so on).

The regular hosts of *Loveline* include Dr. Drew Pinsky, a board-certified physician who specializes in addiction medicine, and Adam Carolla, a comedian who participates in dispensing advice, even at odds with that of his medical professional cohost. Staff members on remote location and in the studio help solicit questions and also provide advice and opinions. Celebrity guests also figure prominently. Actors and musicians promote their recent work in music videos, television, or film and participate with Dr. Drew and Adam in discussions of the issues raised by those seeking advice. Thus *Loveline* draws on the basic strategies of *Good Sex! with Dr. Ruth Westheimer* but intensifies them in televisual, performative, and discursive terms. The roles of confessor and interlocutor are redivided and dispersed among an even wider possible range of participants, the conflation of medical authority and media celebrity is even more acute, and the sense of (multi)media simulation and of performance is increasingly blatant.

While advice gets offered, it results from drawn-out conversations that are variously snide, ironic, humorous, and/or serious on the part of the program hosts and their celebrity guests. This mixture of responses is an explicit strategy, promoted especially by Adam, who is more than willing to deride any caller. The regular hosts and their on-stage guests often express divergent opinions about callers and their questions. As a result, no one position holds sway in all cases. Instead, the nature of advice, input, and authority depends on the particular situation and the degree to which the various hosts participate in the discussion. Adam is at once the comedian and the "regular guy" while Dr. Drew represents medical expertise and authority. Celebrity guests tend to supplement and expand the range of points of view. As stars within the world of MTV viewers, their celebrity confers on them status of "extra-regular" individuals, able to articulate norms and opinions with authority or interest because of their star status.

As a discursive procedure, confessional performance remains the heart of the program. The proliferation of apparatuses—telephone, computer, remote cameras—facilitates the process, which is met with an expanding network of confessors and interlocutors. The self-conscious mediations and performativity of the confessional transaction are foregrounded as many of the participants—both confessors and interlocutors—appear on screen. In the case of celebrity guests, this extends to the inclusion of film clips and music videos. In all these ways, the discourse of confession is conjoined with the performance aspects of being on TV to produce a therapeutic discourse for public consumption that is at once technologically mediated and performatively embodied.

The result is a confessional transaction that is multivocal, multisubjective, telecommunicative, and performative in nature, with substantial ramifications for how social subjectivity is understood. The participants are implicated in a process that shifts the focus from their particular psychic formations and habits to less personalized, interactive transactions of bodies and subjectivities. This does not mean that normative medical and social values are not invoked to explain and evaluate specific practices and situations. But normative explanations and prescriptive advice are only some of the possible responses that may be provoked by any one person's confession, and the seriousness of any particular response is hardly assured in advance. Adam can go so far as to explicitly propose that callers are either "stupid or lying," to poll his cohost in this regard, and to use these terms as a transition device: "Next caller: Are you stupid or lying?"

As such, the program offers a reevaluation of popular ideas about advice and therapy. *Loveline,* following *Good Sex! with Dr. Ruth Westheimer,* performs short-term interventions rather than initiating long-term analysis. Quick diagnostics, barbed exchanges about what is or is not "normal" behavior, and a range of possible advice is advanced as the appropriate mode of response. But within this context, confessional discourse proliferates the disclosure of personal narratives and the dispensing of commentary—even of a derisive or dismissive nature—dealing with interpersonal social relations and technologies of sex and bodies. This is in fact a requirement of the show, since the program literally could not exist in the absence of confessional performers. The real people who come to the program with their sexual and romantic dilemmas are manifestly displayed as networked performative participants in this therapeutic dynamic. As the nature of therapeutic discourse is transformed, the understanding of a "cure" also undergoes reconstrual. The idea of reaching some kind of self-understanding based on the assumptions of long-term analysis is increasingly irrelevant. It is replaced by successful participation in a performative interplay of celebrity, authority, and media technologies, exactly along the lines provided by the program. Any necessary social "realignment" results from pinpointing specific social or external factors—drug use, childhood sexual abuse—as the cause of behaviors considered aberrant or asocial. In other words, participation in this process provides the context for appropriate "managed" subjectivity, a position that may even be attainable simply by watching television.

Loveline and *Good Sex!* are two variants of the therapy/advice program, and they function in similar terms. Both programs rely heavily on the ongoing participation of real people willing to disclose deeply personal matters in a frankly public, mediated forum. They deploy confessional discourse, divide and multiply the positions of confessor and interlocutor, and address them, along with studio and television viewers, in terms that are variously serious and trivializing, often even at the same time. This is characteristic of a range of talk shows and game shows (such as *The Dating Game* and *The Newlywed Game*), as well as hybrid genre programs such as *Divorce Court, Forgive or Forget,* and other counseling programs.[4] Confession in these terms is combined with repetitive, self-conscious televisual strategies of mediation and simulation, undermining the distinction between fictive and nonfictional perspectives. As is the case with *Loveline,* the televisual aesthetic combines different levels and styles of performance: the low-tech nonprofessionalism of the ordinary individuals who participate, the self-assured, seemingly spontaneous responses of the program hosts, and the highly self-conscious stylistics of camera work, mise-en-scène, and digital image processing. As a result, these programs offer multiple and simultaneous positions of aesthetic implication and identification, sustaining a balance between engagement and disinvolvement, proximity and distance, for participants and viewers. They contribute to a subjectivity that is contradictory and decentered, using ambivalence as a central strategy of therapeutic engagement that captures viewers in the first place.

While the thematics of the programs implicate voyeurism—with their probing of the personal interests and private practices of the couples in question—viewers are held at a distance by self-conscious performances of the hosts, deployments of televisual style, and the very performativity of the participants in the process. At the same time, the presence of viewers, along with program hosts, is authorized by the very deployment of confession for, recalling Foucault, "one does not confess without the presence (or virtual presence) of a partner who is not simply the interlocutor but the authority who requires the confession."[5] Viewers slide among a range of positions afforded, variously participating and judging, as confessor and interlocutor. In this context no singular subject has sufficient coherence—psychic or social—to be probed and cured; instead, one experiences the multiplication of subjects and social configurations to be managed.

All these programs blur the distinction between personal and social, private and public, individual and group, embodiment and performativity, exerting a pressure toward new formulations of subjectivity that are not dependent on these distinctions. Instead these shows delineate the ways in which public and private experience are equally permeated by institutional and impersonal strategies of power—including the community, law, psychiatry, and the star industry—while requiring the involvement and complicity of subjects who will speak for themselves in their capacity as (apparently) free, private individuals. Here, the differences between the private and the public is effaced in favor of a larger consuming social body where subjectivity can be managed and negotiated through confessional strategies. These programs project individuals and couples as the site where private and public interests commingle, and they invite individual viewers to share in this formation of social subjectivity as a performative, consuming, and consumable therapeutic spectacle. In the process, these reality-based television programs contribute to a larger process of redefining what it means to be real.

NOTES

1. Michel Foucault, *The History of Sexuality*, vol. 1, trans. Robert Hurley (New York, Pantheon, 1978), 61–62.

2. Ibid., 61.

3. These genres are discussed in my *Tele-Advising: Therapeutic Discourse in American Television* (Chapel Hill: University of North Carolina Press, 1992). There is an extensive literature on television talk shows expressing a wide range of critical perspectives. Some of the prominent book-length studies include Donal Carbaugh, *Talking American: Cultural Discourses on Donahue* (Norwood, N.J.: Ablex Publishing, 1989); Joshua Gamson, *Freaks Talk Back: Tabloid Talk Shows and Sexual Nonconformity* (Chicago: University of Chicago Press, 1998); Sonia Livingstone and Peter Lunt, *Talk on Television: Audience Participation and Public Debate* (London: Routledge, 1994); Wayne Munson, *All Talk: The Talkshow in Media Culture* (Philadelphia: Temple University Press, 1994); Patricia Joyner Priest, *Public Intimacies: Talk Show Participants and Tell-All TV* (Cresskill, N.J.: Hampton Press, 1995); Gini Graham Scott, *Can We Talk? The Power and Influence of Talk Shows* (New York: Insight Books, 1996); and Jane Shattuc, *The Talking Cure: TV Talk Shows and Women* (New York: Routledge, 1997).

4. Programs of this sort are discussed in greater detail in White, *Tele-Advising*.

5. Foucault, *The History of Sexuality*, 61–62.

About the Contributors

RHONA J. BERENSTEIN, a former associate professor and director of film studies at the University of California, Irvine, currently works in the Internet industry as vice president of marketing and business development for a leading affinity portal. In addition to her numerous articles, she is the author of *Attack of the Leading Ladies: Gender, Sexuality, and Spectatorship in Classic Horror Cinema* (Columbia University Press, 1995).

DANIEL BERNARDI is an assistant professor in the department of media arts at the University of Arizona, where he teaches courses on cultural studies, critical race theory, and new media. He has published in *Film and History, Science Fiction Studies, Stanford Humanities Review,* and in collected works. He is the editor of *The Birth of Whiteness: Race and the Emergence of U.S. Cinema* (Rutgers University Press, 1996) and *Classic Hollywood/ Classic Whiteness* (University of Minnesota Press, 2001) and the author of *Star Trek and History: Race-ing toward a White Future* (Rutgers University Press, 1998).

JOHN CALDWELL is an associate professor in the department of film and television at the University of California, Los Angeles. He is the recipient of awards from the National Endowment for the Arts and Regional Fellowships; his films and videos have been screened in festivals in Amsterdam, Berlin, Paris, and New York and broadcast in the United States and abroad. He is the author of *Televisuality: Style, Crisis, and Authority in American Television,* the editor of *Electronic Media and Technoculture* (Rutgers University Press, 2000), and is currently completing a film on migrant farmworker housing, *Rancho California (por favor),* which will premiere at the Sundance Film Festival.

JODI DEAN is an associate professor in the political science department at Hobart and William Smith Colleges in Geneva, New York. She is the author of *Aliens in America* (Cornell University Press, 1998) and *Solidarity of Strangers* (University of California Press, 1996). She is the editor of *Feminism and the New Democracy* (Sage Publications, 1997) and *Cultural Studies and Political Theory* (Cornell University Press, 2000). She is currently finishing a project on technocultural ideology, *Publicity's Secret* (forthcoming from Cornell University Press).

MARGARET DEROSIA is a Ph.D. candidate in the history of consciousness department at the University of California at Santa Cruz. Her dissertation analyzes representations of race and sexuality in American film noir. She is the author of "An Erotics of Violence: Masculinity and Homosexuality in Stanley Kubrick's *A Clockwork Orange*" (in the Cambridge Film Handbooks' *A Clockwork Orange,* edited by Stuart Y. McDougal, Cambridge University Press, forthcoming).

ARILD FETVEIT is a research fellow at the department of media and communication, University of Oslo. He has worked in reception studies, reality TV, and digitalization of film and photography. Now he is writing a book on the problem of defining documentary and on the discursive possibilities between documentary and fiction film.

JAMES FRIEDMAN is a Ph.D. candidate in the department of film and television at UCLA, a guest lecturer at California State University, Los Angeles, and the manager of the UCLA Film and Television Archive Research and Study Center. His dissertation, "Attraction to Distraction: Live Television and the Public Sphere," examines the formal, temporal, and spatial construction of live broadcasting. He has published in *Screen* and contributed to a number of collected works.

KRISTEN HATCH is a Ph.D. candidate in the department of film and television at UCLA. Her dissertation examines performances of girlhood in American film through the 1930s.

TOBY MILLER is a professor of cultural studies and cultural policy at New York University. He is the author of *The Well-Tempered Self: Citizenship, Culture, and the Postmodern Subject* (1993), *Contemporary Australian Television* (with S. Cunningham, 1994), *The Avengers* (1997), *Technologies of Truth: Cultural Citizenship and the Popular Media* (1998), *Popular Culture and Everyday Life* (with A. McHoul, 1998), *Global Hollywood* (with N. Govil, J. McMurria, and R. Maxwell, 2001), *Globalization and Sport* (with G. A. Lawrence, J. McKay, and D. Rowe, 2001), and *Sportsex* (2001); coeditor of *SportCult* (with R. Martin, 1999), *Film and Theory: An Anthology* (with R. Stam, 1999), and *A Companion to Film Theory* (with R. Stam, 1999); and editor of *A Companion to Cultural Studies* (2001). He edits the journal *Television and New Media.*

ALAN NADEL, professor of literature and film at Rensselaer Polytechnic Institute, is the author of several works, including *Containment Culture: American Narratives, Postmodernism, and the Atomic Age* (1995) and

Flatlining on the Field of Dreams: Cultural Narratives in the Films of President Reagan's America (1997). Currently he is completing a book entitled *Reinventing America in Black and White: Cold War Television and the Legacy of Racial Profiling,* from which the essay in this collection is taken.

GARETH PALMER is a senior lecturer in the School of Media, Music, and Performance where he also manages the Contemporary Documentary Archive. He has published widely on the connections between governmentality and televsion. His book entitled *Governance: Television and Its Public* is to be published by Manchester University Press in 2001–02.

VIVIAN SOBCHACK is an associate dean and a professor of film and television studies at the UCLA School of Theater, Film, and Television, and she was the first woman elected president of the Society for Cinema Studies. Her work focuses on film and media theory and its intersections with philosophy, perceptual studies, and historiography. She has published widely in journals and anthologies, and her books include *Screening Space: The American Science Fiction Film* and *The Address of the Eye: A Phenomenology of Film Experience*; two edited anthologies, *The Persistence of History: Cinema, Television, and the Modern Event* and *Meta-Morphing: Visual Transformation and the Culture of Quick Change*; and a forthcoming collection of her own essays, *Carnal Thoughts: Bodies, Texts, Scenes, and Screens.*

MARITA STURKEN is an associate professor in the Annenberg School for Communication at the University of Southern California. She is the author of *Tangled Memories: The Vietnam War, the AIDS Epidemic, and the Politics of Remembering* (University of California Press, 1997), a British Film Institute monograph on *Thelma & Louise* (2000), and, with Lisa Cartwright, *Practices of Looking: An Introduction to Visual Culture* (Oxford University Press, 2001).

MIMI WHITE is a professor of radio, TV, and film at Northwestern University. She has also taught at the Universities of Helsinki, Tampere, and Jyvaskyla in Finland. She is author of *Tele-Advising: Therapeutic Discourse in American Television* and coauthor of *Media Knowledge: Readings in Popular Culture, Pedagogy, and Critical Citizenship*. She has published articles in *Screen, Cinema Journal, Film and History,* and *Wide Angle* as well as other journals and books; and is coeditor of the Media Topographies book series at Northwestern University Press.

Index

morphing, 158, 173; pornography, 168, 178; and race, 163, 175, 176; structures of, 171
cyborg, 156, 158, 159, 167; manifesto, 178; metaphor and social reality, 157; ontology of, 155

Daquerre, Louis Jacques Mandé, 121
Daughton, Suzanne M., 219n64
Davis, Tom, 316
Davy Crockett, 51, 57, 58, 60
Dayan, Daniel, 144, 153n6
Dean, Jodi, 19
Debord, Matthew, 310n2
decentralization, 299
de Certeau, Michael, 114n19
Deer, Mark, 60
DeLillo, Don, 212
Denison, Merrill, 46n32, 47n50
DeRosia, Margaret, 18
Derrida, Jacques, 305
dialectical: contraction, 110; images, 94, 111, 112, 116n54; shock, 111
Dibbell, Julian, 312n36
Dick Clark's Rockin' New Year's Eve, 140, 141
Dienst, Richard, 116n52
digitalization, 119, 124, 126, 127, 132; of imagery, 136n38; and manipulation, 15, 119, 127, 129–131, 136n34
direct address, 267, 273, 280, 281, 284, 317
direct cinema, 268
discourse: circulation of, 316; confessional, 320, 321; factual, 127, 128; negotiation, 318; public, 195; style of, 145; therapeutic, 19, 284, 313, 320
Disney, Walt, 51, 62
Disneyland (theme park), 54, 56, 57
Disneyland (TV series), 13, 54, 55, 56, 57, 62, 71
Disney Studios, 54, 55, 56, 58, 64
distraction, 86
Divorce Court, 321
Doane, Mary Ann, 254n20
docudrama, 259. *See also* docu-real; docu-stunt

documentary, 123, 128, 221, 224–226, 231–233, 234, 267, 268; in docu-soaps, 224, 225; and fiction, 259, 260, 272; forms of, 225, 284, 285; gaze in, 266, 277–279, 284, 286; interview in, 265, 266, 273; modes of, 281–283; and reality television, 221, 230–232, 297; tabloid, 276, 278; and technology, 264; theory of, 285, 286
docu-real, 269–270, 281, 282–285, 286; deconstruction in, 275, 279, 286, 289; and fiction, 259, 260, 264, 266, 267, 273, 275, 277, 286–289; and narrative, 281, 285; as ontological anchoring, 267; postmodern series as, 270–272; structural patterns in, 263, 279, 284, 287–288; as subgenre, 273, 281
docu-stunt, 259–260, 264, 266–268, 281, 288; and generic conventions, 272, 281, 285, 288; and *The Simpsons*, 270–271
domestic space, 35
Donovan, Pamela, 254n23
Doyle, Aaron, 254n23
drama, 9, 13; depictions of television, 261; based on real life, 9; based on historical events, 13
Duerr, Edwin, 37, 38, 40
Dunlap, Orrin Jr., 34, 43
Dupuy, Judy, 29, 30, 32, 38, 39
Dyson, Ester, 30

Eatwell, Roger, 161, 164
Eddy, William C., 38, 41, 47n53
Eisenstein, Sergei, 113n3
Ellis, John, 27, 42
emplotment, 113n15
Epstein, Michael, 299
ER, 6, 11, 277, 278, 279, 280, 283, 284, 287
Escobar, Arturo, 311n25
evidence, 245, 305; photographic, 123; power of, 119, 122, 125, 128; representation of, 245; visual, 122, 124–126, 129–131, 271; and *The X-Files*, 304, 305
Ewen, Stuart, 46n43